THE

GOSPEL

UNCOMPROMISED

Evangelism From Genesis to Revelation

WILLIAM E. KING

THE

GOSPEL

UNCOMPROMISED

Evangelism From Genesis to Revelation

FOREWORD BY RICO TICE

"Billy King has done the Church an excellent service in reminding us why God has left the Church on this earth for now. In a compelling survey of God's Word, he shows that God's heart is for the nations. The American Church has, for too long, been asleep in the light. This book is a clarion call to "arise, O sleeper!" - we are Jonah, sent with a message but too often silent. I'm thankful for Billy's work here to remind us of God's call on the Church and all who know Christ. I can't commend it to you highly enough!"

Matthew Bradley, Pastor and Church Planter, All Saints Presbyterian Church, Brentwood, TN

"'For God so loved the world'... 'And the Word became flesh and dwelt among us'... Every page of Scripture reveals God's commitment to rescue the lost. This book may be unique in that it is a study throughout the whole Bible on evangelism from Genesis to Revelation, tracing God's plan from the beginning – to bring salvation to the whole world – looking at the threads of redemption through the whole counsel of God. This book provides practical application at every juncture, calling believers to action, to repentance, and asking God for revival. Billy has been greatly used of God throughout South America as he has taught on the subject of evangelism. His teachings now in book form will be a useful resource as ESI equips church leaders in both Latin America and Africa. We thank God for this important book.

This is a MUST READ for all who seek to obey the Great Commission effectively and to lead their friends and loved ones into a saving knowledge of our Lord Jesus Christ."

Kep James, Director, Equipping Servants International, and longtime Missionary

In my 45 years of pastoral ministry, I have been a church planter, pastor, missionary trainer of pastors in Africa, Romania, and Israel over many years. So, I have not been simply sitting in the stands. But something slowly was shrinking. There was much activity, but in some ways it felt like I was losing my first love. Sadly, church ministry can do that to you.

My spiritual journey began under the influence of the late 60's Jesus Movement. I was a rebel at heart and my life revealed my rebellious nature. While I was in a church background that preached the "partial gospel", I really wanted no part of it. That is, until circumstances led to my family changing churches. This change exposed me to the influence of expository preaching and to a collection of high school students who shared the Good News at St. Pete Beach in Florida.

It was that bold power of witness that broke me. In misery I wearied of running from God. I finally asked my youth director if he would teach me how to share my faith. He did and I did. That journey of falling in love with Jesus enough to evangelize changed the course of my entire life. Since that day I have evangelized in multiple countries and cities.

As years of pastoral ministry wore on, **I lost my cutting edge in evangelism.** The fire went to embers. This book was just what the doctor ordered. I was biblically transported back to my former passion for sharing Christ everywhere to anyone. The pages of this book rebuked me through God's grand evangelistic vision and passion for the nations. Billy King reveals the fabric of redemptive history. The message of this book has re-kindled an evangelistic fire in my belly. I warn you, if you are holding this book in your hand, beware of reading too far. You will either experience a similar fire (if you have a spiritual pulse) or you will be hardened. But you won't forget. At the risk of offense, I challenge you, buy the book and read it carefully. If you don't live the Father's passion described in these pages, I dare say things will not end well for you.

William Joel McCall, D.Min., Equipping Leaders International and Associate Pastor at Christ Covenant Church PCA, Knoxville, TN

"In a day when a truncated gospel is popular this book masterfully shows us the whole biblical gospel and the glorious heart of God. It is in more fully knowing Him that we understand God's passion for the lost and see the full scope of the gospel message. This book demonstrates that not just what God says but everything He does, from Genesis to Revelation, point to the cross where Christ removes our curse by Himself becoming this curse for us, carrying upon Himself our sin, and freeing us to share that glory and grace we have so freely experienced with those all around us. It is in truly knowing Him that we ourselves become instruments in His hands, seeking those wandering sheep which we once were."

Walter (Jerry) Cross III, M.Div., D.Min., Seminary Professor, Published Author, Church Planter, Evangelist, and Conference Speaker in Latin America for 45 years

For my wife, Janet,
my treasured companion in life
and follower of Christ

CONTENTS

FOREWORD

Rico Tice, Evangelist

My recent story will explain why this book on evangelism in the Bible by my friend and fellow worker, Billy King, is indispensable. I would even call this book prophetic. As I am writing this foreword at the end of March 2024, I have been a Presbyterian for 10 weeks, but I've come from a Church of England background. I was baptized at St. Michael's Milverton in 1966. I attended a Church of England school and went to countless services at Sherborne Abbey. I worked for a Church of England church in my gap year, St. Peter's, in the inner city of Liverpool. I served as a student worker at Christ Church Clifton in Bristol, and whilst at a Church of England Theological College, Wycliffe Hall Oxford, I attended St. Ebbe's. I then spent 30 years on staff at All Souls Church, Langham Place, London.

I give you this resume because I always thought I would be a "cradle to grave" Anglican. Having been converted at 17, I spent the next 40 years working for the gospel in Church of England churches, yet because of the apostasy of some key leaders in that denomination, I found myself heartbroken but in conscience having to make the difficult decision to leave the Church of England.

As I wrestled with this issue, I reflected on these verses from Jeremiah 23 verses 17 and 18: "They keep saying to those who despise me, 'The Lord says: you will have peace.' And to all who follow the stubbornness of their hearts they say, 'No harm will come to you.' But which of them has stood in the council of the Lord to see or to hear his word? Who has listened and heard his word?"[1] Because of passages like these, I knew I had to distance myself from the leadership of the Church of England.

---

1   All Scripture references in the Foreword are from the New International Version (1984) unless otherwise noted.

As you can imagine such a monumental move out of a denomination I love and have given my life to has caused a tremendous amount of soul searching. These were questions I struggled with for some time: What went wrong with these leaders? How did we lose them? What happened? And I asked those questions because some of the key leaders of the Church of England at one time strongly identified themselves as orthodox evangelicals. These were Bible-believing men and women, not like some of the sneering liberals with whom I was ordained. They appeared to take seriously the promises they made when they were ordained as pastors and Bishops. Here were the questions that were asked of the leaders of the Church of England at their ordination:

Bishop   Do you accept the holy Scriptures as revealing all things necessary for eternal salvation through faith in Jesus Christ?

Answer   I do so accept them.

Bishop   Do you believe the doctrine of the Christian faith as the Church of England has received it, and in your ministry will you expound and teach it?

Answer   I believe it, and will so do.

So again, I ask what has happened to the commitment to the vows of these leaders who took the same vows I took? It was at this point, as I was asking these questions, and in conscience having to prepare to leave the Church of England, that the Sovereign Lord caused Billy King's manuscript to come across my desk. It was a real light-bulb moment reading page 43 about the eight basic elements of the gospel that I found a critical diagnostic tool that exposes the erroneous gospel foundations that we see time and again among ex-evangelicals including the leadership in the Church of England.

You will see as I did in this book that Billy draws out these eight elements of the gospel. He first outlines them in Genesis chapters 1 to 7, but he then shows how they are echoed right through Scripture, in book after book of the Bible.

Here is a brief summary of those eight elements:

1. **God**
In Genesis Chapters 1 to 3 God created everything from nothing. He is our Creator and as his creatures we are subordinate to his authority.

2. **Holiness**
God requires man to live in perfect obedience to his will, Genesis 2 verses 15 to 17. Negatively we are to separate ourselves from all that is evil and positively we are to be consecrated to God. Holiness is the one thing without which no-one will be allowed into God's presence.

3. **Sin**
Adam and Eve violated God's requirement of them by rebelling against his authority over their lives. They wanted to make themselves equal with God, Genesis 3 verses 1 to 6.

4. **Judgment and Wrath**
As a result of their sin and disobedience, God's judgment came down on Adam and Eve, as seen in Genesis 3 verses 8 to 19. As a result of their sin against a holy God, they were immediately separated from God, with the prospect of eternal separation in the fires of hell.

5. **The Cross and Resurrection**
God showed His grace by promising the solution to their sins, the coming of His son Jesus to make payment for their disobedience. God's prophecy in Genesis 3 verse 15, "He shall crush your head and you will strike his heel," reveals how God gave Adam and Eve the promise of a deliverer, who would rescue them from their sin.

6. **Grace**
Adam and Eve deserved only wrath and condemnation, but God acted in grace. In Genesis 3 verse 21, we have a portrayal of the blood sacrifice of Jesus: "The Lord God made garments of skin for Adam and his wife and clothed them."

7. Counting the Cost

There is a cost to following the Deliverer, Genesis 3 verse 15: "I will put enmity between you and the woman, and between your offspring and hers; he will crush your head, and you will strike his heel." This reveals the introduction of animosity on earth between the offspring of Eve and the offspring of Satan.

8. Repentance and Belief

To be saved, a sinner must turn from their sin and place their trust in God. Adam and Eve had trusted in Satan's word and now they needed to repent and turn away from the lies of Satan and place their trust in God and his word. They had to turn back to God, as the appropriate Ruler of their lives.

This book reveals how these themes are central to the gospel and are pervasive throughout Scripture. Now, when I preach at Christmas, I'm going to be guided by these eight principles, as Billy reveals that they are predominant in the gospel accounts.

Having read Billy's summary of the gospel, my light-bulb moment came as I compared Billy's eight points to the six point gospel outline that I and many leaders today were raised on as young men at Scripture Union camp. Here they are, and I wonder if you can see the gaps:

1. God is the loving Creator and the Ruler of the world.
2. We all reject the Ruler by trying to run life our own way without him.
3. God won't let us rebel forever, God's punishment for rebellion is death and judgment.
4. Because of his love, God sent his Son into the world, and by dying in our place he took our punishment and brought forgiveness.
5. God raised Jesus to life again as the Ruler of the world. Jesus has conquered death, now gives new life and will return to judge.
6. There are two ways to live: reject the Ruler and try to live life our own way, which leaves us condemned by God and facing death and judgment. Or submit to Jesus as our Ruler, rely on his death and resurrection and be forgiven by God and given eternal life.

Can you see what two essentials were missing in the gospel outline and indeed systematic theology, which characterized the instruction that was given to me as a young Anglican evangelical and indeed to future leaders when we were young Christians.

The first missing piece is holiness, point 2. Alarmingly, we were taught that God is Creator, but it was not emphasized that God is holy. Looking back, that was a real blind spot. We went straight from saying God made us to we've rebelled against him. Yet the holiness of God is central to Scripture. Indeed, holiness is mentioned in Scripture twice as much as the love of God is. In the following pages, at one point the focus is on Isaiah Chapter 6. We study the call of the evangelist and Isaiah's encounter with God.

Isaiah 6 verses 1 to 5:

In the year that King Uzziah died, I saw the Lord, high and exalted, seated on a throne; and the train of his robe filled the temple. Above him were seraphim, each with six wings: with two wings they covered their faces, with two they covered their feet, and with two they were flying. And they were calling to one another:

'Holy, holy, holy is the LORD Almighty;
the whole earth is full of his glory.'

At the sound of their voices the doorposts and thresholds shook and the temple was filled with smoke. 'Woe to me!' I cried. 'I am ruined! For I am a man of unclean lips, and I live among a people of unclean lips, and my eyes have seen the King, the LORD Almighty.'

We learn in this text from Isaiah that God's holiness cannot be hidden or controlled by any sinful human. It's something we can't "mold to our own system of human values or fit into our little theological box. It is an active, untamable force" (page 119). I really do not remember this aspect of God's character being taught to us. This should make us tremble with the fear of the Lord.

Currently, as I look at the apostasy of the leadership of the Church of England, this sense of God's holiness is absolutely absent. Indeed the emphasis constantly is on the love of God, which celebrates inclusion but not transformation. So there is no call for repentance in the light of the fact that God is holy. And as I look back on our training as young men, where was the holiness of God in the outline we were taught?

The second missing piece is counting the cost, point 7. There has been a real failure among Anglican evangelicals to count the cost. Again, right through the book, Billy demonstrates that this element is absolutely essential in faithful gospel preaching. On page 87, as we study the life of Moses, Billy writes: "Moses experienced substantial difficulties because he was following God. He led Israel from age 80 until his death at 120. His retirement plan may have been fully funded by the time he reached 80, but he chose to follow God, which added to the hassle factor of his life." Jesus tells us to count the cost of following him, Mark 8 verses 34 to 38, Luke 14 verses 25 to 33. Peter warns, 1 Peter 4 verse 12, "Do not be surprised at the fiery trial, when it comes upon you to test you as though something strange were happening to you" (ESV).

So, as I look back on 40 years as an Anglican, and look forward to the future in a new denomination, what has this book caused me to think about? It makes me wish that the men and women who led me to faith in the 1980s in the Anglican church, and trained me had read a copy of this manuscript. We know the importance of truth from Titus 1 verse 1 which says, "The knowledge of the truth that leads to godliness", and so we have to ask to what degree these two gaping holes about holiness and counting the cost have contributed to the carnage that we now see among many church leaders. What we must not do is make the same mistake again, and that's why, as I reflect on my story, this book could not be more timely.

As I read this manuscript, I was reminded of one of the Time 100 individuals in 2010. He was a young doctor named Atul Gawande and he wrote The Checklist Manifesto. His premise was very simple, in medicine you can significantly reduce human error in complex operations by ticking off a checklist of safety steps. It does seem basic and almost patronizing, simply making sure that you have: 1. Washed hands, 2. Sterilized instruments, 3. Checked location of operation on the body, but as hospitals introduced the checklist a vast number of lives were saved. The medical checklist had a revolutionary effect and was then introduced in other complex professions like aviation and engineering. I certainly will be using Billy's outline as my theological checklist, as I seek to preach evangelistically.

So how do we preach the gospel? We now have it outlined in its fulness, but what are we to expect as we seek to heed the call of 2 Corinthians 4 verse 2: "Rather, we have renounced secret and shameful ways; we do not use deception, nor do we distort the word of God. On the contrary, by setting forth the truth plainly we commend ourselves to everyone's conscience in the sight of God."

And how do we read the Scriptures through the lens of the urgency to get the gospel out? For example, have you ever thought about the one thing Jonah got right? I confess, I'd never seen this, and to quote Billy: "But this is the one thing that Jonah did right! He preached the message God gave him without alteration: 'Yet forty days and Nineveh shall be overthrown!', Jonah 3 verse 4" (page 106).

Before Jonah's day, Noah also faithfully preached the message God had given him, a message that sees wickedness from God's perspective. Though tellingly the two men had very different results. The people of Nineveh repented (which Jesus commends), but in Noah's day they scoffed until the promised day of judgment came and they were drowned. But what the preacher must see is that the message does not change, and nor indeed does the price of preaching it. Billy takes us right through Scripture and shows us that if you speak of judgment, of human wickedness, and of the coming wrath, then you will suffer and be rejected. So John the Baptist, Peter, and Paul all died violently for confronting human beings with their wickedness and their need to repent.

As I was reading this book, I was much helped by the prayer based on Psalm 73 on page 94, which encourages us to keep thinking and speaking the real gospel.

Personalized Confession: "O Lord, there are times when I cannot understand life in the world around me. So many prosper who ignore you, live lives of corruption, and even hate you. I find myself hating them or at best wanting to shut them out of my life and pretend they do not exist. But this is sin on my part. Help me to see unbelievers from your perspective. Help me to see that they live in a 'slippery' place and that 'in a moment' they will be 'swept away utterly by terrors!' (Psalm 73 verses 18 and 19). Please give me the ability to see the lost through your eyes. Give me the strength and the heart to respond as you would have me respond. Right now, I do not want to respond in a gracious way, nor do I want to tell others the good news of your great salvation. Help me to recognize how horrible hell will actually be. O God, please change my sinful heart. Grant me the ability to repent and enable me to 'tell of all your works' and to have compassion on those who are lost."

I confess that in both my gospel content and in my gospel communication I found this book revealing my blind spots. For example, I was staggered by the summary of Spurgeon's preaching (page 50): "In 479 sermons selected from eight full years between 1855 and 1885, words depicting God's wrath were present more than 15,000 times. That equates to an average of more than 32 times per sermon." Surely those words make us ask ourselves several questions. What is the content of our preaching? What is our model? And what are our blind spots?

So here is the challenge of this most timely book. Have we got the gospel message right and are we personally prepared for what will happen to us when we seek to present this message to a rebellious, wicked, and perishing world?

Rico Tice, Evangelist

PREFACE

The idea for this book emerged out of many evangelism training conferences that I led in nine Latin American countries over several years. I approached Kep James, Director of Equipping Servants International, with the idea of putting the training material into manuscript form. It would then be used as part of a three-year curriculum for more than 1,800 pastors and leaders in training. He liked the idea, and I was off and running.

Early in this undertaking, I asked retired pastor, Jim Barnes, if he would serve as a coach to me through this project. During discussions with Jim at the beginning, I decided to expand the original scope of the book to survey evangelism and the biblical gospel from Genesis to Revelation. This represented a significant expansion of the original concept. Thus, a one-year project became a 4 ½ year journey with a bit of adventure along the way.

Actually, this journey began long before those evangelism conferences in Latin America. In 2003 I was dissatisfied with my own evangelistic efforts and began a search for a solution. That search led me to an encounter with Christianity Explored at All Souls Church in London. The ministry of Christianity Explored equips believers for evangelism and that was exactly what I needed. This training gave me a newfound freedom in evangelism.

I have always found evangelism difficult and still do today. But with clarity of the gospel and a solid biblical foundation for evangelism, it becomes an undertaking that anyone who is living for the Lord can do.

I must confess that I have benefitted from the studies that comprise this book. Everyone needs encouragement in evangelism, and I am no different. Over the years of this endeavor, in the research, writing, and editing of it, I found myself both encouraged and frequently in need of confessing my sins. My shortcomings in evangelism and my failures to love other people enough to engage them with the full gospel, often became apparent. So, if you are reading this book and find yourself encouraged as well as challenged, then you are not alone.

Every chapter of this book was a spiritual wrestling match of sorts for me. The challenge was to interpret the Bible accurately, to apply it in my own life appropriately, and then to write it in a way that is understandable and useful to others. It is my hope that you, the reader, will engage each chapter in a wrestling match of your own. May the Lord use this book, which for the most part is an exposition of Scripture revealing God's passion for the lost, to enable you to be faithful to God's grand overarching purpose for His people in redemption.

William E. King
Nashville, Tennessee
April 6, 2024

ACKNOWLEDGMENTS

I owe a huge debt of gratitude to many. Jim Barnes served as coach, trusted counselor, and initial editor through the more than four years of work on this book. He read every chapter in the early draft stages, spent many hours discussing the text with me, and made many literary recommendations. He also served as a sounding board and theological guide as I wrestled with different concepts and how best to express them. Without his encouragement and sound advice, this book would never have come to its present scope and quality.

David Bond and Matt Bonner read early drafts of every chapter and provided many recommendations for improving the manuscript. They revealed areas that needed clarification and offered edits that made this book much better. Their insights were invaluable.

Matt Bradley, the senior pastor of the church I am a member of, read the finished manuscript and met weekly with me over a six-month period examining each chapter. Matt provided important theological insights and proposed many ways to improve the manuscript.

Dale Ralph Davis graciously read the manuscript and recommended many improvements. He also provided important insights to me on the Old Testament section of this book.

Joel McCall read the manuscript and gave me a better understanding of the usefulness of this book. He has been a great encouragement to me.

Jerry Cross, a longtime friend and missionary in Latin America, is responsible for my first connections to lead evangelism training conferences in Latin America. He provided helpful observations and edits along the way.

David Roach, pastor and author, edited the manuscript. He not only made it a much better read but provided theological insights. This book is far better with his expert touch.

In addition to reading the manuscript and recommending important improvements, Rico Tice taught me the biblical foundation for evangelism many years ago – God's sovereignty, gospel integrity, and my service. This revolutionized my thinking and practice regarding evangelism. I am grateful for Rico and Christianity Explored Ministries, not only for the impact on my life, but on the lives of hundreds of thousands around the world.

Numerous people have prayed for me during this project. Many in my church have prayed often and particularly my shepherding group. A Friday morning prayer group, of Mark Rasmussen, Bruce Cairns, Bob Ralston, Robert Southwick, and Clarke Tungseth, faithfully lifted me and this project before the Lord from the beginning. Many others at various times have prayed. Your prayers were evident in big ways and small as this project unfolded.

Most important of all, I am grateful to my wife, Janet, for her support as I devoted much time over many years to the writing of this book. It would have been a lonely journey without her alongside. Her love, prayers, and faithfulness to the Lord helped carry me to the finish line.

PROLOGUE – IN *MY* BEGINNING

Genesis is a book of beginnings. Yet before looking at the Book of Genesis, here is a short version of my own personal "genesis" in Christ and how the whole gospel played a role in it. I'm still amazed at my conversion when I was redeemed by Christ and came to know intimately and personally this holy God who created the universe. Amazingly, I did not want to follow Christ. I wanted to be saved from hell to be sure but did not want to submit my life to the creator of the universe. I liked being *god* of my own life.

It was a momentous occasion when God's wrath toward me was appeased (propitiated) in Christ and I was reconciled to the Creator of the universe. Knowing for the first time the all-powerful and all-important God of creation as friend was an astonishing experience for me.

Before that moment could take place though, someone had to tell me the gospel. In fact, multiple people needed to speak the gospel to me over a period of many years. I needed to hear it in many voices and in many "languages." Some spoke the gospel to me with a voice of gentleness, and some spoke more forcefully. Some spoke to me in the language of the hard truths of sin, wrath, judgment, and hell, and some drove the love of God into me. I needed to hear the whole gospel for it explained the whole truth of my reality: that I was a sinner, alienated from God, and was on my way to hell for all of eternity. I could never shake the idea of the wrath of God awaiting me at my death. I am extremely grateful to those who took the risk to love me and to offend me for the sake of the gospel.

As a child, my mother taught me the gospel. She taught me the stories of Jesus and impressed upon me the truth of who He really is (God Himself) and the great love He had for me. As a pre-teen my parents taught me the right way to live and instilled in me a sense of right and wrong. During this phase of my life, I became aware that I was a sinner and that I needed God's forgiveness in Jesus. In the early teenage years, it seems my mind was continually plotting to see how much difficulty I could give my parents. Their responses to my misbehaviors were enough to impress upon me the fact that I had sin in my heart. The trouble I gave my parents during this phase was mostly harmless mischief although misuse of alcohol would become a regular part of my later teenage years.

The small Methodist church my family attended in south Mississippi always had a visiting preacher come and lead four or five nights of "revival" meetings each summer. To my consternation and great dismay, my mother would always expect me to attend. Some summers I was able to get off by attending only one of the evenings. But it was at these services that I heard in a powerful way the full gospel proclaimed, including judgment and the wrath of God. There would always be an invitation and time to pray and accept Christ at the end. On one occasion I remember the preacher saying something like this after leading the sinner's prayer, "With everyone's head bowed, if you prayed that prayer, please raise your hand." I remember raising my hand because I had indeed prayed the prayer. But nothing really happened in my life. Nothing changed. I continued living and thinking as I always had.

In retrospect, I realize that nothing happened in my life because genuine repentance had not taken place. I was to some extent sorry for my sins, but I did not want to change my ways. I had merely "voted" not to go to hell. After all, who wants to go to hell. I certainly didn't, but neither did I want to live for Jesus at that point in my life.

As a teenager I learned that God's call on a person's life was a call to follow Jesus and to submit to Him as the sovereign of their life. But my heart was attracted to the things of the world. The things I saw outside the church seemed so much more interesting than what I observed inside the church. I wanted an interesting life, the "shiny" things of the world, none of that boring church stuff.

But during my later years of college, a sense of emptiness began to grow. It was an emptiness that grew larger the more I tried to fill it. The more I tried to find fulfillment, the emptier I became. During a particularly low period, at the end of my junior year of college, I was reading a book, *The Cross and the Switchblade* by David Wilkerson. It told the story of gang members in New York who came to faith in Christ and how Jesus transformed their lives.

In the wee hours of one morning, around 2:30 a.m. in August of 1971, I finished reading that book and knew what I needed to do. I prayed a prayer that went something like this, "Lord, I am sick of my life and this emptiness. There must be something better. If I am honest with you, I don't want to live a Christian life. I don't know how to live the Christian life. But I know that I am a sinner and I ask for your forgiveness. I want to live your way. In Jesus name. Amen."

When I finished praying that prayer, I expected that I would feel something, but my emotions were neutral. I did feel a sense of relief that I was no longer under God's wrath, but I also had a sense of apprehension. I knew I had to change, but I had no clue how that was going to happen. I knew instinctively that I did not have the ability to live the Christian life. But what I did not know at that moment was that God would help me to live the Christian life by giving me His Holy Spirit. He would begin to transform my life.

If C. S. Lewis was the self-described most reluctant convert ever, I was the second most reluctant convert. God was who I needed but did not initially want. He used my deep sense of emptiness to cause me to deal with my sin and the awful tragedy of looming judgment and wrath. He used that emptiness to lead me to bow down before Jesus. I knew the wrath of God was true and that I deserved it. That fact had troubled me greatly. I could never get away from it. Nothing would cover it up. Only the blood of Jesus took that trouble away from me.

Therefore, I am extremely grateful for those who taught me who Jesus really is, taught me about the wrath of God, told me of His grace, and taught me of His death on the cross to pay for my sins. What a jam I would still be in if no one had taken the trouble to offend me and to teach me those important facts of the gospel.

INTRODUCTION

Always and everywhere the servants of Christ are under
orders to evangelize – J. I. Packer[2]

It has been my concern as a follower of Christ that the evangelical church is in danger of missing the most important message of the entire Bible, that being the great message of redemption. This message is not limited to the presentation of the gospel in the New Testament with the coming of Jesus Christ to earth. **It is seen throughout the Old Testament, starting in the first book of the Bible – Genesis.**

The purpose of this book is to remind the church of the centrality of the message of redemption and the call of the church to evangelism that is seen throughout the Bible. We will explore example after example of the gospel as seen in both Testaments. We will study Paul's great manifesto for his model of New Testament ministry in 2 Corinthians 2:14-7:4 and we will consider the power that can be unleashed when we use "one of God's own books about His only Son"[3] in our evangelism efforts (the Gospel of Mark). Hopefully, because of this study, a believer will understand the great message of redemption throughout the Bible and how God presented that gospel. Believers will realize that God's message (the biblical gospel) and purpose (evangelism – a light to the nations) must be the message and purpose of every Christian.

Several themes will emerge that permeate the Bible such as the great disaster of God's wrath and judgment on the lost; the life and death reality in which His followers are involved; the importance of proclaiming the "whole gospel"[4] rather than an incomplete

---

2   J. I. Packer, *Evangelism and the Sovereignty of God* (Downers Grove, IL: InterVarsity Press, 1961, Americanized and Forward, 2008), p. 13.

3   Christianity Explored Ministries, https://www.ceministries.org/.

4   Will Metzger, *Tell the Truth: The Whole Gospel to the Whole Person by Whole People* (Downers Grove, IL: InterVarsity Press, third edition 2002), p. 39. Metzger contrasts the "whole gospel" vs a "shrunken gospel," or a gospel that leaves out certain elements.

version of it; and evangelism as *the chief strategic task* [5] for God's people. The gospel and God's call to witness are both rooted in God's character and emerge out of all His attributes.

One of the challenges of our age, but not new to our age, is the continual pressure on the Christian church to alter the biblical gospel to conform to the values of the culture, to be non-offensive, and even to affirm sin. This deformation of the gospel has been going on since the beginning of time. The perversion of the gospel is occurring across every denomination today in the United States. The same issue was addressed by Jesus in His teachings (Mt. 7:15, 23:13-24, Mk. 2:23-28, 24:11, 24) and was confronted by several writers of the New Testament (2 Cor. 11:12-15, 26, 2 Pet. 2:1-3, 1 Jn. 4:1; Jude 3-4ff). The church in every century has faced this pressure. Many of us today are like the proverbial frog who is incrementally boiled in water. The temptation to change the gospel happens imperceptibly so that the church is boiled before we realize it. We become so steeped in the values of the culture that if we are not careful, it warps the gospel. It is my hope that this book will help you evaluate your own understanding of the gospel and evangelism from a fresh perspective.

The overall focus of the book will be on finding the expression of the gospel in both the Old and New Testaments and in God's requirement to speak the gospel to the lost in every age. Many churches devote time to teaching and studying God's word, spending time in fellowship and caring for one another, and worshipping together. However, only a handful of churches are proficient and faithful in sharing the life-changing message of the gospel. Few churches see unbelievers come to a saving knowledge of Jesus Christ.

The need to focus on telling the gospel is evident when we look at today's church. Thom Rainer in his 1996 book *Effective Evangelistic Churches*, concluded from a study of the approximately 40,000 Southern Baptist churches, that less than 4% are effective

---

5   I am using the word "strategic" to mean "a carefully planned overarching and mostly externally focused task or purpose that is proactively set in motion and to which every member of the organization is dedicated". Later I will contrast "strategic" with "organic" functions. In developing this definition, I conducted an internet search using two different search engines and was particularly influenced by: Macmillan Dictionary, https://www.macmillandictionary.com/us/dictionary/american/strategic; SmartCompany, article by Sue Barrett, April 22, 2012, https://www.smartcompany.com.au/marketing/sales/so-what-does-being-strategic-really-mean/and Cambridge Dictionary, https://dictionary.cambridge.org/dictionary/english/strategic; all accessed 29Mar 2022.

evangelistically.[6] The problem is not unique to Southern Baptists. I asked several pastors in the Presbyterian Church in America if their denomination was any more successful evangelistically than the Southern Baptist Convention and their unanimous response was, "We are most likely worse than that."

Before we look into evangelism as seen throughout the Bible, there are two terms that need definition: gospel and evangelism. My working definition for the gospel is what nonbelievers need to hear of how God acted in history for the redemption of His people. The gospel can be summarized under eight elements:[7] God, holiness, sin, judgment/wrath, the cross and resurrection of Christ, grace, the cost of following Christ, and repentance and belief. It is not less than these eight elements.

One question that emerged during my research and writing of this book was, "Does the term gospel, as used in the New Testament, convey anything other than good news?" In other words, do the writers of the New Testament think of and use the word gospel to include the Bible's view of sin, judgment, wrath, repentance, and the cost of following Christ? Or should believers only use the term gospel to refer to the more evident good news such as love, grace, mercy, forgiveness, justification, and redemption?

The answer is that the writers of the New Testament do include all of those elements in their meaning of the word gospel (Lk. 3:7-18; Rom. 1:16-18ff; 2:16; 1 Cor. 15:1-11; Rev. 14:6-20). And it is used often throughout the New Testament in a way that is synonymous with "message of salvation" (Lk. 9:6; Acts 8:25, 40; 14:7, 21; 16:10; 1 Cor. 15:1-2; Gal. 1:9).

The cross is the heart of the gospel (Rom. 3:21-26; 1 Cor. 1:17-2:5; 15:1-8; Gal. 3:13-14; Heb. 9:22). John Stott writes, "Evangelical Christians believe that in and through Christ crucified God substituted himself for us and bore our sins, dying in our place the death we deserved to die, in order that we might be restored to his favor and adopted into his family...[this] takes us to the very heart of the Christian gospel."[8]

---

6   Thom S. Rainer, *Effective Evangelistic Churches* (Nashville, TN: Broadman & Holman Publishers, 1996), p.50.

7   The idea of breaking down the gospel into elements was precipitated by Will Metzger's book in which he uses "Five Primary Points of the Gospel" (p. 53). His points are excellent. And though what I have developed is different, I believe it is consistent with his view of the "whole gospel". Will Metzger, *Tell the Truth: The Whole Gospel to the Whole Person by Whole People* (chapter 3), pp. 53-86.

8   John Stott, *The Cross of Christ* (with study guide) (Leicester, England: Inter-Varsity Press, 1986, 2004), p. 7.

J. I. Packer writes, "And a gospel without propitiation at its heart is another gospel than that which Paul preached. The implications of this must not be evaded."[9]

Jesus' death on the cross cannot be explained without addressing the reality of God as creator and judge, the holiness of God and his requirement of holiness for everyone, the tragic reality of humans stained by sin, as well as judgment, wrath, the resurrection, grace, forgiveness of sins, the cost of following Jesus, and repentance and faith. These individual components are like interlocking elements that form the structure of the biblical gospel. If we remove one, the structure becomes something other than the gospel of Christ. A gospel separated from the cross, and from the implications of the cross, is a gospel rendered "with words of eloquent wisdom" with the result that "the cross of Christ [is] emptied of its power" (1 Cor. 1:17).

I have provided a more comprehensive examination of the word gospel in the Appendix. There is a table at the end of chapter one and at the end of chapter 14 that provides a grid of these eight elements with Scripture references. Interestingly we find all eight of these gospel elements in Genesis chapters 1-7! And where we find the components of the gospel in Scripture, we will most often find evangelism nearby. This too we will see in the first seven chapters of Genesis.

The second term that needs defining is evangelism. J. I. Packer uses the following definition, adapted from a 1918 Church of England report: "To evangelize is so to present Christ Jesus in the power of the Holy Spirit, that men *may* come to put their trust in God through him, to accept him as their Savior, and serve him as their King in the fellowship of his Church."[10]

This is, of course, a good definition for evangelism. However, I would make one further change in view of the tendency among many churches and individuals today to emphasize grace and love to the exclusion of sin and wrath. I would add the words "the whole gospel of" so that it would read: "To evangelize is so to present *the whole gospel of* Christ Jesus in the power of the Holy Spirit, that men may come to put their trust in God through him, to accept him as their Savior, and serve him as their King in the fellowship of his Church."

---

9 J. I. Packer, Knowing God (Downers Grove, IL: InterVarsityPress, 1973, Americanized 1993), p. 182.
10 Packer, *Evangelism and the Sovereignty of God,* pp. 46-48. Packer changes the word "shall" to "may" as I have used it.

A less formal way of thinking about evangelism is to define it as "having a meaningful conversation of the gospel with a friend." It could be a conversation that covers all elements of the gospel in a single conversation or one or two elements of it. But over time, all elements are covered. Evangelism is teaching these truths and trusting God to transform lives.

Based on the overarching emphasis of the Bible regarding redemption, and what I intend to demonstrate throughout this book, sharing the gospel is the responsibility of every believer. It is an obligation and a privilege for everyone who is born of God. Come join in *loving, living, and telling the good news of Jesus to the ends of the earth!*[11] Become involved in God's great desire and plan to lead lost people to Himself.

---

11 Adapted from Christianity Explored Ministries, https://www.ceministries.org/.

PART ONE

THE OLD TESTAMENT

CHAPTER 1

ADAM TO NOAH

The LORD God said to the serpent,
Because you have done this,
cursed are you above all livestock
and above all beasts of the field;
on your belly you shall go,
and dust you shall eat
all the days of your life.
I will put enmity between you and the woman,
and between your offspring and her offspring;
he shall bruise your head,
and you shall bruise his heel.
Gen. 3:14-15
(Emphasis added.)*[12]*

Most of us are not accustomed to using the words "gospel" and "evangelism" to describe activities in the Old Testament, but these terms are entirely appropriate to use with only a small adjustment in how we understand them. The first seven chapters of Genesis reveal: the life and death reality of gospel proclamation, the gospel being spoken powerfully to lost people, the inextricable linkage of the gospel and evangelism, courage by God's people in telling the gospel, and the urgency of proclaiming this story

---

12 Throughout this book there will be times when selected text or phrases of Scripture are placed in bold. The bolding is not in the original text of Scripture but is used in this book to call attention to certain phrases or words and their special relevance to the points I am making. Every instance of the bolding of Scripture going forward is my emphasis.

of redemption. **It's not an overstatement to say we have the foundations of both the gospel and evangelism in Genesis chapters 1–7!**

If Christians were asked when the gospel "first appeared" in the Bible, most would probably say, "The gospel is first found in the New Testament." However, when one looks at the third chapter of the book of Genesis, the gospel leaps from the text. When we view Genesis as the beginning of the biblical story, we will clearly see how God prophesied the coming of Jesus Christ and His ultimate death to pay for the redemption of sinners. The gospel begins here, in Genesis at the fall, and that is what you would expect from a righteous, holy, loving, and merciful God. The gospel is revealed across the entire Bible, and not only the expression of the gospel, but also the need for God's people of all ages to share it with everyone around them. The Bible is a book about redemption, with Jesus as the centerpiece. When you look for Jesus in the Bible, you will find Him as well as His message of redemption from Genesis to Revelation.[13]

Genesis is a book of beginnings and there are two beginnings that need to be noted. Not only do we have the beginning of creation, but we also have the beginning of redemption. When Adam and Eve sinned and came under God's judgment and wrath, God did not simply destroy what He created. Instead, God responded with a promise of redemption, the gospel.

The story of Adam to Noah reveals with great intensity truths about the gospel and evangelism. We find four evidences of evangelism in Genesis 1-7: Adam and Eve, Seth and Enosh, Enoch and Methuselah, and Noah.

This is a tragic drama in history with a surprise thread of redemption running through it. The suspense in this drama is threefold: Who will find redemption? Who will be swept up in the tragedy of God's wrath? And who will warn those on the path to hell?

As we consider the story of Adam and Eve, I want you to look for the eight elements of the gospel I first mentioned in the Introduction. When each is encountered, a phrase

---

13   Jesus' own words tell us that Genesis to Malachi is about him: "You search the Scriptures because you think that in them you have eternal life; and it is they that bear witness about me" (Jn. 5:39); "And he said to them, 'O foolish ones, and slow of heart to believe all that the prophets have spoken! Was it not necessary that the Christ should suffer these things and enter into his glory?' And beginning with Moses and all the Prophets, he interpreted to them in all the Scriptures the things concerning himself." (Lk. 24:25-27); and "Do not think that I have come to abolish the Law or the Prophets; I have not come to abolish them but to fulfill them." (Mt. 5:17).

or sentence that expresses that element will be placed in italics followed by a number in parentheses corresponding to the table at the end of this chapter.

Adam and Eve

Genesis began with God creating the world (1). He brought everything into existence and gave life to everything that has life. It was an amazing display of power through the mere speaking of a word. He is clearly an other-worldly Being. But how should we think about this God?

The most telling revelations of God's holiness are those occasions in Scripture when a sinful man comes into direct contact with this holy God. The first several chapters of Genesis do not explicitly tell us a lot about God's holiness. Nevertheless, there are some indicators of His character in this early account. First, God spoke the world and universe into existence by a mere word. Pretty impressive stuff which places Him in a category all by Himself! He has no peer. Second, Adam and Eve, when they sinned, were afraid of God's presence and hid themselves, being acutely aware of their sinful condition. God is not like them. They are intimidated. And finally, when God pronounced judgment on Satan, Adam and Eve, and on the creation itself, God was the dominant figure, and everyone and everything was subordinate to Him. No one could withstand His decrees. His judgment was immediately set in motion and became permanent reality for Adam and Eve, for all of creation, and for Satan.

Moving through the timeline of history in Scripture, there are several dramatic examples of God's holiness. Moses in the wilderness saw a burning bush, and as he approached it, God told him to stay back and to take off his shoes for he was standing on holy ground (Ex. 3:3-6). **"Moses trembled and did not dare to look"** at the burning bush (Acts 7:32). **Isaiah came unglued in God's presence and thought his life was about to come to a fiery end** as he recognized his own sinfulness and God's blazing righteousness (Isa. 6:4-7). **The apostle John fell down as a dead man** at the feet of the glorified Christ, whom he had known intimately during His ministry on earth (Rev. 1:17). This almighty God is a "consuming fire" (Heb. 12:29) who must be approached carefully and with great reverence. He existed from eternity past. He never had a beginning and will never have an end. No one compares with the one and only God of creation.

The world that God created was for the man that He would later create. In this new world God would create the perfect environment with the perfect food and the perfect elements to allow man to live forever. God would even provide a tree of life that man could eat to continue to live in this perfectly created world.

In this new world, Adam and Eve could walk with God in the garden and talk with Him directly. They were united with their creator in perfect fellowship, united with one another in perfect unity, and in harmony with the created world around them, including all of God's creatures. It was all perfect.

God, who is holy and infinitely superior to anything in His creation, established the requirements Adam and Eve must adhere to in order to continue in perfect fellowship with Him (2). As the Creator of Adam and Eve, God had the right to make the rules. The only rule God made for Adam and Eve was they were prohibited from eating of the tree of the knowledge of good and evil. They were to manage the garden and develop it under God's authority. They could eat of every tree of the garden except for the tree of the knowledge of good and evil. *He required complete holiness and perfect obedience to his will (2).* God attached a penalty to any violation of His decrees. If Adam and Eve ate of this tree, the sword of judgment would fall, and they would die that very day. In other words, God's wrath would fall on them.

The Great Disaster

> *Did God actually say, "You shall not eat of any tree in the garden?...*
> *You will not surely die...you will be like God"* – **Satan**
>
> *Gen. 3:1-5*

What Adam and Eve did not realize was they had an enemy in the garden who wanted them to fall from their perfect relationship with God. *Adam and Eve violated the arrangement God made with them* (3), and it brought about The Great Disaster – God's judgment and wrath. This is the life-and-death reality of the gospel. Here is how it happened. Satan entered the scene, in the form of a serpent,[14] and cast doubt on God's word with his clever distortions.

---

14   See also Rev. 12:9 for identification of Satan with the serpent of Genesis.

Adam and Eve trusted the word of Satan, the liar. Their sin was not merely a mistake in managing the garden. It was not that they planted too many tomato plants and not enough broccoli. Their sin was breaking the rule, which God established for them, governing their conduct. Their actions amounted to open rebellion and insurrection against the King of the universe. They were not victims of something outside their control, but perpetrators of an offense against a holy God. *As a result, God fulfilled His promise of judgment and death (4).* God always keeps His word. Death immediately occurred and manifested itself in the form of separation from God, separation from each other, and separation from the created world around them. The harmony and unity with everything they had enjoyed was shattered. Physical death and the consuming fires of God's wrath for all of eternity awaited them.

Rico Tice says it well:

> *What does the devil do? He denies God's goodness: "Did he re-*
> *ally say you must not eat or touch it? You can't trust Him." The*
> *devil denies God's holiness: "You won't surely die, there will be no*
> *judgment." And he denies God's otherness: "You will be like God*
> *knowing good and evil." That's always what the devil does. He*
> *denies God's goodness, God's holiness, and God's otherness. "You*
> *can't trust Him to know what is best for you." That's how people*
> *leap into sin.*[15]

There are many kinds of disasters that have come upon the earth in its long history – wars, worldwide pandemics, droughts, famines, hurricanes, tornadoes, earthquakes, and man-made disasters of all kinds. As bad as these catastrophes are, none is as terrible as the judgment and wrath of God falling on a person's life. The others don't even compare. God's wrath falling on Adam and Eve was the disaster of all disasters. From that moment in history, judgment was always on the horizon for every human. From

---

15   Rico Tice, *Preaching Sin in a Hostile World,* Plenary Session 3 at the annual Christianity Explored USA conference: How Will They Hear?, May 4, 2019, Nashville, TN. Audio: 29:30-31:35.

that moment in history, mankind was in need of salvation. Every person outside of Christ is under wrath and only held from the fires of hell by the thinnest of threads (Deut. 32:35[16]; Jn. 3:36).

Satan, the serpent, was judged, humiliated, and condemned. God's wrath was poured out on Adam and Eve. It came in the form of spiritual death and alienation from God immediately, with physical death and eternal death in the future. In their sinful, unclean, and unholy condition, they were without hope, dead to God with no ability to restore their relationship to Him. A dead man can do nothing, and they were dead.

The Great Salvation

"But God, being rich in mercy"[17], proclaimed to Adam and Eve *the first and greatest Messianic prophecy ever given in all of Scripture, on which the entire Bible would rest (5).*[18] *Adam and Eve deserved only God's wrath, but God acted out of grace (6).* Amazingly, a Deliverer, a Savior was promised to come from the offspring of Eve – a human being (Gen. 3:15). God, speaking to Satan, said in Gen. 3:15, "He shall bruise your head," meaning the Deliverer would deal a death blow to Satan. We know from later Scripture that at the end of the world he will be thrown into the lake of fire. God continued speaking to Satan, "And you shall bruise his heel," meaning Satan would strike the heel of Messiah, which symbolically refers to his death and actually was fulfilled when Christ died on Golgotha at the hands of Roman soldiers where they drove a spike into the heel of Jesus as He was put on the cross. This proved to be a non-fatal blow when Jesus rose from the dead on the third day. Whereas the crushing of the head is a fatal blow to Satan, the bruising of the heel was a temporary wound to Jesus.[19] Archaeology confirms

---

16   Jonathan Edwards, in his famous (and loving) sermon, *Sinners in the Hands of an Angry God,* warned sinners of the danger they were in apart from Christ and urged them to turn to Christ and be saved. "You hang by a slender thread, with the flames of divine wrath flashing about it, and ready every moment to singe it, and burn it asunder" Jonathan Edwards, *Sinners in the Hands of an Angry God,* (Enfield, MA, July 8, 1741), p. 6.

17   Eph. 2:4.

18   This is the first time the gospel is spoken in the Bible, Genesis 3:15, and is often referred to as the pro-to-evangelium (Latin for "the first gospel" or "first good news").

19   New Testament passages that support the "bruising of the head" as referring to what Jesus accomplished on the cross and support the identification of Satan as the serpent are: Rom. 16:20; Gal. 4:4; Col. 2:13-15; 1 Jn. 3:7-10, 3:11-15; and Rev. 12:9, 20:2.

a link to the crucifixion through a discovery in 1968 of the remains of a person who was crucified in Jerusalem with a spike still embedded in their heel.[20]

As part of the judgment pronounced by God, enmity (hostility, animosity, hatred) was installed between the offspring of Eve and the offspring of Satan and is part of our present reality today (7). One way this manifest itself is in the opposition to Christians and Christianity that many nonbelievers have. For example, Cain killed his brother Abel because God did not accept his offering and had accepted the offering of Abel.

After the pronouncement of judgment and offer of salvation, Adam and Eve had a decision to make. Would they continue trusting in Satan's word? They saw how well that worked out. Or would they repent of trusting Satan's word and place their faith (trust) in what God promised them? *The evidence in the text shows us they repented of their sin, placed their trust in God's word, and were saved from His wrath (8).*

Adam's faith can be seen in the naming of Eve in Gen. 3:20 – "The man called his wife's name Eve, because she was the mother of all living." God promised that Eve would have "offspring," and Adam demonstrated his faith in God's promise by naming his wife "life giver." Eve had never borne children, and Adam believed God's promise that she would become a mother. That was an act of faith.

Eve's faith can be seen in Gen. 4:1 and 4:25, when she celebrated the arrival of her offspring Cain, and later Seth. She celebrated the birth of Cain by saying, "I have gotten a man with the help of the LORD" (4:1). She celebrated the birth of Seth when she "called his name Seth,[21] for she said, 'God has appointed for me another offspring instead of Abel, for Cain killed him.'" (4:25).[22] She initially thought Cain was the line through which the Savior would come, but he turned out to be a murderer. Eve's words demonstrated her faith in God's promise.

We see a parallel to Adam and Eve's faith in Paul's teaching on the salvation of Abraham. Paul states that Abraham was saved by faith: "just as Abraham 'believed God, and it was counted to him as righteousness'" (Gal. 3:6). Paul was citing Gen.

---

20 Lisette Bassett-Brody, *Etched in Stone,* (Washington, D.C.: WND Books, 2017), p. 210-213; and https://jamestabor.com/crucifixion-nails-our-latest-evidence/, April 11, 2018, Accessed August 17, 2020.

21 The ESV footnote reads: "*Seth* sounds like the Hebrew for *he appointed.*"

22 James M. Boice, *Genesis: An Expositional Commentary, Volume 1, Genesis 1-11* (Grand Rapids, MI: Baker Books, 2005), pp. 230-31.

15:6: "And he (Abraham) believed the Lord, and he (God) counted it to him as righteousness." It is entirely appropriate to equate what Adam and Eve experienced to Abraham's experience.

Immediately following Adam's act of faith, Scripture tells us that God "clothed" both Adam and Eve in skins of animals. Nakedness after the fall in Gen. 3:7-11 signifies the guilt and shame of their sin. The death of an animal to provide clothing for them foreshadowed the promised Savior's death on the cross as a propitiation[23] of God's wrath. This first prefiguring of Christ's death on the cross followed the first promise of a Savior, which was followed by the repentance and faith of Adam and Eve. God's clothing them in the skins of animals was symbolic of "imputing"[24] His righteousness to them. The promise of Gen. 3:15 and the sacrifice of 3:21 are related. It gives us a first, though somewhat obscure, glimpse of what the Savior would accomplish. It would be salvation through judgment. Judgment falls on the innocent animal (prefiguring Jesus' death on the cross) and salvation is achieved for Adam and Eve. We, in the 21st century, know the cross was gruesome, and for Adam and Eve, the sight of the first animal being killed to give them clothing must have been a traumatic event. They had never seen anything, or anyone die, and now an animal's blood was shed on their behalf.

This early portrayal of the cross does not contain the many details that are revealed progressively in Scripture, beginning with Isaac and the ram in Gen. 22:13 and continuing as we progress through the Old Testament into the New. But it communicates the same basic message as more vivid instances of foreshadowing do, such as the Passover lamb during the exodus (Ex. 12:1-20), whose blood on the doorposts spared the firstborn of the household from God's wrath and death.[25]

---

23 Propitiation means an appeasement of God's wrath. For an extensive discussion of this word see John Stott, *The Cross of Christ (with study guide)*, (Leicester, England: Inter-Varsity Press, 1986, 2004), pp. 168-75; (additional references – O.T.: Ex 12:1-20; Isa. 52:13-53:12; N.T.: Rom. 3:25; Heb. 2:17; 1 John 2:2, 4:10).

24 Imputed righteousness is the idea that righteousness is attributed by God to the sinner who repents and turns to Him for salvation. "The sinner's guilt is imputed to Christ; the latter's righteousness is imputed to the sinner." William Hendriksen, *Exposition of Paul's Epistle to the Romans (Vol. 12–13)*, (NTC), (Grand Rapids: Baker Book House, 1980, 1981), p. 130.

25 For additional references in scripture of blood sacrifices, here is a short list: Gen. 22:1-19, Lev 16, John 1:29, 36; Rev. 5:6, 9, 12; 13:8.

The Foundation of the Gospel

Eight Basic Elements of the Gospel (See table at the end of this chapter.)

In the fall of Adam and Eve, we see the eight basic elements of the gospel revealed. Additional details are made known going forward in the Old Testament and into the New Testament, but all the ingredients are here. The narrative shows us the real-life context, as it played out in the lives of Adam and Eve. It shows us what is at stake and opens the gospel to us both intellectually as well as emotionally.

1. **God.** In Genesis chapters 1–3 God created everything from nothing. He is a holy God without equal and without peer. He is our creator, potentially our Father, and will be our judge (Gen. 1-2; 3:8-19, 22-24). Every human and all of creation are subordinate to his absolute authority. He is the sole ruling monarch of his creation.

2. **Holiness.** God is holy and requires of man complete holiness, sinless perfection, and perfect obedience to his will. He is transcendent (supreme, preeminent, without peer) over His creation and morally perfect in His character. He rules and reigns in "sovereign majesty and power" over creation.[26] When Adam and Eve sinned against God they lost the intimacy they previously enjoyed with Him because they were no longer holy. It was a great loss. (Gen. 1:26-27; 2:15-17).

3. **Sin.** Adam and Eve violated God's requirement by rebelling against his authority. They ate the forbidden fruit and essentially decided to make themselves equal with God. They committed treason against the King of Creation, and it was deadly. They found themselves naked, which after the fall signifies the guilt and shame of sin (Gen. 3:7, 10-11; 2 Cor. 5:3; Heb. 4:13; Rev. 3:17). They died spiritually that very day, were alienated from God, and were under his wrath (Gen. 3:6-7, 9-11).

---

26 Walter A. Elwell (General Editor), *"Holiness," Baker Encyclopedia of the Bible* (Grand Rapids, MI: Baker Book House, 1988), p. 984.

4. **Judgment and Wrath.** As a result of sin and disobedience Adam and Eve (as well as all their biological and spiritual children) were guilty, separated from God, and children of wrath. God's judgment came down on Adam and Eve (Gen. 3:8-19; 6:5-8, 13). The punishment ("you shall surely die") would be spiritual death which meant separation from God immediately and separation from God for all of eternity suffering his wrath in the fires of hell commencing at physical death.

5. **The Cross and Resurrection.** But God promised Adam and Eve a Savior who would rescue them from their sin and God's wrath. The cross and resurrection were prophesied in Gen. 3:15 in the bruising of Jesus' heel, a non-fatal blow, the cross. The bruising of Satan's head predicts a fatal blow to be inflicted on him by the Savior through the cross. The effect of this for Adam and Eve, as they repented and trusted in God's promise, is seen when God clothed them with the skins of animals. This symbolized their being clothed in the righteousness of Jesus and that God's wrath was averted. (Gen. 3:15, 21). They were rescued from his wrath and restored to union with God.

6. **Grace.** Adam and Eve deserved only God's condemnation and wrath, but God acted out of his love in grace. He gave them the promise of a Savior, their only hope of a rescue from the result of their sin. "And the *Lord God made* for Adam and for his wife garments of skins and clothed them" (Gen. 3:21). God did this out of his great mercy and undeserved favor (grace). (See also Gen. 6:8).

7. **Counting the Cost of Following Christ.** There is a cost of following the Savior and it began at the Fall. Enmity was introduced on the earth between the offspring of Eve and the offspring of Satan. The cost is three-fold: a.) sin must be forsaken, b.) one's self-determination must be abandoned and replaced with living for the glory of Christ, and c.) there is opposition from the offspring of Satan toward those who follow Christ (i.e., Cain's murder of Abel, Gen. 3:15; 4:1-26; 6:11-13). "In evangelism there's a huge problem of us not calling people to see this as a precondition of repentance. We repent and believe as we become Christians having counted the cost. Of course, it's then a daily part of discipleship, but it's getting the un-

derstanding in at the beginning that is so often critical to facing suffering and persecution (see Lk. 14:25-33)."[27]

8. **Repentance and Faith.** To be saved, a sinner must turn from their sin and place their trust in God. Adam and Eve trusted in Satan's word, and it proved disastrous. They needed to turn away from their sin, turn away from the lies of Satan, and trust in God and his word. Repentance does not mean to stop sinning. No one can do that perfectly. It means to have sorrow for sin, to feel remorse, to have revulsion toward it and to give it up. This sorrow and revulsion is "accompanied by a true change of heart toward God."[28] "The emphasis...seems to be more specifically the total change, both in thought and behavior, with respect to how one should both think and act."[29] Repentance and faith entail turning to Christ for his mercy and forgiveness and following him as Lord (Gen. 3:20; 4:25; 6:9, 22).

The Foundation of Evangelism

The gospel and evangelism are two sides of the same coin. The *"good news"* and *"telling"* the good news cannot be disconnected if we wish to be consistent with Scripture. If we grasp what occurred in the first three chapters of Genesis – judgment and wrath was poured out on Adam and Eve because of their sin – it should be inconceivable to us that God would withhold the message of hope and deliverance from Adam and Eve. That would not be consistent with God's holiness and His character. Since God provided the promise of a Savior to rescue them from His righteous wrath, would He not communicate that reality? Of course, He would! The same dynamic applies to the people who are His offspring and who are made in His image to reflect His character.

God was the one who evangelized Adam and Eve. There was obviously no one else available in that unique situation. It is important to notice how God spoke the whole

27 This insight provided to me by Rico Tice in an email on January 11, 2024.

28 Spiros Zodhiates, General Editor, *The Complete Word Study Dictionary: New Testament (electronic edition),* (Chattanooga, TN: AMG Publishers, 2000), μετανοέω (metanoéō), word no. 3340.

29 Johannes P. Louw and Eugene Albert Nida, *Greek-English Lexicon of the New Testament: Based on Semantic Domains* (New York: United Bible Societies, 1996), 41.52, p. 509.

gospel into their lives and did not shy away from what we consider the hard parts. In fact, God began and ended with the hard parts of sin and wrath and folded the promise of grace and salvation into it. The order of His "evangelism presentation" was: (1) God called them to account and exposed their sin (3:9-13); (2) judgment was pronounced (3:14-15); (3) God inserted enmity into life on earth, the first wave of judgment and an escalation of the cosmic conflict between good and evil. Now there would be a cost of following the Savior (Gen. 3:15); (4) He gave hope through a promise of salvation, a Savior who would save them from their sin and from God's wrath (Gen. 3:15); and (5) God made additional pronouncements of judgment, spelling out the implications of it (3:16-19). There are five parts to this "evangelism" moment, and four of them are negative. There are 321 words (ESV) in this gospel presentation. Ninety-six percent of these words are devoted to holding them accountable for their sin and pronouncing judgment on them. Only 4 percent are devoted to the hope of salvation. In today's environment one might sarcastically ask, "Didn't God know He might hurt Adam and Eve's feelings with all this negative talk of sin and judgment? Was He trying to scare them into the kingdom?" Well, *yes* to both of those questions. They needed to be humbled, and they needed to be fearful of God's coming wrath.

After hearing the whole gospel story, including the consequences of what they had done, Adam and Eve repented and were restored through their trust in God's word. God responded to their faith and clothed them in righteousness (3:21). We know from later illumination in Scripture that God's righteousness only comes through faith (Gen. 15:6; Rom. 4:3; Eph. 2:8-9) by "the blood of the lamb" (Rev 7:14; 12:11).

The order and content of God's gospel presentation to Adam and Eve is important. I am not suggesting it is a model template of the *order* in which we must speak the gospel into people's lives. But I am suggesting it shows us the necessary *content and emphasis*. It demonstrates what needs to be communicated if we are to faithfully speak and teach God's message to others. ***Any presentation of the gospel that does not adequately illuminate sin, judgment, wrath, repentance, and counting the cost of discipleship as well as the love of God, grace, and forgiveness is inadequate and incomplete.*** And it is actually worse than that. It is false teaching, and God abhors false teaching. Just ask Hananiah, who preached grace and eliminated wrath (Jer. 28). This account has a unified message with an emphasis that God intended.

What Can We Learn About the Gospel and Evangelism from Adam and Eve?

The early unfolding of the gospel and evangelism gives us vivid images that reveal the drama of life. Let's consider three ways we should be impacted by this narrative: understanding the life and death reality, speaking the whole gospel, and taking seriously God's word.

First, the life and death reality. The story of Adam and Eve dramatizes the seriousness of relating properly to a holy God. Every person born after the fall is born into a state of alienation from God as a sinner by nature and under the curse of eternal death. "And you were dead in the trespasses and sins in which you once walked...and were by nature children of wrath, like the rest of mankind" (Eph. 2:3). God's promise that the Savior would endure a "bruised heel" in the process of crushing Satan's head is the most precious promise God has ever given. "Whoever believes in the Son has eternal life; whoever does not obey the Son shall not see life, but the wrath of God remains on him" (John 3:36).

This makes the issue of being rightly related to God the most important issue our friends and family will ever face. It is more than a mere personal preference or one choice among many good options. It is the ONLY good option! How a person responds to God's offer of salvation determines where they will spend eternity. **We must view others through the lens of this ultimate reality.** Only when we comprehend this life and death reality will we join the Apostle Paul in "great sorrow and unceasing anguish in my heart" (Rom. 9:2) over those who stand separated from God and under His wrath. **This is compelling motivation for believers to organize their lives to win some to Christ!** (1 Cor. 9:19-23).

Second, the whole gospel. God, in evangelizing Adam and Eve, spoke to them the whole gospel. In holding them accountable for their sin and warning them of the coming judgment and wrath, God was acting in love. If believers fail to warn people of the consequences of their sin and fail to urge them to repent and place their trust in God's promised Savior (Jesus), they reveal coldness toward God and toward others. Jesus says in Mt. 24:12 that in the last times "the love of many will grow cold." Yet "the one who endures to the end will be saved. And this gospel of the kingdom will be proclaimed throughout the whole world...and then the end will come" (Mt. 24:13-14). If we genuinely love God (meaning our love has not grown cold), we will speak the hard truths of the gospel in love. It is not kindness to refuse to speak of God's wrath. It is the exact opposite.

Many in today's evangelical church preach and teach a severely "truncated gospel."[30] Many teachers and evangelists teach God's love, mercy, grace, and forgiveness but practically ignore sin, judgment, wrath, repentance, and the cost of following Jesus. The difficult doctrines of sin, judgment, wrath, repentance, and the cost of discipleship **should** be of equal prominence in our telling of the gospel as the love of God, grace, forgiveness, and faith. If we integrate the love of God with the fact that "he is angry with sin and will punish those who persist in it," the "love of God is given a backbone."[31]

J. I. Packer in his classic work *Knowing God* writes about the tendency to neglect the doctrine of God's wrath. "The modern habit throughout the Christian church is to play this subject down. Those who still believe in the wrath of God (not all do) say little about it; perhaps they do not think much about it. To an age which has unashamedly sold itself to the gods of greed, pride, sex, and self-will, the church mumbles on about God's kindness but says virtually nothing about his judgment. How often during the past year did you hear, or, if you are a minister, did you preach, a sermon on the wrath of God?"[32]

In the same chapter, Packer adds: "Clearly the theme of God's wrath is one about which the biblical writers feel no inhibitions whatever. Why then, should we? Why, when the Bible is vocal about it, should we feel obliged to be silent? What is it that makes us awkward and embarrassed when the subject comes up, that prompts us to soft-pedal it and hedge when we are asked about it? What lies at the bottom of our hesitations and difficulties?...What really is the trouble here?"[33]

The people who spent the most time with Jesus on this earth and were most impacted by His ministry used words reflecting God's wrath (e.g., wrath, fire, judgment, condemnation, hell, etc.) an astounding 350 times in 300 different verses in the New

---

30   Metzger, *Tell the Truth,* p. 39. The author devotes nearly two chapters, 54 pages, to the necessity of teaching the whole gospel; highly recommended.

31   Metzger, *Tell the Truth,* p. 39.

32   Packer, *Knowing God,* p. 148.

33   Packer, *Knowing God,* p. 150.

Testament. They are on practically every page of the New Testament. Paul writes in Rom. 11:22, "Note then the kindness and the severity of God: severity toward those who have fallen, but God's kindness to you, provided you continue in his kindness." It is not either/or, but both. If we teach a gospel that includes God's grace but leaves out His wrath, it is no longer the biblical gospel.

C. H. Spurgeon was a great example of how to preach the whole gospel. His sermons were heavy on sin, wrath, the coming judgment, repentance, hell, etc. They were also filled with grace, mercy, love, and pleadings to sinners to repent and turn to Christ. Here are two examples:

> O, sinners, do not think because we come tonight to preach free grace and dying love to you, and proclaim full pardon through the blood of Jesus, that therefore God winks at sin. No, he is a terrible God, and will by no means spare the guilty. As surely as fire consumes the stubble so does his wrath burn against wickedness, and he will utterly destroy it from off the face of the earth, for 'God is angry with the wicked every day.' [34]

From another sermon.

> There is perfect pardon to be had by the vilest transgressor; immediate and irreversible pardon is freely given according to God's infinite mercy and abounding grace to the very chief of sinners. He waits to bestow mercy on the sons of men, and, therefore, if you have it not it is not because God is hard to propitiate. He delighteth in mercy; to the ends of the earth he makes proclamation 'Let us reason together, though your sins be as scarlet, they shall be as white as snow.' [35]

---

34 C. H. Spurgeon, *Amazing Grace in The Metropolitan Tabernacle Pulpit Sermons* (Vol. 22), (London: Passmore & Alabaster, Electronic Edition), p. 101.

35 Spurgeon, *Reasons for Parting with Sin in The Metropolitan Tabernacle Pulpit Sermons, (Vol. 22)*, p. 94.

In 479 sermons selected from eight full years between 1855 and 1885, words depicting God's wrath were present more than 15,000 times.[36] That equates to an average of more than 32 times per sermon. To say the least, Spurgeon was not shy about teaching this distressing doctrine of the gospel. Instead of turning people away, the truth of the gospel resonated with his listeners and drew them into Christ. When people heard Spurgeon preach, they knew he was telling them the truth of the biblical gospel.

Spurgeon had a monumental worldwide impact that was not limited to his home country of the United Kingdom. Beginning in 1855, a Spurgeon sermon was published every week until his death in 1892. The distribution grew to include more than 30 countries. "An English author writing in 1903 declared, 'The total number of Spurgeon's sermons issued in print during half a century must be between two and three hundred millions!'" In a world of hard copy-only publishing, that was a staggering number of sermons distributed.[37]

Here is one example of the impact Spurgeon had. "In many countries where people lived at a distance from a church, groups of people gathered each Lord's Day to hear the reading of one of Spurgeon's sermons. He tells, for instance, of hearing from such a company in some remote district of England. The letter stated that approximately two hundred persons had been converted in such a gathering, and they wanted a minister to come and form them into a church. Likewise there were out-of-the-way areas in Scotland where people had no idea who was the Prime Minister of Great Britain, but they all knew about Spurgeon through the reading of his sermons."[38]

(Spurgeon's sermons are available free online[39] and can be purchased in hard copy or in electronic form through various Bible software programs.)

For those of you who preach, teach, or tell the gospel to others, I would encourage you to undertake this exercise: Analyze the content of your presentations, whether they

---

36   C. H. Spurgeon, *The New Park Street Pulpit Sermons* and *The Metropolitan Tabernacle Pulpit Sermons*, (Vols. 1, 6, 10, 15, 20, 22, 26, and 31), (London: Passmore & Alabaster). These sermons were for the years 1855, 1860, 1864, 1869, 1874, 1876, 1880, and 1885. Words searched were: anger, angry, curse, cursed, condemnation, condemned, condemn, darkness, death, deliver, destruction, destroy, destroyed, fire, fury, hell, judgment, judged, judge, perish, perishing, saved, save, vengeance, and wrath.

37   Arnold A. Dallimore, *Spurgeon: A Biography*, (Edinburgh, UK: Banner of Truth, 1984, reprinted 2018), pp. 193, 195.

38   Dallimore, *Spurgeon*, pp. 194-195

39   There are several websites that make Spurgeon sermons available free electronically such as *The Spurgeon Center* at https://www.spurgeon.org and *Spurgeon Gems* at https://www.spurgeongems.org.

are sermons, lessons, or conversations with nonbelievers. Use the eight elements of the gospel that I presented earlier as a grid for comparison. Then select a period of time, such as the last four sermons or lessons or the last three months or 12 months and analyze how well you covered all eight elements of the gospel message. It is relatively easy to teach the truths of God's love and grace and Christ's sacrificial death on the cross. But are you giving equal "airtime" to teaching the truths of sin, judgment, wrath, hell, repentance, and counting the cost of following Christ? Based on my limited observations, I believe spiritual leaders have ceased to teach and speak these hard truths of the gospel. If that is true, we must reclaim the gospel in a way that is pleasing to God and biblically correct. Here is a form you can use to evaluate the gospel content of your teaching and preaching.

Whole Gospel Checklist

	Elements of Gospel	Week 1	Week 2	Week 3	Week 4	Summary
1	God (Creator, Father, Judge)					
2	Holiness (God's standard)					
3	Sin					
4	Wrath/Judgment					
5	Cross and Resurrection					
6	Grace					
7	Count the cost of following Jesus					
8	Repent and Believe					
	Total Doctrines Covered					

Why is it so crucial that we speak, teach, and preach the whole gospel? Let me summarize: (1) faithfulness to God and His word, (2) love for our neighbor, and (3) personal integrity. We want people to know we love them and to know we are telling them the truth.

Third, God's word is not to be trifled with. God always does what He says He will do. Satan perverted God's word. Adam and Eve responded foolishly based on that perversion and were broken by their sin and by God's judgment. They had violated His word. God's word is not influenced by popular culture or personal opinions. **We may**

try to make the biblical message more acceptable to our culture, but when we do, we mislead and deceive.

God commands His servants to never compromise His word. The prophet Jeremiah was angry at God and discouraged at the high cost of faithfully proclaiming God's word (Jer. 15:10-21). God's word to him was sweet initially (v. 16), but it became bitter as he met with persecution and reproach from his society (vv. 10, 15, 17). Jeremiah complained to God and harshly accused God of being a "deceitful brook" and "like waters that fail" (v.18). He basically called God a liar and accused Him of being unreliable. Jeremiah "had forgotten God's word [and] like many today...[had written] his own job description."[40] As we might expect, God rebuked Jeremiah and called him to repent. God set out the conditions for his reinstatement: (1) Jeremiah must repent, (2) he must speak only what God gives him to speak, and (3) he must not allow the message to be contaminated by cultural, societal, nor political influence (v. 19). He must not alter God's word to suit those around him no matter how powerful they may be. He was to influence them and was not to allow their influence to compromise God's word. (v. 19). If Jeremiah would agree to God's conditions, He would restore him to his position as God's spokesman and God would make him as "a fortified wall of bronze" (v. 20) and would rescue him from the hand of his "ruthless" enemies (v. 21). The cost of being faithful to God's word would be great – "they will fight against you" (v. 20) – as Jeremiah would have powerful enemies. However, his words would be worthless if he altered them. He knew the cost and re-surrendered to God's demands.

The book of Revelation has a somber warning for those who would change the word of God (Rev. 22:18-19). It is drawn from Deuteronomy (cf. Deut. 4:2; 12:32; 29:19-20). These warnings, from early in the Bible to the end, put all of us on notice that God's word is not under our authority. Everyone who speaks, teaches, or preaches the gospel is held to this standard. It is His word and not our own which has the power to transform lives.

> *But this is the one to whom I will look:*
> *he who is humble and contrite in spirit*
> *and trembles at my word.*
> *Isaiah 66:2*

---

40 F. B. Huey, *Jeremiah, Lamentations* (NAC) (Nashville: Broadman & Holman Publishers, 1993), p. 162.

Seth (and Enosh)

And Adam knew his wife again, and she bore a son and called his name Seth, for she said, 'God has appointed for me another offspring instead of Abel, for Cain killed him.' To Seth also a son was born, and he called his name Enosh. **At that time people began to call upon the name of the LORD.**

Gen. 4:25-26

It is interesting that people began calling on the name of the Lord around the time Seth's son Enosh was born. Seth and Enosh were in the line of God's promised Messiah. Given that the promised Savior would be an offspring of Eve, it would have been natural for a *birth* to generate renewed focus on the promise given to Adam and Eve 235 years earlier.[41] We celebrate the birth of THE Savior – Jesus – at Christmas every year 2,000 years after the fact. We remind ourselves of the fulfillment of God's promise and remember His coming to save us from our sins. I am not aware of any Scripture relating the birth of Enosh to Jesus' birth, but it is an interesting parallel.

Adam was 130 years old when Seth was born, and Eve recognized him as God's appointed one. Though her statement at the birth of Cain evidenced her faith, her faith was more mature at the birth of Seth. She saw more clearly God's hand in his birth. He came through the line of promise. She stated, "God has appointed for me another offspring instead of Abel, for Cain killed him" (Gen. 4:25). God received full credit for the birth of Seth. See Timeline below.

In another 105 years, when Adam was 235 years old, Seth had a son, Enosh. Something extraordinary happened around that event. "People began to call upon the name of the Lord" (Gen. 4:26). It had been 235 years since God gave Adam and Eve the promise of a Savior, and hope in this promise was still alive. Notice that "people" (plural) were "calling on the name of the Lord."

---

41   The number of years and spans of time I have calculated assume there are no time gaps in the genealogy of Gen. 5. I have provided these to give a general sense of the spans of time. We should not assume precision as there could be gaps which would mean the time spans were longer.

Evangelism from Adam to Noah

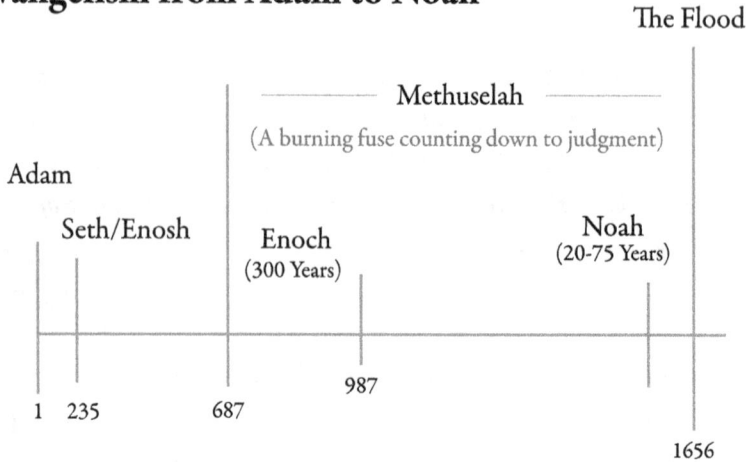

The Flood

Methuselah

(A burning fuse counting down to judgment)

Adam

Seth/Enosh

Enoch
(300 Years)

Noah
(20-75 Years)

987

1   235   687

1656

What Can We Learn about Evangelism from Seth and Enosh?

This passage makes us think of Rom. 10:13 which says, "Everyone who calls on the name of the Lord will be saved." Paul is quoting Joel 2:32, which is also cited in Acts 2:21. We tend to think of the phrase "calling on the name of the Lord" as unique to the New Testament, but it is definitely not. Its origins are in the Old Testament (e.g., Ps. 116:17; Joel 2:32; Zeph. 3:9; Zech. 13:9).

In Romans 10, Paul makes clear that God's primary way of bringing people into His kingdom is through the telling of the gospel story. "How then will they call on him in whom they have not believed? And how are they to believe in him of whom they have never heard? And how are they to hear without someone preaching?... So faith comes from hearing, and hearing through the word of Christ" (Rom. 10:14-17).

Calling on the name of the Lord is synonymous with people being saved. In the line of Seth and Enosh, a mini-revival seems to have occurred. Was Adam acting as the first high priest, telling the gospel story to his children, grandchildren, and others, urging them to turn to God? Was this the first church of God's people?[42] Many tantalizing questions arise from this passage, and we are left to wonder. But it is clear there was a movement of people coming to God.

---

42   Boice, *Genesis: An Expositional Commentary*, Volume 1, p. 275.

Regardless of the geographical or numerical scope of people calling on the Lord, we know that **God's people were telling the story of His promise of redemption.**[43] The flip side of the gospel coin – evangelism – also was taking place. The people of God are people of the good news. The good news was being proclaimed at this very early point in world history, and **"people began to call on the name of the LORD" (Gen. 4:26).**[44]

Enoch (and Methuselah)

When Enoch had lived 65 years, he fathered Methuselah. Enoch walked with God after he fathered Methuselah 300 years and had other sons and daughters. Thus all the days of Enoch were 365 years. Enoch walked with God, and he was not, for God took him.

Gen. 5:21-24

Enoch is one of the most amazing characters in the Bible. Three passages about him enable us to put together a brief profile of his life and ministry – Gen. 5:21-24; Heb. 11:5; and Jude 14-15. He was one of only two humans to enter heaven without dying (Gen. 5:24; Heb. 11:5). Elijah was the other, and we know what a powerful force he was as a proclaimer of God's message. Enoch too, quite possibly on the magnitude of Elijah, was a proclaimer of God's message. He warned of the Lord's coming in judgment against the ungodly because of their sin. He called out the sins of his generation and of his culture, specifically naming their "deeds" of ungodliness and the "harsh things" said by the ungodly against God (Jude 14-15).

43　Some theologians prefer to translate the last sentence of Gen. 4:26 as "Then it [offspring] began to be called by the name Yahweh." John D. Currid, *Genesis*, vol. 1 (Darlington, England, Grand Rapids, MI: EP Books, 2003), p. 158. "There is a holy, godly line and it is known by Yahweh's name" (Currid, p. 158). In either case, people *began* publicly talking about and/or identifying with the name of the Lord.

44　More on the phrase "call on": "The verb *qārā*, 'call,' can be used for naming (cf. 4:17, 25), reading, proclaiming, summoning, and praying. Usage of this expression in the Pentateuch supports the idea of proclamation more than praying (cf. Gen. 12:8; Exod. 34:6; Lev. 1:1)...The idea of this line is that people began to make proclamation about the nature of the Lord ('began to make proclamation of the Lord by name'). This record informs the reader that some who traced their lineage to Seth, God's replacement for Abel, began to proclaim their faith. They, as well as Noah, Abram, and others, proclaimed the Lord by their worship and their words." Allen P. Ross, *Creation and Blessing: A Guide to the Study and Exposition of Genesis*, (Grand Rapids, MI: Baker Books, 1998), p. 169.

The sins of the world at the time of Noah (Gen. 6) most likely characterized Enoch's earlier timeframe as well. The New Testament tells us Enoch preached, "Behold, the Lord comes with ten thousands of his holy ones, to execute judgment on all and to convict all the ungodly of all their deeds of ungodliness that they have committed in such an ungodly way, and of all the harsh things that ungodly sinners have spoken against him" (Jude 14-15). Enoch warned of an overwhelming and obliterating judgment, and it is safe to assume that he would have called out specific sins by name: false teaching ("harsh things" against God), sexual promiscuity (6:1-4), hearts set on evil continually (6:5), corruption in society, a culture filled with violence (6:11-12), murder, revenge, and boasting about it (4:23-24).[45]

Enoch was pleasing to God (Heb. 11:5). In other words, God was pleased about his faithfulness, his naming of sins and calling sinners to repent. He was pleased that Enoch warned of the coming judgment. It would be a judgment that no one would escape outside of God's redemption. The corollary is that **God cannot be pleased when we *fail* to call out sin, and especially when we *redefine* sin. He cannot be pleased when we fail to warn of the coming judgment.**

Enoch was a proclaimer of the gospel in his day. He pleased God by his faith, a faith that drove him to speak the hard truths of the gospel.

What Can We Learn from Enoch about the Gospel and Evangelism?

First, Enoch spoke the whole gospel message into a world dominated by darkness and sin. He spoke as God directed him, and God directed that the whole of reality be declared. His message included sin, judgment, wrath, and the only hope available which was trust in the Savior. **Redemption cannot be understood apart from the context of sin and wrath.**

In our day there is a persistent failure to preach and teach about sin and wrath. If we fail to teach the doctrine of sin and name sins, that is tantamount to redefining sin. If we fail to warn of God's wrath, that is tantamount to redefining God's character. If sins defined by Scripture are no longer sins by our reckoning, then we are saying two

---

45 Jude is citing from the non-canonical book *1 Enoch,* and he is not indicating that he believed all of *1 Enoch* to be part of the canon of Scripture. Jude "believed that the portion he quoted represented God's truth…Jude simply drew from a part of the work that he considered true." This is similar to what Paul did in Acts 17:28 and Tit. 1:12. Thomas R. Schreiner, *1, 2 Peter, Jude* (NAC) (Nashville: Broadman & Holman Publishers, 2003), pp. 469–470.

things: (1) God is no longer a righteous God, and (2) God's word cannot be trusted. The righteous response to sin is wrath, and if God is not angry at sin, then He is no longer a righteous God. *The church's failure to name sin and warn of God's wrath in our generation is an absolute failure of faith and obedience to God and His Word.*

The brief summary of Enoch's message in Jude indicates that he named the sins of his generation and warned them of an overwhelming judgment to come. The 21st century environment in the United States (and in most countries of the world) is similar to the time of Enoch. James Montgomery Boice, writing about the time of Enoch, draws the application well: "If these are such days and if the future coming of the Lord Jesus Christ will be a judgment comparable even to the flood, should not our preaching and witnessing be as filled with condemnation of sin as was the preaching of Enoch and equally as insistent in warning people to flee from the wrath to come?"[46]

Second, Enoch displayed significant courage and love in his message. The same courage required of Enoch to walk with God, call out sins, and warn of coming judgment is required in our day. It takes courage to walk faithfully with Christ and to warn others about the coming judgment.

In Rev. 21:8, God speaks from the throne and says, "But as for **the cowardly,** the faithless, the detestable, as for murderers, the sexually immoral, sorcerers, idolaters, **and all liars,** their portion will be in the lake that burns with fire and sulfur, which is the second death." In contrast to those who have conquered and who will enjoy the new heavens and the new earth, God describes the kinds of sinners who will be cast into the lake of fire. He begins the list with "cowards" and ends it with "liars." G. K. Beale observes,

> *By introducing the list of sins with "cowards" and concluding it with "liars,"*
> *he shows that these vices primarily indicate failures of so-called Christians*
> *facing the threat or reality of persecution…so that the cowardly are those who*
> *have been professing Christians. They are those in the visible community of*
> *faith who have "'turned back in the holy war" with the world and have not*
> *demonstrated courageous faith in the battle against the beast.*[47]

---

46 Boice, *Genesis: An Expositional Commentary*, Volume 1, p. 287.
47 Beale, *The Book of Revelation*, p. 1059.

This may be one of the most shocking passages in the Bible because of who is included in the lake of fire. It is disturbing that "the cowardly" make the list of those with whom Jesus will be ashamed (see Mk. 8:34-38). I am not implying that those who fail to share the gospel with others are consigned to hell. I do believe however that this passage is referring to those who ultimately deny Christ out of fear of suffering for the sake of the gospel. And it is perhaps a shorter step than we imagine from merely fearing to share the gospel to a denial of Christ to avoid suffering.

It is shocking to our delicate sensibilities because it cuts through the false lives of many who are in the visible church today. And if the Bible is true, many who attend church every Sunday, are racing toward a most horrific eternity. That harsh fact of reality is what disturbs me. It hits too close to home. But, if we are to please God through a genuine biblical faith like Enoch's, we must follow his example. We must courageously, driven by love, faithfully follow Christ and that includes faithfulness to his gospel. If we are habitually not telling the gospel to others and have resolved that evangelism is for someone else, then maybe our love has grown cold. It does take courage to follow Christ. May the Lord give us courage for our times and grant us repentance. "Remember therefore from where you have fallen; repent, and do the works you did at first. If not, I will come to you and remove your lampstand from its place, unless you repent" (Rev. 2:5).

A Living Legacy

As a final note, Enoch left a legacy for his generation. It was a living parable acted out in the life of his son. The name Methuselah means "when he is dead, it shall come."[48] Methuselah died the same year of the great flood. This is not a coincidence. He was like a burning fuse counting down to the coming judgment. God had set a date, and humanity was moving rapidly toward that date with judgment. It was an apt parable that the world's longest living human should represent God's great longsuffering and patience and, at the same time, reveal that God would bring about His promised judgment. His patience with the wicked would come to an end.

We too are living in an age where God has set a date for the final judgment – "now he commands all people everywhere to repent, because he has fixed a day on which he

---

48   Boice, *Genesis: An Expositional Commentary*, Volume 1, p. 291.

will judge the world in righteousness by a man whom he has appointed; and of this he has given assurance to all by raising him from the dead" (Acts 17:30-31). God is not mystified, nor is He puzzled about when that judgment will occur. He has fixed the date. It is on His calendar. Only God knows the date. The fuse is lit and burning down to this massive outpouring of wrath on unbelievers and the magnificent rescue of His faithful followers at the second coming of Christ. God is patiently waiting for men and women to repent of their sin and call on the name of the Lord while His faithful ones warn them of this coming event and plead with them to run to the Savior.

Noah

But Noah found favor in the eyes of the Lord.

These are the generations of Noah. Noah was a righteous man, blameless in his generation. Noah walked with God. And Noah had three sons, Shem, Ham, and Japheth.

Now the earth was corrupt in God's sight, and the earth was filled with violence.

Gen. 6:8-11

Noah's World

If there has ever been a story in the Bible that reveals how a holy God feels about man's sin, it is the story of Noah. The world at that time was dark, with ungodliness dominant. The earth was totally "corrupt" and "filled with violence." It seems that Satan had been productive during the first 1,600 years of history. He certainly had a vested interest to destroy the promised Savior of Gen. 3:15 and avoid having his head bashed in, figuratively speaking. The way to destroy God's appointed Savior was to destroy the godly line coming through Seth. Noah, of course, was in that line and a target of Satan's.

In Noah's day sexual promiscuity was rampant (Gen. 6:1-2), wickedness was great (Gen. 6:5), the intention of man's heart was "only evil continually" (Gen. 6:5), there was total corruption on the earth (Gen. 6:11, 12), and the earth was filled with violence (Gen. 6:11, 13). Men and women "did not obey, when God's patience waited in the days of Noah, while the ark was being prepared" (1 Pet. 3:20). It sounds a lot like our own world. People today seek liberation from God and self-fulfillment through the idolatries of sexual freedom, power, fame, materialism, career, "personal peace and affluence,"[49] lives that are filled with nonstop activities and entertainment, and various other narcissistic endeavors. But real fulfillment and real liberation do not come from the license to do anything one desires. They come only from being forgiven of sins and reconciled to God through child-like faith in the Savior.

Noah's environment illustrates the characteristics and result of sin. Sin is not a "mere imperfection, but something thoroughly hostile to God's purposes and thoroughly infecting, like poison in drinking water."[50] The generation of Noah's day was thoroughly poisoned. God was angry about it and decided to bring judgment on the entire world (Gen. 6:5-7).

God Called Noah

God can be angry and merciful at the same time. God interrupted Noah's life, and the Bible tells it in this understated way – "But Noah found favor in the eyes of the LORD" (Gen. 6:8). "While 'Noah found favor' is the only way in which the words can be translated, they actually mean that 'favor found Noah.'"[51] And this "favor" or grace was a transformational explosion in Noah's life. It caused him to do things that he would have never considered doing. This grace moved him in the opposite direction of his culture. The first step was to live an upright life. Following God's act of salvation, "Noah was a righteous man, blameless in his generation. Noah walked with God" (Gen. 6:9). The Book of Hebrews adds that Noah "became an heir of the righteousness that comes by faith" (Heb. 11:7), which is a way of articulating his salvation. He lived differently than the corrupt people around him.

---

49 Francis Shaeffer, *The Complete Works of Francis A. Shaeffer: A Christian Worldview*, Volume Five, *A Christian View of the West, How Should We Then Live? (1976),* (Wheaton, IL: Crossway Books, 1982, 2nd Edition) p. 211.

50 Boice, *Genesis: An Expositional Commentary*, Volume 1, p. 314.

51 Alec Motyer, *6 Ways the Old Testament Speaks Today: An Interactive Guide,* (Wheaton, IL: Crossway, Kindle Edition, 2016), p. 130..

But that was only the beginning of the countercultural steps Noah would be required to take. Next, Noah was commanded to build an embarrassingly large ship[52] on dry land with no means of moving it to water. He could not really hide this thing. "And God said to Noah, 'I have determined to make an end of all flesh, for the earth is filled with violence through them. Behold, I will destroy them with the earth. Make yourself an ark of gopher wood'" (Gen. 6:13-14). Noah "in reverent fear constructed an ark for the saving of his household" (Heb. 11:7). "He did all that God commanded him" (Gen. 6:22). None of this made sense in his cultural environment.

The final step God charged Noah to take was warning people of an imminent judgment to come and proclaiming the righteousness of God. Noah likely heard about the powerful preaching of his great grandfather Enoch from his father Lamech and grandfather Methuselah. Enoch had been taken to heaven 69 years before Noah was born. But Noah's father and grandfather, both of whom would likely have heard Enoch's preaching firsthand, were alive for nearly 600 years of Noah's lifetime.

The apostle Peter tells us that Noah was a "herald of righteousness" (2 Pet. 2:5). The Greek word for herald, *kĕrux*, means one who proclaims, a crier. "A *kĕrux*, messenger, was the public crier and reader of state messages such as the conveyor of a declaration of war."[53] This means Noah proclaimed the "state message" of God. He called out the sins of his generation and warned people of the coming judgment. He pleaded with his generation to turn from their sins and call on the name of the Lord. He was a solitary figure standing against an ungodly world. This took courage.

Noah was part of a tiny remnant of God's people – eight people out of the whole population – who would survive the flood of God's wrath. Noah was a descendant of Seth. The line of Seth, carrying the seed of the Savior, was dependent on the survival of Noah and his sons.

---

52 "Assuming a 'cubit' of about eighteen inches, the vessel was approximately 450 feet long, 75 feet wide, and 45 feet high (6:15)." Kenneth A. Matthews, *Genesis 1-11:26*, Vol. 1A (NAC), (Nashville, TN: Broadman & Holman Publishers, 1996), p. 364.

53 Spiros Zodhiates, General Editor, *The Complete Word Study Dictionary: New Testament (electronic edition)*, (Chattanooga, TN: AMG Publishers), Word No. 2783.

The Great Flood

How did the people Noah preached to respond? What happened to them? More than likely, they laughed at Noah. More than likely they scoffed and reviled Noah and his family. They probably threatened violence and may have attacked Noah and his family. Remember, these were not nice people. They were evil, corrupt, and violent.

Noah strongly urged people to repent and trust in God for their salvation. He did this for many years during the building of the ark. Noah's preaching most likely spanned 70 to 100 years and maybe as many as 120 years.[54] While Noah warned them of coming judgment, people lived as if life would go on forever. They continued in the normal course of their lives, marrying, raising children, giving their children in marriage, worshipping false gods, celebrating whatever festivals they enjoyed, raising crops, buying, selling, conducting commerce, building houses, and doing all the things people do. Life seemed normal. "What had gotten into Noah?" they must have thought. "He's not like everyone else." "He is nothing but a hate monger telling us we will be destroyed."

After they refused to respond to Noah's preaching, God kept His promise and flooded the earth. Genesis 7:11-12 tells us how God flooded the entire earth. "In the six hundredth year of Noah's life, in the second month, on the seventeenth day of the month, on that day all the fountains of the great deep burst forth, and the windows of the heavens were opened. And rain fell upon the earth forty days and forty nights" (Gen. 7:11-12). "Subterranean waters 'burst forth,' and the cloudbursts are overwhelming so that they are like the 'floodgates of the heavens' (i.e., sky) flung open."[55] The "floodgates" remained open for "forty days and forty nights."

It was worse than any hurricane, tsunami, flash flood, or weather event that anyone living today can imagine. It was all of those combined into one event that covered the entire earth. The floodgates above were opened, and the ground exploded in geysers of water. Millions of cubic feet of water from below and from above. Tons of water in an unstoppable force of destruction was unleashed. Millions of people died. Millions of animals died. Homes, previously seen as safe havens from the elements, were obliterated. Weddings and festivals may have been in progress when suddenly everything changed.

---

54   Various lengths of time are estimated by scholars for the constructing of the ark. Estimates range between 20 and 120 years.

55   Kenneth A. Matthews, *Genesis 1-11:26*, Vol. 1A (NAC), p. 376.

We can imagine people outside of the ark, when the rains began, beginning to wonder, "Did I make a mistake in taunting Noah and his family?" When they heard the explosions of water from the ground they may have thought, "Should I have listened to Noah?" As the waters began to rise, people may have knocked on the door or sides of the ark, calling for Noah to let them in. But God had shut the door. "And the Lord shut him in" (Gen. 7:16). When God shut them in, it was too late.

One must ask, "Did God really flood the entire earth and kill all of those people?" Yes, He did. The only eight people on earth who believed and were saved from this worldwide catastrophic flood were Noah and his family. Jesus confirms this in Matthew 24:36-41 and tells us that His second coming will be for those who have rejected Him a catastrophic judgment on this same order of magnitude.

"For 120 years Noah built the ark and exhorted the people to repent. Yet no one accepted his teaching, for everyone perished."[56]

The Gospel and Evangelism From Adam to Noah

There is a pattern, in this period from Adam to Noah, of the destructive effect of sin, the resulting judgment of God, the escape offered through repentance and faith, and the proclamation of God's salvation. Here are a few applications we should draw from this text.

First, the period of history from Adam to Noah is framed by judgment. It begins with the disastrous judgment at Adam's fall and ends with the massive judgment of the great flood. Judgment is the demarcation of this period of history and defines the ultimate reality of it. In truth, judgment defines the ultimate reality of every age and every life. All of us will one day die and then we will face judgment. "It is appointed for man to die once, and after that comes judgment..." (Heb. 9:27). Those who wish to remove the doctrine of judgment from the gospel message, often in the name of reaching a postmodern generation, are gutting the gospel of its offense and displaying a lack of courage. The cross itself was a brutal judgment for our sins that fell on Jesus.

---

56   Simon J. Kistemaker, *New Testament Commentary: Exposition of Peter and Jude* (Vol. 16), (Grand Rapids: Baker Books, 1987), p. 288. See also footnote 43 above.

God and His People
(Proclaiming the Gospel!)

Judgment (Death)					Judgment (The Flood)

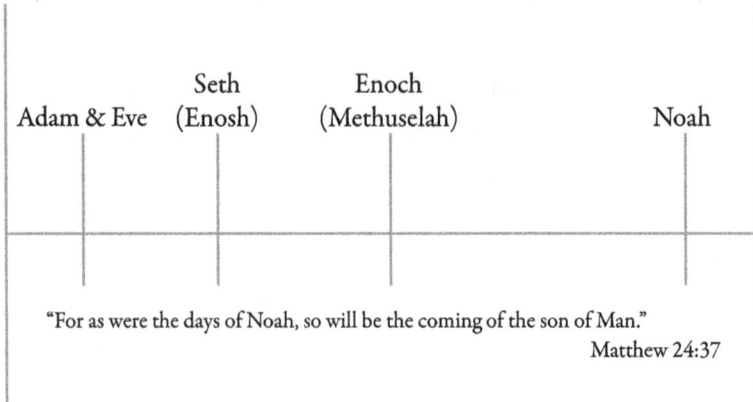

| Adam & Eve | Seth (Enosh) | Enoch (Methuselah) | | Noah | |

"For as were the days of Noah, so will be the coming of the son of Man."
Matthew 24:37

Second, in the account we have of this period, God and His people proclaimed the gospel. A quick review shows: (1) God "evangelized" Adam and Eve in year one; (2) evangelism occurred around the birth of Enosh to Seth in year 235; (3) Enoch burst onto the scene with his ministry in year 687 and preached the gospel for 300 years through 987. Enoch also left behind the legacy of Methuselah whose name means "when he is dead, it shall come" (He died in 1656, the year of the flood); and (4) Noah proclaimed the gospel for an unknown time, but likely 70 to 100 years, before the flood. It is significant that God's people proclaimed, told, and pleaded for others to call on the name of the Lord and be saved while God Himself patiently waited until the day of wrath.

Third, perhaps the most obvious lesson from the story of Noah is that God did judge the world according to His righteousness. There should be no confusion about this. And according to Jesus' own words in Matthew 24, not only has He judged the world before, but He will do it again. As Jesus said about the period of Noah's ministry, people were going about their life, "eating and drinking, marrying and giving in marriage." The people in Noah's day thought that their lives would go on forever. Can you imagine how these same people of Noah's day felt once the earth's core burst forth with water and the millions of tons of water fell from the sky? Can you imagine people floating on logs beating on the door of the Ark to get in and wanting to repent? In a few days or weeks, every living person or animal would be dead. Please note that the God of the Old Testament is the God of the New Testament. Both testaments warn us of a judgment.

Most people today are blind to the reality of God's wrath. But Jesus is not blind to it, nor are the writers of the New Testament. Four New Testament writers in five books draw upon Noah and tell us the lessons we should learn (see Mt. 24:36-39; Luke 17:22-30; Heb. 11:7; 1 Pet. 3:20; 2 Pet. 2:4-10).

- "For as were the days of Noah, so will be the coming of the Son of Man. For as in those days before the flood they were eating and drinking, marrying and giving in marriage, until the day when Noah entered the ark, and they were unaware until the flood came and swept them all away, so will be the coming of the Son of Man" (Mt. 24:37-39; also Lk. 17:26-27).
- "By faith Noah, being warned by God concerning events as yet unseen, in reverent fear constructed an ark for the saving of his household. By this he condemned the world and became an heir of the righteousness that comes by faith" (Heb. 11:7).
- "...when God's patience waited in the days of Noah, while the ark was being prepared, in which a few, that is, eight persons, were brought safely through water" (1 Pet. 3:20).
- "If he did not spare the ancient world, but preserved Noah, a herald of righteousness, with seven others, when he brought a flood upon the world of the ungodly...the Lord knows how to rescue the godly from trials, and to keep the unrighteous under punishment until the day of judgment" (2 Pet. 2:4-10).

Judgment is the dominant theme and context. Jesus and these writers want us to recognize the prominence that judgment and God's wrath should have in gospel ministry. The wrath of God is more than a doctrine. It is the horrendous reality for all who have rejected Jesus as Lord and Savior. In Hebrews 11:7, the context is faith and how it plays out in a sinful and dangerous world. Telling the gospel is an act of genuine faith. **It is impossible to understand grace apart from a clear understanding of God's wrath.**

Here is what Paul says about the coming judgment when Jesus returns:

God considers it just to repay with affliction those who afflict you, and to grant relief to you who are afflicted as well as to us, when the Lord Jesus is revealed from heaven with his mighty angels in flaming fire, inflicting vengeance on those who do not know God and on those who do not obey the gospel of our Lord Jesus. They will suffer the punishment of eternal destruction, away from the presence of the Lord and from the glory of his might, when he comes on that day to be glorified in his saints, and to be marveled at among all who have believed, because our testimony to you was believed.

2 Thess. 1:6-10

Fourth, the flood is a real-life tragic parable. Those who know the Lord Jesus and who are on the earth when He returns will tremble with joy and will marvel at His presence. For those who do not know the Lord, it will be the worst day of their lives, a day of absolute terror. For them, it will be the tragedy that never ends.

Four times in Gen. 7:16-24, we are told "the waters prevailed." "Waters," of course, represent God's judgment. Wrath prevailed and no one escaped except the seven people on the ark with Noah. The waters of Christ's judgment at His second coming will be: unexpected, all-encompassing, overpowering, inescapable, and righteous. No one will escape except those who are in the "ark" of Jesus Christ.

Unbelievers are warned about that event so they will call on the name of the Lord. Believers are warned about it to motivate evangelism. If our love has not grown cold, this knowledge will motivate us to speak the whole gospel message, in love, to all who do not know Christ as God gives us opportunity.

As terrible as The Great Disaster was and is, greater is The Great Salvation in this great Deliverer – Jesus!

And the LORD God made for Adam and for his wife garments of skins and clothed them.

Gen. 3:21

Elements of the Gospel Table

	Description	Gen. 1 – 7	New Testament	Gospel of Mark
1	God – creator, father, judge	Gen. 1-2; 3:8-19	Jn. 4:25-26; Mt. 6:9-13; Acts 17:22-34; Col. 1:15-20; 2 Tim. 4:1; Heb 1:2-3; Rev. 4:11	1:1, 11; 9:2-8; 13:24-27; 14:62; 16:1-8; 21 miracle accounts.
2	Holiness – God is holy and requires absolute holiness and sinless perfection of mankind	Gen. 2:15-17	Mt. 5:48; 22:34-40; 2 Cor. 7:1; Col. 1:21-23; Heb. 12:4; James 2:10; 1 Pet. 1:14-16.	1:9-11; 8:34-38; 9:2-8; 10:17-31; 12:29-31; 16:1-8.
3	Sin	Gen. 3:6-7, 9-11	Rom 1:18-23; 2:1-29, 3:9-20, 3:23; 5:18-19, 6.23.	4:1-20; 7:14-23; 8:14-21, 33; 9:33-37, 42-50; 11:12-21; 12:1-11, 38-40.
4	Judgment and wrath	Gen. 3:8-19, 22-24; chapters 6 & 7	Mt 13:36-43; Jn. 3:16, 36; Rom 1:18, 2:5, 8, 16; 5:9; Eph 2:3, 5:6; Col 3:6; 2 Thess. 1:5-10; Rev 6:12-17; 11:18; 19:15-16; 20:15; 21:7-8.	9:42-50; 11:12-25; 12:1-12; 13:1-2; 24-27.
5	The cross and resurrection	Gen. 3:15, 21	Rom. 3:21-26; 4:24-25; 5:6-11, 19; Eph. 2:14-16; Col. 1:20; 2:14; 1 Pet. 2:24-25, 3:18; (also in OT Isa. 52:13-53:12).	8:31-32; 9:31,10:32-34; 10:45; 14:1-2, 22-25; 15:1-47; 16:1-8.
6	Grace	Gen. 1:1, 3:15, 3:21; 6:8	Rom. 3:21-26; 4:13-25; 5:2; Gal. 2:15-21; 3:10-14; 5:4-6; Eph 2:8-9, Titus 3:4-5.	1:40-45; 2:1-12, 13-17; 10:13-31; 10:46-52; 21 miracle accounts.
7	Counting the cost of following Jesus	Gen. 3:1-7, 15; 4:1-26; 6:11-13	Mt. 8:18-22; Lk. 14:25-33; Jn. 15:18-16:4; Rom. 8:17; 2 Cor. 2:14-16; 6:4-10; 7:1-4; Phil. 1:29-30; 1 Thess. 1:6; 3:2-4; 2 Thess. 1:3-12; 2 Tim 3:12; 1 Pet. 1:6-9; 4:1-2, 12-19; Rev. 1:9.	6:14-29; 8:34-38; 10:28-31; 13:5-37.
8	Repentance and faith	Gen. 3:20, 4:1, 25-26; 6:9, 22	Luke 13:1-5; 15:1-32; Acts 2:14-41; 3:19; 17:30-31; Rom 10:9-13; 2 Pet 3:9.	1:4-5, 14-15; 8:34-38.

The logic of these individual components flows like this:

God is our creator, our judge, and may become our Father. God is holy and requires of everyone perfect holiness, sinless perfection, and perfect obedience, yet all have sinned and are under God's judgment and wrath. But there is hope, for God sent his Son as a ransom for many by his death on the cross and rose from the dead on the third day as proof that God's anger at sinners was appeased. This salvation by grace through faith is received freely by all who, having understood the cost of following Him, repent of their sins and trust Jesus as Lord.

CHAPTER 2

ABRAHAM TO MOSES

Now the Lord said to Abram, "Go from your country and your kindred and your father's house to the land that I will show you. And I will make of you a great nation, and I will bless you and make your name great, so that you will be a blessing. I will bless those who bless you, and him who dishonors you I will curse, **and in you all the families of the earth shall be blessed."**

So Abram went, as the Lord had told him... From there he moved to the hill country on the east of Bethel and pitched his tent, with Bethel on the west and Ai on the east. **And there he built an altar to the Lord and called upon [proclaimed] the name of the Lord.**

Gen. 12:1-4, 8

God revealed the chief strategic purpose for His people in the calling of Abraham. When God redeemed Israel out of Egyptian slavery, He shouted His great name to the entire world. The strategic mandate for God's people was (and is) to be a witness to His glory and to proclaim His great name to every nation on earth. This is the legacy of the church. It emerged in history in clear expression with Abraham.

Abraham

"God so loved the world that he called Abraham."[57] This is the title of chapter 1 of Ralph Davis' expositions of Genesis 12-25. God's call of Abraham inaugurated a plan to carry the redemptive purpose of God *to the whole world.* It began as a tiny "seed," the promise of God to Abraham, and would grow in size and scope over the next 4,000 years. There would be two prominent milestones – the forming of the descendants of Abraham into a nation at the exodus from Egypt and the arrival of the Savior that marks the beginning of the last days. This plan will produce what Rev. 7:9-10 predicts, "a great multitude that no one could number, from every nation, from all tribes and peoples and languages, standing before the throne and before the Lamb, clothed in white robes, with palm branches in their hands, and crying out with a loud voice, 'Salvation belongs to our God who sits on the throne, and to the Lamb!'"

The channel of God's blessing initiated with Abraham can be compared to the Mississippi River, with its humble beginnings and massive expansion. At the headwaters of the Mississippi River at Lake Itasca in Minnesota, a person can easily wade across its 20-foot width and three-foot depth. By the time it reaches the Gulf of Mexico 2,320 miles later, it is more than a half mile wide and as much as 200 feet deep, with an average annual discharge of up to 700,000 cubic feet of water per second. It is a massive river system impacting millions of lives along its route.

According to many biblical scholars, Abraham may be the most important person in the Bible other than Jesus Christ.[58] In Genesis, 14 chapters are devoted to him. In the New Testament, his name is mentioned 72 times (32 in the Gospels and 40 in the rest of the New Testament). Matthew begins his gospel by tracing Jesus' genealogy back to Abraham. Paul presents Abraham as his preeminent example of genuine saving faith. All of Romans 4 and most of Galatians 3 – 4 are devoted to Abraham. James points to Abraham as a profoundly honorable example of the obedience of genuine saving faith (James 2:21-24). The writer of Hebrews devotes the largest section of chapter 11 to Abraham, as a man who walked by faith and obeyed God – "By faith Abraham obeyed when he was called to go out to a place that he was to receive as an

---

57   Dale Ralph Davis, *Faith of Our Father: Expositions of Genesis 12-25,* (Fearn, Scotland: Christian Focus Publications, 2015), p.9.

58   Boice, *Genesis: An Expositional Commentary, Volume 1,* p. 435.

inheritance" (Heb. 11:8, see also 11:8-19). The seed planted with Abraham, though tiny when initiated, continues to grow today. It is a massive river system on its way to impacting every family of the earth. God's purpose of reaching the nations for Christ flows through this river.

God Called Abraham

Abraham was living in Haran, to the north and slightly east of Canaan, at the time God called him. He "was advanced in years, probably prosperous and settled, but in a thoroughly pagan world."[59] There is nothing especially remarkable about Abraham until God intrudes into his life. Although Abraham was in the line of Shem through Noah, "the evidence seems rather clear that Abram had an idolatrous background."[60]

But God disrupted Abraham's comfortable pagan life. God appeared to him and called him to leave his country, his extended family, and "go" to a strange "land that I will show you" (Gen. 12:1). God gave Abraham only promises. There was nothing tangible that Abraham could touch and feel. All that God gave Abraham were these promises: (1) his descendants would become a great nation, (2) he would be given land, (3) he would be protected – "I will bless those who bless you, and him who dishonors you I will curse..." (Gen. 12:3), and (4) he would have a grand strategic purpose – "in you all the families of the earth will be blessed" (Gen. 12:3).[61]

These promises were quite outlandish. God's plan to turn "descendants" of Abraham into a "nation" seemed absurd. After all, Abraham's wife Sarah was barren and an old woman. A promise of offspring numbering more than the stars in the heavens and more than the sand on the seashore (Gen. 15:5) was laughable. Adding to the difficulty, the lands Abraham was to possess were under the control of pagan nations who were known as fierce warriors. Abraham was called to a cosmic battlefield and not to safe pastures for his retirement leisure. It would be a physical field of battle with a fourth dimension, the spiritual component.

How well did Abraham actually know this God? Was this God trustworthy? Was He prone to change His mind? God had no references Abraham could check

59   Ross, *Creation and Blessing*, p. 259.
60   James M. Boice, *Genesis: An Expositional Commentary*, Volume 2, Genesis 12-36, p. 438.
61   Dale Ralph Davis, *Faith of Our Father: Expositions of Genesis 12-25*, p.10.

since there were no other followers nearby that we know of. Melchizedek, who was a believer and could have been that reference check, may have had a small clan of believers in Canaan at this time, but Abraham did not know him yet. (He would meet him later in Gen. 14:18.) Abraham had no say in establishing the terms of this arrangement with God.

Can you imagine what Abraham told his father Terah, who worshipped other gods (Josh. 24:2)? That conversation may have gone something like this: "Sarah and I have been called by almighty God to go to Canaan where He is going to give us land as well as protection. He also has told me I will father a great nation." Terah would have been skeptical of these improbable expectations. But Abraham believed God. He trusted Him and left Haran for the 400-mile trek to Canaan.

> *And Abram took Sarai his wife, and Lot his brother's son, and all*
> *their possessions that they had gathered, and the people that they*
> *had acquired in Haran, and they set out to go to the land of Canaan.*
> *Gen. 12:5*

Abraham left Haran and went from one pagan environment to another. But he was a different man: Abraham, the gospel carrier. "And the Scripture, foreseeing that God would justify the Gentiles by faith, preached the gospel beforehand to Abraham, saying, 'In you shall all the nations be blessed'" (Gal. 3:8). We normally do not think of Abraham as carrying the gospel, but Paul sees him as doing just that – "so that in Christ Jesus the blessing of Abraham might come to the Gentiles" (Gal. 3:14).

When Abraham arrived at Shechem, 400 hundred miles from Haran, the Lord appeared to him again and said, "To your offspring I will give this land" (Gen. 12:7). So Abraham built an altar, which implies he offered sacrifice and worshipped the Lord publicly. He then moved to a parcel of land between Bethel and Ai not far from Jerusalem. "And there he built [another] altar to the Lord and *called upon the name of the Lord*" (Gen. 12:8). And yet a third time, after travels through Egypt and after separating from his nephew Lot, Abraham settled in Hebron to the south of Jerusalem and built an altar, sacrificed, and proclaimed the name of the Lord (Gen. 13:18). According to Allen P. Ross, the phrase "called upon the name" may be better translated, "made proclamation of the Lord by name…Martin Luther translated it 'preached' [*predigte*], a good rendering in this context."[62] The word can mean either depending on its context. Whether Abraham "called upon" or "proclaimed" the name of the Lord, he was publicly "making [the name of] the Lord famous in Canaan."[63] It took courage to do this in enemy-controlled land.

Abraham's Childlessness

Why did God choose Abraham and Sarah to begin this nation of His people? If God had called upon me to go to Haran around 2100 BC and search to find the best candidates with whom to inaugurate God's plan for evangelism, Abraham and Sarah would not have made the list of couples to interview. Sarah was barren. But God seemed to take pleasure in this predicament. Genesis records an interesting conversation between God and the couple. Here is how Frederick Buechner describes the scene:[64]

> *The place to start is with a woman laughing. She is an old woman, and, after a lifetime in the desert, her face is cracked and rutted like a six-month drought. She hunches her shoulders around her ears and starts to shake. She squinnies her eyes shut, and her laughter is all China teeth[65] and wheeze and tears running down as she rocks back and forth in her kitchen chair. She is laughing because she is pushing ninety-one hard and has just been told she is going to have a baby. Even though it was an angel who told her she can't control herself, and her husband can't control himself either. He keeps a straight face a few seconds longer than she does, but he ends by cracking up, too. Even the angel is not unaffected. He hides his mouth behind his golden scapular, but you can still see his eyes. They are larkspur blue*

---

62   Ross, *Creation and Blessing*, p. 267.

63   Ross, *Creation and Blessing*, p. 267.

64   See Gen. 15:4; 17:15-21; 18:9-15.

65   False teeth were once made of porcelain and Buechner appears to be referring to the fact that Sarah is so old that her false teeth no longer fit properly. https://forum.wordreference.com/threads/their-china-teeth-slip-a-notch.785418/. Accessed 22Sept2023.

and brimming with something of which the laughter of the old woman and her husband is at best only a rough translation.[66]
(Ref: Gen. 12:1-3; 17:15-21; 18:9-17; 21:1-7)

It is a truly remarkable story that often is underappreciated. This issue of barrenness is an important key to understanding how God's purpose is accomplished. In Abraham's family, barrenness does not stop with Abraham and Sarah. All three of the Patriarchs (Abraham, Isaac, and Jacob) were married to women who were initially unable to have children. (So, how in the world is God going to give Abraham descendants?) Throughout the Old Testament God does things His people could not do. It is striking that in God's plan of building a nation of His people, to carry the seed of redemption and its story to the world, He starts with not one, but three barren couples in His chosen line. Unless God acts, it is not going to happen.

Abraham's Significance

It is hard to overstate the importance of Abraham in Scripture. Many Christians fail to fully grasp the importance of what God did through him. The writers of the New Testament had no such lack of understanding. They recognized Abraham's strategic singularity. In Matthew's genealogy of Jesus, beginning with Abraham, we can hear "echoes...of God's promises to Abraham that his offspring would bless all the peoples of the earth (Gen 12:1–3)."[67] Later in his Gospel, Matthew drew that link even more emphatically when he ended with a parallel to Gen. 12:1-3. "The words of Jesus to His disciples in Matthew 28:18-20, the so-called Great Commission, could be seen as a Christological mutation of the original Abrahamic commission – 'Go... and be a blessing...and all nations on earth will be blessed through you.'"[68] The figure below is an illustration of the parallels between the two "commissions."

---

66   Frederick Buechner, *Telling the Truth: The Gospel as Tragedy, Comedy, and Fairy Tale* (New York: HarperCollins Publishers, 1977), pp. 49-50.

67   Craig L. Blomberg, *Matthew*, Vol. 22 (NAC), (Nashville: Broadman & Holman Publishers, 1992) p. 53.

68   Christopher J. H. Wright, *The Mission of God: Unlocking the Bible's Grand Narrative* (Downers Grove, IL: InterVarsity Press, 2006), p. 213.

The Two "Commissions" *(comparing Gen. 12:1-3 with Mt. 28:18-20)*

All authority in Heaven and on Earth

God to Abraham

➡ **Go**
    Nation
    Land
    Protection
    (Those who bless you...)

➡ **All The Families
of the Earth**

Jesus to the Church

➡ **Go**
    Church
    Inheritance
    Protection
    (I am with you always...)

➡ **Make Disciples
of all Nations**

The people of God in the Old Testament were distinguished by a national identity. In the New Testament God's people no longer have a single national identity, but take on an identity as small groups of believers (the church) around the world. Physical land in the New Testament takes on a less prominent place, and inheritance in Christ emerges as the key focus. Protection takes a new form with Jesus' promise, "I am with you always, to the end of the age" (Mt. 28:20). The believer's protection is in the resurrection of Christ.

The apostle Paul gives a commentary on the call of Abraham in Galatians 3-4. "And the Scripture, foreseeing that God would justify the Gentiles by faith, ***preached the gospel beforehand to Abraham,*** saying, 'In you shall all the nations be blessed'" (Gal. 3:8). "It is the climax of God's promise to Abraham. It is also a pivotal text not only in the book of Genesis but indeed in the whole Bible. So important is it in Genesis that it occurs five times altogether, with minor variations of phraseology (Gen. 12:3; 18:18; 22:18; 26:4-5; 28:14)."[69]

Notice that Paul referred to God's call of Abraham as the "gospel." Paul connects two things in this one word: (1) **the good news** of Jesus ("offspring") and (2) **the proclamation** of this gospel to the entire world (Gen. 18:18; cf. Gal. 3:16). In Paul's view they are inseparably linked. The fact of it and the telling of it cannot be disconnected.

---

69   Wright, *The Mission of God,* p. 194.

Paul also is explicit as to the meaning of "offspring" in Gal. 3:16, "Now the promises were made to Abraham and to his offspring. It does not say, 'And to offsprings,' referring to many, but referring to one, 'And to your offspring,' who is Christ" (cf. Gen. 12:7; 22:18). It cannot be clearer than that. God's promise to Abraham was the promise of Messiah, and Messiah is the One who will bless all the nations.

It was the first time a structure for God's purpose in redemption was installed. It was not the first time redemption had been promised or proclaimed. We saw the promise of a Savior for the first time in Gen. 3:15, and we examined four examples of evangelism in the first seven chapters of Genesis. But in the first 11 chapters of Genesis there was no formal structure in place to nurture and model redemption to the world. Those chapters cover many centuries which were characterized as a mostly dark time marked by the fall, the flood, and the Tower of Babel. But God inserted a structure for redemption with Abraham and it would change everything.

What Can We Learn About Evangelism from Abraham?

First, the strategic purpose established with Abraham continues in the church – "in you all the families of the earth shall be blessed" (Gen. 12:3). It is affirmed multiple times from Genesis to Revelation. In the Old Testament we have these examples: Ex. 9:14; Ps. 67:1-2; 96; 98:2-3; Isa. 12:4-5; 43:8-13; 45:4-6; 49:6; 66:19; Jer. 1:5; Ez. 36:23; 37:27; Mal. 1:11. In the New Testament, in addition to the Matthew passage noted earlier, it is affirmed by Luke (Lk. 24:45-49; Acts 1:7-8; 3:25-26), John (Jn. 15:26-27), Peter (1 Pet. 2:9-10), and Paul (2 Cor. 5:18-20; Gal. 3:8, 16).

There is a difference between organic tasks and strategic tasks. Organic tasks are those that have to do with the living and breathing of an organism. For example, an athlete training for an event eats the right foods, trains their body for the skills needed, and gets the right amount of sleep. But the athlete's strategic purpose is the athletic event itself.

> *The church must be a healthy body of Christ, learning the Scriptures, living morally upright lives, loving one another, caring for one another, and worshipping the Lord. It must be a healthy body so that it can fulfill its strategic purpose.*

John Stott, in speaking of the top priorities of the church, notes four key elements of a biblical church based on Acts 2:42-47. The congregation is to be: (1) a learning church with teaching and study of the word; (2) a caring church full of fellowship and love for one another; (3) a worshipping church full of joyful reverent worship of the Lord; and (4) an evangelizing church. Stott states that if all a church possesses is the first three – study, worship, and fellowship – and it leaves out the fourth, "It's like an ingrown toenail – self-regarding."[70] Many churches may be attentive to the first three but are poor at or have totally forsaken the fourth. The first three elements are organic in nature, and the fourth is strategic. Proclaiming the great name of Christ is an intentional movement outward beyond the existing body of believers. It is easy for a church to become wrapped up in the organic functions so that it totally neglects its strategic mandate. We must not stop with the organic functions but press on to fulfill God's strategic purpose.

Second, Abraham is a model of what genuine saving faith looks like. The Genesis account tells us how he was saved: "And he believed the LORD, and he counted it to him as righteousness" (Gen. 15:6). Paul comments on this account as he uses Abraham as an example to teach justification by faith alone (Gal. 3:1-18). James uses Abraham as an example of what genuine saving faith looks like – saving faith lives out the truth of its confession (Jas. 2:21-24). Salvation in the Old Testament and in the New Testament is by grace alone through faith alone (Eph. 2:8-10).

We must not miss the fact that genuine saving faith responds in obedience. God told Abraham to "go" and gave him promises, assurances, and a purpose. Going requires leaving and leaving includes suffering (see Mk. 8:34-38). So Abraham packed his bags and left his paganism behind. Four hundred miles later he arrived in Canaan and began proclaiming the name of the Lord in the middle of pagan territory. Trusting God resulted in a significant upheaval in his life, including a transformation of purpose.

God demands radical transformation of every life, a total reorientation of life's purpose under the kingship of Christ. Jesus said to all who would be His followers, "If

---

70   John Stott, *The Marks of a Renewed Church*, https://www.preachingtoday.com/sermons/sermons/2013/april/marks-of-renewed-church.html, 2013, accessed June 16, 2020.

anyone would come after me, let him deny himself and take up his cross and follow me." (Mk. 8:34). Luke's account says, "take up his cross *daily*" (Lk. 9:23). This is an evangelistic call. It is a call to "followership" of Christ. It is a radical call to a radically different purpose in life.

Third, God's kingdom grows and advances through "barrenness," not human power. Abraham had no hope that he and Sarah would produce an heir. So, he took matters into his own hands initially. At the suggestion of Sarah, he conceived a child through Hagar, Sarah's Egyptian servant. But that proved disastrous (Gen. 16; 21:8-21). At the proper time, God delighted in supernaturally giving Sarah the ability to bear a son in her old age as promised. Isaac demonstrated a better response to the same dilemma than his father Abraham did. "And Isaac prayed to the LORD for his wife, because she was barren. And the LORD granted his prayer, and Rebekah his wife conceived" (Gen. 25:21).

In the work of evangelism, God alone is the One who brings forth new life. Certainly, believers must use biblical methods of evangelism and biblical gospel content, all while trusting God to bring about the result. Yet God is the only one who can soften hard hearts and bring about the new birth in a person's life.

Moses and the Exodus

*But for this purpose I have raised you [Pharaoh] up, to show you my power, **so that my name may be proclaimed in all the earth.***

Ex. 9:16

The exodus event was a spectacular display of God's ability to keep His promises and of His unmatched ability to save. The Exodus account restated God's purpose given to Abraham and recalled His promise to make of Abraham a great nation. The "nation" was in seed form in Genesis 12, and in the exodus the seed emerged as a young nation.

This event occurred in about 1447 BC,[71] 600 years after the promise to Abraham. Jacob and the rest of the family had joined Joseph in Egypt four centuries earlier, due

---

71   Tremper Longman III and Raymond B. Dillard, *An Introduction to the Old Testament*, (Grand Rapids, Michigan: Zondervan, 2*nd* edition 2007), p. 66. Many dates in the Bible are debated, and this one is especially so.

to the famine in their own land, in about 1875 BC. Joseph died about 30 years later. Over time, a new king arose over Egypt "who did not know Joseph" (Ex. 1:8). Israel suffered as slaves under the subsequent kings, and their stay in Egypt was a total of 430 years (Ex. 12:40-41).

> *During those many days the king of Egypt died, and the people of Israel groaned because of their slavery and cried out for help. Their cry for rescue from slavery came up to God. And God heard their groaning, and God remembered his covenant with Abraham, with Isaac, and with Jacob. God saw the people of Israel—and God knew.*
>
> Ex. 2:23-25

God Called Moses

Moses was born into a Hebrew family who were slaves in Egypt. He was under a death sentence at his birth because Pharaoh, concerned about the growing numbers of the Israelites and their risk to national security, commanded the midwives to kill all newborn males born to Hebrew women. The midwives refused and Moses' mother contrived a way for her newborn son to be noticed and "rescued" by a compassionate Egyptian. The daughter of Pharaoh saw him floating in a basket "among the reeds by the river bank" (Ex. 2:3) one day and adopted him as her own. He was raised and edu-cated in the palace, but as a grown man murdered an Egyptian for beating an Israelite. Pharaoh put out a warrant for his arrest, and Moses fled to the wilderness of Midian where he would spend the next 40 years as a shepherd.

In Midian Moses was 80 years old and minding his father-in-law's sheep. He was not looking for God. Life was good. He had comfort, peace, and a good wife and family. It may have been a demotion from his position in the royal family in Egypt, but with much less hassle. He was tending sheep in the wilderness of Midian and had given up those foolish ideas of alleviating the suffering of his people that he had entertained as a much younger man. But God appeared to him in a bush that was on fire yet was not consumed. As Moses approached to get a closer look, God warned him, for his own safety, to stand back and remove his shoes. He was standing on holy ground. It was a dangerous thing to get too close to this holy God. Moses did as he was told, and with trembling he hid his face because he was afraid to even look at it (Ex. 3:3-6; Acts 7:30-34).

Then God introduced Himself to Moses as the God of Abraham, Isaac, and Jacob and began to communicate to Moses God's purpose for his life (Ex. 3:7-10). This would involve Moses being sent back to Egypt to free the Israelites and take them out of Egyptian bondage. God would use him as part of the fulfillment of His promise to Abraham and its worldwide objective (Gen. 12:1-3). He would lead God's people out of Egyptian bondage, and they would become a nation who would worship God in their own land. "Come, I will send you to Pharaoh..." (Ex. 3:10).

After this conversation with God, Moses responded with a list of self-protecting and tiresome excuses for why God should send someone more qualified:

1.   I am a nobody (3:11)
2.   I don't even know your name (3:13)
3.   they will not believe me or listen to me (4:1)
4.   I don't have the ability and cannot even speak well (4:10)
5.   and my heart is not really in it (4:13)[72]

God answered every complaint, but in response to the last one, "my heart is not really in it," Moses may have felt some extra heat coming out of the burning bush as God responded in anger. It must have been like a solar flare when God's anger was "kindled" against him (Ex. 4:13). Moses eventually capitulated, as he was exhausted and out of excuses for why someone else should go. So, he trusted God and set out for Egypt.

The Drama

After arriving in Egypt, Moses and Aaron, as instructed, made their first appearance to Pharaoh and requested he let Israel go into the wilderness for three days of feasts and sacrifice to the Lord. They received the response that Moses had dreaded, and it was even worse than he had anticipated. Pharaoh not only refused to let them go but intensified the pressure on God's people. He made their burden more unbearable than

---

72   Jim Barnes, *Old Testament Series: Seeing God in the Old Testament "The Call of God" (Moses)*, pp. 5-11.

it had been. By following Moses, who was following God, life for the people of Israel went from bad to worse. The people complained to Moses. Then Moses complained to the Lord and even accused God of doing "evil" to the people. Moses lashed out at God, "Why did you ever send me?" (Ex. 5:22-23). God responded with the equivalent of, "Now we are ready. Now I have Pharaoh where I want him. You are going to see an amazing demonstration of what real power looks and feels like" (Ex. 6:1-9). God's response included this purpose statement for the entire event:[73]

> *Say therefore to the people of Israel, "I am the Lord, and I will bring you out from under the burdens of the Egyptians, and I will deliver you from slavery to them, **and I will redeem you with an outstretched arm and with great acts of judgment.** I will take you to be my people, and I will be your God, and **you shall know that I am the LORD your God**, who has brought you out from under the burdens of the Egyptians. I will bring you into the land that I swore to give to Abraham, to Isaac, and to Jacob. I will give it to you for a possession. I am the Lord. "*
>
> *Ex. 6:6-8*

Thus began the 10-round encounter between God and Pharaoh. It was like a heavyweight boxing match, but there was a heavyweight (God) in one corner of the ring and a lightweight (Pharaoh) in the other. Pharaoh thought he was the heavyweight, but he was overmatched. The struggle of God's people, Israel, would be solved by God's sending 10 plagues in increasing severity. The final plague was the most serious and deadly.

Pharaoh and the Egyptians did not know this God of the Hebrews. But before it was all over, many of the Egyptians would become "believers" in Him, and a few may have become real believers and members of the people of God.

The final round was preceded by the first Passover. God would redeem and set His people free through the blood of the lamb. The 10th plague would take the life of the firstborn of every family in Egypt who did not have the blood of the lamb smeared on

---

73   Christopher J. H. Wright, *The Mission of God: Unlocking the Bible's Grand Narrative*, p. 76.

the doorpost of their home. It's the enduring dramatization of Christ's blood shed on the cross to free sinners from the penalty of their sins.

Before, during, and after the 10 plagues, there were many purpose statements revealed and multiple responses to God's proclaiming of His great name. He proclaimed His great name so loudly that Rahab, a prostitute in the city of Jericho, even heard it 40 years later and 250 miles away. Statements like, "you shall know" and "the Egyptians shall know" show up often in the narrative. "Clearly, the motivation from God's point of view was not only the liberation of His enslaved people but *this driving divine will to be known to all nations* for who and what he truly is."[74]

The Exodus

The significance of the exodus event should be understood in view of God's call of Abraham (Gen. 12:1-3). When Abraham received God's call and promises, the nation was only a "seed." In 1447 BC, God was now ready (600+ years after His promise to Abraham) to bring His fledgling nation out into the open. God is the one who had made these promises to Abraham, and it was His reputation that was at stake. But the *strategic purpose* in the redemption of His people (Israel) from Egyptian bondage was based on God's desire for His name to be known in all the earth (Ex. 9:16), as stated in Gen. 12:3. The structure and purpose, as given to Abraham, was about to exert itself in the world in a major way.

Here is a listing of most of the statements in Exodus revealing this "driving divine will to be known to all nations":[75] These statements are highly significant.

- "you shall know that I am the LORD your God" (Ex. 6:7) – Moses to the people of Israel
- "The Egyptians shall know that I am the LORD" (Ex. 7:5) – God to Moses
- "By this you shall know that I am the LORD" (Ex. 7:17) – Moses to Pharaoh
- "So that you may know" (Ex. 8:10) – Moses to Pharaoh

---

74 Christopher J. H. Wright, *The Mission of God: Unlocking the Bible's Grand Narrative*, p. 95. (Emphasis mine.)
75 Wright, *The Mission of God*, p. 95

- "that you may know" (Ex. 8:22) – Moses to Pharaoh
- "so that you may know" (Ex. 9:14) – Moses to Pharaoh
- "so that you may know" (Ex. 9:29) – Moses to Pharaoh
- "that you may tell in the hearing of you son" and "that you may know" (Ex. 10:2) – God to Moses
- "that you may know" (Ex. 11:7) – Moses to Pharaoh
- "the Egyptians shall know" (Ex. 14:4) – God to Moses
- "the Egyptians shall know" (Ex. 14:18) – God to Moses

The sheer number of times these statements were made regarding God's desire to be known (evangelism) is overwhelming. Once would have been a clear revealing of God's will. **But eleven times indicates God really did mean what He promised to Abraham: "in your offspring [Jesus] shall all the nations of the earth be blessed" (Gen. 22:18; Gal. 3:16).** It is an extraordinary emphasis of His strategic purpose. And the importance of the exodus, with its modeling of redemption and its expressed purpose statements, is the reason the exodus event was often in the minds and words of the prophets throughout the Old Testament and why it is portrayed or alluded to often in the New.[76] The exodus impacted more than just the nation of Israel. It had an impact on the Gentiles as well, as it was intended to do.

This brings us to a logical question. Did anyone pay attention and come to know the LORD through this event? The answer is yes, and we are given in the exodus account some interesting responses.

- **"But the Hebrew midwives feared God and did not do as the king of Egypt commanded them**...And because the midwives feared God, he gave them families." (Ex. 1:17, 21) – The word for "God" used here is *Elohim*, a general word for God; this does not necessarily mean saving faith,

---

76 "For indeed it is the exodus that provided the primary model of God's idea of redemption, not just in the Old Testament, but even in the New, where it is used as one of the keys to understanding the meaning of the cross of Christ." "The exodus, of course, was not God's only redeeming act or even (in a full biblical perspective) his greatest. But it is the first that is described as such in the Bible, and the rest of the Bible clearly takes it as paradigmatic." Wright, *The Mission of God*, pp. 265 and 275.

although it could indicate saving faith, but at a minimum, it shows they had enough respect for a supreme being to risk their lives because they feared this God of the Hebrews more than they feared Pharaoh.

- **"Then the magicians said to Pharaoh, '*This is the finger of God.*'** But Pharaoh's heart was hardened, and he would not listen to them, as the Lord had said." (Ex. 8:19) – This statement was made to Pharaoh by the magicians when Moses unleashed the third plague of gnats. The magicians tried but failed to make it go away with their magic. Their response was not of saving faith, but it is fascinating that these pagan magicians got into the act of speaking God's truth into the life of Pharaoh. We do not expect it from them.

- **"Whoever feared the word of the Lord among the servants of Pharaoh hurried his slaves and his livestock into the houses."** (Ex. 9:20) – This does not necessarily indicate saving faith, but it does mean these individuals recognized that when Moses told Pharaoh that God was about to do something, they believed it would happen.

- **"A mixed multitude also went up with them."** (Ex. 12:38) – This group is ethnically diverse, not descended from Abraham, and they basically joined Israel, the people of God, and departed Egypt with them. Many could have been genuine converts.

- **"And Jethro rejoiced for all the good that the Lord had done to Israel"** and he **"brought a burnt offering and sacrifices to God; and Aaron came with all the elders of Israel to eat bread with Moses' father-in-law before God."** (Ex. 18:9, 12) – Moses' father-in-law Jethro was converted and turned from his pagan gods; he brought a burnt offering and sacrifice, which was at "the heart of obedient worship"[77] and reflected forgiveness

---

77   Douglas K. Stuart, *Exodus*, Vol. 2 (NAC) (Nashville: Broadman & Holman Publishers, 2006), p. 413.

through the death of another.[78] He ate a meal with Moses, Aaron (the religious leader of Israel), and all the elders of Israel.[79] This "signified the formal admission of Jethro into Israel."[80]

John Currid describes what we witness in the interaction of Moses and Jethro:

> *What a wonderful family conversation we are witnessing! Moses and Jethro are not talking about the weather, sheep-herding, or the latest caravan gossip or news. No, but they are talking about the wondrous works of God. Moses is telling Jethro of the marvelous deeds of Yahweh—it is Moses' testimony, his sharing of the good news with his father-in-law. How profitable is this type of conversation! Each of us ought to consider the manner in which we deal with our families—what do we talk about around the dinner table? In what do we rejoice when we hear of it? I believe Moses' evangelistic efforts put many of us to shame.*
>
> *Jethro's response to the good news is also astounding. Whereas the Israelites murmured and grumbled throughout their wanderings, here is a Midianite rejoicing over God's goodness to Israel! The faith of the Gentile is putting to shame the faith of the Hebrew. What Jesus says about the Roman centurion in Matthew 8:10 could be said about Jethro: 'Truly I say to you, I have not found such great faith with anyone in Israel.'*[81]

---

78   Stuart, *Exodus*, Vol. 2 (NAC), p. 413

79   "We would say that Jethro came to faith, that he was converted—and the response of the Israelite leadership shows that Jethro was officially affirmed in the faith he had professed (12b). He exemplified the words of Paul in the New Testament that, 'The Gentiles are heirs together with Israel, members together of one body' (Eph. 3:6)." Alec Motyer, *The Message of Exodus: The Days of Our Pilgrimage* (Nottingham, England: Inter-Varsity Press, 2005), 170.

80   Stuart, *Exodus*, Vol. 2 (NAC), p. 413

81   John D. Currid, *A Study Commentary on Exodus: Exodus 1–18* (Vol. 1), (Darlington, England; Carlisle, PA: Evangelical Press, 2000), p. 380.

- **Rahab said: "I know that the LORD has given you the land... for the LORD your God, he is God in the heavens above and on the earth beneath... Now then, please swear to me by the LORD...that you will save alive** my father and mother, my brothers and sisters, and all who belong to them, and deliver our lives from death." (Josh. 2:9-13) – Rahab had heard about the rescue of Israel from Egypt and recounted to the spies the miracle of crossing the Red Sea. At some point she became a convert and pleaded with the spies to save her and her family when they conquered Jericho. It is an amazing story that crossed several decades and many miles. What is equally amazing is that Rahab, through marriage, became part of the royal line of Judah from which Jesus was descended. She is listed in the genealogy of Christ in the Gospel of Matthew (Mt. 1:5). Rahab was the mother of Boaz, the grandmother of Obed, the great grandmother of Jesse, and the great, great grandmother of King David.

- **Finally, and tragically Pharaoh came to know God** through the destruction of his firstborn son and through the destruction of all his horses, chariots, and horsemen. Pharaoh's rebellion against God resulted in the destruction of Egypt.

What Can We Learn About Evangelism from Moses and the Exodus?

First, the major driving force in the life of God's people, the church, should be: "that [His] name may be proclaimed in all the earth" (Ex. 9:16; also Mt. 28:18-20; 2 Cor 5:18-20). The foundations of evangelism are in place in the Old Testament even though it is in an early stage of development, not unlike the young nation of Israel, the body of God's people at that time. When we get to the New Testament, evangelism comes into full bloom. It has never been an optional activity for God's people in either the Old or New Testament periods. It was and remains a strategic mandate. Yet most churches in the United States are apathetic about it at best. The heritage of the church and its purpose have come down to us from the seed planted with Abraham and restated by Jesus. This purpose grows on the vine, which is Jesus (John 15:16).

The ruling body of every church, whether it is an elder, deacon, or other named leadership body, has the obligation to lead the church in faithfulness to this strategic mandate. If believers are to be a biblical church, they will embrace and guard this purpose of God. It is not an elective.

Second, evangelism is an individual responsibility as well. Moses was personally doing evangelism with his father-in-law Jethro. He witnessed to what he saw the God of Israel doing. Others were also witnessing to His great acts of redemption and judgment.

J. I. Packer articulates this responsibility well:

> *Christ's command to his disciples, "Go...and make disciples of all nations" (Mt. 28:19), was spoken to them in their representative capacity; this is Christ's command, not merely to the apostles, but to the whole Church. Evangelism is the inalienable responsibility of every Christian community, and every Christian person. We are all under orders to devote ourselves to spreading the good news, and to use all our ingenuity and enterprise to bring it to the notice of the whole world."* [82]

Believers are often like Moses when God called him out of his world of comfort and peace. We should examine the "structure" of our lifestyles and determine if we are in alignment with God's purpose. Work, career, vacations, retirement, how we spend our money, hobbies, and how we spend our time are all to be placed under the Kingship of Christ. That means following Christ is more than simply living a moral life and attending church regularly.

Third, there is a cost of following God. The cost is most conspicuous in a believer's life when the proclaiming of Christ is operative in that life. Moses experienced substantial difficulties because he was following God. He led Israel from age 80 until his death at 120. His retirement plan must have been fully funded by the time he had reached 80, but he chose to follow God, which added to the "hassle" factor of his life.

---

82 Packer, *Evangelism and the Sovereignty of God*, p. 34.

He encountered many crisis moments along the way. He could have been minding sheep in Midian and avoided the hassle. Jesus tells us to count the cost of following Him (Mt. 8:18-22; Lk. 14:25-33). Paul tells us what to expect as disciples of Christ (Rom. 8:17; 2 Cor. 7:4; Phil. 1:29-30; 2 Tim. 3:12). And Peter understood this as well when he wrote, "Do not be surprised at the fiery trial when it comes upon you to test you, as though something strange were happening to you" (1 Pet. 4:12).

CHAPTER 3

THE PSALMS

Oh sing to the LORD a new song;
sing to the LORD, all the earth!
Sing to the LORD, bless his name;
tell of his salvation from day to day.
Declare his glory among the nations,
his marvelous works among all the peoples!

Psalm 96:1-3

God's structure of redemption, inaugurated with Abraham, was still developing and advancing more than 1,000 years after Abraham and more than 400 years after the exodus. In this chapter we will see how the Psalms nurture this structure. As we move through time, God's purpose remains constant, and more specifics are revealed about how it is being accomplished.

The dates of the Psalms range from Moses through David to after the Babylonian exile, which is a span of about 1,000 years.[83] They were a compilation of works by several authors.

The Psalms

The Book of Psalms speaks to the heart of God's people and was designed to be used for praise and comfort, to be absorbed, meditated on, prayed, sung, and used in worship. Many Psalms are expressions of the believer's deepest feelings and aspirations.

---

83   R. C. Sproul, General Editor, *The Reformation Study Bible (ESV)*, (Sanford, FL: Reformation Trust Publishing, 2015), pp. 826-827.

The Psalms also reflect the deepest feelings of God's heart. They encourage us to pray for that same heart of God to be expressed through our hearts. According to Pastor Keith Miller, **the glory of God and the strategic purpose of God for His people** "are like 'strands of DNA'...[and] are his two highest priorities from the dawn of creation to new creation, and serve as the DNA of Scripture."[84] The Psalms reveal this DNA of God, which flows out of His righteous character.

God's purpose for His structure of redemption, installed with Abraham as expressed in Genesis 22:18, "in your **offspring** shall all the nations of the earth be blessed," is highly visible in the Psalms. Here are a few examples that express **how far geographically and ethnically** God's "blessing" (salvation) is to extend:

- **Psalm 2:8** – "Ask of me, and **I will make the nations your heritage, and the ends of the earth** your possession." – This Messianic Psalm shows Jesus reigning over all of the earth; the gospel is the means through which He is spreading His reign prior to His second coming.
- **Psalm 22:27** – **"All the families of the nations** shall worship before you." This is another Messianic Psalm predicting all the nations worshipping Messiah (Jesus).
- **Psalm 48:10** – "As your name, O God, so your praise reaches **to the ends of the earth.**" – Praise will come from all corners of the earth.
- **Psalm 98:3** – **"All the ends of the earth have seen the salvation of our God."** – God's purpose is not carried out in a closet.

(Additional examples in the Psalms of the geographic and ethnic scope of God's salvation can be found in 18:49-50; 22:30-31; 59:13, 65:5, 8; 67:2, 7; 72:8, 11, 17; 117:1-2.)

---

84   Keith James Miller, "A Missional Pathway For Highly Dysfunctional and Dying Churches Within The Converge Rocky Mountain District" (A Dissertation for Doctor of Ministry, Biblical Theological Seminary, 2015), p.29. The full quote is: "Furthermore, it is the researcher's observation that the glory of God and the mission of God are like the strands of DNA, with the high points of redemption the base pairs making the double helix, which means that the DNA of all Scripture is indeed the glory and mission of God. A survey of the Scriptures will reveal that the glory of God and the mission of God are his two highest priorities from the dawn of creation to new creation, and serve as the DNA of Scripture."

The following are examples from the Psalms of **exhortations to "tell" and "proclaim"** God's glory:

- **Psalm 22:31 – "They** [believers] **shall come and proclaim his righteousness** [the cross; the gospel] **to a people yet unborn, that he has done it"** – Psalm 22 is a messianic psalm and is a "Psalm of the Cross."[85] The psalm ends with a parallel to Jesus' final statement on the cross, "that he has done it"; see John 19:30, "It is finished";[86] believers in Christ will proclaim His gospel, the message of the cross.
- **Psalm 40:9 – "I have told the glad news of deliverance** in the great congregation" – gospel language ("glad news") and proclamation of salvation ("deliverance") on display.
- **Psalm 51:15 – "O Lord, open my lips, and my mouth will declare your praise."–** This comes out of one of the great psalms of confession, forgiveness, and restoration, all of which results in proclaiming God's great salvation.
- **Psalm 96:2b-3a – "Tell of his salvation from day to day. Declare his glory among the nations"** – This is explicit, direct, and bold.
- **Psalm 145:4 – "One generation shall commend your works to another, and shall declare your mighty acts."** – We must tell the gospel to the next generation, our children, and grandchildren; it must be passed on.

(Additional encouragements to proclaim His great name and tell of His glory can be seen in Psalms 9:11; 30:9; 35:28; 40:5, 9-10; 48:13; 66:16; 67:1-7; 71:15, 17, 18; 78:4, 6; 96:1-13; 105:1; 145:4-7, 10-13; 148:13.)

What Can We Learn About Evangelism from the Psalms?

If the two dominant features of God's DNA are that He acts for His glory and for His purpose, we should expect these features to be expressed consistently in His

---

85 James M. Boice, *Psalms 1–41: An Expositional Commentary* (Grand Rapids, Baker Books, 1994, 2005), p. 191.

86 Boice, *Psalms 1–41: An Expositional Commentary,* p. 203.

revelation of Himself from Genesis to Revelation. The Psalms teach believers to pray that all of God's character traits, including the telling of His message of redemption, are to course through the veins of their hearts.

One of the exercises that believers can do is to pray through the Psalms and to confess where we specifically fall short. All of Scripture is useful for this purpose, and the Psalms are a great place to start. Here is an example of how to personalize and pray a passage of Scripture. Consider this passage for confession, especially confession of our failure in evangelism. It challenges how we think about wealth, talents, time, and other blessings.

Example 1:

> *May God be gracious to us and bless us*
> *and make his face to shine upon us,*
> ***that your way may be known on earth,***
> ***your saving power among all nations.***
> *Psalm 67:1-2*

Personalized Confession: "O Lord, so often I have used the blessings you have given me for selfish purposes. I have often used my knowledge of you, my talents, my time, and my material blessings without regard for the salvation of my friends and family or for others around the world. Please, O Lord, forgive me of this sin and transform my heart to have a heart like yours, to have the desire to make your saving power known to others. In Jesus' name. Amen."

Example 2:

The next passage, Psalm 96:1-2, is from one of the most obvious of the Psalms regarding evangelism. It explicitly calls the whole world to worship Him, it is filled with singing, and it characterizes evangelism as a joyful purpose. Under the LORD's righteous reign, the whole of creation will rejoice in the LORD, "Then shall all the trees of the forest sing for joy." Psalm 96 also contains six of the eight elements of the gospel, with the other two implied. See if you can find them (the answer is in the footnote below).[87]

> *Oh sing to the LORD a new song;*
> *sing to the LORD, all the earth!*
> *Sing to the LORD, bless his name;*
> **tell of his salvation from day to day.**
> **Declare his glory among the nations,**
> **his marvelous works among all the peoples!**
> *Psalm 96:1-2*

Personalized Confession: "O Lord, I am so often caught up in my own small world and fail to see that many around me are currently under your wrath. I tend to block from my mind that if unbelievers die without knowing you, they will spend eternity forever in torment. As your child, please give me the courage to *tell of your salvation* at every opportunity and to *declare your glory to others*. Fill me with joy as I engage others. In Jesus' name. Amen."

Example 3:

The final passage to consider, Psalm 73, is a Psalm of Asaph, of the tribe of Levi who was in charge of worship under David (1 Chron. 6:39).[88] In this Psalm the writer gives us an honest look at his wrestling match with the age-old question, Why do the wicked prosper?

Initially the psalmist fell into the trap of comparing his life with the arrogant and wicked (73:3). They were doing quite well in life and enjoyed prosperity. But this only made him envious and bitter. It turned his heart into chaos and made him foolish and senseless (73:21-22).

The psalmist only found resolution to this struggle when he saw the wicked from God's perspective. When he entered the "sanctuary of God" and "discerned their end,"

---

87   Eight elements of the gospel linked to Ps. 96: (1) God (v. 1), (2) holiness (vv. 6, 9), (3) sin (vv. 5, 8), (4), wrath/judgment (vv. 10, 13), (5) the cross/resurrection (v. 2), (6) grace (vv. 2, 8 implied), (7) the cost of following God (v. 5 implied), (8) repent/believe (vv. 7-10).

88   James M. Boice, *Psalms 42–106: An Expositional Commentary* (Grand Rapids, MI: Baker Books, 1996, 2005), p. 610.

he found relief from his struggle. He saw that their end was horrible. This motivated him to renew his trust in God and to "tell of all your [God's] works."

This is an important Psalm. Envy and hatred of believers toward unbelievers is a real problem. But when we understand the ultimate end of the lost, it changes us.

> *But when I thought how to understand this,*
> *it seemed to me a wearisome task,*
> ***until I went into the sanctuary of God;***
> ***then I discerned their end.***
>
> *Truly you set them in slippery places;*
> *you make them fall to ruin.*
> ***How they are destroyed in a moment,***
> ***swept away utterly by terrors!***
>
> *But for me it is good to be near God;*
> *I have made the Lord God my refuge,*
> ***that I may tell of all your works.***
> *Psalm 73:16-19, 28*

Personalized Confession: "O Lord, there are times when I cannot understand life in the world around me. So many prosper who ignore you, live lives of corruption, and even hate you. I find myself hating them or at best wanting to shut them out of my life and pretend they do not exist. But this is sin on my part. Help me to see unbelievers from your perspective. Help me to see that they live in a 'slippery' place and that 'in a moment' they will be 'swept away utterly by terrors!' (Ps. 73:18-19). Please give me the ability to see the lost through your eyes. Give me the strength and the heart to respond as you would have me respond. Right now, I do not want to respond in a gracious way, nor do I want to tell others the good news of your great salvation. Help me to recognize how horrible hell will actually be. O God, please change my sinful heart. Grant me the ability to repent and enable me to 'tell of all your works' and to have compassion on those who are lost."

These are simply three examples of praying God's word and confessing our lack of faithfulness in evangelism. When we pray God's word, it aligns our heart with His heart, our desires with His desires, and our purpose with His purpose. It is an exercise in using God's own words to shape our petitions to Him. It must please God to hear His own words prayed back to Him by His children.

The Book of Psalms is full of the longings, not only of human hearts, but also the longings of God's heart. We can relate to them with our emotions. We can feel them. Since our lives are driven by what we value, the Psalms give believers a stream of water to drink from that will transform our hearts so that we value what God values.

CHAPTER 4
JONAH

You pity the plant...And should
I not pity Nineveh...?

Jonah 4:10-11

Many Christians do not believe that the gospel was ever shared during the time of the Old Testament. If there ever was a doubt that the Old Testament expressed God's call to evangelism, the Book of Jonah answers that question. The Book of Jonah is one of the clearest examples of evangelism to lost people in the entire Old Testament. As this book presents a case for evangelism in the Old Testament, the Book of Jonah should solidify that position.

The Book of Jonah takes place during the first half of the eighth century BC during the reign of Jeroboam II.[89] The only thing that could hinder God's purpose of evangelism was unbelief. Jonah certainly tried to derail God's plan, but even his rebellion could not stop it. God never changes His purpose to suit a rebellious people because "all the families of the nations shall worship before [Him]" (Ps. 22:27).

The Book of Jonah is the story of an evangelistic outreach by the "world's worst missionary"[90] who delivered a powerful gospel message to a lost people. It was not the standard practice in the sense of God sending one of His prophets to call a Gentile people to repentance. Massive worldwide outreach with the gospel would not be unleashed until the Book of Acts. But it was certainly not, the only time God sent a

---

89   Sproul, *The Reformation Study Bible (ESV)*, pp. 1560-1561.
90   John MacArthur, *Sermon: The World's Worst Missionary* (https://www.gty.org/library/sermons-library/80-111/the-worst-missionary, February 14, 1993).

prophet to another country or issued prophetic pronouncements regarding named Gentile nations.[91]

The Ninevites were a horrible and wicked people. We would think of them in today's terms as a terrorist nation known for committing unspeakable human atrocities. The Ninevites were known for mutilating their victims while still alive. "Archaeology confirms the biblical witness to the wickedness of the Assyrians. They were well known in the ancient world for brutality and cruelty."[92] "Nineveh was a second Sodom, the epitome of wickedness, which merited divine retribution."[93]

Nineveh was a threat to Israel. It was "one of the capitals of the Assyrian empire and at the height of that empire one of the great cities of the world."[94] During Jonah's time, Israel, the northern kingdom, along with Judah, the southern kingdom, were strong and prosperous politically speaking. Under Jeroboam II, Israel enlarged the northern borders "to where they had been in the days of David and Solomon...Spiritually, however, it was a time of poverty; religion was ritualistic and increasingly idolatrous, and justice had become perverted. Peacetime and wealth had made her bankrupt spiritually, morally, and ethically."[95] Prior to Jonah, Assyria under Shalmaneser III (859-824 BC) made frequent military raids against Israel and/or the surrounding nations.[96] At the time of Jonah, Assyria was ascendant and though not at the height of its powers was a real threat to Israel. "Jonah's prophetic mission to this languishing foreign nation

---

91   God sent Elijah to Zarephath in Phoenicia to hide for a time from wicked King Ahab (1 Kgs. 17:8-24). Elijah was sent to Damascus in Syria to anoint Hazael as king over Syria (1 Kgs. 19:15). Isaiah issued oracles regarding several Gentile nations and cities in Isa. Chs. 13-19 and 21 including Babylon, Assyria, Philistia, Moab, Damascus, Cush, Egypt, Duma, and Arabia. Jeremiah was referred to as a "prophet to the nations" (Jer. 1:5) and sent a word from God to the kings of several nations and cities including Edom, Moab, Ammon, Tyre, Sidon, Egypt, Philistia, Damascus, Kedar, Hazor, Elam, and Babylon (Jer. 27:1-11; Chs. 46-51). Both Isaiah's and Jeremiah's prophecies of judgment on these nations would have been carried by envoys from or emissaries to these nations (Isa. 33:7; 39:1; Jer. 27:3; 49:14). Jeremiah commanded Seraiah to take his pronouncements of disaster on Babylon that were written on a scroll, to Babylon. Once there, he was to read the scroll and to perform an acted parable of judgment against them (Jer. 51:59-64). Obadiah pronounced God's judgment on the Edomites and Nahum issued pronouncements of judgment on Nineveh about a century after Jonah. These nations were warned and could have repented as Nineveh did and be saved from God's wrath.

92   Billy K. Smith and Frank S. Page, *Amos, Obadiah, Jonah (NAC)* (Nashville: Broadman & Holman Publishers, 1995), p. 225.

93   James E. Smith, *The Minor Prophets* (Joplin, MO: College Press, 1994), p. 103.

94   Elwell, "Nineveh", *Baker Encyclopedia of the Bible* (Vol. 2), pp. 1553-1554.

95   John MacArthur, *The MacArthur Study Bible (NASB)*, p. 1264.

96   Elwell, "Shalmaneser," *Baker Encyclopedia of the Bible* (Vol. 2), p. 1935.

resulted not only in their repentance and deliverance but ultimately also in Israel's destruction."[97] Jonah apparently recognized that possibility.

God Called Jonah

"Now the word of the LORD came to Jonah the son of Amittai, saying, 'Arise, go to Nineveh, that great city, and call out against it, for their evil has come up before me'" (Jonah 1:1-2). This was a signature phrase to indicate a direct revelation from God to Jonah. It was the message of a holy God who was opposed to all that is evil. It was also a message of a righteous God who was giving the wicked people of Nineveh an opportunity to repent and come under His gracious mercy.

God's sending Jonah to Nineveh was an unthinkable idea, and Jonah was not happy about it. His nationalistic view of the world would have caused him to view Ninevah as a threat to Israel's safety. He would have preferred for God to destroy them rather than warn them of a coming judgment.

Jonah Responded With: "No!"

Jonah responded "no" with a giant exclamation point! As a righteous Jew, the prophet Jonah did not want to obey God's call to go and evangelize Nineveh. In actuality, what Jonah truly wanted was for God to destroy the Ninevites. God, however, did not see the Ninevites as Jonah did, for He cared about the lost people there.

So, to express his disobedience to God's call, Jonah did the opposite of what God wanted him to do. For, instead of traveling to Nineveh, which was 500 miles to the east, Jonah purchased a one-way ticket for Tarshish some 2,000 miles to the west.[98] That was about as far away in the known world as one could go. It was in the opposite direction of Nineveh. What is clear is that Jonah was not prepared to obey God in this matter.

Please observe that there was a downward spiral for Jonah that began with his refusal to obey God. The text says he went "down to Joppa" (1:3), found a ship that he went "down into" (1:3), went "down into the inner part of the ship" (1:5), and lay "down" (1:5). The downward trajectory continued as he went down into the water (1:15) and down into the

---

97   Billy K. Smith and Frank S. Page, *Amos, Obadiah, Jonah* (NAC), p. 205

98   The most reliable location for Tarshish is in southern Spain. Elwell, "Tarshish," *Baker Encyclopedia of the Bible*, p. 2036.

belly of the fish (1:17) and down into the "belly of Sheol" (2:2). Responding with "No" to God led Jonah to the displeasure of God, which is unavoidable with "no."

God Responded to "No" With Judgment

Because Jonah disobeyed God, God was angry at Jonah and "hurled" a storm at him (Jon. 1:4). *God's judgment came down on Jonah, and it placed those around him in great danger.* One irony of the event was that Jonah wanted judgment to fall on Nineveh but in his disobedience, God's judgment fell on him. The sad part of God's judgment upon Jonah was that the storm sent to Jonah also affected the lives of innocent sailors on the ship.

When God's storm hit, the sailors did everything in their power to save themselves. The ship was about to break apart, so they threw the cargo overboard. They "cried out" to their pagan gods. The captain rebuked Jonah for being asleep in the hold of the ship and for not praying to his god. When the sailors cast lots and the lot fell on Jonah, they asked him why he brought all this trouble on them. Jonah told the sailors that he was running away from God and to toss him overboard so that the sea would quiet down. This made the sailors even more terrified. And they appear to be alarmed at the utter foolishness of Jonah which placed their lives in danger.

Showing greater virtue than Jonah, the sailors did not initially follow Jonah's instructions because they did not want his blood on their hands. So, they continued rowing, trying hard to get back to shore, but the conditions of the sea only grew worse. Eventually the sailors were without hope and gave in to Jonah's instructions to throw him overboard. When they did, "the sea ceased from its raging" (Jon. 1:4-15).

Jonah thought his life was over as he went flying over the side of the ship into the angry sea. He had resigned himself to drowning. But it would actually get far worse than Jonah could have ever imagined. As Jonah passed over the side of the ship and entered the water, he soon found himself going into the open mouth of a great fish. As he passed through the lips and down the hatch of this large fish, to his horror, he realized he was being eaten. What a nightmare!

But in the judgment of Jonah, God still had mercy. There is a movement up in the story and not just down for Jonah. "And the Lord appointed [or "ordained"][99] a great

---

99   Billy K. Smith and Frank S. Page, *Amos, Obadiah, Jonah (NAC)*, p. 239.

fish to swallow up Jonah. And Jonah was in the belly of the fish three days and three nights" (Jonah 1:17). And that would be **three stinking days and three stinking nights.** It was one of those upside down acts of mercy. Jonah was totally removed from all human comforts and described himself as being in the "belly of Sheol" (Jonah 2:2), a term meaning in the "place of the dead" and "separated from God."[100] God's judgment and subsequent rescue involved his languishing in the belching stomach gases of this "ordained" giant for three days. It must have seemed like an eternity to Jonah.

Many people find this part of the story too farfetched to be believable and refer to it as "allegory, parable, legend, novella, satire, etc."[101] In order to come to that conclusion, one must ignore Jesus' own statements about it. Jesus said of Jonah in Matthew 12:40, "For just as Jonah was three days and three nights in the belly of the great fish, so will the Son of Man be three days and three nights in the heart of the earth." What Jesus was doing here was comparing one supernatural physical event to another – the miracle of Jonah surviving the great fish to His own supernatural resurrection from the grave. The cross and resurrection of Jesus were not fiction, nor were they satire. Jesus' rising from the dead on the third day was equally "impossible" and even more supernatural than was Jonah's surviving the large fish. James Montgomery Boice says, "Jesus referred to the experience of Jonah as a historical illustration of His own literal resurrection, thus reinforcing the truthfulness of this narrative."[102] Later Boice adds, "Yet the book is true, and it is only when we regard it as true that it speaks to us forcefully"[103] (See Mt. 12:38-42 and Lk. 11:29-32).

We must also realize that there have been sea creatures large enough to swallow a man without destroying his body. History recalls several accounts of people actually being swallowed by large fish and living to tell about it.

As to whether a man could survive in a whale's stomach, the Britannica article maintains that he certainly could, though in circumstances of very great discomfort. There would be air to breathe, of a sort. It is

---

100 Smith and Page, *Amos, Obadiah, Jonah*, p. 245.
101 Smith and Page, *Amos, Obadiah, Jonah*, p. 210.
102 James M. Boice, *The Minor Prophets: An Expositional Commentary, (Vol. 1) Hosea – Jonah* (Grand Rapids, MI: Baker Books, 2002), p. 262.
103 Boice, *The Minor Prophets (Vol. 1)*, p. 262.

needed to keep the animal afloat. But there would be great heat, about 104–108°F. Unpleasant contact with the animal's gastric juices might easily affect the skin, but the juices would not digest living matter; otherwise they would digest the walls of the creature's own stomach.[104]

Another validation:

Dr. Harry Rimmer, President of the Research Science Bureau of L.A. said they found an account of an English sailor swallowed by a giant Rhinodon in the English Channel in the Literary Digest. Apparently they were trying to harpoon the giant sharks when this sailor fell overboard. Before he could be pulled back in the boat the shark turned around and swallowed him up. 48 hrs after the incident the shark was found and killed. When the shark was opened by the sailors they were amazed to find their friend alive and unconscious. They rushed him to the hospital where they found that he only suffered from shock. He was perfectly healthy and fit otherwise. In 1926 Dr. Rimmer met the man and said that his body was devoid of hair and patches of yellowish-brown color covered his entire skin.[105]

God gave Jonah some time in this disgusting, nauseating, and frightening environment. He had three days and three nights to think about how angry God was at his refusal to tell the gospel to the lost people of Nineveh. Jonah clearly recognized he was under the hand of God's judgment.

"Jonah prayed to the LORD his God from the belly of the fish" (Jonah 2:1). In this prayer, he prayed back to God, God's own words using phrases found in 14 or more different Psalms. He put together a patchwork quilt of Scripture from memory that was

---

104 Boice, *The Minor Prophets (Vol. 1)*, p.283.

105 https://considertheevidence.wordpress.com/2010/06/01/could-jonah-survive-3-days-in-a-fish/, accessed October 27, 2020. "There are at least 2 known monsters of the deep that could easily have swallowed Jonah. They are the Balaenoptera Musculus or sulphur-bottom whale, and the Rhinodon Typicus or whale shark. Neither monster has any teeth. They open their enormous jaws and take in water at an incredible speed, then strain out the water and swallow whatever is left."

stunning in its composition and eloquence. Using Scripture, he articulated his experience of being under the judgment of God and of experiencing God's great salvation. Jonah was a brilliant theologian with a hard heart who was under God's judgment.

Here is Jonah's psalm based on his real-life experience compared with Scripture he was likely drawing from:

	Jonah 2:2-9	Psalms
1	called out to the Lord, out of my distress, and he answered me; out of the belly of Sheol I cried, and you heard my voice.	In my distress I called to the Lord, and he answered me. (Ps. 120:1) But you heard the voice of my pleas for mercy when I cried to you for help. (Ps. 31:22b)
2	For you cast me into the deep, into the heart of the seas, and the flood surrounded me; all your waves and your billows passed over me.	because of your indignation and anger; for you have taken me up and thrown me down. (Ps. 102:10) I have come into deep waters, and the flood sweeps over me. (Ps. 69:2) all your breakers and your waves have gone over me. (Ps. 42:7)
3	Then I said, "I am driven away from your sight; yet I shall again look upon your holy temple."	I had said in my alarm, I am cut off from your sight. (Ps. 31:22a) I will bow down toward your holy temple in the fear of you. (Ps. 5:7)
4	The waters closed in over me to take my life; the deep surrounded me; weeds were wrapped about my head	For the waters have come up to my neck. (Ps. 69:1) The cords of death encompassed me; the torrents of destruction assailed me; the cords of Sheol entangled me; the snares of death confronted me. (Ps. 18:4-5)
5	at the roots of the mountains. I went down to the land whose bars closed upon me forever; yet you brought up my life from the pit, O Lord my God.	who redeems your life from the pit (Ps. 103:4)
6	When my life was fainting away, I remembered the Lord, and my prayer came to you, into your holy temple.	When my spirit faints within me (Ps. 142:3) I remember the days of old (Ps. 143:5) Let my prayer come before you (Ps. 88:2)
7	Those who pay regard to vain idols forsake their hope of steadfast love.	I hate those who pay regard to worthless idols (Ps. 31:6)

	Jonah 2:2-9	Psalms
8	But I with the voice of thanksgiving will sacrifice to you; what I have vowed I will pay. Salvation belongs to the Lord!	I will offer to you the sacrifice of thanksgiving (Ps. 116:17) I will pay my vows to the Lord (Ps. 116:18) Salvation belongs to the Lord (Ps. 3:8)

Jonah knew God's word, but he did not know God's heart. His prayer gives us a glimpse into his biblical knowledge and theology. Jonah totally misunderstood God's love. He totally misunderstood God's purpose of salvation for the Gentiles as well as for Israel. His big failure was not a failure of doctrine, but a failure of the heart. Real love and compassion matter.

However, for three days and nights, God supernaturally preserved the life of Jonah in the belly of the "ordained" fish. God's judgment on Jonah was a judgment not to accomplish his death. In God's anger toward Jonah, He bestowed grace on him, and God would extend grace to the Ninevites, using this tragic prophet to proclaim the gospel to them.

So, after three days the fish "vomited" Jonah out somewhere near the shore and he must have spent the next few days getting the fish smell out of his hair (if he had any left), clothing, and nostrils. He may have borne the marks of his misadventure on his skin for the rest of his life. God's disciplining judgment never leaves anyone feeling elegant and dignified. Jonah survived a humiliating and dangerous adventure, by the grace of God.

Proclaiming the Gospel

Jonah eventually arrived in Nineveh, a city of either 120,000 people, or as many as 600,000 people,[106] and proclaimed the gospel to them. He was not happy about being in Nineveh. But he did as God commanded him. We do not know if we have been given his full message or not, but we can identify in the narrative the impact it had on his hearers.

*Jonah began to go into the city, going a day's journey. **And he called out, "Yet forty days, and Nineveh shall be overthrown!" And the***

---

106 Scholars are divided as to whether "120,000 persons who do not know their right hand from their left" (Jon. 4:11) means the population of children only or the entire population who are characterized as ignorant of their Creator God and His ways. See Smith and Page, *Amos, Obadiah, Jonah (NAC)*, pp. 282-283.

people of Nineveh believed God. They called for a fast and put on sackcloth, from the greatest of them to the least of them.

The word reached the king of Nineveh, and he arose from his throne, removed his robe, covered himself with sackcloth, and sat in ashes. And he issued a proclamation and published through Nineveh, **"By the decree of the king and his nobles: Let neither man nor beast, herd nor flock, taste anything.** *Let them not feed or drink water, but let man and beast be covered with sackcloth,* **and let them call out mightily to God. Let everyone turn from his evil way and from the violence that is in his hands. Who knows? God may turn and relent and turn from his fierce anger, so that we may not perish."*

Jonah 3:4-9

The Pulpit Commentary gives us a vivid picture of how this event might have seemed from a ground-level eyewitness perspective.

An Eastern city sleeps in the rosy morning light. Its moated ramparts tower a hundred feet in the air, and, dotted with fifteen hundred lofty towers, sweep around it a length of over sixty miles. Already the gates are open for the early traffic, and conspicuous among the crowd a stranger enters. The stains of travel are on his dress, and he looks with curious awe at the figures of winged colossal bulls that keep silent symbolic guard over the gate by which he passes in. Within, things new and strange appear at every step. The houses, sitting each in its own grounds, are bowered in green. The streets are spanned at intervals with triumphal arches, whose entablature is enriched by many a sculptured story. On every eminence is a palace, or monument, or idol temple, guarded by symbolic monsters in stone, and adorned in carving of bas-relief with sacred symbols. The markets fill, the bazaars are alive with multifarious dealing, soldiers and war-chariots parade the streets, and the evidences of despotic power and barbaric wealth and heathenish worship, with their inevitable accompaniments of luxury, corruption, and violence, abound on every side. The stranger is deeply moved. Surprise gives place to horror, then horror warms into righteous indignation; and with trumpet voice and dilating form and eye of fire he utters the words of doom, "Yet forty days, and Nineveh shall be destroyed." Through street, and park, and barrack, and bazaar the direful message rings. There is momentary incredulity, then swift alarm, then utter consternation. Like wildfire the news, and with it the panic spreads. It reaches the nobles in their palaces. It penetrates to the king upon his throne. It moves society to its depths. And the result is the scenes of mourning and self-abasement our text records.[107]

It must have been an amazing scene. Scripture records a one-dimensional message of coming judgment that Jonah spoke. His message could have been only the "one liner" the text gives us (eight words in the ESV and five in the original Hebrew).[108] But it could have included more details about repentance and faith. We just do not know. **But this is the one thing that Jonah did right! He preached the message God gave him to preach without alteration.**

> *Yet forty days, and Nineveh shall be overthrown!*
> Jonah 3:4

The announcement by Jonah of imminent judgment precipitated significant actions. Here are the actions which followed, given to us in the order of the text:

1. **"The people of Nineveh believed God"** (Jon. 3:5):
   a. Called for a fast and
   b. Put on sackcloth

---

107 H. D. M. Spence (Ed.), *Jonah,* The Pulpit Commentary (London; New York: Funk & Wagnalls Company, 1909), p. 67.
108 Boice, *The Minor Prophets, Vol 1*, p. 296

2. **Word reached the king, and he (Jon. 3:6-9):**
    a. Got off his throne in humility
    b. Removed his robe
    c. Covered himself in sackcloth
    d. Sat in ashes
    e. And issued a decree that everyone should:
        1. Fast
        2. Put on sackcloth
        3. Call out mightily to God
        4. Repent – "turn from his evil ways and from the violence"
        5. Hope in God – maybe He will "turn from his fierce anger, so that we may not perish."

This response was nothing short of a supernatural miracle. The king removed his royal robes and got off his royal throne, the position of power and authority, put on sackcloth and sat in ashes, a position of humiliation and subjection. Kings in the ancient world were not inclined to intentional public humiliation. It was an amazing response by so wicked a people. Please note what God did as a result of their response.

> *When God saw what they did, how they turned from their evil way,*
> *God relented of the disaster that he had said he would do to them,*
> *and he did not do it.*
>
> *Jonah 3:10*

Jesus himself confirmed genuine repentance and saving faith by the Ninevites. Any confusion about this being an actual revival should be settled when we read Matthew 12:41, **"The men of Nineveh will rise up at the judgment with this generation and condemn it, for they repented at the preaching of Jonah, and behold, something greater than Jonah is here."** This statement by Jesus showed that He believed the Ninevites to be real people, part of an historical event, who repented at hearing the gospel, and that they would on Judgment Day condemn the generation He was speaking to for their failure to repent and believe. William Hendriksen says of Matthew 12:41,

"Since it is the teaching of Scripture (Dan. 7:22; Mt. 19:28; 1 Cor. 6:2; Rev. 15:3, 4; 20:4) that God's children are going to participate in the final judgment (for example, by praising God in Christ for His judgments), this statement of Jesus about the role of certain Ninevites in that Great Assize is understandable if their repentance was genuine."[109] Craig Blomberg takes a similar position regarding Matthew 12:41-42 saying, "But in this case, he compares those rejecting him with those Gentiles who actually repented and heeded God's Word favorably—the Ninevites (see Jonah 3) and the Queen of Sheba (see 1 Kgs 10:1–10). Such Gentiles will join with believers of every time and place on Judgment Day to condemn all who reject Jesus."[110] (See also Luke 11:29-32.)

This statement by Jesus stands in contrast to His statement of judgment made to Bethsaida, "But it will be *more bearable in the judgment* for Tyre and Sidon than for you" (Lk. 10:14). That is different terminology (**"bearable"**) than what He used regarding Nineveh and the Queen of Sheba (**"rise up…and condemn it, for they repented"**). The people of Nineveh and the Queen of Sheba are in a different category – saved – as compared with the people of Tyre and Sidon – unsaved.

Although opinions differ whether this was a genuine revival or not, John MacArthur and James Montgomery Boice describe this event respectively as "the greatest revival in history"[111] and "nothing less than the greatest mass conversion in history."[112]

Jonah's Hatred

After Jonah had finished preaching his message throughout Nineveh, he went outside the city and found an optimal viewing location from which to enjoy the judgment of God falling on Nineveh. Jonah hoped to see God's wrath rain down on this enemy of Israel. But Jonah would be disappointed, for instead of wrath God showed mercy to Nineveh.

"But it displeased Jonah exceedingly, and he was angry" (Jonah 4:1). The literal translation is, "It was evil to Jonah with great evil."[113] There are two Hebrew words

---

109 William Hendriksen, New Testament Commentary: *Exposition of the Gospel According to Matthew* (Grand Rapids: Baker Book House, 1973), p. 536.

110 Craig L. Blomberg, *Matthew (NAC)* (Nashville: Broadman & Holman Publishers, 1992), p. 207.

111 John MacArthur, Sermon: *Running Away from God's Will* (https://www.gty.org/library/sermons-library/1221/running-away-from-gods-will, March 25, 1973).

112 Boice, *The Minor Prophets, Vol. 1* p.291.

113 Billy K. Smith and Frank S. Page, *Amos, Obadiah, Jonah (NAC)*, p. 271.

describing Jonah's anger in the sentence, which meant he was in a rage at God. He was angry to the point of asking God to end his life. God's extending grace to Nineveh "was exceedingly evil to Jonah."[114]

Notice the paradox surrounding this "man of God." God had extended grace to Jonah when he reprehensibly disobeyed God. Yet Jonah was excessively angry at God for extending grace to the reprehensible Ninevites. Jonah was as much in need of and a beneficiary of God's grace as the Ninevites were. His hard heart toward the lost people of Nineveh was exposed and his hatred of lost people was on full display. God had love for Nineveh, but Jonah did not. Jonah and God were not on the same page.

What was most tragic about the story of Jonah was not only his disobedience to God's commission, but his lack of compassion for the Ninevites. In the days following Jonah's preaching in Nineveh, God orchestrated events for Jonah that were designed to show him his callousness toward the lost (Jonah 4:5-11). A poignant part of the conversation between God and Jonah was when God pointed out to Jonah that he (Jonah) had compassion for the plant that had given him protection from the heat, while He (God) had compassion for the people of Nineveh. It is a dramatic contrast, and the story ends with this tension between Jonah and God unresolved. Sadly, Jonah was used as an evangelist against his will and despite his lack of love for the lost.

What Can We Learn About the Gospel and Evangelism from the Book of Jonah?

First, the strategic purpose revealed in Abraham's call and commission was demonstrated dramatically in this event. In Chapter 2 of this book, we looked at Genesis 12:1-2 where, "the LORD said to Abram, 'Go from your country and your kindred and your father's house to the land that I will show you. And I will make of you a great nation, and I will bless you and make your name great, so that you will be a blessing.'" Later in Genesis 22:18, God revealed more specifically to Abraham what that "blessing" was to be: "in your **offspring** shall all the nations of the earth be blessed." "Offspring," in the singular, is a reference to Christ, as Paul tells us in Galatians 3:16. The blessing of Abraham, Christ,

---

114 Footnote no. 4 to Jon. 4:1 in *The Holy Bible: English Standard Version*, (Wheaton, IL: Crossway Bibles, 2016).

was for "all nations" and not exclusively for Israel. It never was exclusively for Israel. Jonah did not regard that idea as proper, and he was not on board with it.

God's call of Jonah and sending him to Nineveh was a dramatic example of God's purpose in action. Jonah being sent to Nineveh was the strategic and redemptive purpose of God carried to the nations. God's people today, the church, have the same call – given to Abraham, dramatized by Jonah, and restated by Jesus in Matthew 28:18-20. However, the church has almost totally abandoned that call and is more like Jonah than anyone cares to imagine. In many ways Jonah is a picture of the church today. We are Jonah. We have convinced ourselves that there is no downside to ignoring God's purpose and call and that we can take it or leave it based on personal preference. Whereas Jonah ran from God by boarding a ship to faraway destination, church people today run from God by ignoring God's call to share the gospel with the lost.

It is easy to lose sight of God's central purpose for His people. Too many in the church have fallen in love with the things of this world, and their eyes have become blinded to the biblical message and to the biblical purpose of God for His people. The apostle John warns us of this danger in his first epistle.

> *Do not love the world or the things in the world. If anyone loves the world, the love of the Father is not in him. For all that is in the world—the desires of the flesh and the desires of the eyes and pride of life—is not from the Father but is from the world. And the world is passing away along with its desires, but whoever does the will of God abides forever.*
>
> *I Jn. 2:15-17*

Many churches today have embraced the idols of the world such as materialism, wealth and affluence, entertainment, hobbies, sports, the values and philosophies of the culture, and various immoralities.

> *Idols are the things that capture the passions of our hearts and re-place God as the central love of our life. All of the idols of this world are enemies of the gospel. All of them extinguish real love of Jesus.*

Second, Jonah did one thing right. He did not alter the biblical gospel message. It was a hard message to deliver, and one dominated by judgment.

> *"Arise, go to Nineveh, that great city, and call out against it the message that I tell you."...And he called out, "Yet forty days, and Nineveh shall be overthrown!"*
>
> *Jonah 3:2-4*

This was not a feel-good message that God gave Jonah to deliver. It was a truthful message. God had set the day of judgment for Nineveh – in 40 days – and sent Jonah to deliver that message. Jonah delivered the message without changing it.

In our own day, God has set the day of judgment. "The times of ignorance God overlooked, but now he commands all people everywhere to repent, because **he has fixed a day on which he will judge the world** in righteousness by a man whom he has appointed; and of this he has given assurance to all by raising him from the dead" (Acts 17:30-31). The day of judgment is on God's calendar. He is not trying to figure out when He is going to wrap up the history of the world. That decision has already been made. The date is set.

The biblical gospel message differs significantly from the typical message delivered from most pulpits in America today. Pastors, teachers, and believers delude themselves if they think they are doing anyone a favor by making the message of the Bible more "acceptable" to modern ears. By eliminating the disturbing parts of the gospel, we are in effect withholding crucial information from our listeners. By failing to expose sin, warn of judgment, and call for genuine repentance, we are obfuscating the only way a person can be saved from God's wrath. We must act in genuine love and incorporate the whole gospel message. **Incorporating the whole gospel message is an act of genuine love.**

Third, God judged Jonah for refusing His command to evangelize Nineveh. The severity of God's hand on him and the use of the fish show us how displeased God actually was that Jonah was not willing to warn them of judgment.

Jonah did not lack courage, as evidenced by telling the sailors to throw him into the raging sea (Jonah 1:12). But he was clearly lacking in love and compassion. He lacked compassion for lost people, as God stated in Jonah 4:10-11. Jonah was afflicted by his nationalistic idols, which destroyed compassion for others. Jonah's blindness and hardness of heart were severe. Sin and idolatry in the lives of believers will extinguish their love for God, their love for the lost, and harden their hearts toward the purpose of God.

Believers in the church today can relate to Jonah, for many find evangelism difficult or inappropriate. Believers have a variety of reasons why not to evangelize. The average believer and the average church have become creatively busy at finding ways to avoid it. Churches have become so busy with good things, such as ministry to their own members or ministry to the poor, that they have lost sight of God's call to evangelize. It is tragic to think that it is okay to neglect God's call to evangelize and that we can do so without consequences.

An important question is this, "Is there a judgment of God on the church today when the church refuses to evangelize the lost?" This is a question I have pondered for some time. **My conclusion is that *God is angry* when believers, individually and corporately, do not share the gospel with the lost and that there is a judgment for this disobedience.** So, what is that judgment? The answer is found in Revelation chapter 2:1-7.

> *To the angel of the church in Ephesus write: "The words of him who holds the seven stars in his right hand, who walks among the seven golden lampstands.*
>
> *"I know your works, your toil and your patient endurance, and how you cannot bear with those who are evil, but have tested those who call themselves apostles and are not, and found them to be false. I know you are enduring patiently and bearing up for my name's sake, and you have not grown weary.* **But I have this against you, that you have abandoned the love you had at first. Remember therefore from where you have fallen; repent, and do the works you did at first. If not, I will come to you and remove your lampstand from its place, unless you repent.** *Yet this you have: you hate the works of the Nicolaitans, which I also hate. He who has an ear, let him hear what*

the Spirit says to the churches. To the one who conquers I will
grant to eat of the tree of life, which is in the paradise of God."

Rev. 2:1-7

The "love you had at first" relates to love for Christ that overflows to others, including lost people. It is a love that emulates Christ's ministry of witness. It is a love overflowing from God's grace reaching into our own life and rescuing us from our sins. It is a love overflowing from Jesus' love invading our life with His undeserved favor and flowing to the lost. G. K. Beale writes:

> *Although they were ever on guard to maintain the purity of the apos-*
> *tolic teaching, the Ephesian Christians were not diligent in witnessing*
> *to the same faith in the outside world... This is what is meant when*
> *Christ chastises them for having left their "first love." The point is not*
> *primarily that they had lost their love for one another, as argued by*
> *most commentators... Nor is the point merely that they had lost their*
> *love for Christ in general (as some commentators also think; cf. Jer.*
> *2:2; Ezek. 16:8). The idea is that they no longer expressed their former*
> *zealous love for Jesus by witnessing to him in the world. This is why*
> *Christ chooses to introduce himself as he does in v 1. His statement*
> *that he "walks in the midst of the seven golden lampstands" is intended*
> *to remind the introverted readers that their primary role in relation to*
> *their Lord should be that of a light of witness to the outside world.* [115]

If we love Jesus, we will love everything He is and everything He stands for. It is easy to love a figment of our imagination of Jesus and not the Jesus of the Bible. If our love is truly fixed on Him, our lives will display His character traits and we will emulate His ministry of witness.

Christ called the people of Ephesus to "repent and do the works you did at first. If not, I will come to you and remove your lampstand from its place, unless you repent."

---

115 Beale, *The Book of Revelation* (NIGTC), p. 230.

The lampstands are the seven churches (Rev. 1:20), and a lampstand symbolizes witness and testimony for Christ. The warning of judgment to the church at Ephesus was that Jesus would remove their lampstand and they would no longer exist as a church. They may continue to meet and own a building, but they would no longer be a church in God's eyes.

So, the answer to the question is "yes," there is a judgment of God for disobedience to His commission to evangelize. Jonah is a dramatic demonstration of that judgment and Rev. 2:1-7 is a specific articulation of it.

Fourth, Jonah lacked love and compassion for the lost. Jonah thought he was being a righteous and faithful member of God's people. Jonah's theology was good, he knew God's word, he hated sin, he lived a righteous life, and he loved his country. But God punctured his delusion. God ordained a plant, a worm, and a scorching wind (4:6-8) as the setup for a conversation with Jonah and to reveal to him his hardness of heart. Jonah valued the plant more than he valued a human life. God challenged Jonah's sin directly: "You pity the plant...should I not pity Nineveh?" **Lack of compassion for the lost is sin!** God exposed this sin in Jonah's life.

Here is an example of praying God's word based on what we find in the Book of Jonah.

> *Lord, you had compassion on the Ninevites. I must confess that I find it difficult to have your compassion for the lost. Please change my heart and give me the ability to care about the eternal destination of those who do not know you. Help me to care enough about them to endure the hassle that comes with trying to share the gospel with them. Please give me a joy and a boldness to engage others for your kingdom. You are their only hope. In Jesus name, amen.*

CHAPTER 5

ISAIAH

It is too light a thing that you should be my servant
to raise up the tribes of Jacob
and to bring back the preserved of Israel;
I will make you as a light for the nations,
that my salvation may reach to the end of the earth.

Isaiah 49:6

The prophet Isaiah is one of the greatest gospel proclaimers of all time, and he makes one of the most powerful gospel presentations in all of Scripture. "Indeed, so plain is the gospel message set forth in Isaiah's prophecy that Philip Melanchthon, preaching at the funeral service of Martin Luther, could claim that the pure gospel had been most clearly set forth by five men: Isaiah, John the Baptist, Paul, Augustine and Luther! For Melanchthon, at least, Isaiah was a preacher of the gospel *par excellence!*"[116] The Book of Isaiah is an invaluable resource to observe the biblical gospel proclaimed, evangelism practiced, as well as a biblical model of evangelism. Every generation of the church should learn the lessons of evangelism from the prophet Isaiah.

Isaiah is a lengthy book[117] that feels very New Testament-like. There is a reason for that, for references to Isaiah can be found throughout the New Testament. It actually is the book of the Old Testament most often cited or alluded to in the

---

116 Derek Thomas, *God Delivers: Isaiah Simply Explained* (Darlington, UK; Auburn, MA: Evangelical Press, 1991), pp. 14-15.

117 Isaiah, at 25,608 words, is the 6th longest book of the bible by word count in the original languages behind (1) Jeremiah, (2) Genesis, (3) Psalms, (4) Ezekiel, and (5) Exodus. Rounding out the top ten behind Isaiah are (7) Numbers, (8) Deuteronomy, (9) 2 Chronicles, and (10) 1 Samuel. *https://overviewbible.com/longest-book-of-the-bible/,* accessed January 27, 2021.

New Testament, as there are 166 citations and allusions from Isaiah used in the New Testament.[118]

Isaiah prophesied to God's people during the period of the divided kingdom, with Israel in the north and Judah in the south. Isaiah's ministry focused primarily on Judah from his home in Jerusalem. He was an evangelist, prophet, historian, literary virtuoso, and follower of God. "Isaiah was a well-educated aristocrat by birth, with access to the king and the royal court."[119] He spoke God's message to a rebellious people, from about 740 to 690 BC.[120] His ministry spanned the reigns of four kings (Isa. 1:1). The setting was 100+ years in advance of the national calamity of the Babylonian captivity.

In this chapter, we will study Isaiah as a model evangelist, his call to gospel ministry, his telescoped view into evangelism in the last days, his reprimand of God's people for failure to witness, the "Greatest Commission," and the extraordinary ending to the Book of Isaiah which is a field trip to the cemetery of the lost.

The Call (and Life) of an Evangelist – Isaiah 6

In the year that King Uzziah died I saw the Lord sitting upon a throne, high and lifted up; and the train of his robe filled the temple. Above him stood the seraphim. Each had six wings: with two he covered his face, and with two he covered his feet, and with two he flew. And one called to another and said:

"Holy, holy, holy is the Lord of hosts;
the whole earth is full of his glory!"

*And the foundations of the thresholds shook at the voice of him who called, and the house was filled with smoke. **And I said: "Woe is me!***

---

118 *Parallel Passages in New Testament Quoted from Old Testament,* Blue Letter Bible, accessed August 15, 2020, https://www.blueletterbible.org/study/misc/quotes.cfm. The Psalms are second at 146 followed by Genesis (95), Exodus (89), and Deuteronomy (66).

119 R. C. Sproul, General Editor, *The Reformation Study Bible (ESV)* (Sanford, FL: Reformation Trust Publishing, 2015), p. 1114.

120 John N. Oswalt, *The Book of Isaiah, Chapters 1-39* (Grand Rapids, MI: Wm. B. Eerdmans Publishing Co., 1986), p. 26.

For I am lost; for I am a man of unclean lips, and I dwell in the midst of a people of unclean lips; for my eyes have seen the King, the Lord of hosts!"

And I heard the voice of the Lord saying, "Whom shall I send, and who will go for us?" Then I said, "Here I am! Send me." And he said, **"Go, and say to this people:**

> *Keep on hearing, but do not understand;*
> *keep on seeing, but do not perceive.*
> *Make the heart of this people dull,*
> > *and their ears heavy,*
> > *and blind their eyes;*
> *lest they see with their eyes,*
> > *and hear with their ears,*
> *and understand with their hearts,*
> > *and turn and be healed.*
> *Then I said, "How long, O Lord?"*
> *And he said:*
> *"Until cities lie waste*
> > *without inhabitant,*
> *and houses without people,*
> > *and the land is a desolate waste,*
> *and the Lord removes people far away,*
> > *and the forsaken places are many in the midst of the land.*
> *And though a tenth remain in it,*
> > *it will be burned again,*
> *like a terebinth or an oak,*
> > *whose stump remains*
> > *when it is felled."*
> *The holy seed is its stump.*

Isa. 6:1-13

In this section we will focus on three aspects of Isaiah's life: his encounter with God, the meaning of his call, and his environment. Understanding these factors will enable us to better comprehend the message of this book.

Isaiah's encounter with God was an intensely disturbing experience for him. There was nothing in his life experience that could have prepared him for it. He was worshiping in the temple when he experienced this vision. He was brought into the presence of the "Holy One of Israel" (Isa. 12:6) and saw that:

> *the train of his robe filled the temple – the seraphim covered their*
> *faces and feet and called "Holy, holy, holy," – the foundations of the*
> *thresholds shook at the voice of him who called – the house was filled*
> *with smoke.*
>
>

Isa. 6:1-4

It was an intimidating sight, and we can better understand holiness as we observe two things: how the seraphim responded and how Isaiah responded to it. The seraphim, *sinless* creatures, were in awe of God's holiness. "Even sinless seraphs cover face and feet (v. 2b). So holiness is not mere sinlessness—It is beyond that."[121]

Ralph Davis reveals an insight from the seraphim that can be easily overlooked – the aggressive nature of holiness.

> *The seraphs also tell us that* **holiness is something aggressive:**
> *'his glory is what fills all the earth' (v. 3b). 'Glory' is what holiness*
> *is like when it's visible; 'glory' is holiness with a wrapper around it.*
> *And this glory either does (if the text implies present time) or is going*
> *to (if future) fill the whole earth. God's holiness is going to take over.*
> **Holiness is not some tame, docile, dormant, reclusive quality**
> **in God—it is going to go on display throughout the earth**
> *(Hab. 2:14).[122] (emphasis mine)*

---

121 Davis, *Stump Kingdom: Isaiah 6–12*, pp. 11-12.
122 Davis, *Stump Kingdom*, p. 13.

From Isaiah's text we see that God's holiness cannot be hidden or controlled by any sinful human. Holiness is not something we can mold to our own system of human values or fit into our little theological box. **It is an active, untamable force.**

We also learn from Isaiah's response to God's holiness, *sinful* creature that he was, as he cried out in utter despair and thought that his life was abruptly coming to an end. Isaiah realized immediately he was in a dangerous place and, unless someone came to his rescue, he would be destroyed by this mere brush with Holiness. At this overwhelming moment, the seraph brought a burning coal and touched his lips. This coal represented the atoning work of the coming Messiah. Whether or not this was Isaiah's conversion experience, it is a portrayal of conversion. The effect of the applied coal, the imputed righteousness of Christ, was the only reason that the prophet Isaiah was not totally consumed by being in God's presence.

Ralph Davis describes Isaiah's experience.

> *One can simply be glad it was Isaiah. That way we can read about it and watch—hopefully—at a distance. Isaiah's report of his call is very sense-oriented; he focuses on what he sees, feels, and hears. But the privilege of the vision Isaiah has (v. 1) brings him smack up against the terror of God's holiness. If Isaiah says, 'I saw the Lord' (v. 1), he also has to say, 'I am destroyed' (v. 5).* [123]

> *Clearly, Isaiah did not think this was 'just the neatest experience' but the most dreadful moment of his life.* [124]

Isaiah was mercifully spared destruction by the atoning touch of the "burning coal." As a result of this act of grace from a holy God, he went from being in grave danger of destruction to experiencing the tender comfort of God. He was transformed: energized and eager to serve God.

---

123 Davis, *Stump Kingdom,* p. 11.
124 Davis, *Stump Kingdom,* p. 14.

Isaiah's call (6:8-13) was an evangelistic call that would have a hardening effect – "**Go, and say** to this people…" (Isa. 6:9). It was an unusual call to say the least. So, how can we understand it?

First, Israel was an idolatrous nation – "Their land is filled with idols; they bow down to the work of their hands, to what their own fingers have made" (Isa. 2:8). Isaiah's call included a reference to the idolatry of the nation and the judgment it brings: "And though a tenth remain in it, it will be burned again, like a terebinth or an oak" (Isa. 6:13). Sinful, idolatrous people become blind to the things of God as the Psalmist shows us, "Those who make them [idols] become like them" (Ps. 115:8). If the people of Israel spurned Isaiah's "evangelism" efforts, God would not be mocked. If Isaiah's naming of sins and his continual calling for repentance was met by Israel's burying their hearts deeper in their sin, the words of God would harden their hearts beyond remedy. These words of Isaiah are delivered with poetic intrigue and are somewhat perplexing. Yet "these expressions can be understood more precisely as metaphors of idolatry applied to the disobedient nation **as a retributive taunt** in order to impress upon them the fact that they would be punished for their idolatry by being judged in the same manner as their idols. Both the idols and the people would undergo destruction" (emphasis mine).[125] It is similar in impact to Galatians 6:7, "Do not be deceived: God is not mocked, for whatever one sows, that will he also reap". Isaiah's message would be a message of exposing sin, calling for repentance, and warning of God's wrath. Some would be saved but more would be hardened.

Second, we can look at how Isaiah responded to this call. He responded by speaking the gospel message again and again over the course of a 40-year career, and he spoke God's message clearly, plainly, and bravely.[126]

And **third,** God was preparing Isaiah for the difficult task of speaking God's word into the lives of people who were blinded by their sin and hardened in their idolatry. God wanted him to know it would not be easy. Here is how Ralph Davis describes Isaiah's call relative to a story from the life of Jonathan Edwards:

---

125 G. K. Beale, *Isaiah VI 9–13: A Retributive Taunt against Idolatry,* Vetus Testamentum 41 (Jul., 1991), p. 277.

126 J. Alec Motyer, *The Prophecy of Isaiah: An Introduction & Commentary,* (Downers Grove, IL: InterVarsity Press, 1993), p. 79.

*In principle it reminds me of what Jonathan Edwards told Elihu
Parsons when he asked for the hand of Edwards' daughter Sally in
marriage. Edwards told him plainly of her 'unpleasant temper'. Parsons
persisted with 'But she has grace, I trust?' (i.e., she is converted after all,
isn't she?) Edwards retorted, 'I hope she has, but grace can live where
you cannot.' As if to say, 'Do you realize what a hornets' nest you'd be
walking into? I'm sure I wouldn't want to deal with that nasty temper
day after day.' Not exactly a complimentary thing to say about one's
daughter, but, from another angle, a very kind and gracious warning to
Mr. Parsons.[127]*

Like Jonathan Edwards' caution to Elihu Parsons, God's warning to Isaiah was an act of kindness. It established realistic expectations for Isaiah. He would not be surprised by opposition and few results. He would need a laser-like focus and confidence deeply rooted in God because he would be torpedoed repeatedly by those in the culture around him.

Isaiah's environment was saturated with sin and idolatry. Idolatry is not only the worship of an image or material object as a deity, but also is when a person loves something more than God. Here is Isaiah's short description of God's people which precedes a rather detailed look at the range of specific sins that characterized them:

> *Ah, sinful nation,*
> *a people laden with iniquity,*
> *offspring of evildoers,*
> *children who deal corruptly!*
> *They have forsaken the Lord,*
> *they have despised the Holy One of Israel,*
> *they are utterly estranged.*
>
> *Isa. 1:4*

---

127 Davis, *Stump Kingdom*, p. 19.

He proceeded from there to give a detailed analysis of the state of God's people through the first five chapters. This served as his "preface...[and was] the 'backdrop' to the whole book."[128] Isaiah identified sins 65 times in this section as he moved between general and specific.

It is important that we appreciate the state of the society he lived in because most people in the world today live in a similar environment. After the summary he proceeded to specifics such as immorality (1:10), sin-polluted worship (1:13), violence (1:15), prostitution (1:21), bribery (1:23), injustice (1:23), idolatry (1:29), arrogance, (2:11), man exalted above God (2:22), oppression of one another (3:5), youth insolent to elders (3:5), people of bad character contemptuous of honorable people (3:5), leaders who obscured and deceitfully hid the right way (3:12), leaders who plundered the nation's wealth (3:14), women arrogantly and wantonly driven by narcissism drawing attention to themselves (3:16), society that produced godless results (5:2, 4), the wealthy misusing their wealth (5:8), the people calling evil good and good evil (5:20), the people rejecting God's ways in general (5:24), and the people despising the word of God (5:24).

But even in these first five chapters, which are dominated by the naming of sins, Isaiah held out hope. He pleaded with them to turn to God: "O house of Jacob, come, let us walk in the light of the Lord" (2:1-5), and "though your sins are like scarlet, they shall be as white as snow" (1:16-19). He urgently warned them that continuing their present course would result in a collision with God's judgment, "but if you refuse and rebel, you shall be eaten by the sword; for the mouth of the Lord has spoken" (Isa. 1:20); "the haughty looks of man shall be brought low, and the lofty pride of men shall be humbled, and the Lord alone will be exalted in that day" (Isa. 2:11). It was an ugly anatomy of God's people. If they failed to repent and spurned His grace, they would not escape His wrath.

What Can We Learn About the Gospel and Evangelism from Isaiah 6?

First, holiness is "aggressive" and requires that God's greatness be made known throughout the world. Sometime during the 20th century, the connection was severed between the biblical obligation to tell the gospel and expectations for living a godly life. In other words, evangelism was deemed unnecessary for living a godly life. That

---

128 Motyer, *The Prophecy of Isaiah*, p. 40.

is a false dichotomy never taught in Scripture. In fact, the opposite is taught (see Isa. 6:3; 12; 43:8-13; 49:6; 66:19; Mt. 28:18-20; Acts 1:8; 13:47; Rom. 1:14-17; 15:8-12; 2 Cor. 5:18-20; 1 Pet. 2:9-10; Rev. 1:2, 5-6, 9; 2:1-7).

Here are three passages that demonstrate the point.

- **"the whole earth is [or will be]**[129] **full of his glory!"** (Isa. 6:3)
- "Sing praises to the Lord, for he has done gloriously; **let this be made known in all the earth."** (Isa. 12:5)
- "But you are a chosen race, a royal priesthood, a holy nation, a people for his own possession, **that you may proclaim the excellencies** of him who called you out of darkness into his marvelous light" (1 Pet. 2:9). Peter is citing from Isa. 43:21 among other Scriptures.

Throughout Scripture God uses His people to spread His gospel to all parts of the world. But more than that, as God's holiness pervades the lives of believers, they too will be inspired and qualified to tell this story. To separate holiness and evangelism is to conform God to *our* own image.

Second, Isaiah modeled evangelism under the direct supervision of God. The prophet Isaiah had a good tutor, as God specifically told him what to say to the people of Israel. God has also told us what to say to unbelievers. We have it in His word. Since Isaiah's environment is similar to our own today, believers should emulate Isaiah in the way he evangelized. We should learn how he integrated proclaiming the grace of God while specifically exposing sins, coupled with urgent warnings of judgment.

Isaiah preached and taught a fully loaded gospel (or full biblical gospel), for He preached a gospel of God's mercy as well as a judgment of God's wrath. **He exposed sin and warned of its devastating consequences.** His warnings of judgment were matched with offers of salvation. He gave King Ahaz the choice of whether to trust the One to be born of a virgin (Immanuel) or to experience the consequences of his rebellion, judgment at the hands of the king of Assyria (Isaiah 7:14-17). Ahaz could have either

---

129 Davis, *Stump Kingdom,* p. 13.

Immanuel or the King of Assyria. He rejected Immanuel and received instead the King of Assyria "to his detriment" (2 Chron. 28:20-27).[130]

Isaiah had been urging Ahaz to trust God in the midst of a national crisis, telling him that God would keep Judah safe. When Ahaz rejected God's promise of safekeeping, Isaiah rebuked Ahaz with a judgment "sandwich." In the middle of that "sandwich" is the Messianic prophecy of the incarnation of Jesus Christ to be born of a virgin. The church today celebrates the fulfillment of that prophecy every year during the Christmas season, as well we should. But I have never heard a sermon on the full context of that passage. We conveniently leave out the part about judgment of God's wrath on those who reject Messiah. I fear we have sentimentalized Isaiah's great prophecy and have cleaned it up so that it will be more presentable to the modern audience. The Isaiah context gives us an unvarnished narrative, and we tamper with it to our own peril.

Isaiah made a similar contrast when he issued the next Messianic prophecy. The promise of "Wonderful Counselor, Mighty God, Everlasting Father, Prince of Peace" to come and rule in Isaiah 9:6 was contrasted with the alternative of being devoured by the Syrians and Philistines in Isaiah 9:12. Isaiah urged Judah to trust in the "Wonderful Counselor" but warned of judgment by God at the hands of the Philistines.

These two prophecies (7:14 and 9:6-7) were magnificent Messianic promises that the church still celebrates today. In the masterful hand of Isaiah, the blessings of Messiah were held in tension against the consequences of rejecting Him. In the hands of the modern church, I fear these promises and warnings have been sanitized and sterilized to conform to cultural sensibilities.

The doctrines of the gospel were presented by Isaiah in a tension that found release only in Messiah. Nonbelievers *should* feel bad about their sin. They *should* be afraid of judgment. The pastor, teacher, "teller" of the gospel *should* bring the same level of tension between God's grace and God's wrath, as Isaiah delivered, and the same release point – the "root of Jesse" Jesus the Christ (11:1, 10; also Rev. 5:5; 22:16). "For even the Son of Man came not to be served but to serve, and to give his life as a ransom for many" (Mk. 10:45).

Third, sin blinds God's people to the gospel and silences their voice. God's people easily drift away from the center of God's purpose. This has been happening since the be-

---

130 Davis, *Stump Kingdom*, p. 30.

ginning of time, and the visible church in the 21st century is no different than God's people of Isaiah's day. Sin must be continually **exposed.** Jeremiah, who began his ministry about 60 years after the end of Isaiah's ministry, also understood the integral role of exposing sin. He wrote in Lamentations 2:14, "Your prophets have seen for you false and deceptive visions; **they have not exposed your iniquity** to restore your fortunes, but **have seen for you oracles that are false and misleading."** If we fail to expose sin, we have moved into the territory of false teaching. Isaiah never drifted into this territory. The ***word "sin"*** must be used, of course, but more importantly the ***doctrine of sin*** must be taught, AND ***specific sins*** must be named and warned against. Biblical preachers and teachers cannot be biblically faithful if the doctrine of sin is not preached and taught, with sins exposed.

Another example of the blinding effect of idolatry is how the visible church today speaks about hell. The church has lost its voice on this essential component of the gospel. What is the reason for this? It could be because the visible church today is riddled through and through with idolatry. People set their love on affluence, materialism, personal peace, power, around-the-clock entertainment, and other narcissistic self-serving pursuits. It seems we have an idolatry infestation of the heart. As a consequence, the voice of the church is mainly silent on sin, wrath, judgment, and hell. It has been decades since I've heard the doctrine of wrath, judgment, or hell preached or taught. Instead, many preachers and Bible teachers present only grace, feel-good sermons, and God's love. Many sermons that Christians hear today are nothing more than bedtime stories for adults. Idolatry has a way of silencing the gospel. But idolatry will also be actively and contemporaneously judged by God.

Fourth, gospel ministry requires courage and perseverance to walk in the untamable holiness of God. The authors of the four gospels each cited Isaiah's call (6:9-10) in their respective accounts (Mt. 13:14-15; Mk. 4:12; Lk. 8:10; Jn. 12:40); plus, it is cited in Acts 28:26-27. Each citation of this passage occurred in the same context, as an explanation of the rejection of Jesus' teaching.

Paul, speaking to the Jews in Rome said this to them:

The Holy Spirit was right in saying to your fathers through Isaiah the prophet:
^{26} Go to this people, and say,
'You will indeed hear but never understand,

and you will indeed see but never perceive.'

²⁷ For this people's heart has grown dull,

and with their ears they can barely hear,

and their eyes they have closed;

lest they should see with their eyes

and hear with their ears

and understand with their heart

and turn, and I would heal them."

²⁸ Therefore let it be known to you that this salvation of God has been sent to the Gentiles; they will listen.

Act. 28:25-28

That this puzzling call of Isaiah is cited five times and the concept of blindness alluded to many times in the New Testament (Mk. 8:18; Rom. 11:8, 10; Rev. 2:7, 11, 17, 29; 3:6, 13, 22) is a clear indication of how important the message is for today's church. Isaiah's call prepares believers for the difficult task before them. Believers should not be surprised when they are rejected after sharing the gospel with the lost. Isaiah understood this and demonstrated courage and perseverance throughout his ministry. We too must exhibit courage.

After citing Isaiah 6:10, in the Gospel of John, the author John said,

> *Isaiah said these things because he saw his [Jesus'] glory and spoke of him [Jesus]. Nevertheless, many even of the authorities believed in him, but for fear of the Pharisees they did not confess it, so that they would not be put out of the synagogue; for they loved the glory that comes from man more than the glory that comes from God.*
>
> *Jn. 12:41-43*

Lost people love "the glory that comes from man" more than the glory that comes from God. Everyone sharing the gospel will face resistance and opposition. This is a partial explanation for the difficulty faithful followers of Christ will face, and these principles are part of the real-life context of evangelism in the New Testament.

Isaiah "Telescopes" to the Book of Acts – Isaiah 12:1-6

You will say **in that day:**

"I will give thanks to you, O LORD,
   for though you were angry with me,
your anger turned away,
   that you might comfort me.

Behold, God is my salvation;
   I will trust, and will not be afraid;
for the LORD GOD is my strength and my song,
   and he has become my salvation."

With joy you will draw water from the wells of salvation.
And you will say in that day:

"Give thanks to the LORD,
   call upon his name,
make known his deeds among the peoples,
   proclaim that his name is exalted.

Sing praises to the LORD, for he has done
     gloriously;
   let this be made known in all the earth.
Shout, and sing for joy, O inhabitant of Zion,
   for great in your midst is the Holy One of Israel."

Isa. 12:1-6

The first five chapters of Isaiah dealt with the sins of Israel. Salvation for Isaiah emerged out of the dark forbidding reality of God's wrath against all that is unrighteous. For Isaiah, salvation produced a certain result. Those who became believers in God, were transformed from being under His anger to enjoying His comfort.

In this chapter, Isaiah "telescoped" to the New Testament. By "telescoped" I mean that Isaiah saw into the distant future as if looking through a telescope at a distant object. He brought into view God's people, beginning in the Book of Acts, and gave us a double portrait of them in the time of Messiah. He showed us a portrait of an individual believer as well as a group of believers and revealed that worship and evangelism are on equal footing.

The power of context is often remarkable when closely examining a passage of Scripture. In the texts leading up to chapter 12, Isaiah issued a triad of Messianic prophecies (in chapters 7, 9, and 11) as steppingstones to chapter 12. They were placed within the framework of Isaiah speaking God's word to God's hard-hearted people as they wrestled with the best way to cope with an impending invasion.

Isaiah, in chapter 7, addressed the disastrous foreign policy of King Ahaz, who was placing his trust in the northern kingdom allied with Assyria and was not placing his trust in God (7:1-9). Isaiah warned the king to turn away from that false trust and place his faith in God. God had a plan, but Ahaz did not like God's plan. Three separate prophecies of Messiah followed, interspersed among warnings of judgment: (1) "the virgin shall conceive and bear a son" who will be called "Immanuel" (God is with us) (7:14); (2) a child will be born of the royal line of David whose name will be "Wonderful Counselor, Mighty God, Everlasting Father, Prince of Peace" (9:6-7); and (3) a "shoot from the stump of Jesse" (11:1) shall be salvation for all the nations (11:10-12). In other words, **Isaiah prophesied (1) the incarnation of Christ, who would be a human born of a virgin and fully God, (2) a Royal King was coming who would rule forever, and (3) this Royal King, "the root of Jesse," would accomplish a massive worldwide salvation.**

In a bit of irony that may have been lost on the original hearers, Messiah would emerge as an insignificant "shoot" or a "twig" in contrast to an impressive oak or sequoia tree. He would seem insignificant in the eyes of the world. But this "twig" would accomplish a worldwide salvation far bigger than the exodus of Israel out of Egypt (Isa. 11:10-12)!

Armed with these promises, King Ahaz and Israel could know that God would keep the nation safe. But Ahaz refused God's promises and kept God's people on a collision course with judgment. Reading through chapters 6-11 we come to the "epilogue"[131] of the section, chapter 12, which contains a double portrait of God's people. Chapter 12 reveals an individual believer and a group of believers. Isaiah dramatizes the motivating and driving forces in play, reveals God's highest priorities, challenges some cherished ways of thinking, and shapes the individual and group lives of God's people. It is a powerful though short chapter.

Chapter 12 is a scene of what will happen when the "the root of Jesse" arrives. "In that day" of 12:1 links to "in that day" of 11:1 and 11:10-11.[132] The poem comprises two songs (vv. 1-2 and 4-5), each "followed by prophetic commentary (12:3, 6)."[133] The first song is of an individual, as indicated by the singular *you* in verse 1.[134] We see the individual's conversion. His fear of God turned to comfort as God became his salvation, his strength, and his song (12:1-2).

The second song is of a group, as indicated by the plural *you* in verse 3.[135] The group of believers "with joy draw water from the wells of salvation." Fueled by these "waters," they are guided by five imperatives (12:4-6):

- ***give thanks*** – "Give thanks to the Lord" (v. 4)
- ***call upon*** – "call upon his name" (v. 4)
- ***make known*** – "make known his deeds among the peoples" (v. 4)
- ***proclaim*** – "proclaim that his name is exalted" (v. 4)
- ***sing*** – "Sing praises to the Lord" (v. 5)

These imperatives lay out for believers the godly response to God's great salvation.[136]

Chapter 12 closes with a shift back to the individual (as indicated by the singular *you* in verse 6).[137] The phrase "for great in your midst is the Holy One of Israel"

131 Motyer, *The Prophecy of Isaiah*, p. 127.

132 Motyer, *The Prophecy of Isaiah*, p. 128.

133 John L. Mackay, *A Study Commentary on Isaiah: Chapters 1–39* (Vol. 1) (Darlington, England; Carlisle, PA: EP Books, 2009), p. 307.

134 The ESV footnote reads: "the Hebrew for *you* is singular in verse 1."

135 The ESV footnote reads: "the Hebrew for *you* is plural in verses 3, 4."

136 Gary V. Smith, *Isaiah 1–39* (NAC) (Nashville: B & H Publishing Group, 2007), p. 283.

137 The ESV footnote reads: "the Hebrew for *you* is singular in verses 6."

embodies the same concept as the name "Immanuel" (God is with us) of 7:14. He is "with us" first as an individual and then as a group as the individual unites with the group. These imperatives give shape to the believers' response and purpose as part of God's kingdom.

The timeframe of this scene from the prophecy of Isaiah is affirmed by the New Testament.

- **The Incarnation (Mt. 1:22-23 citing Isa. 7:14)** – *All this took place to fulfill what the Lord had spoken by the prophet: "Behold, the virgin shall conceive and bear a son, and they shall call his name Immanuel" (which means, God with us).*

- **A Mighty King (Lk. 1:32-33 alluding to Isa. 9:6-7)** – *He will be great and will be called the Son of the Most High. And the Lord God will give to him the throne of his father David, and he will reign over the house of Jacob forever, and of his kingdom there will be no end."*

- **A Shoot of Jesse (Rom. 15:12 citing Isa. 11:10)** – *And again Isaiah says, The root of Jesse will come, even he who arises to rule the Gentiles; in him will the Gentiles hope;* (**Rev. 22:16 alluding to Isa. 11:1, 10**) – *I am the root and the descendant of David, the bright morning star. (Also Rev. 5:5.)*

What Isaiah saw was the inaugurated kingdom. We know the kingdom is not yet fully consummated, but the consummation will occur at the second coming of Christ. This epoch, the inaugurated kingdom, was initiated by Jesus; and His followers were fully incorporated into it with the giving of the Holy Spirit in the Book of Acts. For additional references on the inaugurated kingdom see Mt. 4:17; 12:28; Mk 1:15; Col. 1:13; and Rev. 1:6.

What Can We Learn About Evangelism from Isaiah 12?

First, worship and evangelism are both mandates of equal priority. The Christian church cannot choose one and neglect the other. God revealed His standard for His people of the last days, 700 plus years in advance of the arrival of the "root of Jesse."

Gary V. Smith:

> *In this picture, **worship and evangelism are connected at the hip, inextricably joined as two sides of the same coin.** Evangelism is joyfully shouting about the exalted glory of God and retelling his wonderful deeds. Worship is joyfully shouting about the exalted glory of God and retelling his wonderful deeds. **For worship to become evangelism it has to be done outside of the four walls of a church, where non-believers can hear God's praise.***[138] (emphasis mine)

Worship and evangelism are mandates of equal importance and spring from atonement of sins and "the wells of salvation."

Second, the phrase "let this be made known in all the earth" means literally "'a thing worthy to be made known' or 'this must be made known in all the earth.'"[139] Worship is an *organic* function and is part of the living and breathing of believers. Evangelism is a *strategic* purpose, and it is clear from this passage it is ***the chief strategic purpose*** of God's people.

Third, the power source to accomplish this purpose is "water from the wells of salvation" (12:3). Jesus is the "living water" for believers (Jn. 4:10). He is also the vine (Jn. 15:1). Both metaphors in their contexts reveal the source of nourishment and the purpose of it. His people are to "bear fruit" that shall "abide" or "remain."

> *You did not choose me, but I chose you and appointed you that you should go and bear fruit and that your fruit should abide...*
>
> *Jn. 15:16*

Here is what D. A. Carson has to say about John 15:16:

> *The fruit primarily in view in this verse is the fruit that emerges from mission... **The fruit, in short, is new converts...** the focus on*

---

138 Gary V. Smith, *Isaiah 1–39* (NAC), p. 284.
139 Motyer, *The Prophecy of Isaiah*, (p. 130).

evangelism and mission is truly central...the union of love that joins believers with Jesus can never become a comfortable, exclusivistic huddle that only they can share.[140]

Fourth, Isaiah challenges our traditional view of the purpose of the church. All of us have a personal theology of what the ideal church should be. For example, if you and your family were to move to a new city and begin a search for the "right church," you would have certain attributes in mind for this "right church." The list would likely include interesting sermons, inspirational worship and singing, exciting youth programs, people you would like to be friends with, a convenient location, nice facilities, a coffee shop/café onsite, etc.

All of those may be good things, of course. But if we incorporated Isaiah's mandates for God's people, how would they influence our search criteria for a new church? Under Isaiah's watchful eye, we would elevate the following attributes and try to discover a group of believers who:

- Spend time and energy giving thanks for all God has done
- Spend time faithfully in prayer calling upon His name
- Depend on God as their true source of power
- Faithfully preach and teach the full biblical gospel
- Sing beautiful, God honoring songs that exalt God and cause believers' spirits to turn to Him
- Actively proclaim the greatness of His name inside and outside the church
- Are motivated and active in telling the gospel outside of the church

There is no perfect church of course, but it is useful to have a biblical template in mind to assist in the search. We should be biblically discerning.

---

140 D. A. Carson, *The Gospel According to John (Pillar NT Commentary)* (Leicester, England; Grand Rapids, MI: Inter-Varsity Press; W.B. Eerdmans, 1991), p. 523.

Church leadership can use these concepts, drawn from Isaiah, to examine the life of their local body of believers. Is the church on track with God's purpose or has it drifted off center?[141]

Isaiah Chastised God's People for Not Witnessing – Isaiah 43:8-13

Bring out the people who are blind, yet have eyes,
  who are deaf, yet have ears!
All the nations gather together,
  and the peoples assemble.
Who among them can declare this,
  and show us the former things?
Let them bring their witnesses to prove them right,
  and let them hear and say, It is true.
"You are my witnesses," declares the LORD,
  "and my servant whom I have chosen,
that you may know and believe me
  and understand that I am he.
Before me no god was formed,
  nor shall there be any after me.
I, I am the LORD,
  and besides me there is no savior.
I declared and saved and proclaimed,
  when there was no strange god among you;
  and you are my witnesses," declares the LORD, "and I am God.
Also henceforth I am he;
  there is none who can deliver from my hand;
  I work, and who can turn it back?"

Isa. 43:8-13

---

141 The seven bullet points above are drawn from Isaiah 12. For a more complete listing of the indicators of a healthy church, please refer to Mark Dever's material on the "9 Marks of a Healthy Church." https://www.9marks.org/about/the-nine-marks/. Accessed September 27, 2021.

The familiar song "This Little Light of Mine" emerged onto the American scene in the 1920s and has been used by Christian groups as well as secular organizations and people around the world ever since. Children sing it in churches all over the US every year.[142]

There are slight variations of the lyrics, but here is a typical example:

> *This little light of mine, I'm going to let it shine...All around the neighborhood, I'm going to let it shine...Hide it under a basket? No! ... Don't let Satan blow it out! I'm going to let it shine.*[143]

This little song expresses good theology. The modern version of it goes back some 100 years. But the idea is not a 20th century idea. Isaiah had a sarcastic version of this song for the adults of Israel. It was a biting rebuke for failing to "sing" this song.

"You are my witnesses" (Isa. 43.10) was spoken to a group of blind and deaf people – God's people (42:18-19). They had become blind through the judgment that happens imperceptibly when a person places their love and trust in something other than God. "Those who make them [idols] become like them; so do all who trust in them" (Ps. 115:8).

In Isaiah 43:8-13, Isaiah called out the people of Israel, in a theoretical "courtroom drama,"[144] by saying, "Bring out the people who are blind, yet have eyes, who are deaf, yet have ears!" (Isa. 43:8). The blind and deaf were the nation Israel (Isa. 42:18-20) who were blinded and silenced by their own sin and idolatry. God then exclaimed, "'You are my witnesses,' declares the Lord, 'and my servant whom I have chosen'" (43:10). God's servants have the obligation of witnessing to God's greatness, but "the prompting...has apparently been met by silence on the part of the blind and deaf."[145] God must be His own witness.[146] In the emotion of the scene and in the drama of the poetry, it feels like

---

142 Wikipedia, *https://en.wikipedia.org/wiki/This_Little_Light_of_Mine,* November 17, 2020.

143 https://www.lyrics.com/track/3203784/Cedarmont+Kids/This+Little+Light+of+Mine, December 1, 2020.

144 Motyer, *The Prophecy of Isaiah,* p. 333. "Isaiah uses again a favourite literary form, the courtroom drama."

145 Motyer, *The Prophecy of Isaiah,* p. 335.

146 Motyer, *The Prophecy of Isaiah,* p. 335.

a cosmic exclamation that burst forth from God, **"I, I am the LORD, and besides me there is no savior"** (43:11).

Three times in the broader section of Isaiah 43 the Lord declared, "You are my witnesses" (43:10, 12; 44:8). God told them they were a people whom He formed for Himself (43:21). He had preserved them and nourished them so "that they might declare [His] praise" (43:21). **But they had become like their idols – blind, deaf, and silent.** (See Ps. 115:4-8 and 135:15-18).

What Can We Learn About Evangelism from Isaiah 43:8-13?

Much of Isaiah is focused on exposing sin, warning of judgment, and urging people to turn to God and trust His salvation for their lives. Here the focus is on the purpose God has for them and their abject failure to fulfill that purpose.

God's people today are capable of drifting into modern day idolatry. When that happens, voices for the full biblical gospel go silent. If believers, individually and as a church body, are silent about the gospel to the world around them, it is time for a thorough spiritual and biblical self-examination. Silence of today's church regarding man's sins is a gigantic red flag. Peter captured the essence of God's purpose for the people of Israel and applied it to God's people under the New Testament.

> *But you are a chosen race, a royal priesthood, a holy nation, a people for his own possession, that you may proclaim the excellencies of him who called you out of darkness into his marvelous light.*
>
> *1 Pt 2:9*

Peter was citing from and alluding to several Old Testament passages, including Isaiah 43:20-21 and Exodus 19:5-6.[147] Peter saw holiness as driving the proclamation of the gospel. We can flip that around. Peter saw proclaiming the gospel as the logical extension of holiness and of being part of the people of God. Holiness is not an end in itself. Holiness is not merely living a moral life, as is popularly thought. It is the platform

---

147 G. K. Beale *and* D. A. Carson, *Commentary on the New Testament Use of the Old Testament* (Grand Rapids, MI; Nottingham, UK: Baker Academic; Apollos, 2007), pp. 1030–1033.

from which effective witness occurs. It is the foundation from which God's purpose in the world is lived out. Holiness is not a formula to supercharge business success, raising children, achieving political power, or the accumulation of wealth. **Genuine holiness is lived out by people who are set apart for *God's purpose*.**

D. A. Carson, quoting Karen Jobes, writes about the believer's obligation expressed in 1 Pet. 2:9:

> *The kingdom of God is composed of believers who must think of themselves as holy with respect to the world, **set apart for purity and a purpose demanded by God.** This is the priesthood that serves the King of the universe.*[148]

This "purity and purpose" is lived out by God's people both individually and collectively.

The Father's Great Commission to the Son – Isaiah 49:6

> *and he [God] says, 'It is too light a thing that you should be my servant to raise up the tribes of Jacob,*
> > *and to bring back the preserved of Israel;*
> **so I have set you as a light to nations,**
> **to be my salvation to the end of the earth.**'[149]
>
> > > > > > > Isaiah 49:6

God the Father was speaking to God the Son ("my servant") in Isaiah 49:6. This was one of those big moments in history. The Father issued a charge to the Son, **"I have set**

---

148 Beale, *Commentary on the New Testament Use of the Old Testament,* p. 1031.

149 This is John Mackay's translation of this passage from his commentary: John L. Mackay, *A Study Commentary on Isaiah: Chapters 40–66* (Vol. 2) (Darlington, England; Carlisle, PA: EP Books, 2009), p. 248. Motyer says, "The Hebrew resists the NIV's *that you may bring my salvation* and requires 'that you may be my salvation,' for in the parallelism of the verse, 'that you should be my servant' and 'that you should be my salvation' balance each other. The thought is not that the Servant is the agent in communicating salvation but that he is in his own person the salvation the world needs, and, in the same way, the world's *light*." Motyer, *The Prophecy of Isaiah,* pp.388-389.

you as a light to nations, to be my salvation to the end of the earth."[150] Messiah's role is twofold: light and salvation. First, He was a light of verbal witness and example. Second, He was our salvation by His atoning death on the cross. John introduced Jesus in Revelation 1:5 in a way that captures both light and salvation when he referred to Him as "the faithful witness (light), the firstborn of the dead (salvation), and the ruler of kings on earth." He "persevered as a faithful witness to the Father in the face of persecution,"[151] He conquered death through His death on the cross and resurrection from the dead, and He reigns now as "the cosmic ruler."[152] This passage is the Father's charge to the Son – Jesus Christ. It is a big moment and established the purpose of His first coming.

What Can We Learn About Evangelism from Isaiah 49:6?

Isaiah 49:6 stands out as one of those passages with an extra level of strategic significance. At the same time, it contains an extra level of real time relevance to today. Luke recorded how Simeon identified this passage with Jesus in Luke 2:32 and revealed in Acts 26:17-18 how Jesus made the application to Paul.[153] In a stunning move, the apostle Paul cited this verse in Acts 13:47 as the basis for his taking the gospel to an audience far wider than the Jews. It was a turning point in Paul's ministry as he shifted from carrying the gospel primarily to ethnic Israel, to a focus of taking the gospel to the Gentiles.

When Paul went to Antioch in Pisidia, a predominantly Gentile city,[154] he went to the synagogue on the Sabbath and began teaching the gospel (Acts 13:13-52). The people listened with interest and invited Paul to speak to them again the following Sabbath. Word spread and practically the whole city turned out the next sabbath to hear what Paul had to say. But the Jews were jealous of salvation being offered to the Gentiles and began to contradict Paul and his message (Acts 13:44-45). "The Jews of Pisidian Antioch could not accept a Messiah who embraced the Gentiles. In rejecting Paul's witness to the Gentiles, they thus rejected their Messiah as well."[155]

---

150 Mackay, A Study Commentary on Isaiah (Vol. 2), p. 248
151 Beale, The Book of Revelation (NIGTC), p. 190.
152 Beale, The Book of Revelation (NIGTC), p. 190.
153 John Stott, The Message of Acts (Downers Grove, IL: InterVarsity Press, 1990), p. 227.
154 John B. Polhill, Acts (NAC) (Nashville: Broadman & Holman Publishers, 1992), p. 308.
155 Polhill, Acts (NAC), p. 308.

*And Paul and Barnabas spoke out boldly, saying, "It was necessary that the word of God be spoken first to you. Since you thrust it aside and judge yourselves **unworthy of eternal life**, behold, we are turning to the Gentiles. For so the Lord has commanded us, saying,*

> **'I have made you a light for the Gentiles,**
> **that you may bring salvation to the ends of the earth.'"**

Act. 13:46-47

The implication of what is happening here is staggering. By rejecting a Messiah who offered open arms to the Gentiles, they were rejecting Jesus as their savior and, with that, they were discarding eternal life for themselves. Rejecting God's strategic purpose had significant implications for the Jewish population in Antioch of Pisidia.

It is remarkable the ease with which this strategic purpose of Jesus flowed seamlessly from Him into and through the lives of Paul and Barnabas. They were a living illustration of how Isaiah 49:6 was to be applied in the lives of believers. Paul made the Son's great commission his own great commission. Paul saw himself as a light (witness) and as bringing salvation (telling the gospel) to the "ends of the earth." These roles flowed from Isaiah to Paul and then to all of God's people today. Evangelism is among the core values of genuine believers in Jesus Christ.

Far too many Christians and churches today reject God's purpose of witness to the Gentiles, those who are outside the church. They minimize the Great Commission Jesus conveyed to all believers through the Apostles. This rejection occurs both by neglect and by explicit denunciation of it. Regardless of our opinion, evangelism is God's chief strategic purpose for His people to the world.

Isaiah Calls for World-Wide Gospel Proclamation – Isaiah 66:18-23

And the time is coming to gather all nations and tongues. And they shall come and shall see my glory, and I will set a sign among them. And from them I will send survivors to the nations...that have not heard my fame or seen my glory. **And they shall declare my glory among the nations.**

Isa. 66:18-19

Isaiah pointed to a time in the future when the glory of God would be declared to all nations and tongues. People would be drawn to Him who had never heard of His fame. God promised to set a "sign" among them. The "sign" is the cross. "Knowing as we do that this passage refers to the interim between the comings of the Lord Jesus, the 'sign' can only be his cross."[156]

In the New Testament Jesus referred to the cross as a "sign." When the Pharisees were trying to goad Him into performing a miracle on demand, He responded, "No sign will be given to it except the sign of the prophet Jonah. For just as Jonah was three days and three nights in the belly of the great fish, so will the Son of Man be three days and three nights in the heart of the earth" (Mt. 12:39-40). Other references that support this conclusion are Mt. 16:1, 4; Lk. 2:34; 11:30.

"Survivors" or "escapees" are those who have escaped captivity by the world's false gods. They have escaped God's judgment and have become His redeemed. These are the ones who will carry the message of God's fame and glory to the nations.[157] They are the remnant of God's people. Not all of ethnic Israel is true Israel (Rom. 9:6-7). In the same way, **not all who claim to be Christians are saved believers** (Mt. 13:24-30, 36-43).

Similar to what we saw in chapter 12, Isaiah once again peered into the age we are in right now and revealed that declaration of the gospel will occur. This is the second time Isaiah predicted gospel proclamation during the time of Messiah. When that epoch arrives, the "escapees" will declare God's glory among the nations. "God is intending to expand the church beyond the confines of the Jewish state. The nations of the world are to flood in."[158] This expansion will not be by military might, but by *proclaiming* His glory. Gospel proclamation at that time will be in full bloom (Mt. 28:18-20; Acts 1:8).

---

156 Motyer, *The Prophecy of Isaiah,* p. 541.

157 Motyer, *The Prophecy of Isaiah,* p. 541-542.

158 Thomas, *God Delivers: Isaiah Simply Explained (electronic ed.),* pp. 393.

What Can We Learn About Evangelism from Isaiah 66:18-23?

First, the primary change in witness from the Old Testament to the New Testament is *how* the witness occurs. "For the most part, the Old Testament thinks of the world as won by attraction; [Isa.] 2:2–4 is a paradigm. On the other hand, the New Testament [church] lives under the great commission to go out with the gospel. Together these constitute the missionary obligation of the church: to create a magnetic community **and** to share a saving message." [159] (emphasis mine)

Second, God's "survivors" (or escapees) will tell God's lifesaving story. Those who have escaped the idolatry of this world, His redeemed, will proclaim the full gospel.

Third, this promise of God given through Isaiah would have been an encouragement to God's people of that day. As dark as the times were in the eighth century BC, God would not be on the losing side of history. God was going to reign supreme, and His fame would be carried to every corner of the world. Those faithful to Him would enjoy His ultimate victory. Believers today are encouraged by His promises and look forward to the consummation of His kingdom.

"Sinners in the Hands of an Angry God" [160] – Isaiah 66:24

As we come to the end of Isaiah, and to the very last verse, we are shown a disturbing picture. The concept of God's wrath was not introduced here of course, as Isaiah had been warning of God's wrath from the beginning of his book (1:5; 1:10-11, 12-15; 2:10-11, 19, 20-21). He issued warnings on practically every page of it. **But God had Isaiah conclude his book with this unsettling scene, like something out of a horror movie.**

> *And they shall go out and look on the dead bodies of the men who have rebelled against me. For their worm shall not die, their fire shall not be quenched, and they shall be an abhorrence to all flesh.*
>
> *Isa. 66:24*

---

159 Motyer, *The Prophecy of Isaiah*, p. 541.

160 The title of the sermon preached by Jonathan Edwards, *Sinners in the Hands of an Angry God* (Enfield, MA, July 8, 1741)

Isaiah brought his book to a close by presenting a graveyard with dead bodies. It is counterintuitive to our 21st-century sensibilities that he would end this way. We want to ignore it, change it, or resist it. Nevertheless, this is how Isaiah chose to leave it with us. "Remarkably, there is a cemetery beside the city. Always as they come to worship, the redeemed deliberately make themselves face (*go out and look*), vividly, horribly, the fate from which they have been spared."[161]

These are the dead bodies of those who have rebelled against God, and they will be in plain view in their tragic state of perpetual decay. Those who reside here are always suffering in this place of never-ending torment and they will never be able to leave. **The fire will never go out in this stinking place of organic decomposition.** It will be a distressing sight, a terrible scene. It is meant to be "loathsome."[162]

The redeemed will walk past this cemetery and see those who have rebelled against God. But surely this field trip past the cemetery is not for gloating.[163] This walk past the cemetery will be a reminder of the greatness of God's salvation. It will continually reveal why the cross of God's Son, where the wrath of God was poured out on Jesus as the substitute for those who are saved, was so horrible and why it was so necessary. It will enrich the worship of God's people. It will magnify God's glory.

Still, it is astonishing that Isaiah ends his book like this. I think he leaves it this way so we will ponder the serious consequences for those who rebel against God. Our first reaction, as a reader, is to avert our eyes, but we cannot. And we must not!

In one sense it gives a certain resolution to the whole book. If we compare this last verse of Isaiah with the very beginning (Isaiah 1:2, "Children have I reared and brought up, but they have rebelled against me"), the conflict is resolved. But, in another sense the struggle continues. It's Isaiah's way of making clear what is at stake and his way of passing the torch to us.

What Can We Learn About the Gospel and Evangelism from Isaiah 66:24?

First, we learn that hell and everlasting torment is real and is a vital part of the presentation of the biblical gospel. After all, Jesus Christ may have talked more about

---

161 Motyer, *The Prophecy of Isaiah*, p. 543.
162 Motyer, *The Prophecy of Isaiah*, p. 544.
163 Motyer, *The Prophecy of Isaiah*, p. 544.

hell than anyone else in all of Scripture. The church cannot eliminate the teaching of eternal punishment and still maintain biblical integrity. As we see in this verse, God has not even banished the view of hell from heaven, yet many churches and denominations have banished hell from their teachings. Jesus, on the other hand, believed Isaiah knew what he was talking about. "On the lips of Jesus these verses will become the vehicle of the doctrine of eternal loss (Mk. 9:43–48)."[164] Jesus gave His stamp of approval of the way Isaiah finished his book. By His words, Jesus conveys to us the truth that hell is not old fashioned, irrelevant, nor out of date.

Many in the United States do not believe in hell. Ligonier Ministries' State of Theology survey reveals that of those who never attend church, 56% believe that hell is *not* a real place where certain people will be punished and another 18% are not sure. Only 26% of the "never attenders" believe hell is a real place. Below is more detail from the survey.[165]

Hell is a real place where certain people will be punished forever. *True or False*

	Entire Population	Evangeli-cals	Mainline	Roman Catholic	Never Attend Church
Strongly Agree	39%	64%	34%	39%	15%
Somewhat Agree	20%	18%	22%	29%	11%
Not sure	12%	8%	16%	12%	18%
Somewhat Disagree	8%	4%	13%	10%	9%
Strongly Disagree	21%	6%	15%	10%	47%

Satan is engaged in this life-and-death combat. He has been propagating the lie that there will be no judgment and no hell since the beginning of time. Remember what Satan said to Eve: "But the serpent said to the woman, 'You will not surely die'" (Gen. 3:4). Satan lied to Eve. He is a liar and has always been a liar. Only the lies of Satan would move us to eliminate hell from our preaching, teaching, **AND** one-to-one telling of the gospel.

---

164 Motyer, *The Prophecy of Isaiah*, p. 544.
165 Ligonier Ministries and Lifeway Research, *The State of Theology,* https://thestateoftheology.com/, survey completed in January 2022, accessed website on January 5, 2024.

Second, the reality of hell for the lost sinner is a valid motivation for the believer to tell the gospel to the lost. Paul understood the awfulness of hell and was motivated by it. To the Romans he wrote: "I am speaking the truth in Christ—I am not lying; my conscience bears me witness in the Holy Spirit—that **I have great sorrow and unceasing anguish in my heart. For I could wish that I myself were accursed and cut off from Christ for the sake of my brothers,** my kinsmen according to the flesh" (Rom. 9:1-3). Paul was saying he would do anything to convince his Jewish friends to turn to Christ and avoid eternal punishment.

Jesus told a parable, recorded in Luke 16:19-31, that bears on the reality of hell and the motivation of those who fully comprehend its abhorrence. This parable of the rich man and Lazarus is part of a dialogue Jesus had with the Pharisees who were "lovers of money" (Lk. 16:14). He directed this parable to them as a warning of what they faced if they continued on their path. In the second half of the parable, the rich man, from the torment of hell, begs Father Abraham to send Lazarus to warn his five brothers so their fate will not be as his. The rich man was highly motivated by the intense suffering of his final and never-ending state of suffering. He knew the horror of "this place of torment" (Lk 16:28). If we as believers fully understand the terrible physical and mental anguish of hell, it will drive us to overcome our apathy and to climb over obstacles to point others to Christ.

> *The irony in this parable is the rich nonbeliever is more highly motivated to warn of hell than the average Christian in the United States.*

Third, as believers, we are engaged in a cosmic struggle of life-and-death significance. Because of this eternal issue that everyone must deal with, believers have a responsibility of great importance. Paul said those of us who have this good news in our possession are obligated to share it with others.

> *I am under obligation both to Greeks and to barbarians, both to the wise and to the foolish. So I am eager to preach the gospel to you also who are in Rome.*

*For I am not ashamed of the gospel, for it is the power of God for sal-
vation to everyone who believes, to the Jew first and also to the Greek.
For in it the righteousness of God is revealed from faith for faith, as it
is written, "The righteous shall live by faith."*

Rom. 1:14-17

Jonathan Edwards was actively engaged in this cosmic battle. He understood what
was at stake. Here is an excerpt from his famous sermon *Sinners in the Hands of an
Angry God*, preached on July 8, 1741, when he was 37 years old. He had preached it at
least once before in June at his own church in Northampton with little apparent effect.
But on this occasion, he was unable to finish his sermon because the Holy Spirit was
so extraordinarily powerful, and his listeners were making such a clamor wanting to
know how they could be saved and escape the terrors of hell.[166]

The sermon is centered on the phrase I have placed in bold from Deut. 32:35, "To me
belongeth vengeance, and recompence; **their foot shall slide in _due_ time**: for the day of
their calamity *is* at hand, and the things that shall come upon them make haste" (KJV).
It refers to the fact that sinners are always on a slippery slope and only held from the
fires of hell by the mercy of God. His mercy may be withdrawn at any moment. In the
following excerpt, toward the end of the sermon, Edwards draws from Isaiah 66:23-24.

*Thus it will be with you that are in an unconverted state, if you
continue in it; the infinite might, and majesty, and terribleness of
the omnipotent God shall be magnified upon you, in the ineffable
strength of your torments. You shall be tormented in the presence of
the holy angels, and in the presence of the Lamb; and when you shall
be in this state of suffering, the glorious inhabitants of heaven shall
go forth and look on the awful spectacle, that they may see what the
wrath and fierceness of the Almighty is; and when they have seen it,
they will fall down and adore that great power and majesty.[167]*

166 George M. Marsden, *Jonathan Edwards: A Life* (Harrisonburg, VA: R. R. Donnelley and Sons, 2003),
Kindle loc. 3156-74.
167 Jonathan Edwards, *Sinners in the Hands of an Angry God* (Enfield, MA, July 8, 1741), p. 8.

This is an aspect of reality that no one enjoys talking about. Yet ignoring it does not make it go away. The Christian life is not merely a happiness parade, even though the believer has an inner joy that is not dependent on circumstances. It is through this joy, the power of the Holy Spirit, that we "draw water from the wells of salvation" (Isa. 12:3) so that we can warn others they are in danger and make known this great salvation in Jesus.

It is okay that we mourn certain things and even necessary that we grieve and fear at times. Sadness and fear for ourselves, if we have not placed our faith in God – and for our family and friends who do not know Christ. It sits heavily on us. Our mourning and grieving have a positive outlet – praying and telling. Jeremiah grieved and mourned over the rebellious people of God even as he warned them of the danger they were in. "My joy is gone; grief is upon me; my heart is sick within me" (Jer. 8:18). Read the entire section of Jeremiah 8:18 to 9:11.

In my own coming to grips with the fact of eternal wrath, I have often wondered what my former friends or associates who are not saved would think of me if they should die in an unsaved condition. What will they think when they see me walking past their cemetery, they in their putrid state of decay and me in my glorified body like Christ's body? My hope is that if one of my former friends sees me, they will not be able to say, "Oh, I wish he had warned me of this terrible place and had told me the gospel."

It is fitting that I close this chapter as Isaiah closed his book. May it stir our hearts.

And they shall go out and look on the dead bodies of the men who have rebelled against me. For their worm shall not die, their fire shall not be quenched, and they shall be an abhorrence to all flesh.

Isa. 66:24

CHAPTER 6
MALACHI

My name will be great among the nations – Malachi 1:11

The Book of Malachi was written approximately 50 to 100 years following the Babylonian exile, probably in the first half of the fifth century BC[168] and possibly in the 460s BC.[169] He was a contemporary of Nehemiah. The spiritual state of the nation was tragic as God's people had become disobedient and spiritually apathetic.

One irony of Malachi's day was the people of God were complaining that God had mistreated them. They "saw [their] current economic and social troubles as a sign of God's unfairness or unfaithfulness. They deserved divine blessings, they thought, but were receiving divine afflictions instead [2:17]. Ignoring their own sins...[and] complaining of divine injustice,"[170] they were the ones God was going to judge (3:5).

The people of Malachi's day should have taken note of Daniel's prayer in Daniel 9, which was written during the Babylonian captivity. In that prayer Daniel confessed his own sins along with the sins of his people as he implored God to rescue him and God's people out of Babylonian captivity. This was not the attitude of the people of God in the Book of Malachi.

Like Isaiah, the prophet Malachi specifically exposed the sins of God's people numerous times (more than three dozen). Half of the sins described by Malachi were committed by the clergy (the priests), and the rest were committed by all of God's people.

---

168 Richard A. Taylor and E. Ray Clendenen, *Haggai, Malachi*, vol. 21A (NAC) (Nashville, TN: Broadman & Holman Publishers, 2004), pp. 204-207.

169 Joyce G. Baldwin, *Haggai, Zechariah and Malachi: An Introduction and Commentary* (Downers Grove, IL: InterVarsity Press, 1972), pp. 227-228

170 Taylor and Clendenen, *Haggai, Malachi* (NAC), p. 370.

In actuality, the people of God were so disobedient to God's law during the time of Malachi, the last prophet of the Old Testament, that at the conclusion of this book, God did not speak again to His people for 400 years – until Jesus' birth was announced and the prophet John the Baptist, a prophet of the magnitude of Elijah (Lk. 1:17), burst onto the scene. Some theologians call this period the intertestamental period where "the heavens were as brass."[171] The disobedience of God's people in the Book of Malachi greatly confirmed Israel's true spiritual need, the need of a savior, a Messiah, the Lord Jesus Christ.

Malachi is relevant to us today because "His teaching, both negative and positive, strikes at the heart of nominal, easygoing Christianity as it did at that of Judaism."[172]

The Narrative

As the prophet Malachi began his book, he quickly confronted the sins of God's people. He addressed the people of Israel who were questioning God's love for them. "How have you loved us?" they said (1:2). However, God, speaking through the prophet Malachi, reminded Israel of His covenantal love for Jacob. From there He proceeded to demonstrate their lack of love for God by specifically naming their sins. He started with the sins of the priests. The clergy did not honor nor fear God (1:6), despised God's name (1:6), offered polluted and evil sacrifices (1:7-8), worshipped God in vain (emptiness) (1:10), profaned God's name by despising His ways (1:12), considered service to God a weariness (1:13), violated God's regulations for worship (1:13), exhibited hearts hardened toward God's ways (2:2), violated God's covenant with Levi (2:4), turned aside from God's ways (2:8), corrupted God's message (2:8), caused many to stumble (2:8), and sought to be popular and to please men with their message (2:9). Those were the rebukes addressed to the priests, and they were many. Malachi correctly addressed the heart of the spiritual problem in Israel, the lack of godly leaders.

Then, to all of God's people, Malachi rebuked these sins: they had profaned the sanctuary (2:11); married women who were not followers of God (2:11); they lived a

---

171 This expression seems to come from Deuteronomy 28:23 in the King James Version, "And thy heaven that is over thy head shall be brass," meaning there is no Word from God due to God's displeasure with His people.
172 Baldwin, *Haggai, Zechariah and Malachi*, p. 233.

lifestyle openly in violation of God's ways while worshipping in God's temple (2:12); they were faithless in marriage (2:14); they called evil good and good evil (2:17); they hypocritically asked, "Where is the God of justice?" (2:17); they engaged in sorceries, oppression of the weak, lying, fraud, and mistreatment of immigrants, with no fear of God (3:5); they failed to tithe (3:7); and with hard words against God, they said it was vain to serve Him and there was no profit in it (3:13-14).

Malachi's purpose was to expose the sins of Israel's priests and people so that they would turn to God in repentance and trust. It actually was an act of love on God's part, warning of danger and pointing to the great salvation He offered those who turned away from their sin. Even though Malachi's warnings were an act of love, his words could not have made Malachi popular. His teachings would likely have generated opposition and created many enemies.

Embedded in Malachi's naming of Israel's specific sins was a significant purpose statement. Malachi addressed God's purpose that was being damaged and hindered by the sins of His people. God was emphatic on this point and cried out forcefully in defiance of His rebellious people:

> *For from the rising of the sun to its setting* **my name will be great among the nations,** *and in every place incense will be offered to my name, and a pure offering.* **For my name will be great among the nations,** *says the Lord of hosts... For I am a great King, says the Lord of hosts, and* **my name will be feared among the nations.**
>
> *Mal. 1:11, 14*

God's purpose from the beginning was to bless all the nations in His Son Jesus Christ and to use His people Israel, and later the church, to accomplish that purpose. We saw this in God's call and promise to Abraham in Genesis 22:18 – "and in your offspring shall **all the nations of the earth** be blessed." The apostle Paul confirms in Galatians 3:16 that God was speaking about Jesus in His promise to Abraham – "Now the promises were made to Abraham and to his offspring...who is Christ." **This very same purpose statement given to Abraham burst forth from God in Malachi's day out of God's great exasperation with the clergy (Mal. 1:11, 14)!** The emphatic statement that "my name will be great (or feared) among the nations," **declared three times**, reminds us that what was first expressed in the calling of Abraham (Gen. 12:3) was still very much a part of God's purpose for His people – despite their unfaithfulness.

At the conclusion of Malachi 2, the reader may begin to wonder if they will find any good news at all in the Book of Malachi. But there was exceptionally good news embedded in God's words to Israel. **Notice first,** in Malachi 3:1 we have the prediction of a "messenger" who "will prepare the way before me [God]" for someone called "the Lord." In fact, the books of Matthew, Mark, and Luke each cite this passage (Mt. 11:10; Lk. 7:27; Mk. 1:2). This messenger was clearly John the Baptist. (See also Mal. 4:5 compared to Mt. 11:14).

Second, and also in Malachi 3:1, Malachi prophesied the coming of the Messiah. He is the second "messenger" in the verse. "And the Lord whom you seek will suddenly come to his temple; and the **messenger of the covenant** in whom you delight, behold, he is coming, says the Lord of hosts." Jesus is the "messenger of the covenant." Jesus was predicted by Malachi to come to His temple and was to be preceded by John the Baptist. In a book so dominated by the listing of sins committed by the clergy and by all of Judah, this passage is a light of hope to those who will repent and trust in the Lord.

Third, there is another bright spot in the book in Malachi 3:16-17. Promises were given to the remnant who feared God. This remnant was a minority and must have wondered, **"What will happen to us?"** They felt God had forgotten them, but God had not forgotten them.

> *The Lord paid attention and heard them, and a book of remembrance was written before him of those who feared the Lord and esteemed his name. **They shall be mine, says the Lord of hosts, in the day when I make up my treasured possession, and I will spare them as a man spares his son who serves him.** Then once more you shall see the distinction between the righteous and the wicked, between one who serves God and one who does not serve him.*
>
> *Mal. 3:16-17*

Those who fear God's name are His treasured possession. Those afflicted by society because they were following God, when most around them were living self-obsessed lifestyles, would not regret it in the long run. **To be treasured by the Creator of the Universe is beyond special. They were God's treasure. God was their salvation and comfort.**

What Can We Learn About the Gospel and Evangelism from Malachi?

First, God's gospel message is **not to be changed** (altered through removal or de-emphasis of the unpopular parts such as sin, wrath, repentance, and the cost of following Him), **selectively applied** (made to be pleasing to men and women), **nor corrupted** (made to say what it does not say). The prophet Malachi was clear in his preaching about the sins of Israel. Certainly, he was not applauded for being so direct in the confronting and exposing of their sins.

James Montgomery Boice gives this account of a message delivered by Billy Graham:

> *In 1966 at the first World Congress on Evangelism, held in Berlin, Germany, Billy Graham addressed the more than twelve hundred evangelical delegates from more than one hundred countries on the theme "Stains on the Altar," suggesting that many of even these outstanding evangelical leaders had been offering God defiled sacrifices in these areas:*

(The following are two of the seven areas in which Graham challenged pastors.)

> ***Their message.*** *Countless preachers offer a watered-down, man-pleasing message instead of the true and disturbing message of the Word of God.*

> ***Their evangelism.*** *One of the great old preachers said, "I preach always as a dying man to dying men." Yet many preachers talk as if life is unending, hell is a fantasy, and faith in the Lord Jesus Christ*

is unnecessary for salvation. How can ministers of the Word of God become so unconcerned, so careless?[173]

These comments by Billy Graham were made in 1966! We are now in the 21st century, and not much has changed. The prosperity gospel preachers continue to lie to people, rake in their money, and create false expectations about the relationship of faith and wealth on the way to destroying authentic faith. Megachurches pull in millions of people and billions of dollars. But do they produce disciples who make disciples, or are they more like a secularized entertainment venue?[174] Do they produce disciples who follow Jesus when the music is turned off? Do they train disciples who are willing to follow Christ even when it proves difficult? Mainline denominations provide "safe spaces" for people to retreat to avoid the ugliness of society. And so we wander and slumber. Many believers ignore God's purpose of sharing the gospel with the lost and wonder why He does not fix the problems in the world around them.

Malachi speaks very clearly into our circumstances today. Using the prophet Malachi, God pointed to Levi as a model of leadership that should be emulated. Moses and Aaron were from the tribe of Levi, and under God's covenant Levi was the priestly tribe which served the tent of meeting and later the temple. In Malachi 2:4-7, God celebrated Levi because he:

1. Feared the Lord (2:5)
2. Stood in awe of God's name (2:5)
3. Taught accurately God's word (2:6)
4. Did not teach error (2:6)
5. Walked with God in peace and integrity (2:6)
6. Turned many away from sin (2:6)

---

173 Boice, *The Minor Prophets, Vol. 2*, p. 580.

174 "...the process of secularization is far more pervasive than theological differences between conservatives and liberals. It is not secular humanists but we ourselves who are secularizing the faith by transforming its odd message into something less jarring to the American psyche. This may mean, however, that precisely the most numerically successful versions of religion will be the least tethered to the biblical drama of redemption centering on Christ." Michael Horton, *Christless Christianity: The Alternative Gospel of the American Church*, (Grand Rapids, MI: Baker Books, 2008), Kindle edition, p. 15-16.

7. Protected and guarded God's message (2:7)
8. Delivered accurate application of God's word into individual circumstances (2:7)

In this profile of Levi, we see the same tension in the gospel we have seen elsewhere in Scripture. Warnings of wrath and judgment with calls for repentance stand in tension with offers of grace and salvation. In proclaiming the word, salvation, love, and hope are integrated with the exposure of sin, warnings of judgment, and calls to repent. It takes courage, passion, grace, and faithfulness to the truth of God's word for preachers and believers to share the full gospel to the world around them, and especially to the visible people of God. That is every believer's charge and not only the clergy's. The "full gospel" or "whole gospel" is a gospel with a "backbone."[175]

Second, God's purpose in the 21st century is unchanged from Malachi's day. God's people then and now are to walk in holiness before Him and to "make his name great among the nations" (1:11). Effectively, the church in America today has removed from its purpose the making of His "name great among the nations." Many churches no longer engage this purpose. Instead, it seems that many churches have engaged in making their *own* name great among the nations. This is a tragedy.

Many pastors fail to teach their congregations what God's purpose for the church is and how to achieve that purpose. Consequently, elders and deacons fail to lead their churches to fulfill the Great Commission. Pastors and elders are typically diligent about the general operations of the church, the quality of worship, and making sure all the funerals, weddings, and hospital visits are covered, **but they have no plans to evangelize the lost with the gospel. This is an outrageous failing.** There is no other honest way of assessing our current condition. A great many pastors are in a massive state of failure, and congregations are completely happy (and naïve) about it. Pastors, elders, and congregations are all to blame.

Apathy, affluence, and neglect appear to do greater damage to the spread of the gospel than persecution. Take for example Iran, a country of approximately 84 million people and the only Islamic theocracy in the world.[176] Iran is a religious

---

175 Metzger, *Tell the Truth,* p. 39.
176 Sarah Eekhoff Zylstra, *Meet the World's Fastest Growing Evangelical Movement* (The Gospel Coalition, U.S. Edition, February 8, 2021), https://www.thegospelcoalition.org/article/meet-the-worlds-fastest-growing-evangelical-movement/, accessed February 16, 2021.

dictatorship where nothing of consequence can occur without approval of the Islamic rulers.[177]

> *In Iran, anyone who shares their faith, publishes Christian litera-ture, or holds church services in the common language of Farsi can be arrested – and they are. Punishment is often prison, and sentences are long. Last year two Christian converts were flogged 80 times for drinking communion wine, then sentenced to several years in prison for organizing house churches. In 2018, four Christians were sen-tenced to 10 years in prison—one of them had originally been sen-tenced in 2010 to die by hanging.[178]*

Yet evangelism is taking place in Iran, and the church is growing.

> *"About 20 years ago, the number of Christian converts from a Muslim background was between 5,000 and 10,000 people," Paul Crabtree said (a Christian source close to the region; not his real name). "Today that's between 800,000 to 1 million people. That's massive growth." According to Operation World, Iran has the fastest growing evangelical movement in the world.[179]*

Evangelism is done primarily by the "non-professionals," ordinary believers.

> *Whenever two or three people came to the Lord, Alizadeh's church would connect them with each other and help them begin to evange-lize. Over the past 20 years, this church has planted about 25 other small groups in 12 cities. About 500 people have committed their lives to Jesus.[180]*

---

177 Jason Mandryk, *Operation World* (Colorado Springs, CO: Biblica Publishing, 2010), p. 465.

178 Zylstra, *Meet the World's Fastest Growing Evangelical Movement.*

179 Zylstra, *Meet the World's Fastest Growing Evangelical Movement.*

180 Zylstra, *Meet the World's Fastest Growing Evangelical Movement.*

We must awaken to God's call to share the "disturbing message"[181] of the gospel. God has equipped all believers with the Holy Spirit to give them the courage, passion, grace, and faithfulness to carry out this call. Believers cannot carry out this gospel call in their own strength, nor does the Lord expect us to. It is sin to even try. We are called to share the good news of His great salvation by the power of His Holy Spirit.

Third, God is "taking names" (Mal. 3:16). It may seem as if God had turned a blind eye to the spiritual apathy of His people and was ignoring those who remained faithful to Him. But that was not the case. In the Book of Malachi God had the names "of those who feared the Lord and esteemed his name" placed in a "book of remembrance," which means God knows who they are, and they will not be forgotten.

What should pastors and believers do in today's church or denominational cultures that are predominantly apathetic or opposed to evangelism? Many of God's people find themselves in that state of reality. In that situation "those who fear the Lord" must possess an intense concentration on God and His purpose. However, the believer must not slip into anger or respond in arrogance to the spiritual apathy and disobedience of fellow believers who refuse to share the gospel. The believer must recognize there may have been a time in their own life when they were not faithful to be a witness. The believer must also recognize they are not the perfect witness as Jesus was. Humility, love, courage, and perseverance are required to help fellow believers be faithful to Christ in sharing the gospel.

It is okay to mourn the fact that many of God's people have abandoned all pretense of obedience to the Great Commission. However, this mourning must be channeled into something positive, such as prayer for the awakening of His people. The faithful believer's prayer must be accompanied by the confession of their own sins.

> *I prayed to the LORD my God and made confession, saying, "O Lord, the great and awesome God...we have sinned and done wrong and acted wickedly and rebelled, turning aside from your commandments and rules. We have not listened to your servants the prophets, who spoke in your name..."*
>
> *Dan, 9:4-6*

---

181 Boice, *The Minor Prophets*, Vol. 2, p. 580.

We can engage in constructive conversations about sharing the light of Christ with those who are lost. We can speak about the importance of teaching the whole gospel. It is my hope that more people will mourn over the state of the visible church today and pray for God's people to regain their first love (Rev. 2:5).

Finally, the Book of Malachi is a good source of Scripture to pray. Below are two examples of praying God's word using Malachi.

> *Lord, I acknowledge your desire that "your name will be great among the nations." You are "a great King" and your "name will be feared among the nations." Too often I have lived for enhancement of my reputation and not yours. I have desired the approval of men and not your approval. Please forgive me of this sin. I acknowledge that I cannot live to make your name great without you giving me that ability. I do not have within my own strength the power of living for your glory. I confess my inability and the weakness of my flesh. But you have given me the Holy Spirit to enable me to live for your glory. Please transform my life in this way and enable me to have a strong heart's desire to see others come to know what "a great King" you are.*
>
> *Mal. 1:11, 14*

Another:

> *Lord, I acknowledge your praise of Levi who had "true instruction... in his mouth and no wrong was found on his lips." "He turned many from iniquity." He exposed sin in people's lives. He taught your word accurately and made piercing applications into the lives of others whether or not it was popular. He spoke your truth without "partiality." I confess my lack of courage to speak your word in such a bold fashion and to expose sin in the lives of others. I confess that failing to do so is sin in my life. Please forgive me and give me the courage, passion, and love to speak the whole truth of your word into the lives of*

those around me. Without your empowering Spirit, I can do nothing for your kingdom.

Mal. 2:6, 7, 9

PART TWO

THE
GOSPELS

CHAPTER 7

ARRIVAL
OF THE SAVIOR

*Joseph, son of David, do not fear to take Mary as your wife, for that which is conceived in her is from the Holy Spirit. She will bear a son, and **you shall call his name Jesus, for he will save his people from their sins.***

Matthew 1:20-21

When the Old Testament came to an end with the Book of Malachi, the spiritual condition of Israel was extremely poor, as they were a rebellious people of God and He was angry with them. Because of God's disappointment with their rebellion, He did not speak to them for almost 400 years. When Jesus entered the picture, they were still an unfaithful people. We learn specific details about Israel's contemptuous disrespect of God from Jesus during His public ministry. For example, He accuses the religious leaders of having hearts full of "greed and wickedness" (Lk. 11:39). They give great emphasis to man-imposed trifles but neglect the far more important "justice and the love of God" (Lk. 11:42). They love sitting in places of honor and receiving glory to themselves in public places (Lk. 11:43). But their hearts are hard toward God, and they are no different than their forefathers who murdered the prophets (Lk. 11:47-51). They distort God's word by redefining it, adding unnecessary burdens to it, and consequently hiding the true way of salvation by grace through faith (Lk. 11:46, 52; Mk. 7:6-8; Gal. 3:1-14; Gen. 15:6), thus "shutting the kingdom of heaven in people's faces" (Mt.23:13). The fruit of their corruption is that they produce disciples who are "twice as much a child of hell" as they themselves are (Mt. 23:15). The people who go by God's name are shrouded in a thick cloud of darkness fueled by their own sin.

But in this spiritual darkness, God once again takes steps in accord with His earlier promises to Adam and Eve, Abraham, Moses, and David. He acts to fulfill His predictions through Isaiah, Jeremiah, Daniel, Malachi, and all the prophets of the Old Testament to send a Savior to rescue mankind from the tragedy of its sin.

God has been preparing for this Savior by controlling and shaping history for more than 3,000 years. History must fall in line with the detailed predictions God has made through His prophets. When God breaks the 400-year silence, it is most interesting to see whom He chooses to use to communicate this spectacular news. He selects an "exclusive" group of mainly B-list actors. The A-listers, those with political power, social status, and impressive religious pedigree, are mostly missing. There are 12 individuals or groups of individuals that God chooses to use. God uses nobodies in this historic event to reveal His one and only Son and His purpose in coming to earth.

The Arrival

God's supernatural hand is prominent in this account of events as history plays out in the lives of real people. If God is to accomplish the salvation He has promised, He must be in complete control of history. This story is a powerful demonstration of His active, ongoing rule over the details of history. We will follow the series of events in a mostly chronological fashion, drawing from all four Gospels.

The **genealogies** of Matthew and Luke are a witness of God's outworking of redemption in history (Heb. 12:1). Its witness is important to the story since in it we can see God's sovereign hand fulfilling His promise of a savior, which was first made to Adam and Eve. Only a God in control of history can make a promise and predict the historical details of how that promise will be fulfilled hundreds of years in advance. God's first promise of a Savior was that He would be **an offspring of Eve**, meaning a human (Gen. 3:15). Through the centuries God made His promises more specific with more details, including naming people from whom the Savior would be descended. God promised that He would be a **son of Abraham** (Gen. 22:18; Gal. 3:16), **"a shoot from the stump of Jesse"** (Isa. 11:1), and **"the son of David"** (Mt. 1:1). All the specifics God predicted are fulfilled in the person of Jesus Christ.

Out of the blue, four hundred years after Malachi in the autumn of 6 BC,[182] about 15 months before the birth of Jesus, **Gabriel** is sent by God to break the silence. He appears to **Zechariah** in the temple "standing on the right side of the altar of incense" (Lk. 1:11). No one other than Zechariah was supposed to be in that room. Zechariah is a priest of the lineage of Aaron and is married to Elizabeth who has not been able to bear children. They are both in their old age now. As far as we know, Zechariah is an ordinary priest among the approximately 18,000[183] priests who served the temple. He and Elizabeth are described by Luke as "righteous before God" and "blameless" (Lk. 1:6). Otherwise, he is of no known prominence, and was not well prepared for Gabriel's intrusion into his "once in a lifetime"[184] privilege of conducting "the most solemn part of the entire liturgy [which] was the burning of incense"[185] in the temple.

Gabriel's unexpected appearance is obviously terrifying to Zechariah, even as a priest, "and fear fell upon him" (Lk 1:11-12). Gabriel's message is equally shocking. First, he tries to calm Zechariah down and tells him not to be afraid. He then tells him that his prayer has been answered, "and your wife Elizabeth will bear you a son, and you shall call his name John" (Lk. 1:13). Gabriel adds some additional details and tells him that John "will be great before the Lord…and he will be filled with the Holy Spirit, even from his mother's womb…he will turn many of the children of Israel to the Lord their God, and he will go before him in the spirit and power of Elijah…to make ready for the Lord a people prepared" (Lk. 1:15-17).

All of this is more than Zechariah can handle, and he responds to Gabriel with, "How shall I know this? For I am an old man, and my wife is advanced in years" (Lk. 1:18). Based on Gabriel's response, it is as if Zechariah said, "Are you out of your mind? What planet are you from?" *(My very loose paraphrase of Lk. 1:18)*. Gabriel answers him with dignity and seriousness, "I am Gabriel. I stand in the presence of God, and I was sent to speak to you and to bring you this good news. And behold, you will be

---

182 Colin Duriez, *AD 33: The Year that Changed the World* (Downers Grove, IL: InterVarsity Press, 2006), p. 226. This announcement date is extrapolated based on the dating of Jesus' birth by Duriez as January 4 BC (or December 5 BC).

183 Robert H. Stein, *Luke* (NAC) (Nashville: Broadman & Holman Publishers, 1992), p. 74.

184 William Hendriksen, *Exposition of the Gospel According to Luke* (NTC) (Grand Rapids: Baker Book House, 1978), p. 68.

185 Hendriksen, *Luke* (NTC), p. 67.

silent and unable to speak until the day that these things take place, because you did not believe my words, which will be fulfilled in their time" (Lk. 1:19-20). Zechariah's failure to believe earns him a nine-month silent retreat.

Zechariah's response reminds us of Abraham's wife Sarah and how she responded when she overheard the Lord tell Abraham that she was going to have a son. Sarah was so shocked at this news that she laughed. And when the Lord asked why she laughed, she denied it because she was afraid (Gen. 18:12-15). Sarah, like Elizabeth, was well beyond childbearing years and initially could not believe God's promise of a supernatural conception. Thus, Elizabeth will not be the first older barren woman to give birth.

The supernatural did not stop with Abraham and Sarah as both Isaac and Jacob, Abraham's son and grandson respectively, were also married to barren wives. God had made specific promises starting with Abraham that Messiah would come through their descendants. In order for this prophecy to be fulfilled, God would perform three miracles of birth utilizing barren women. God's purpose of Messiah coming through the line of Abraham and David would not be thwarted, and it would happen by His power and not by human power. God preserved His chosen line century after century, often in miraculous ways. God is now acting again supernaturally in redemptive history.

Six months after Gabriel appears to Elizabeth, He also visits **Mary,** a young virgin living in the small insignificant town of Nazareth. She is a poor young teenage Jewish girl betrothed to Joseph. "At this time Mary likely was no more than fifteen years old, probably closer to thirteen, which was the normal age for betrothal."[186] But Gabriel has some stunning news for her, "Greetings, O favored one, the Lord is with you!" But she is greatly troubled at the saying (Lk. 1:28-29). She is as troubled as Zechariah at the sight of Gabriel and at his message. The angel tries to put her at ease, as he did with Zechariah, and says to her: "Do not be afraid, Mary, for you have found favor with God. And behold, you will conceive in your womb and bear a son, and you shall call his name Jesus. He will be great and will be called the Son of the Most High. And the Lord God will give to him the throne of his father David, and he will reign over the house of Jacob forever, and of his kingdom there will be no end" (Lk. 1:30-33).

---

186 Stein, *Luke (NAC)*, p. 82.

This is an overwhelming weight of information for Mary and enough to cause shock to anyone's system. Mary feels the strain of this encounter and is "deeply troubled... very much upset."[187] But unlike Zechariah, Mary does not disbelieve the angel Gabriel. Though perplexed, Mary asks Gabriel a clarifying question. It is not the question of a doubter, and Gabriel can see this in Mary and gives her an explanation. Mary responds by trusting God's promise given to her through Gabriel and humbly submits to God's actions in her life. But God's grace falling on a person's life brings its own set of issues. The first one for Mary is that she must explain to her family and to Joseph that she is pregnant. How does a young teenage Jewish girl tell her family she is pregnant by the Holy Spirit? What will she say to the man to whom she is betrothed?

To understand the impact of Mary's situation, we must understand the steps of a Jewish marriage. The first step was the engagement period. In this stage, the parents chose a mate for their son. This engagement stage lasted one year, during which the couple would decide if they wanted to continue into marriage. The second stage required the couple to enter the betrothal stage. This stage was the legal stage as a Jewish couple would actually be considered married. What was unique in a Jewish marriage was that, though legally married, the couple had not consummated their marriage. If the couple did not want to go to the third stage in the marriage, they would have to get a legal divorce. The final stage in the Jewish marriage was the wedding ceremony, after which the couple would consummate their marriage. It was in this second stage, the betrothal stage, where the angel appeared to Mary—and soon Mary was pregnant.

Mary goes "with haste" (Lk. 1:39) to visit **Elizabeth** in the hill country of Judah and stays with her for about three months. When Mary greets Elizabeth, "the baby [John] in [her] womb leaped for joy" (Lk. 1:44). Elizabeth tells Mary how honored she is that "the mother of my Lord should come to me." Elizabeth states that the baby in Mary's womb is the Lord Himself and extols Mary for trusting the promise of God given to her through Gabriel. Mary's trusting response to Gabriel's message stands in contrast to Zechariah's disbelief and reveals a tender heart toward God. With her heart she could hear God's voice in Gabriel's message. Zechariah was apparently as crusty in his old heart as he was in outward appearance.

---

187 Louw and Nida, *Greek-English Lexicon of the New Testament*, 89.23, p. 314.

Mary, during her meeting with Elizabeth, gives us her beautiful song of praise, popularly known as "The Magnificat" (Lk. 1:46-55). She begins with "My soul magnifies[188] the Lord" (1:46). She rejoices in "God my savior" (1:47) and exclaims that God is a mighty, holy, and merciful God (1:49-50). She proclaims that He "has shown strength with his arm," "scattered the proud," "brought down the mighty from their thrones," and "exalted the humble" (1:51-52). He is acting in "remembrance of his mercy, as he spoke to our fathers, to Abraham and to his offspring forever" (1:54-55). These are the words of one who is filled with the Holy Spirit, and Mary honors God's great works.

We learn three things about Mary from her song of praise. First, she is a sinner in need of a savior herself and rejoices in God's provision of this savior. Her statement reflects a practical response to the angel's statement to Joseph regarding the purpose of Jesus – "he will save his people from their sins" (Mt. 1:21). Mary applies this truth to her own life by trusting God as her savior. Second, she tells us about her status in society. She is of "humble estate" (Lk. 1:48). The Greek word is ταπείνωσιν (tapeinosin), which means "someone in humble circumstances"[189] or "a humble origin or lowly estate."[190] This speaks of her humble status politically, socially, and economically. And third, she is blessed by God. "From now on all generations will call me blessed" (Lk. 148). She is the recipient of a great blessing by God.

The salutation by Gabriel to Mary is "Greetings, O favored one" (Lk. 1:28). The Greek word translated "O favored one" is κεχαριτωμένη (kecharitomene) and literally means "one who has been favored (by God)."[191] It is the action of a holy God bestowing His favor upon Mary who was undeserving of this favor. The statement by Gabriel to Mary is similar to Gen. 6:8, "But Noah found favor in the eyes of the Lord." As noted in Chapter 1 of this book, "While 'Noah found favor' is the only way in which the words can be translated, they actually mean that 'favor found Noah.'"[192] And just as God's grace acted upon Noah's

---

188 The Greek word translated "magnifies" is Μεγαλυνει (megalunei) which means "to cause to be held in greater esteem through praise or deeds, *exalt, glorify, magnify, speak highly of.*" William Arndt et al., *A Greek-English Lexicon of the New Testament and Other Early Christian Literature* (BDAG) (Chicago: University of Chicago Press, Third Edition, 2000), p. 623.

189 Arndt et al., *A Greek-English Lexicon of the New Testament* (BDAG), p. 990.

190 Zodhiates, *The Complete Word Study Dictionary: New Testament,* Word No. 5014.

191 Arndt et al., *A Greek-English Lexicon of the New Testament* (BDAG), p. 1081. The root word is χαριτόω (charitoo) and is used one other time the NT in Eph. 1:6.

192 Motyer, *6 Ways the Old Testament Speaks Today,* p. 130.

life and changed his plans, so Mary's life is totally interrupted by God's grace acting on her life. The good plans she has for her life are totally changed as she is given an entirely new purpose for her life. It will not be easy for her, just as it was not easy for Noah.

Mary, a young ordinary person in out-of-the-way Nazareth, is of no particular prominence before God's intervention in her life. It is God's favor (grace) falling on her life that gives her prominence. Mary trusts God and God receives the glory for her life. Mary has no power emanating from herself. It is God's power and glory that are on display.

We are not told how Mary communicated this shocking information to her family or to **Joseph**, but we do know that Joseph was troubled by the news and did not believe the story as initially communicated to him by Mary. We are also not told the reaction of her family to this news, but there is no reason to expect them to have responded any differently than Joseph. This is a scandal in progress for this small Jewish community and would have been troubling news to any Jewish family of that day.

Joseph seems to be wrestling with how to handle the situation and "being a just man and unwilling to put her to shame, resolved to divorce her quietly" (Mt. 1:19). It is clear that before the angel communicates to him, Joseph does not believe Mary's story of a conception by the Holy Spirit. We can see that Joseph is a kind man but is not willing to marry someone who has been unfaithful to him before their marriage is consummated. But while Joseph is still contemplating this whole matter (Mt. 1:20), he is brought into the inner circle by an unnamed angel of the Lord and told what is going on. The angel says to him in a dream, "Joseph, son of David, do not fear to take Mary as your wife, for that which is conceived in her is from the Holy Spirit. She will bear a son, and you shall call his name Jesus, **for he will save his people from their sins**" (Mt. 1:20-21). Matthew adds here in the text that Mary is the virgin of Isaiah 7:14 and that the son she shall bear will be called "Immanuel," meaning "God with us" (Mt. 1:23).

"When Joseph woke from sleep, he did as the angel of the Lord commanded him: he took his wife, but knew her not until she had given birth to a son. And he called his name Jesus" (Mt. 1:24-25). Joseph immediately submits his life to the Lord and to whatever cost it may have on his life. The first cost would be the cost to his reputation. Most people in the community would likely not have believed the "conceived by the Holy Spirit" explanation. They would have considered that Mary had an immoral encounter with a man. If Joseph divorced her, they would speculate that it must have been someone other than Joseph. If he married her, they would assume Joseph was the father. In either case, people would likely think immorality must have been involved. Joseph's submission to the Lord made him part of the scandal. He could have walked away, but he did not. Mary was embroiled in the controversy either way. So, Joseph acts in faith and takes her into his home under his protection and provision.

We need to realize why God called a virgin to be the mother of Messiah. It was prophesied in Isa. 7:14, "Behold, the virgin shall conceive and bear a son, and shall call his name Immanuel" (cited in Mt. 1:23). No virgin, prior to nor after this event, has ever borne a child in the history of the world. This is part of the evidence enabling the world to identify Messiah. It is one of God's many attestations of Jesus' messianic identity.

Zechariah's tongue has been silenced for nine months since his encounter with Gabriel. At the birth and naming of his son, John the Baptist, he is not only full of words that need to come out, but he is full of the Holy Spirit and gives us some amazing information about what is occurring. He tells us that God "has visited and redeemed his people and has raised up a horn of salvation for us in the house of his servant David" (Lk. 1:68-69). The phrase "horn of salvation" is equivalent to "a mighty Savior"[193] and conveys that a powerful Savior is coming. Zechariah, as Mary did, proclaims that what is unfolding is in fulfillment of God's covenant with Abraham (Lk. 1:73). He goes on to tell us John "will be called the prophet of the Most High; for you will go before the Lord to prepare his ways, **to give knowledge of salvation to his people in the forgiveness of their sins**" (Lk. 1:76-77).

A few months later **Jesus** enters human history as a helpless baby born into poverty in a stable while His parents are away from home. They use a manger, a feeding trough for animals, for His bed. This is not how we expect Messiah, the savior of the world, to arrive. His name (Jesus) "means *Yahweh is salvation* or 'the Lord saves' (NIV marg.)."[194]

---

193 I. Howard Marshall, *The Gospel of Luke* (NIGTC) (Exeter: Paternoster Press, 1978), p. 91.

194 Blomberg, *Matthew* (NAC), p. 59.

God does not end the communication of this event with the immediate families of John and Jesus. Others become involved.

The high priest and his family, on the night Jesus was born, are awakened by an angel who appears in the courtyard of their home. They all tumble out of their comfortable beds to hear a multitude of angels give them the most wonderful concert any humans had ever experienced and announce the momentous news that a Savior Christ the Lord has been born that day in the city of David... **No, no, no! That is not what happened!**

The high priest and his family slumbered as God chose to celebrate this occasion with a group of unimportant, dirty, smelly **shepherds** on a lonely hillside near Bethlehem. "And an angel of the Lord appeared to them, and the glory of the Lord shone around them, and they were filled with great fear" (Lk. 2:9). The unnamed angel calmed them down and told them the great news that "unto you is born this day in the city of David a Savior, who is Christ the Lord" (Lk. 2:11). Notice the three titles: Savior, Christ, and Lord. He is from the royal line of David born in the city of David. This is lofty revelation from God given first to lowly shepherds. God is honoring them with this privilege, and how appropriate that the birth of the "good shepherd" (Jn. 10:11) is first announced to...shepherds. They, not the high priest and his family, received the greatest concert ever heard on earth by a "multitude of the heavenly host praising God" (Lk. 2:13). The high priest missed out on it. The greatest news to ever come from heaven, announcing the arrival of the Messiah and that man's sins could be forgiven, was delivered to some of the lowest people in all of Jewish society. It was not an oversight by God.

Simeon comes into view, 40 days after Jesus' birth, as Joseph and Mary bring Jesus to the temple for their purification and His consecration. This is the only time Simeon is mentioned in Scripture, and we know very little about him. But God had revealed to Simeon, a "righteous and devout" man (Lk. 2:25), through the Holy Spirit that he would not die before he had seen Messiah. That day when Simeon comes into the temple "in the Spirit" (Lk. 2:27), he sees the parents with Jesus and:

he took him up in his arms and blessed God and said,

"Lord, now you are letting your servant depart in peace,

> *according to your word;*
> **for my eyes have seen your salvation**
> *that you have prepared in the presence of all peoples,*
> **a light for revelation to the Gentiles,**
> **and for glory to your people Israel."**
>
> *Lk. 2:28-32*

Simeon is overjoyed at the privilege of holding in his own arms the "Salvation" of the world. It is the Salvation that all the Old Testament prophets longed to understand (1 Pet. 1:10). Perhaps Simeon is a representative standing in for all of the Old Testament prophets on this marvelous occasion. But Simeon also speaks to Mary some difficult facts about this Son she has borne.

> *And Simeon blessed them and said to Mary his mother, "Behold,*
> *this child is appointed for the fall and rising of many in Israel, and*
> *for a sign that is opposed (and a sword will pierce through your own*
> *soul also), so that thoughts from many hearts may be revealed."*
>
> *Lk. 2:34-35*

Simeon's message to Mary is of great joy, but it also has a hard edge to it. God has "appointed" or purposed that: (1) Jesus will be a line of demarcation ("the fall and rising of many"); He "is history's watershed, its dividing ridge";[195] (2) He will be "opposed," "contradicted or contested"[196] by many; (3) there will be "piercing anguish of heart"[197] for Mary; and (4) He will reveal the sinful hearts of many, and they will be either for Him or against Him.[198]

---

195 William Hendriksen, *Luke* (NTC), p. 175; "[T]here is a double significance to Jesus' ministry. For the humble and poor it is positive, salvation; for the haughty and rich it is negative, judgment. This twofold aspect of the coming Messiah is found both in the OT (Isa 8:14; 28:16–17) and the NT (Rom 9:33; 1 Pet 2:6–8)." Stein, *Luke* (NAC), p. 117; "In other words a person's relation or attitude toward Jesus would be absolutely decisive of his eternal destiny." Hendriksen, *Luke* (NTC), p. 170.

196 Marshall, *The Gospel of Luke* (NIGTC) (Exeter: Paternoster Press, 1978), 122.

197 Hendriksen, *Luke* (NTC), p. 176.

198 Hendriksen, Luke (NTC), p. 170.

For thousands of years God prophesied that He would send the answer, the solution, and the complete payment for the sins of mankind, beginning in the garden of Eden with the fall of Adam and Eve into sin. Now that moment has arrived.

Anna, a prophetess in her later years of life, is also in the temple at the same time. She too comes up and adds her voice to that of Simeon and begins to speak about God "to all who were waiting for the redemption of Jerusalem" (Lk. 2:28). "The 'redemption of Jerusalem' (cf. 1:68, 'redeemed his people') serves as a synonym for the 'consolation of Israel' in 2:25...and 'salvation' in 2:30."[199] God revealed to her that this baby is the long-awaited Salvation of the world. According to both Simeon and Anna, this is the greatest news the world could ever hear. Sinful man's need of a savior is finally provided.

Sometime later, **"Wise men** from the east" (Mt. 2:1) appear in Jerusalem and create quite a stir looking for the one "who has been born king of the Jews" (Mt. 2:2). They were most likely prominent figures in their society from Persia who "combined astronomical observation with astrological speculation...[and] played both political and religious roles" in their land.[200] They get King Herod's attention as they ride conspicuously into town, as well as the attention of the power brokers of the Jews, the chief priests and scribes. Herod views this news as a threat to his kingly position, as the leaders of the Jews may also have done. In one sense it is surprising that Gentiles have come to worship the newborn King, but in reality He is their King and their only hope of salvation as well. This King is for the whole world. Even the pagan world recognizes who has been born in Bethlehem.

"Herod the Great [is] a half-Jew, half-Idumean."[201] Opposition to Jesus begins early – at His birth. Herod is troubled by what he learns from the wise men and seeks to find out where he can lay his hands on this would be king. "Despite his role as legally installed ruler of Israel and his professed conversion to Judaism, Herod rejects the newborn king and plots to destroy him."[202] The fingerprints of Satan are all over Herod's thinking and actions.

---

199 Stein, *Luke* (NAC), p. 118.
200 Blomberg, *Matthew* (NAC), p. 62.
201 Blomberg, *Matthew*, p. 62.
202 Blomberg, *Matthew*, p. 61.

Herod lies to the wise men, telling them to let him know where they find this baby so he can worship him too. But God warns the wise men in a dream not to return to Herod, so after worshipping Jesus in Bethlehem, they return home by a different route. When Herod learns the men from the east are not going to return to him, he is "furious" (Mt. 2:16). He orders his men to kill all the male children in Bethlehem two years old and under. Herod, the liar and murderer, is doing a good job as Satan's man in Jerusalem. We must realize that while God has foreordained that His Son will be born and will grow up to be the solution to man's sins, Satan does not want this to happen.

Before Herod's rampage, God warned Joseph in a dream to take Jesus and Mary and flee to Egypt. Joseph did this as he had become accustomed to listening to God and putting his faith in God's word. The family stayed in Egypt until after Herod's death. After Herod was dead, they returned to Nazareth where they presumably moved into a normal life.

After living a life in His parents' home and working in His father's carpenter shop, it is time for Jesus to begin His earthly ministry. To prepare people for His ministry, God provided a prophet, "the voice of one crying in the wilderness" (Mk. 1:3; Isa. 40:1-3). **John the Baptist** enters the scene as an enigmatic figure with a powerful presence. He has been filled with the Holy Spirit since he was in his mother's womb, and he comes as a powerful Elijah-like figure. John is charged with building a "highway" (Isa. 40:3), and he is an expert highway builder. This highway (the gospel) leads to God and is paved with the only materials qualified for its construction: (1) exposure of sins, (2) the call to confess sins, (3) warnings of God's wrath and fierce anger, (4) the call to repentance, and (5) the call to trust Jesus as the only solution for sin and the only rescue from God's wrath (Mt. 3:1-17; Lk. 3:1-22; Jn. 1:6-34).

One day after John baptized Jesus, he saw him walking by and exclaimed, **"Behold, the Lamb of God who takes away the sins of the world!"** (Jn. 1:29, 36). This may have seemed an odd expression to John's hearers. The Jordan River, where John baptized, was about 20 miles from Jerusalem where thousands of lambs were sacrificed every year. Those sacrifices prefigured Jesus' death on the cross. But did those hearing John that day make the connection? The popular expectation of Messiah was of a Roman-crushing ruler and not a suffering Servant. It may have been a puzzling statement. John, himself, may not have fully understood the implications of his own statement, but he received it from the Lord and proclaimed it.[203] Over the course of his short ministry, John proved to be a courageous and powerful proclaimer of the gospel (see Lk. 3:1-20) and is described by Philip Melanchthon as one of the greatest gospel proclaimers of all time.[204]

What Can We Learn About the Gospel and Evangelism from His Arrival?

First, up to this point in history Jesus' birth was the biggest event in the history of the world. It is the fulfillment of many prophecies in the Old Testament (spanning 3,000 years), including the very first gospel promise, which God gave to Adam and Eve in Gen. 3:15, "He shall bruise your head, and you shall bruise his heel." That statement was spoken directly to Satan as judgment on him, and for Adam and Eve as a hope-filled promise. This is also the fulfillment of God's promise to Abraham, as we saw in Chapter 2 of this book (Gen. 12:7; 22:18; cf. Gal. 3:16). The head crusher of Satan, the long-awaited Savior had arrived. Now He would do His work.

Second, we see once again the full gospel message. It is revealed with remarkable clarity in the arrival of the Savior. It takes on a special power and eloquence as it unfolds through the lives of the participants and reaches a climax in the preaching of John the Baptist. Here are some of the key points of the gospel revealed in the birth of Jesus.

1. **Jesus as God:** The identification of Jesus as God is explicit. "He will be great and will be called **the Son of the Most High.** And the Lord God will give to him the throne of his father David, and he will reign over the house of Jacob forever, and of his kingdom there will be no end...therefore **the child to be born will be called holy—the Son of God**" (Lk. 1:32-33, 35). (Also Mt. 3:17; Lk. 2:11; Jn. 1:1-5.)

2. **Holiness:** The angel, Gabriel, told Mary that Jesus "will be called holy – the Son of God" (Lk. 1:35). Zechariah includes God's requirement of holy liv-

203 D. A. Carson, *The Gospel according to John* (PNTC) (Leicester, England; Grand Rapids, MI: Inter-Varsity Press; W.B. Eerdmans, 1991), pp. 148-151.

204 Philip Melanchthon as cited by Derek Thomas, *God Delivers: Isaiah Simply Explained,* pp. 14-15.

ing in his prophecy at the birth of John: "that we...might serve him without fear, **in holiness and righteousness** before him all our days" (Lk. 1:74-75). John the Baptist's preaching about sin highlighted the great divide between sinful man and a holy God.

3. **Sin:** No one has lived a sinless life, other than Jesus, and we are all in need of a savior. "[Y]ou shall call his name Jesus, for **he will save his people from their sins**" (Mt. 1:21). "[A]nd they were being baptized by him [John] in the river Jordan, **confessing their sins**" (Mt. 3:6).

4. **Wrath/Judgment:** Because of sin, the wrath of God awaits everyone outside of Christ. This includes both the religious and the non-religious. "But when he [John] saw many of the Pharisees and Sadducees coming to his baptism, he said to them, '**You brood of vipers! Who warned you to flee from the wrath to come?...Every tree therefore that does not bear good fruit is cut down and thrown into the fire**...His winnowing fork is in his hand, and he will clear his threshing floor and gather his wheat into the barn, **but the chaff he will burn with unquenchable fire**'" (Mt. 3:7, 10, 12).

5. **The Cross and Resurrection:** On the cross Jesus paid for the sins of all who believe in Him. The cross is in view in these early statements about Jesus. "She will bear a son, and you shall call his name Jesus, **for he will save his people from their sins**" (Mt. 1:21). "[A]nd a sword will pierce through your own soul also" (Lk. 2:35). This is possibly a veiled reference to the cross and the pain that Mary will experience as she sees her son "pierced" for her sins and for the sins of the world (see Isa 53:5; Jn. 19:34; Rev. 1:7). "**Behold, the Lamb of God, who takes away the sin of the world!**" (Jn. 1:29). Lambs were one of the central animals of the temple sacrificial system. Jesus is the real "lamb of God."

6. **Grace:** God in mercy bestows grace (unmerited favor) on those who believe in Him. "**And his mercy is for those who fear him...**" (Lk. 1:50). "[T]o **show the mercy** promised to our fathers and to remember his holy covenant, the oath that he swore to our father Abraham" (Lk. 1:72-73). "[A]nd on earth peace among those with whom he is pleased" (Lk. 2:14).

7. **The Cost of Following Jesus:** Mary was not exempt from the cost of following Jesus. Simeon's words are sobering, "Behold, this child is appointed for the fall and rising of many in Israel, and **for a sign that is opposed (and a sword will pierce through your own soul also)**, so that thoughts from many hearts may be revealed" (Lk. 2:34-35). Serious opposition will begin quickly as Joseph must take Mary and Jesus and flee to Egypt from Herod's attempt to kill Jesus. Herod murders all the baby boys two years old and under in Bethlehem (Mt. 3:13-18). Those who follow Jesus will encounter opposition aimed at Jesus as they live out following Him.

8. **Repent and Believe:** Both John and Jesus preach a message of repentance and faith. "In those days John the Baptist came preaching in the wilderness of Judea, '**Repent, for the kingdom of heaven is at hand**'" (Mt. 3:1-2). "And he [John] went into all the region around the Jordan, **proclaiming a baptism of repentance for the forgiveness of sins**" (Lk. 3:3). When Jesus began His public ministry, His message was identical: "Now after John was arrested, Jesus came into Galilee, proclaiming the gospel of God, and saying, 'The time is fulfilled, and the kingdom of God is at hand; **repent and believe in the gospel**'" (Mk. 1:14-15). "Bear fruit in keeping with repentance" (Mt. 3:8).

Third, John the Baptist plays a major role in this historic event. God thought this news important enough to predict in advance the announcer of it. There is much we can learn from John, particularly from the content of his message and how he engaged people with it. He consistently preached the full unvarnished biblical gospel, and he consistently applied it to everyone in his audience regardless of social standing, educational attainment, or religious connections. He preached the same gospel to the crowds of ordinary people as he did to the hated tax collectors. And he preached the same gospel message to the Gentile Roman soldiers as to the privileged religious leaders. "The scandal of John's ministry was that he called, not merely Gentiles, but Israelites [God's people] to be baptized, indicating that Israel was also unclean"[205] and in need of a savior.

---

205 R. C. Sproul, *What is Reformed Theology?: Understanding the Basics,* (Grand Rapids, MI: Baker Books, 2006, Third Printing), Loc. 1284-85.

One of the reasons John's message was so powerful was that he did not remove the difficult and unpopular features of the gospel. **John was not concerned merely about the *felt needs* of his listeners. He was concerned about the *real needs* of his listeners.** Unless a sinner recognizes their sin sickness before a holy God and their need for His salvation, they will be eternally lost. But when a sinner confesses their sins and is forgiven by God, there is a release from the guilt of that sin. Felt needs are met as the root cause of guilt is resolved.

The message of John and Jesus was in exact agreement. They both preached the love of God and His great mercy, but they both preached God's wrath as a warning to those who rejected Him. Even in what may be the most famous verse in the entire Bible, John 3:16, there is the expression of love along with a warning of wrath. "For **God so loved the world**, that he gave his only Son, that whoever believes in him **should not perish** but have eternal life."

It takes great love and great courage to proclaim the full gospel message as John the Baptist did. That is the calling of every believer – to have great love and great courage in following Christ to tell lost people the truth. Every believer can and should learn from John's example, especially his use of gospel content. His example is not only for pastors and evangelists, but also for all of us.

CHAPTER 8
THE PURPOSE OF JESUS CHRIST AS LIGHT

And Jesus said to them, "Follow me, and I will make you become fishers of men."

Mark 1:17

The title I really wanted to use for this chapter is, "The Passion of Jesus Christ for the Lost and His Purpose for His Followers, which is also His Purpose and which He Transfers to His Disciples and which He Tells Potential Followers Upfront if they will Only Pay Attention." That's 39 words and a bit too much, but it is a good summary of the focus of this chapter.

While we saw over and over in the Old Testament the fall of man into sin, as well as promises of the coming solution to man's sin, we now enter the actual ministry on earth of the promised Savior – Jesus Christ. If God is going to act consistently with His established pattern, Jesus' ministry will both bring salvation and announce that salvation. He will be both the salvation and the light that the world needs (Isa. 49:6).

In this chapter we will examine how Jesus defines the purpose of His life and the purpose for His followers. We will survey several episodes in the life of Jesus and focus on: (1) Jesus' life with a purpose, (2) preparing the disciples for being a light to the nations, (3) the Great Call of Jesus, and (4) parables that illuminate evangelism.

1. Jesus' Life with a Purpose

God made a big deal out of the birth of His son to the virgin Mary. He does the same with the beginning of His earthly ministry. In many ways it's an even bigger deal. He is now ready to engage in the purpose for which He came to earth.

John the Baptist – A Pivotal Character

According to Old Testament scriptures, before the Messiah is revealed, His herald must first appear to announce His arrival. John exploded onto the scene like something out of the Old Testament. He had one foot in the Old Testament and one foot in the New. He emerged into history out of the prophecies of Isaiah and Malachi.

> *A voice cries. "In the wilderness prepare the way of the Lord; make straight in the desert a highway for our God."*
>
> *Isa. 40:3*

> *Behold, I send my messenger, and he will prepare the way before me.*
>
> *Mal. 3:1*

> *Behold, I will send you Elijah the prophet before the great and awesome day of the Lord comes. And he will turn the hearts of fathers to their children and the hearts of children to their fathers, lest I come and strike the land with a decree of utter destruction.*
>
> *Mal. 4:5-6*

These passages are cited and alluded to in all four Gospels multiple times (cf. Mt. 3:3; 11:10-14; 17:10-13; Mk. 1:2-3; 9:11-13; Lk. 1:17; 3:4-6; 7:27; Jn. 1:23).

John was a strange and powerful figure. He wore strange clothes and ate a strange diet (Mt. 3:4). He lived outside of refined society (Lk. 1:80). Filled with the Holy Spirit from his mother's womb (Lk. 1:15), he was nothing short of a phenomenon: an exceptional and extraordinary person speaking the whole gospel message with great power, clarity, and effect. His message was a message of "repentance for the forgiveness of sins" (Mk. 1:4).

People from Jerusalem, Judea, and all the region around the Jordan River (Mt. 3:5) were coming to hear his message and many were "baptized by him in the river Jordan, confessing their sins" (Mt. 3:6). Even the refined religious leaders ventured to the Jordan River to investigate what John was all about. When John saw these arrogant, self-righteous, and oppressive religious leaders coming to him, he had a ready greeting for them:

You brood of vipers! Who warned you to flee from the wrath to come? Bear fruit in keeping with repentance. And do not presume to say to yourselves, "We have Abraham as our father," for I tell you, God is able from these stones to raise up children for Abraham. Even now the axe is laid to the root of the trees. Every tree therefore that does not bear good fruit is cut down and thrown into the fire.

Mt. 3:7-10

John was fearless and faithful. He did not compromise God's message for anyone. **He had a single purpose: to shine an intensely bright light on Jesus' identity and His purpose.**[206] He did not hesitate to call these lost religious leaders to repentance and faith. They faced a terrible eternity under the wrath of God if they continued on their current path. John extended a kindness to them by issuing them this warning.

John is a pivotal character with a megaphone, standing at the three-way intersection of (1) all of the Old Testament promises, portrayals, and expectations of Messiah, (2) the time for redemptive action in history by the Father's treasured Son incarnate, and (3) sinful humanity desperately in need of salvation.

The first encounter Jesus had in His public ministry was with His cousin, John. This was not a chance meeting, but one preordained. John the Baptist had an integral role to play in revealing Jesus' true identity and helping to inaugurate His mission.

Like the throngs who were flooding to John in the wilderness, Jesus came to be baptized in the wilderness. John initially resisted baptizing Jesus saying, "I need to be baptized by you, and do you come to me?" But Jesus answered him, "Let it be so now, for thus it is fitting for us to fulfill all righteousness" (Mt. 3:14-15). Only then did John yield to Jesus, the sinless son of God, and baptize Him in the river Jordan.

Immediately Jesus went up out of the water, and "the heavens were opened to him, and he saw the Spirit of God descending like a dove and coming to rest on him; and behold, a voice from heaven said, **'This is my beloved Son, with whom I am well pleased'**" (Mt. 3:16-17). **God the Father affirms Jesus' identity and purpose,** citing

---

206 Carson, *The Gospel according to John* (PNTC), p. 121.

"excerpts of Ps. 2:7 and Isa. 42:1. Both texts were taken as messianic by important segments of pre-Christian Judaism...Together they point out Jesus' role as both divine Son and Suffering Servant."[207]

Jesus' baptism by John was to "fulfill all righteousness" (Mt. 3:15). Though we are not expressly told what that means, it seems that Jesus is "placing Himself alongside the sinners He came to save." His action "may involve a commitment to do what He will call others to do".[208] It is one of the many ways Jesus modeled obedience to the Father. Perhaps John, being the son of Zechariah and Elizabeth, both of "priestly stock"[209] and descendants of Aaron (Lk. 1:5), is acting in a priestly role as he presents Jesus as "the Lamb of God, who takes away the sin of the world!" (Jn. 1:29).

In submitting to John's baptism **Jesus "identifies with and endorses John's ministry...and his message."**[210] Many pastors and other believers today hesitate to speak about God's wrath and warn the lost about the path they are on. But John had no such reluctance. Jesus gave His stamp of approval to John's message (see also Jn. 5:32-35). So why do we gloss over the message God has endorsed?

Jesus' baptism by John launched His earthly ministry and defined His purpose consistent with "Old Testament expectations."[211] Jesus cannot be detached from Old Testament promises and predictions. He cannot be separated from the Old Testament images, portrayals, and purpose. He will not allow Himself to be disconnected from the Old Testament gospel message.

Jesus Anointed to Evangelize

Early in Jesus' ministry, during the Galilean period and at least several months after His baptism by John, Jesus goes to the synagogue in His hometown of Nazareth. He has an important announcement to make. "The scroll of the prophet Isaiah" (Lk. 4:17) is handed to Him and He reads from Isaiah 61:1-2. "The Spirit of the Lord is upon

---

207 Blomberg, Matthew (NAC), p. 82.

208 John Nolland, *The Gospel of Matthew: A Commentary on the Greek Text* (NIGTC) (Grand Rapids, MI; Carlisle: W.B. Eerdmans; Paternoster Press, 2005), p. 154.

209 Marshall, The Gospel of Luke (NIGTC), p. 52.

210 Blomberg, Matthew (NAC), p. 81.

211 France, Matthew, p. 101.

me, **because he has anointed me to proclaim good news to the poor…"** (Lk. 4:18). In this event, Jesus focuses on His having been commissioned by the Father from long ago to proclaim the message of salvation.

This is one of the twin purposes expressed in Isaiah 49:6 – salvation and light – **"so I have set you as a light to the nations, to be my salvation to the end of the earth."**[212] This dual purpose – **Salvation:** Jesus' sacrificial death on the cross for the sins of the world (Mk. 8:31; 9:31; 10:33-34; 10:45), and **Light:** proclaiming far and wide this momentous message (Mt. 4:23; 24:14; Lk. 4:43; 8:1; 16:16; Jn. 8:12) – permeates all four Gospels. God the Father, who established this dual purpose and announced it through the prophet Isaiah 700 years in advance of Jesus' earthly ministry, now sends His Son to fulfill and accomplish this mission.

Given John's and Jesus' statements about Jesus, it is clear that Jesus is not only the **"Lamb of God,"** but He is also the **"Lamp of God"**[213] (Mk. 4:21-22). It is the twin purpose of being God's salvation and of proclaiming the good news about it. Broadcasting the good news is the task for which the disciples will join Jesus in His ministry. They will soon be in training to assist Him in that task. Like Jesus' disciples, all who are saved by the cross of Christ join the work of telling the good news of this great salvation.

We saw in the Old Testament how God's provision of salvation and the proclaiming of it are inextricably connected. **In Jesus, these two mandates come together in their full and perfect expression.**

2.   Preparing the Disciples to be a Light to the Nations

From the beginning of Jesus' ministry, He was upfront about His purpose for His followers. In the very first invitation to the first disciples, He is explicit about what they will be doing. "And Jesus said to them, 'Follow me, and I will make you become fishers of men'" (Mk. 1:17). We will see numerous purpose statements like this throughout His time on earth.

---

212 Translation by Mackay, *A Study Commentary on Isaiah* (Vol. 2), pp. 248-249.
213 James R. Edwards, *The Gospel According to Mark* (PNTC) (Grand Rapids, MI; Leicester, England: Eerdmans; Apollos, 2002), p. 139.

Jesus Calling Disciples to Assist in Evangelism

Jesus spent approximately the first 12 to 18 months of His public ministry most-ly in Jerusalem and Judea before moving to the area in and around Galilee.[214] The disciples' first introduction to Jesus occurred right after His baptism (Jn 1:35-42). Later, possibly a few months into His Galilean ministry, He called the first disciples to a greater time commitment in following Him (Mt. 4:18-22; Mk. 1:17). Perhaps in the instance of Mt. 4:18-22 and Mk. 1:17, they became "the Lord's more steady companions."[215] A short time later "they left everything and followed him" (Lk. 5:11).[216] Whereas the gospel accounts give us a condensed summary of it, their going from first introduction to full time following likely occurred over a period of about 18 months.[217]

Often, I have thought that the purpose Jesus has for His people is hiding in plain sight, and this is a good example. In His calling of the first disciples, as noted in Mk. 1:17, there is a clear statement of purpose. The purpose of evangelism is embedded in this call to discipleship. This task is full of hardship and trouble, and Jesus introduces it simultaneously with the call to discipleship. Following Jesus and "fishing for men" are nearly synonymous. He will be more explicit about this purpose later in His ministry.

Jesus Sends Out the Twelve

During the Galilean ministry, Jesus sends the 12 for some on-the-job training. It is an evangelistic training exercise that foreshadows their coming responsibilities (Mt. 10:1-15; Mk. 6:7-13; Lk. 9:1-6). "So they went out and proclaimed that people should repent" (Mk. 6:12). We are only given a summary of the message they proclaimed,[218] but

---

214 Hoehner, *Chronological Aspects of the Life of Christ* (Grand Rapids, MI: Zondervan Publishing House, 1977), pp. 60-61.

215 William Hendriksen, *Exposition of the Gospel According to Matthew* (NTC) (Grand Rapids: Baker Book House, 1973), p. 245-246. Robert L. Thomas, *Charts of the Gospels and the Life of Christ*, pp. 17, 23.

216 Hendriksen, *Luke* (NTC), p. 285. Thomas, *Charts of the Gospels and the Life of Christ*, ,p. 23.

217 The time span estimates in this chapter are approximations and are based mainly on Hoehner, *Chrono-logical Aspects of the Life of Christ*, p. 60 and Hendriksen, *Exposition of the Gospel According to Matthew* (NTC), pp. 245-246. Both estimate a similar span of time. Even though Hendriksen prefers AD 30 (p. 620) as the year of Jesus' death and Hoehner prefers AD 33 (p. 114), they agree on the amount of time which transpired in these events.

218 R. T. France, *The Gospel of Mark: A Commentary on the Greek Text* (NIGTC) (Grand Rapids, MI; Carlisle: W.B. Eerdmans; Paternoster Press, 2002), p. 250.

Jesus is preparing the 12 for their life's work in the kingdom. It is a further illumination of what it means to follow Jesus.

Jesus Sends Out the Seventy-Two

In the later Judean ministry,[219] Jesus sends out a larger group of 72 disciples for an on-the-job training exercise. They are to proclaim the kingdom of God in preparation for Jesus' visit to the surrounding villages (Lk. 10:1-24). There is no reason to think their message is any different than that of Jesus or John the Baptist. It is another training exercise with the practical value of preparing the villages for a visit by Jesus. But like the sending of the 12, it prepares the disciples for their life's work as it illuminates what it means to be a disciple of Jesus.

"The earlier missions of the Twelve (Luke 9:1–6) and the seventy-two (10:1–12) were a [foreshadowing and a] foretaste of the future mission of Jesus' witnesses after the resurrection."[220] **This demonstrates that evangelism is not exclusive to the twelve**, who would later be appointed apostles. **Evangelism is both for leaders and for ordinary followers of Jesus. (It was as true in the first century as it is now in the 21st century.)** Every believer has a role. Evangelism is a corporate (church-wide) responsibility as well as an individual responsibility.

3. The Great Call of Jesus

This event occurs about 6 to 12 months before the cross. At this point Jesus begins to prepare the disciples for the cross. He begins to spend more time with them alone and less time with the large crowds. Crowds still follow Him, but His focus has changed. Jesus and the disciples go to the area of Caesarea Philippi (Mk. 8:27), a predominantly non-Jewish area about 25 miles north of Capernaum, on the north shore of the Sea of Galilee.[221] It was over 100 miles from Jerusalem, the center of Jesus' most powerful enemies. There would be fewer distractions in this location.

It is the first time Jesus teaches the disciples the divine necessity of the cross. But they are not buying into it. "And he began to teach them that the Son of Man

---

219 Thomas, *Charts of the Gospels and the Life of Christ*, p. 18.
220 Robert H. Stein, *Luke*, vol. 24 (NAC) (Nashville: Broadman & Holman Publishers, 1992), p. 621.
221 Edwards, *The Gospel According to Mark* (PNTC), p. 246.

must suffer many things and be rejected by the elders and the chief priests and the scribes and be killed, and after three days rise again" (Mk. 8:31). They are shocked by this statement, and Peter rebukes Jesus (Mk. 8:32). Jesus in turn rebukes Peter for "not setting [his] mind on the things of God but on the things of man" (Mk. 8:33).

Immediately following that exchange, Jesus issues what I have come to think of as *The Great Call of Jesus*. It is an invitation to anyone and everyone who will follow Him. We could also label it *The Great Requirement*. It is not a call to full-time ministry, but a call to salvation. It is relevant not only to those in full-time ministry or to leaders and the highly motivated, but to every believer. It is fundamental to following Jesus and a concise statement of what it means to be a Christian. **It lays out the conditions for anyone and everyone who will be part of His kingdom.** This evangelistic call to salvation is complete with an explanation and warnings. It is a call with the purpose for His people identified. This purpose was also included by Jesus in His call of the first disciples when He said, "Follow me and I will make you become fishers of men" (Mk. 1:17).

In this encounter in Mark 8:34-38, Jesus is evangelizing a small crowd of people and issues an invitation to them.

> *34 And calling the crowd to him with his disciples, he said to them, "If anyone would come after me, let him deny himself and take up his cross and follow me. 35 For whoever would save his life will lose it, but whoever loses his life for my sake and the gospel's will save it. 36 For what does it profit a man to gain the whole world and forfeit his soul? 37 For what can a man give in return for his soul? 38 For whoever is ashamed of me and of my words in this adulterous and sinful generation, of him will the Son of Man also be ashamed when he comes in the glory of his Father with the holy angels."*
>
> *Mk. 8:34-38*

This passage, I fear, has been neglected and not well understood by many in the church. It has not been well taught in the church either. Yet it contains the basic demands of discipleship for every believer. There is a tendency by many to turn Scripture into polite, feel-good stories for adults that can only lead to a superficial happiness. But this passage refuses to cooperate in that endeavor. It is intended to be intrusive and personal and will not yield its sharp edge. It is one of those passages where we must meet Jesus on His terms and not ours.

Let's look at it more closely and break it down into its components. The context begins with Jesus teaching a small group of disciples (8:31-33). It shifts when Jesus turns from them to the crowd that is present. He tells the crowd, "If anyone would come after me, let him deny himself and take up his cross and follow me" (8:34). It is a statement that needs an explanation and receives one from Jesus in verses 35-38. Here are the five phrases of 8:34 that we should master.

First, "And calling the crowd to him with his disciples." This signals a break from the conversation He was having with the smaller band of disciples. Jesus opens His teaching to the wider audience, which would have certainly included non-believers in this predominantly non-Jewish area. This means the context is an evangelization setting.

Second, "he said to them, 'If anyone would come after me.'" The word "anyone" widens the application of this statement to all who are lost and wish to be part of God's kingdom. The "harsh demands"[222] that follow are not merely for the inner circle of Jesus' closest disciples, but are "an essential element in discipleship."[223]

Third, "let him deny himself." This phrase "implies perhaps to refuse to be guided by one's own interests, to surrender control of one's own destiny...What Jesus calls for here is thus a radical abandonment of one's own identity and self-determination, and a call to join the march to the place of execution follows appropriately from this. Such 'self-denial' is on a different level altogether from giving up chocolates for Lent. 'It is not the denial of something to the self, but the denial of the self itself.'"[224] **It is not a call to a life of asceticism but a call to a repurposed life.** It is a life pleasing to God and, as we will see in vv. 35-38, it is about telling the good news of the great salvation available in Jesus.

---

222 France, *The Gospel of Mark*, p. 339.
223 France, *The Gospel of Mark*, p. 339.
224 France, *The Gospel of Mark*, p. 340.

Fourth, "take up his cross." This is a reference to the new purpose of one's life and also to the possibility of actual physical death or, at the very least, physical and/or mental hardship in the act of following Jesus. He is saying, "If you want to be a Christian, you have to be willing to pick up that crossbeam and follow Me."[225] It is not the call to self-sacrifice solely for the purpose of personal holiness. Based on the explanation that follows in vv. 35-38, it is a call to be a witness for the gospel of Jesus Christ. It is also a clear advisory of the potential danger of following Jesus.

Fifth, "and follow me." This speaks of Jesus' sovereign rule over the life of His followers. He is the controlling authority of the believer's life. **He establishes the lifestyle and the purpose.** Jesus is master and Lord of the believer's life.

Immediately following 8:34, Jesus provides specifics of what following Him means. **He makes two statements of explanation, and both come with warnings** (vv. 35, 38). He poses two very personal questions (vv. 36, 37) in between the two statements.

The first statement is, "For whoever would save his life will lose it, but whoever loses his life for my sake and the gospel's will save it" (8:35). It is a paradox that confronts wrong-headed thinking about life. We find salvation ("saving" ourselves) only by losing our self-purpose ("losing" ourselves) in Christ. To "save" ourselves we must first "lose" ourselves. This also is a powerful statement connecting evangelism with the new purpose of those who are being saved – "for my sake **and the gospel's.**" Genuine loyalty to Jesus is accompanied by sharing the good news of His great salvation with others. **Loyalty to Him and sharing the gospel are inextricably connected.**

> *The one for whom the way of Jesus is more important than his own existence will secure his eternal being; but the one whose existence is more important than Jesus will lose both Jesus and his existence.*[226]

Next, He poses two questions: (1) "For what does it profit a man to gain the whole world and forfeit his soul?" and (2) "For what can a man give in return for his soul?"

---

225 R. C. Sproul, *Mark* (St. Andrew's Expositional Commentary) (Orlando, FL: Reformation Trust, 2011), p. 204.
226 Edwards, *The Gospel According to Mark* (PNTC), p. 257.

(8:36-37). These questions are self-evident. They contrast the value of enticing things in this world with something of far greater value – the eternal destination of one's soul. Clinging to and possessing the entire wealth of the world for the span of one's life is basically worthless and leads to spending eternity under the wrath of God. It is a warning that the great things of this world pale in comparison to eternal life in the glorious kingdom of God.

The second statement is a restatement of the first with additional details included. "For whoever is ashamed of me and of my words in this adulterous and sinful generation, of him will the Son of Man also be ashamed when he comes in the glory of his Father with the holy angels" (8:38). The added information is that Jesus will be ashamed of the one who is ashamed of Him and His words when He comes to judge the world. As in the first statement, Jesus connects the gospel ("my words") with loyalty to Him. Any separation of loyalty to Jesus and faithfulness in sharing the gospel is a false dichotomy.

> *When confronted by the call to discipleship, disciples do not have a "both ... and" choice—both Christ and their own lives. They stand before an "either ... or" choice. The claim of Jesus is a total and exclusive one. It does not allow a convenient compartmentalization of natural life and religious life, of secular and sacred. The whole person stands under Christ's claim.*[227]

Being ashamed of Jesus can play out in a wide variety of ways, some subtle and some not so subtle. Some people say they "believe" in Jesus but never darken the door of a church. Some never identify themselves with Jesus to their friends. Some never tell their family and friends of the saving grace of Jesus available to them. Some have friends at work who have no idea they are a Christian. These are just a few of the numerous ways people can be ashamed of Jesus.

To summarize, Jesus' call on our life is a call to a new purpose for living. Jesus' followers will live for His sake and for the sake of the gospel. He warns that if a person

---

227 Edwards, *The Gospel According to Mark* (PNTC), p. 258.

lives only for themself, they will lose their soul forever. Jesus warns that if a person is ashamed of Him and His words (the gospel), He will in turn be ashamed of them when He returns to judge the world. This important message is foundational to salvation, evangelism, and discipleship. If we water it down by removing purpose from calling, we redefine what it means to be saved. Sadly, many pastors, leaders, and church organizations have done just that.

4.   Jesus Uses Parables to Teach Evangelism

There are more than 30 parables recorded in the Gospel accounts that Jesus used in His teachings. "A parable is like a modern political cartoon."[228] "They tend to puzzle as much as enlighten, and are designed to shock and challenge rather than to offer reassuring explanations or illustrations of moral platitudes."[229] Parables approach each listener through the window of the mind's imagination.

Jesus Illustrates His Love for the Lost

Jesus moves closer to the cross and, as seems normal for His ministry, some seemingly despicable sinners are flocking to Him (Lk. 15:1). The "Pharisees and scribes" (Lk. 15:2) complain that Jesus is associating socially and even eating with people like the "tax-collectors [who] were extortioners and traitors."[230] This was totally unacceptable in their eyes. But Jesus challenges and confronts the thinking and the lifestyle of these religious elites with three parables. The parables of the lost sheep, the lost coin, and the lost son bring them (and us) face to face with the importance of God's purpose for His people (Lk. 15). They challenge all of us regarding the desperation associated with the lost and their precarious situation. Jonathan Edwards recognized their danger and said they are held by "a slender thread" over the "great furnace of [God's] wrath".[231] Again Edwards says, "There is nothing that keeps wicked men at any one moment out of hell, but the mere pleasure of God."[232] Jesus must have walked around with a broken heart

---

228 France, *The Gospel of Mark*, p. 183.

229 France, *The Gospel of Mark*, p. 183.

230 Hendriksen, *Luke* (NTC), p. 744.

231 Edwards, *Sinners in the Hands of an Angry God* (Enfield, MA, July 8, 1741), p. 6.

232 Edwards, *Sinners in the Hands of an Angry God*, p. 1.

every day. Make no mistake about it, Jesus and His followers are in a battle against Satan for the lives of the lost.

In the story of the lost sheep, the owner conducts **an intense search** for one lost sheep. When it is found, the owner invites his friends and neighbors to rejoice with him. Jesus ends the story by telling us there is more joy than that in heaven when one sinner repents and turns to Christ (Lk. 15:1-7).

In the story of the lost coin, a woman conducts **an intense search** for one silver coin she has lost. When the coin is found, she invites her friends and neighbors to rejoice with her. Jesus also links this story to the kind of joy in heaven when one sinner repents (Lk. 15:8-10).

And in the story of the lost sons, better known as the "Parable of the Prodigal Son," a rebellious son deeply wounds his father, but when he returns in humble repentance and confession of his sins, the father throws a great celebration which reveals **the intense longing** he had for his son who was lost. The meaning is clear: this same type of celebration occurs in heaven when one sinner repents and turns to Christ (Lk. 15:11-32).

In the first two parables, there is an intense search for that which is lost. In the story of the prodigal, there is an intense longing for the rebellious son who is lost. All three end in celebration over what was lost but was eventually found. Heaven rejoices when one sinner turns to Christ. It is a big deal.

We see several of God's attributes in these three parables, including love, mercy, grace, and goodness. But we especially see that God is a seeking-out-the-lost kind of God. One divine attribute prominently on display is not only that He longs for sinners to turn to Him, but that He actively seeks them out. God takes the initiative. **He is a God who is actively, intentionally, and intensely seeking out sinners.** If we are made in His image and if we are redeemed by Christ and called to follow Him, we too will take the initiative. Jesus challenges our thinking and our lifestyles with these three parables.

Real Life Seeking of a Lost Sheep

As Jesus approaches Jerusalem through Jericho, on His way to the cross, He encounters Zacchaeus. Jesus tells us this is a divine appointment when he says, "Zacchaeus, hurry and come down, for I **must** stay at your house today" (Lk. 19:5). "The 'must' (*dei*) implies a divine necessity to do so."[233] This is similar to the divine necessity that Jesus "had to pass through Samaria" (Jn. 4:4) to meet with the lost woman at the well, where the same Greek word is used.

Zacchaeus is a corrupt tax collector working under the authority of the Roman government. He is a "chief tax collector" (Lk. 19:2) with other tax collectors working for him. He is rich, as many such collectors extorted more taxes than the legally required amount, thus enriching themselves in the process. They were hated and despised by everyone and "were regarded as traitors and crooks."[234]

Jesus takes the initiative "by inviting himself to the house of Zacchaeus."[235] Many people grumbled about Jesus' associating Himself with this terrible sinner, but Jesus seems to glory in it. Zacchaeus is a changed man at hearing the gospel and displays genuine repentance. The language used in the text ("Today salvation has come to this house...", Lk. 19:9) likely indicates many in the household were saved. It reminds us of the account of Lydia and her household being saved in Acts 16:14-15 and the Philippian jailer and his household in Acts 16:31-33. Luke concludes the story with this purpose statement by Jesus – **"For the Son of Man came to seek and to save the lost"** (Lk. 19:10). This assertion is reminiscent of His earlier statement when calling some of the disciples, "Follow me, and I will make you become fishers of men" (Mk. 1:17). Jesus is modeling what "fishing for men" looks like. And He expects His followers to do the same. As we will see in the next sections, Jesus also tells us what it means to "sow" the gospel and to be a "lamp."

Jesus Illuminates Evangelism with Parables

The parables of Mark 4 strongly imply God's purpose for His people. These parables are included in Mark to explain why some are accepting the message of Jesus and why

---

233 Stein, *Luke* (NAC), p. 467.

234 William Hendriksen, *Exposition of the Gospel According to Luke* (NTC) (Grand Rapids: Baker Book House, 1978), p. 855.

235 Marshall, The Gospel of Luke (NIGTC), p. 694.

others are rejecting it even in the face of Jesus' miraculous actions.[236] This is necessary preparation for the disciples' life work. They will need to understand the dynamics involved in telling the good news.

These parables reveal how the kingdom of God expands. They show that the kingdom grows through sowing and giving light. And the purpose of parables is revealed: parables enlighten those with receptive hearts, and they harden those with hearts of obstinate resistance to Jesus. For those with hardened resistance, parables can drive them deeper into darkness (Mk. 4:10-11; Isa 6:9-10).

Parables in general are loaded with "elements of paradox and of challenge."[237] Properly understood, they are a confrontation of our thinking and our lifestyles, "constantly upsetting [our] fundamental assumptions and demanding a program of re-education."[238] There are several key teachings and applications that can be drawn from these parables. One important application is that the five parables in this section challenge our thinking about the purpose of the church. If the kingdom of God grows through sowing – why are most churches sitting on their hands and letting their fields lie fallow?

The following five parables have a common thread and help to illuminate each other. These parables serve an important role in preparing believers for the work of evangelism. Here is a brief summary of each:

1. The parable of the sower (Mk. 4:1-20) demonstrates **there is seed (the gospel) to be sown and good soil will bear the fruit of the kingdom.** The seed sown will elicit responses that range from rejection to full acceptance. This parable is saying, "Disciples, be prepared for difficulties and poor responses, but the seed must be sown. It will achieve God's desired result."

2. The parable of the lamp (Mk. 4:21-22) shows that **the message of the kingdom is to be revealed.** It is not to be hidden. The lamp is to be placed on a lampstand because "lamps are meant to give as much light as possible."[239]

236 France, *The Gospel of Mark*, p. 182.
237 France, *The Gospel of Mark*, p. 184.
238 France, *The Gospel of Mark*, p. 184.
239 France, *The Gospel of Mark*, p. 208.

In this parable, "the lamp" is a metaphor for Jesus.[240] "Jesus is the **lamp of God** who has come to bring light and revelation (John 1:5; 8:12)"[241] (Emphasis mine). Jesus said John the Baptist "was a burning and shining lamp" (Jn. 5:35). John was a faithful proclaimer of the gospel message. And recall Isaiah quoting God the Father commissioning Messiah and saying, "I will give you as a light to the nations, that my salvation may reach to the end of the earth" (Isaiah 49:6). **Disciples are to shine the story of Jesus with life and words**

3. The parable of the measure (Mk. 4:24-25) is **an exhortation to listen very carefully** because much is at stake. How a person listens – with humility, contrition, open mindedness, etc. – will determine what is revealed to them or not revealed to them. If a person brings a hard, skeptical heart to Jesus, they may receive an in-kind response and even what knowledge they have of God may be taken away. There is a "principle of reciprocity" and proportionality at work.[242]

4. The parable of the seed (Mk. 4:26-29) shows the purpose of God's kingdom is that **the seed (the gospel) be scattered.** God will see that it produces a harvest.

5. In the parable of the mustard seed (Mk. 4:30-32), we learn that the kingdom of God, **which is spread through the sowing of a little seed,** appears at times to be quite insignificant, but will in fact surpass in significance all of the great things of the world. The tiny mustard seed of the gospel will produce something of greater significance than that which is produced by all of the billionaires the world over. Disciples must not be deceived into thinking the things of this world are more important than the purpose of God, nor must they think that their contribution in sharing the gospel with another, small as it may be, will not amount to much.

---

240 According to James R. Edwards, Mark 4:21 should be translated, "Does the lamp come in order that it might be placed under the bowl or under the bed?" The lamp is the subject, and the verb is come. Mark "refers to the lamp using the definite article 'the.'" The "reference to the lamp coming (Gk. *erchetai*) is more suitable of a person than an object." Edwards, *The Gospel According to Mark* (PNTC), p. 139.

241 Edwards, *The Gospel According to Mark* (PNTC), p. 139.

242 France, *The Gospel of Mark*, pp. 210-211.

The implication is that **God's people are the means He will use to "scatter" the seed of the kingdom.** The kingdom of God grows not by political power nor by the power of military conquest, but by a seemingly insignificant little seed. No seed that a Christian sows is too inconsequential. We are to sow the seed and let God take care of the rest. The gospel is sown by His servants in love and in weakness as compared to the grand powers of the world. Many will reject this good news, and believers should prepare themselves for that. But some will accept it and be saved from the wrath of God. That is how God has chosen to expand His kingdom.

What Can We Learn About Evangelism from the Gospels?

First, when we pull all these episodes, events, and parables together, they form a compelling image. Jesus was given the special assignment to proclaim the same good news John the Baptist proclaimed. The kingdom of God was compared to sowing, and we examined Jesus' sending the 12 disciples and the larger group of 72 disciples through a training exercise of sowing the seeds of the gospel in the surrounding villages. The parables of the lost sheep, coin, and son, along with the encounter with Zacchaeus, illustrate the divine compulsion Jesus was under from the Father "to seek and to save the lost" (Lk. 19:10). Jesus' great call in Mark 8:34-38 makes clear that those who are saved become part of the same "divine necessity" Jesus was under to speak this good news.

Second, when you think you are saved, but do not have any heart for the lost, do you really understand the gospel? Has it really taken root? When a person experiences a conversion, they become a new creation in Christ. They begin to align their thinking with God's way of thinking. They begin to reflect God's attributes and to reflect His character in their lifestyle. They begin to act in a Christ-like manner. God's character includes great compassion for the lost. Just ask Jonah.

Third, Christ's supernatural pursuit of sinners is the ultimate reason evangelism succeeds. There is a great poem by Francis Thompson, "The Hound of Heaven,"[243] which paints a striking image of Christ pursuing lost sinners. John Stott, in his book *Why I Am a Christian*, enumerates several reasons for his coming to faith. But he states that the "most significant factor" "is due ultimately neither to the influence of my

---

243 Francis Thompson, "The Hound of Heaven," 1890.

parents and teachers, nor to my own personal decision for Christ, but to 'the Hound of Heaven'. That is, it is due to Jesus Christ himself, who pursued me relentlessly even when I was running away from him in order to go my own way. And if it were not for the gracious pursuit of the Hound of Heaven I would today be on the scrapheap of wasted and discarded lives."[244]

244 John Stott, *Why I Am a Christian* (Downers Grove, IL: InterVarsity Press, 2003), pp. 14-15.

CHAPTER 9

JESUS MODELS EVANGELISM

I am the bread of life; whoever comes to me shall not hunger, and whoever believes in me shall never thirst.

John 6:35

Jesus was an amazing evangelist. But surprisingly, His preaching seems to have turned more people away from Him than were drawn to Him. Why was that the case? The parables of Mark 4 give us part of the answer. But He also valued telling people the truth as opposed to telling them what they wanted to hear.

In this chapter we will survey examples of Jesus' evangelizing. We will examine the content of Jesus' gospel and how He engaged the lost with it. In John 3-10, there are eight different evangelistic encounters Jesus engages in. They are: (1) Nicodemus in Jerusalem (3:1-21), (2) a woman in Sychar of Samaria (4:1-42), (3) the Jews in Jerusalem (5:1-47), (4) at the synagogue in Capernaum (6:22-71), (5) large crowds in Jerusalem (7:1-8:59), (6) a man born blind in Jerusalem (9:1-41), (7) the Jews who witnessed the healing of the man born blind (9:1-10:21), and (8) the Jews at the Feast of Dedication (10:22-39).

Some of those encounters will reveal a significant amount of detail about Jesus' view of the gospel. Collectively, they will reveal how Jesus employed a different manner in different settings but communicated the same gospel message in every setting.

Jesus displays genuine love for the lost in His evangelism encounters. He tells people the truth even when it results in opposition. **In all but one case, Jesus exposed the lostness of the people He encountered, confronted their sins, and encouraged them to trust in Him.** The one exception is the man born blind, in which case we are not given many details. What follows is an examination of these encounters.

Jesus Evangelizes a Religious Leader (Jn. 3:1-21)

Early in Jesus' public ministry, after His baptism by John, a Pharisee seeks out Jesus. Nicodemus is one of about 6,000 Pharisees[245] and one of 71 members of the Sanhedrin,[246] which was the "highest judicial body in the land"[247] under Roman authority. He is an elite of the elite, a member of the Jewish ruling class. He comes to Jesus at night to make an inquiry of Him and says, "Rabbi, we know that you are a teacher come from God, for no one can do these signs that you do unless God is with him" (Jn. 3:2). Nicodemus must have felt good about how he phrased his respectful approach to Jesus, but Jesus turns Nicodemus upside down theologically speaking. Jesus basically responds by telling Nicodemus that he is lost and doesn't really know anything. He tells Nicodemus that if he desires to "see" (3:3) and "enter" (3:5) the kingdom of God, he will need to be born a second time. There is no other way to enter God's kingdom. Jesus is in effect saying to Nicodemus that his legalistic "ruler of the Jews" heart will not be enough to save him. Jesus is conveying to Nicodemus that his great learning and rigorous keeping of the law will never gain him entrance into Heaven. This leaves Nicodemus astonished and surprised.

Jesus' priority with Nicodemus is Nicodemus' eternal destination, so he goes straight after Nicodemus' chief problem, his heart. Nicodemus has the intellect and education to comprehend Jesus, but not the heart because his heart is blinded by his own sin. He has followed all the religious rituals of the Jewish people. He has obeyed the law and studied the word of God, but that is not enough. He needs a new heart, and a new heart only comes as a miraculous act of God. Jesus said to him, "Do not marvel that I said to you, 'You must be born again'" (Jn. 3:7). The "you"[248] is plural which means Jesus is saying that not just Nicodemus but the Jewish people in general need to be born again. Further in the conversation Jesus tells him, "As Moses lifted up the serpent in the wilderness, so must the Son of Man be lifted up, that whoever believes in him may have eternal life" (Jn. 3:14-15; see also Nu. 21:4-9). Jesus then speaks what may be the most famous verse in all of the Bible: "For God so loved the world, that he gave

---

245 Carson, *The Gospel According to John*, p. 145.
246 Carson, *The Gospel According to John*, p. 420.
247 Carson, *The Gospel According to John*, p. 420.
248 ESV footnote 4, Jn. 3:7 – "The Greek for *you* is plural here".

his only Son, that whoever believes in him should not perish but have eternal life" (Jn. 3:16). Jesus isn't trying to build a social justice coalition to deal with the issues of the day. He is doing personal evangelism with a lost man who will spend eternity in hell if he does not trust in Jesus.

Nicodemus' blindness is religious. He is a highly respectable sinner on his way to hell and powerless to save himself. But Jesus is lovingly intervening by telling him the truth. Although Nicodemus seems perplexed, he does not appear to be angry. Later in the Gospel of John, Nicodemus is found with Joseph of Arimathea burying the body of Jesus after the crucifixion. We cannot determine with total certainty if Nicodemus was saved or not, but this strongly suggests he did come to understand and believe.

Jesus Evangelizes a Godless Woman (4:1-43)

After Jesus spent the first months, and possibly more than a year,[249] of his public ministry mostly in Jerusalem and Judea, he departed for Galilee. The text "And he had to pass through Samaria" suggests a divine appointment in this region. As He is passing through Samaria, He pauses to rest outside of a town named Sychar (4:5, 28). He sends His disciples into the town. While resting at the well, He engages a woman in conversation who has come to draw water and He directs the conversation to Himself in the context of eternal life (4:14) and salvation (4:22). As their exchange progresses, she becomes more and more intrigued with who this man can possibly be. She is especially intrigued after He exposes her ungodly and sinful lifestyle by saying to her: "You are right in saying, 'I have no husband'; for you have had five husbands, and the one you now have is not your husband. What you have said is true" (4:17-18). Jesus does this gently and without condemnation, but He unmasks her less than forthright answer and brings her face to face with her sin.[250]

The woman may have been taken aback by this statement. That is probably why she redirected the conversation. However, she may had begun to suspect Jesus was Messiah and was inviting him to tell her more. Regardless of her intent, she was happy to talk

---

249 Hoehner, *Chronological Aspects of the Life of Christ,* pp. 60-61.

250 Carson, *The Gospel According to John,* p. 221.

about anything other than their own sin, and she was happy to talk about Messiah. It was a more interesting subject to her. She said to Him: "I know that Messiah is coming (he who is called Christ). When he comes, he will tell us all things" (4:25). At this point Jesus made a rare verbal acknowledgement that He was indeed Messiah. "Jesus said to her, 'I who speak to you am he'" (4:26).

In the middle of the conversation, the disciples return and interrupt. The woman leaves her water jar at the well and goes back into town to tell people about her encounter with someone she has come to suspect is Messiah. The disciples are wondering why Jesus has been talking with a Samaritan woman. This was against the social norms of the Jews. It was especially unusual for a woman to have a theological discussion with a rabbi.

In this interlude, before the woman and townspeople come out to the well, the disciples urge Jesus to eat. He responds with, "I have food to eat that you do not know about" (4:32). They are confused and wonder where He found something to eat. He clarifies, "My food is to do the will of him who sent me and to accomplish his work" (4:34). He then points them to the harvest that is His work and is also their work. "For here the saying holds true, 'One sows and another reaps.' I sent you to reap that for which you did not labor. Others have labored, and you have entered into their labor" (4:37-38). This is **a significant disclosure of purpose as Jesus once again incorporates the disciples into this purpose of sowing and reaping.**

According to Jesus, He had "food" that fueled His life. That "food" was to do the will of God, and that will was prophesied by Isaiah: "I will make you as a light for the nations, that you may be my salvation to the end of the earth" (Isa. 49:6).[251] Jesus is conveying to His disciples the purpose of being a "light for the nations," which is evangelistic sowing and reaping: "you have entered into their labor" (4:38). They are "in" that labor whether or not they fully understand it at this point. It is to become their "food" too. Years later, the Apostle Paul will use that verse in Isaiah as his purpose in taking the gospel to the Gentiles (Acts 13:47). But on this occasion these young Jewish men are way out of their social comfort zone in evangelizing Samaritans.

---

251 Translation by Alec Motyer in Motyer, *The Prophecy of Isaiah,* p.388-389.

After the interlude the story continues: "So when the Samaritans came to him, they asked him to stay with them, and he stayed there two days. And many more believed because of his word" (4:40-41). Sometime during His two-day stay, the people of the town said to the woman, "It is no longer because of what you said that we believe, for we have heard for ourselves, and we know that this is indeed the Savior of the world" (4:42). It is a surprising harvest of souls.

The Samaritan woman's source of spiritual blindness is immorality, but even though she initially tried to hide her sin, she did not run away from it. Jesus' revealing of her sin did not harden her. She is unlike most Pharisees, who run away from their sin, as will be seen in Jesus' next evangelistic encounter. When they deny their sin, it only makes their hearts grow more hardened.

This account of the Samaritan woman at the well is an "evangelism sandwich" with an explicit purpose statement in the middle. Jesus speaks about His purpose and the purpose for His disciples during a pause in the evangelism discussion. The pause gives Him an opportunity to teach the disciples that this is their purpose, too. The embedded purpose statement (4:37-38) gives us greater understanding of how it all fits together. **Jesus is fulfilling His purpose as given by the Father, and in so doing, is modeling evangelism for all believers who will follow Him.**

Jesus Evangelizes Blind and Deaf Religious Leaders (5:1-47)

From Sychar, Jesus travels to Galilee (Jn. 4:43-45) and spends an unknown amount of time there before going back to Jerusalem to attend the unnamed feast mentioned in John 5:1. In this episode, we are given a significant amount of detail about the gospel message Jesus speaks.

In Jerusalem, as Jesus walked by the pool named Bethesda, He saw an invalid lying there. The man had been an invalid for 38 years (5:5). Jesus asked him, "Do you want to be healed?" (5:6). The man believed in the superstition that the pool had magical powers of healing at certain moments in time and responded that he could not get there fast enough to be healed (5:7). "Jesus said to him, 'Get up, take up your bed, and walk'" (5:8). The man immediately picked up his bed and walked. But there was a problem. It was the Sabbath, and the Jews did not take kindly to anyone violating their list of prohibitions regarding the Sabbath. Their list went far beyond anything

Scripture required.[252] The man violated one of their rules by carrying his bed, and Jesus violated one of their rules by performing an act of mercy for this man. Jesus was not violating the Sabbath. He was violating the Pharisees' rules, which were based on an unjust and improper interpretation of Scripture which resulted in an oppressive exercise of authority.

When the Jews learned it was Jesus who healed the man and told him to take up his bed, they were angry at Jesus. "But Jesus answered them, 'My Father is working until now, and I am working'" (Jn. 5:17). This made them even angrier and they "were seeking all the more to kill him because not only was he breaking the Sabbath, but he was even calling God his own Father, making himself equal with God" (Jn. 5:18). But Jesus was not breaking God's rules for the Sabbath. He was breaking the Jews' man-made harsh impositions for the Sabbath. God had never prohibited acts of mercy on the Sabbath, but the Jewish leadership did. They had added their words and their rules to God's word. Jesus responds by proclaiming the gospel to them, the good news that salvation is found only in Him. Here again Jesus is not only the salvation the world needs, but he is also "a light for the nations" (Isa. 49:6). Being a light does not imply that all one needs to do in evangelism is to live a good life for all to see. Living a good life is important, but sharing the message of God's great salvation in Christ is the meaning of being a light. In this situation Jesus acts as a light by speaking His message of salvation as He normally did.

In this particular evangelistic encounter, **Jesus includes several elements of the gospel**. Here are some highlights.

First, Jesus is God. He speaks to the Jewish leaders about God the Father and God the Son, implying they partake of the same divine essence (5:19-23). Both He and the Father have the ability to create life (5:21). Jesus knows the Father (5:19, 20), but they do not know the Father (5:37-38). The Father has given Him "authority to execute judgment" (5:22, 27). Jesus gives eternal life to those who believe in Him (5:24); the Scriptures do not give eternal life – they point to the One who does (5:39-40). And

---

252 "The assumption in the Scripture seems to be that 'work' refers to one's customary employment; but judging by Mishnah (*Shabbath* 7:2; 10:5), dominant rabbinic opinion had analysed the prohibition into thirty-nine classes of work, including taking or carrying anything from one domain to another (except for cases of compassion, such as carrying a paralytic)." Carson, *The Gospel According to John* (PNTC), p. 244. For more details on the 39 regulations see: https://www.ou.org/holidays/the_thirty_nine_categories_of_sabbath_work_prohibited_by_law/, accessed April 21, 2022.

He will raise everyone from the dead – the good to a resurrection of life and the bad to a resurrection of judgment (5:28-29). There is no mistaking who Jesus claims to be.

Second, Jesus names their sin. More than a dozen times He names specific sins of His audience. The Jewish leaders disrespect Jesus (5:23). They are deaf to God (5:37). They are blind to God (5:37). The truth of God's word is not the driving force of their lives (5:38). They reject God's Son who is standing right in front of them (5:38). They created their own way of salvation – studying the Scriptures[253] and perverting the true way of salvation (5:39, 46-47). They refuse to repent of their sin and come to Jesus for salvation (5:40). They do not love God (5:42). They refuse to come to Jesus, who came from the Father (5:43). They are more interested in pleasing men than in pleasing God (5:44). They pervert Moses' writings (5:46) and because they distort Moses, they are blind to Jesus (5:47). Their blindness is religious. They think they are righteous before God because they are serious students of the Scriptures, but nothing could be further from the truth. If they continue to cling to their idol – of studying God's word to achieve salvation – their idol will carry them to an eternity under the wrath of God.

Third, Jesus warns of judgment. He reveals to the Jews that the Father has given all judgment to Him (5:22) and that whoever honors the Son and believes in Him has eternal life and "does not come into judgment, but has passed from death to life" (5:24). The Father has placed into the hands of Jesus all judgment, and He will judge those who have done good and those who have done evil (5:22, 27-29). He is the only one they should fear.

Fourth, Jesus encourages faith in Himself. He says to them, "Truly, truly, I say to you, whoever hears my word and believes him who sent me has eternal life" (5:24). He speaks of eternal life as a present possession for those who believe. Jesus said to them that both He and John the Baptist gave testimony to who He is, **"so that you may be saved"** (5:34). Salvation is the purpose of Jesus' dialogue with them, and yet they refuse to repent of their sins and place their trust in Him. They love the glory that comes from

---

253 The Pharisees studied the Scriptures because they saw that as the way to achieve eternal life. "They spent their time 'diligently study[ing]' the Scriptures *(eraunāte tas graphas)* because the major focus of the rabbis' work was the study of the Torah. It was regarded by them as the dearest part of this life **and their means to the assurance of life in the world to come** *(m. 'Abot* 2:7–8)." (emphasis mine) Gerald L. Borchert, *John 1–11* (NAC) (Nashville: Broadman & Holman Publishers, 1996), p. 246.

man and not the glory that comes from God (5:44). Their sin blinds their eyes and blocks their ability to come to the real source of life. They remain dead in their sins and "the wrath of God remains on" them (Jn. 3:36).

There are many important themes Jesus could have taken up with the Jewish leaders other than their eternal destination. He could have engaged them in a discussion about the many injustices in their society, economic inequality, racial prejudice, corruption in government, etc., but He chose to address the forever destination of their souls and the forever destination of their resurrected bodies. They will be resurrected and receive a body for eternity (Jn. 5: 28-29; 1 Cor. 15). The central question for them is, will they receive beautiful, glorified bodies that live forever in heaven? Or will they receive bodies that forever decay in eternal torment and "be an abhorrence to all flesh" for all of eternity (Isa. 66:24)? That is what is at stake, and Jesus tries to focus them on what matters most.

Jesus Evangelizes an Idolatrous Crowd (6:22-71)

A few months after the encounter described in John 5, back in Galilee, we come to three exodus-linked stories: (a) feeding the five thousand (Jn. 6:1-15), (b) Jesus' walking on water (Jn. 6:16-21), and (c) the "I am the bread of life" dialogue with the Jews (Jn. 6:22-71). These accounts are linked together textually, thematically, and by timeframe.[254] The three stories have strong ties not only to each other but also to the exodus events (Ex. 1-17; Jn. 6:3, 4, 19-20, 31-32, 35). They form a triadic unit that provides mutual illumination and deepens our comprehension.

The three events occur over two consecutive days and around the time of the Passover (Jn. 6:4). It is about one year before Jesus will die on the cross.[255] Taken together the events clearly evoke images of the exodus, with its massive miraculous feeding with manna from heaven and its water miracle of crossing the Red Sea. Jesus uses the Jews' statement that God gave their fathers in the wilderness "bread from heaven to eat" (Jn. 6:31) and employs that miracle to reveal who He is. **He evangelizes this crowd using the Book of Exodus.**

---

254 Borchert, *John 1–11* (NAC), p. 260.
255 Hoehner, *Chronological Aspects of the Life of Christ,* p. 61.

The first of these events, the feeding of the five thousand, takes place on the eastern side of the Sea of Galilee in a wilderness area (Jn. 6:3). Then, overnight Jesus walks on the Sea of Galilee and joins the disciples in their boat. The next day's scene is Capernaum on the northwestern shore (Jn. 6:24). All of the debate of Jn. 6:22-59 seems to occur in the synagogue at Capernaum (6:59).

These events are included here because they show Jesus' modeling evangelism. What He says is instructive. There are numerous teachings in this section, but we will limit the discussion to a review of Jesus' wielding the gospel to lost and idolatrous people. He did not coddle them. He spoke straight at their hard, idolatrous hearts.

The feeding of the five thousand must have had a significant impact on the crowd when they realized what Jesus had done. But the crowd completely misinterprets its meaning. John tells us the crowd was "about to come and take him by force to make him king" (Jn. 6.15). This is no different than Satan tempting Jesus in the wilderness of Mt. 4:1-11. In that meeting Satan's third temptation is to make Jesus king in his own diabolical way: "Again, the devil took him to a very high mountain and showed him all the kingdoms of the world and their glory. And he said to him, 'All these I will give you, if you will fall down and worship me'" (Mt. 4:8-9). Jesus rebuked Satan and told him to "begone." It is like Peter trying to stop Jesus from going to the cross as recorded in Mark 8:31-33. Jesus rebuked Peter (and Satan by name) on that occasion too as He said to Peter, "Get behind me, Satan!" (Mk. 8:33). Jesus would have no part of being made king by Satan or by Peter or by the Jews in Galilee. Mark tells us, "Immediately [after feeding the five thousand] he made his disciples get into the boat and go before him to the other side" (Mk. 6:45). Jesus had to rush the disciples away from the scene so that they would not get caught up in the destructive desires of the crowd.

The chief problem of the Jews in Galilee is that they approach Jesus through the lens of their own idolatry. They see Jesus, not as the Savior who will rescue them from their sins, but as the person who can use His power to make life better for them. He can heal all their diseases, feed thousands, walk on water, raise the dead, and, with that kind of power, He can surely overthrow the overbearing Roman government. But these are self-centered aspirations that view life in a purely human way and not according to God's purpose. Michael Horton, writing about many in the church today, says that we are just like them: "Like his [Jesus'] contemporaries, we want a Messiah we can use: someone who will make all of our dreams come true, here and now, and make his kingdom visible in power and glory in our world."[256]

The bread of life discourse occurs against this background. Jesus greets the Jews who travel from the feeding of the five thousand to find Him in Capernaum not by welcoming them and congratulating them for being so diligent to track Him down, but by confronting their sin. He rebukes them for seeking Him for their own selfish purpose. "Truly, truly, I say to you, you are seeking me, not because you saw signs, but because you ate your fill of the loaves" (Jn. 6:26). "The meaning of 'sign' in this Gospel is that it points beyond the physical, concrete reality to the reality of revelation. It provides insight into who Jesus is."[257] And Jesus chastises them, "Do not work for the food that perishes, but for the food that endures to eternal life, which the Son of Man will give to you" (Jn. 6:27). They are seeking Him with sinful motivations and wrong expectations. Jesus names their sin, exposes it for what it is, and rebukes them for it.

They have invented their own Jesus with misplaced expectations and hopes of what He will do for them. In their minds, they see a Messiah who will bring happiness, prosperity, business success, political power, overthrow of the Roman occupiers, and healing of every disease. Their expectations are similar to those of people today who are pulled into the destructive false teachings of the health-and-wealth prosperity gospel. The so-called prosperity gospel is in fact no gospel at all.[258]

This encounter reveals what happens when people approach Jesus with hearts filled with their own sin and idolatry and expect Jesus to magnify their idols for their personal enjoyment. Jesus urges them to turn away from the "food that perishes" (6:27), their idols, sin, and self-purpose, and turn to Him who is "the food that endures to eternal life" (6:27). Initially Jesus answers their questions with a mix of figurative and non-figurative language (6:28-40). But they "grumble" about Him for two reasons. First, because He is exposing their sin. And second, because they do not believe he has "come down from heaven" (6:41-42). They view Jesus through the lens of their idols

---

256 Michael Horton, *The Gospel-Driven Life* (Grand Rapids, MI: BakerBooks, 2009), pp. 256-257, Kindle. Horton's statement is not specifically in the context of John 6, but in the broader context of Jesus' contemporaries.

257 Borchert, *John 1–11* (NAC), p. 262.

258 For a useful article on the prosperity gospel see Erik Raymond, *The Soft Prosperity Gospel,* https://www.ligonier.org/learn/articles/soft-prosperity-gospel, March 25, 2016, accessed June 22, 2022.

and make Messiah in their own image. In the process they reject Jesus as God and in turn are rejecting the Father.

The longer the dialogue progresses, the more hostile the Jews become toward Jesus. As they become more hostile, Jesus becomes more metaphorical in His response to them.

In John 6:52-59, as questions turn to resistance and resistance turns to hostility, the eyes of these hearers become increasingly opaque as if filled with cataracts. To borrow a phrase from Solzhenitsyn, they "carried within themselves the poison of their imagined superiority."[259] We could rephrase it for this context and say, "They carried within themselves the poison of their self-serving purpose and the poison of their delusional self-righteousness." This type of poison produces spiritual blindness and death. **They fail to see that their greatest need is for a Messiah who will save them from their sins. They want a Messiah who will make all their dreams come true.**

At this point in the dialogue (6:52-59), Jesus transitions to difficult metaphors. His words have the effect of hardening their hearts even further. They are bringing a "measure" (Mk. 4:24) to God that is filled to the brim with their various idols. As they cling to them tenaciously, they are blinded and further hardened by the word of God. The prophet Isaiah predicted this kind of response to the word of God in Isa. 6:9-10, which Jesus affirms by citing it in Mark 4:11-12. Later in this Gospel there is an allusion to it (Jn. 9:39-41) and a citation of it (Jn. 12:40; see also Mt. 13:14; Lk 8:10; Acts 28:26-27; Rom. 11:8).

This example of Jesus evangelizing idolatrous people is painful to watch. His purpose is not to build His own popularity, but to bring glory to the Father. He exhibits a tremendous love for His listeners by telling them the truth. He tells them the truth about their sin and wrong motivations and points to Himself as the Father's divine Son of Man who gives eternal life to those who believe in Him (Jn. 6:27). Superficial faith withers under the glare of the word of God. The source of blindness in this case is idolatrous religion and idolatrous nationalism. These two are a bad mix.

Once again, Jesus valued telling people the truth more than He valued results. Over these two days Jesus had magnificent successes, starting with the feeding of 5,000 people. The crowd was so wowed at this they wanted to make Him King. He would have

---

259 Aleksandr Solzhenitsyn, *In the First Circle* (New York: HarperCollins Publishers, 2009), p. 373. This is a work of fiction.

no part of it. After praying into the night, Jesus walked on water in the middle of a storm to join the disciples in their boat as they were struggling against the storm. Peter even had the privilege of walking on the water to Jesus, but not without faltering. The storm calmed down after Jesus got into the boat. But the next day when Jesus finished speaking the gospel message to the crowd that had followed, the crowd was angry at Him and "many of his disciples turned back and no longer walked with him" (Jn. 6:66).

So, how can that be a model for evangelism?

At a fundamental level, it illustrates that Jesus prioritized speaking the whole gospel truth over and above gaining popularity or adding people indiscriminately to the rolls of the church. He saw gospel integrity as more important than creating superficial and delusional faith and more important than drawing large crowds.

Michael Horton, in his book *Christless Christianity*, makes the following observation about challenges faced by the church in North America:

> *The challenge before us as Christian witnesses is whether we will offer Jesus Christ as the key to fulfilling our narcissistic preoccupation or as the Redeemer who liberates us from its guilt and power. Does Christ come to boost our ego or to crucify our ego and raise us up as new creatures with our identity in him?...By the way, I do not think this means that we simply write off the desire for fulfillment and happiness. The gospel neither meets our narcissistic goals nor denies the truth of which they are a perversion. People were created for meaning, purpose, joy, and fulfillment...Only when God's law – his holiness, majesty, and moral will – creates in us a sense of our moral offensiveness to God does the gospel communicate deeper answers that our felt needs and cheap cravings only mask.*[260]

---

260 Michael Horton, *Christless Christianity: The Alternative Gospel of the American Church* (Grand Rapids, MI: BakerBooks, 2008), pp. 33-34, Kindle.

Jesus Evangelizes Jerusalem (7:1-10:39)

This next passage of Scripture, spans from about September to December of the year before the cross. Jesus' death will occur the following April. The time of Jesus' public ministry is growing short. All of this takes place in Jerusalem, the stronghold of Jesus' enemies. The tension and hostility to Jesus is rising. His closest disciples are most likely nervous and not comfortable with the threat to their personal safety.

We will look at **four separate occasions of evangelism** in this section: (1) the Feast of Booths in September/October (7:1-8:59), (2) healing of the man born blind (9:1-41), (3) the Jews' observing that healing (9:1-10:21), and (4) the Feast of Dedication in December (10:22-39).[261]

The first of these evangelistic encounters is Jesus' evangelizing the crowds in Jerusalem who were there to celebrate the Feast of Booths.[262] Water and light were important symbols used during this joyous celebration that lasted for a week. "On this feast see Lev. 23:33–44 and Numbers 29…besides being a harvest-festival it was also a joyful commemoration of the divine guidance granted to the forefathers in their wilderness-journey."[263] "On the first night of Tabernacles and apparently on each night of the feast except on Sabbath, the worshipers awaited the signal of the special lighting of the festive golden lamps of Tabernacles in the court of women. The lamps were intended to remind worshipers of God's leading the people of Israel through the wilderness at night by a pillar of fire. The lighting of lamps also signaled Israel's recommitment to the God of light…(m. Sukk. 5:1–4)."[264]

Jesus traveled from Galilee to Jerusalem for this celebration. "About the middle of the feast Jesus went up into the temple and began to teach" (7:14). As the Jews "marveled" (7:15) about Him, Jesus engaged them in a dialogue that apparently continued over several days and ended on the last day of the feast (7:16-8:59, also note 7:37).

Over the course of this dialogue, Jesus repeatedly asserts three truths: who He is, who they are, and what they must do. He insists upon His identity as equal to the Father.

---

261 Feast dates are from Elwell, "Feasts and Festivals of Israel," *Baker Encyclopedia of the Bible*, p. 783.

262 Feast of Booths is also referred to as the Feast of Tabernacles, Succoth, or Ingathering. Elwell, "Feasts and Festivals of Israel," *Baker Encyclopedia of the Bible*, p. 783, 787.

263 William Hendriksen, *Exposition of the Gospel According to John,* vol. 2 (NAC) (Grand Rapids: Baker Book House, 1953), p. 4.

264 Borchert, *John 1–11* (NAC), pp. 295–296.

He insists upon their sinful condition and names their sins repeatedly so that they will (hopefully) come to understand their lost condition. That is who they are – lost and in the death grip of sin. He urges them to believe in Him as their only hope of salvation. Jesus interweaves these fundamentals of the gospel multiple times throughout the dialogue. He does not get distracted by other issues because this is the most pressing need in their lives. We will take each of the truths Jesus asserted in turn.

Jesus asserts His identity as equal with the Father. "My teaching is not mine, but his who sent me" (7:16). Again, He states, "He who sent me is true, and him you do not know" (7:28). In that statement, Jesus contrasts His identity with their sinful and lost condition. "You will seek me and you will not find me. Where I am you cannot come" (7:34). He subtly predicts His resurrection, which will occur in about 7 months, and the dark outcome of their spiritual condition – separation from God under His wrath for eternity. "In the presence of the Father there is no room for those who have refused to accept the Son."[265] In 8:12 we have the second of the great "I am" statements of this Gospel: "I am the light of the world. Whoever follows me will not walk in darkness, but will have the light of life." Jesus provides other identifications of His equality with God such as in 8:24-26, 28-29 and the last one in this dialogue in 8:58, "Truly, truly, I say to you, before Abraham was, I am." For this last declaration, "they picked up stones to throw at him, but Jesus hid himself and went out of the temple" (8:59). There is no mistaking who Jesus claims to be.

Jesus confronts their sinful condition. He brings the Jews face to face with the fact that none of them keeps the law (7:19). They are hypocrites for accusing Him of breaking the Sabbath because He "made a man's whole body well" (7:23-24). Multiple times He speaks the hard truth that they do not know God (7:28; 8:19, 54-56), that God is not their father (8:42-47), and that they are of their father, the devil, who is a liar and a murderer (8:44). He tells them they are slaves to sin and will die in their sins unless they believe in Him (8:24). It is an implicit call to repent of their rejection of Him and put their faith in Him. Nearing the end of this dialogue He says to them, "I honor my Father, and you dishonor me" (8:49). It is a ringing rebuke of their self-righteous hardness of heart. Although they don't realize it, they are in great danger.

---

265 Hendriksen, *Exposition of the Gospel According to John*, vol. 2, p. 20.

Jesus offers eternal life to those who believe in Him. Throughout the dialogue, Jesus urges them to believe in Him. "If anyone thirsts, let him come to me and drink. Whoever believes in me, as the Scripture has said, 'Out of his heart will flow rivers of living water'" (7:37-38). "Again Jesus spoke to them, saying, 'I am the light of the world. Whoever follows me will not walk in darkness, but will have the light of life'" (8:12). "If you abide in my word, you are truly my disciples, and you will know the truth, and the truth will set you free" (8:31-32). "Truly, truly, I say to you, if anyone keeps my word, he will never see death" (8:51). These are appeals to put their faith and trust in Him because they can have eternal life in no other way. The more He spoke truth into their lives the more hostile the crowd became.

The largest number of words in this dialogue is devoted to confronting sin. Second is the hostility directed toward Him by His listeners. The Jewish leadership hates Jesus because He testifies about them that their "works are evil" (Jn. 7:7). But it is important that they know not only the truth of who He is, but also the truth about themselves. They have deluded themselves into thinking they have a relationship with God, and they are not open to being proven wrong.

The second of these evangelistic encounters is the healing of the man born blind (9:1-39). John 9:1 seems to follow 8:59. Scholars differ as to when this occurs, but the text gives the impression it immediately follows Jesus' leaving the temple as "they picked up stones to throw at him" (8:59). The setting remains in Jerusalem.

To summarize the story, Jesus heals the man in response to His disciples' asking, "Who sinned, this man or his parents, that he was born blind?" (9:2). Jesus answers that his blindness was not because of sin but so that the "works of God might be displayed in him" (9:3). Jesus then reiterates who He is by saying, "I am the light of the world" (9:5). Jesus anoints the man's eyes with mud and sends him to wash in the pool of Siloam. When the Pharisees learn that Jesus healed this man on the Sabbath, rather than rejoicing that his sight was restored, they are outraged that He broke their distorted rules for the Sabbath. After a lengthy conversation with the man who was healed, they kick him out of the synagogue. Jesus finds the man and reveals Himself to him. The man responds in faith and worships Jesus.

It is a beautiful real-life story that illustrates four truths: (1) Jesus dramatizes His words "I am the light of the world" by bringing light into the man's eyes, (2) Jesus is the only one who can bring people out of spiritual darkness, as illustrated by the healing of the man's blindness, (3) a person must recognize their sin in order to be saved (9:39-41), and (4) the man born blind is a good example of "My sheep hear my voice, and I know them, and they follow me' (10:27).

The third of these evangelistic encounters is with the Jews who were angry about Jesus' healing the man on the Sabbath (9:35-10:21). After the man worships Him, "Jesus said, 'For judgment I came into this world, that those who do not see may see, and those who see may become blind'" (9:39). There is biting irony in Jesus' words. The Jews, who are contending with Jesus, refuse to recognize their sinful condition and their need for Jesus. They are religious leaders who believe they are right with God based on their good works, but they are lost and under God's wrath. They refuse Jesus and reject eternal life. They believe and teach a perversion of the truth that salvation is obtained by keeping the law. "Jesus said to them, 'If you were blind, you would have no guilt; but now that you say, 'We see,' your guilt remains'" (9:41).

The conversation continues in 10:1. "I am the door. If anyone enters by me, he will be saved [from God's wrath] and will go in and out and find pasture" (10:9). Jesus is the only way (the "door") of salvation (10:1, 7), and anyone entering through another way is "a thief and a robber" (10:1, 8). The Jewish leaders are thieves and robbers and lead people along the path to destruction through their distortion of the gospel.

Jesus has drawn a stinging contrast between His teachings ("I am the good shepherd") and the teachings of the Pharisees ("thieves and robbers"). This encounter ends with people sharply divided about Jesus. Some were saying, "He has a demon" and others saying, "Can a demon open the eyes of the blind?" (10:19-21).

The fourth and final of these evangelistic encounters is again with the Jewish leaders in Jerusalem. Although these four events span about two or three months, John has linked all four of them together thematically and textually. This one occurs at "the time of the Feast of Dedication" (10:22) (Hanukkah) which is celebrated in December.[266]

As in the previous encounters, Jesus asserts His equality with God, confronts the sins of the people, holds out eternal life to all who hear His voice and follow Him, and warns of rejecting Him. "My sheep hear my voice, and I know them, and they follow me. I give them eternal

---

266 Borchert, *John 1–11* (NAC), p. 327.

life, and they will never perish, and no one will snatch them out of my hand…I and the Father are one" (10:27-28, 30). The tragic response of the Jewish leadership is to attempt to arrest Him (10:39). Jesus' evangelistic efforts in Jerusalem seems to have caused most of the people to harden in their opposition to Him, though some turned to Him (9:19-21, 10:39-42).

In all four of these evangelistic encounters, we see Jesus: (1) delivering a consistent and whole gospel message, (2) naming sins and calling people to account for their sins, (3) modeling God's purpose of evangelism for His followers, and (4) exhibiting courage and love under pressure. If believers preach, teach, and speak a grace-only gospel and leave out sin, repentance, wrath, and the cost of following Jesus, they will make themselves more popular. But it will distort the gospel message and lead people down a path to their own destruction. The greatest need people had in Jesus' day and have today is redemption from their sins. **The lost can only find redemption if they come to know the truth about themselves and the truth about Christ.**

What Can We Learn About the Gospel and Evangelism from these Encounters?

First, Jesus evangelized His nation and others using the whole gospel message. He did not leave out the hard parts of sin, the call to repent, warnings of judgment and wrath, and the cost of following Him. He did not speak only of grace, love, and mercy. He did not set as His goal the accumulation of large numbers of people. His goal was to speak the entire gospel message and allow God the Father to draw people into His kingdom. He was not interested in drawing followers by creating false expectations. He was not interested in developing followers with superficial faith. He often challenged that kind of faith.

Second, Jesus' approach to lost people fully integrated His love, courage, truth, grace, passion, mercy, and respect. He presented the message of the gospel with words that people could understand. He spoke hard truths into people's lives at the risk of generating anger against Himself. Jesus was a credible witness that people could not dismiss because of His hidden motivations or His deceitful manipulation of the truth. **We as God's witnesses must ensure that we handle gospel truth in the same way that Jesus handled it.**

CHAPTER 10

THE LAST WORDS OF JESUS: THE GREAT COMMISSION

You are my witnesses – Isaiah 43:10
cf. Luke 24:48

Jesus set the stage during His earthly ministry for the disciples' ultimate and ongoing task upon His departure from the earth. Much of His training of the disciples was building to a foreordained conclusion – the launch of the gospel on a worldwide tour de force. According to Jesus' last words to His disciples, there will be an extraordinary responsibility left to them upon His ascension to heaven that will require exceptional ability. Jesus' call to His disciples, to a daunting task, would extend beyond any human capability, but the group of individuals gathered during His ministry was far from exceptional. There were no superstars in this bunch.

> *It was a small group of eleven men whom Jesus commissioned to carry on his work, and bring the gospel to the whole world. They were not distinguished; they were not well educated; they had no influential backers. In their own nation they were nobodies and, in any case, their own nation was a mere second-class province on the eastern extremity of the Roman map. If they had stopped to weigh up the probabilities of succeeding in their mission, even granted their conviction that Jesus was alive and that his Spirit went with them to equip them for their task, their hearts must surely have sunk, so heavily were the*

odds weighted against them. How could they possibly succeed? And yet they did.[267]

As unlikely as it seems, Jesus is passing the baton – His Great Commission (Lk. 4:18) – to these nobodies. During His resurrection appearances Jesus officially authorizes, commissions, and makes provision for their super-human assistance (the Holy Spirit).

In the following three selections of Scripture – Mt. 28:16-20, Lk. 24:44-49, and Acts 1:6-8 – Jesus gives the disciples a formal, fully articulated, and threefold emphasized expression of the chief strategic task of the church and of every believer. In this chapter, we will examine Jesus' declaration and what He expects all believers to do after His ascension. All followers of Jesus are like these nobodies that He charged with the task of the Great Commission.

Matthew 28:16-20. In Galilee, during a post-resurrection appearance, Jesus commissions the disciples.

> *And Jesus came and said to them, "All authority in heaven and on earth has been given to me. Go therefore and make disciples of all nations, baptizing them in the name of the Father and of the Son and of the Holy Spirit, teaching them to observe all that I have commanded you. And behold, I am with you always, to the end of the age."*
>
> *Mt. 28:18-20*

This charge, given to the eleven, seems more formal than the other two articulations of His Commission. What makes Jesus' commission in this text to His disciples feel formal is His carefully chosen language, structure, comprehensiveness, conciseness, and its strategic and historic character. The charge is based on the full authority of Jesus, who transfers His authority to the disciples to carry out His assignment. It includes four specific directives. The scope of the engagement is spelled out and the assurance

---

267 Michael Green, *Evangelism in the Early Church* (Grand Rapids, MI: William B Eerdmans, 1970, 1977), p. 13.

of support is given. It is all a person or organization needs in order to proceed with a monumental task of historic significance.

Some interpreters believe this passage reflects a structure similar to God's call of various people in the Old Testament such as Moses in Ex. 3:1–4:16, Gideon in Jdg. 6:11–21, and Jeremiah in Jer. 1:4–10.[268] As discussed in chapter 2 of this book, there is a strong resemblance to God's call of Abraham and the establishment of God's covenant with him in Gen. 12:1-3.[269] There are covenantal implications in the Great Commission, and it is the hallmark assignment to God's people under the New Covenant. The key points include:

- **A statement of authority** – "All authority in heaven and on earth" (v. 18)
- **A directive** – "Go...make disciples...baptizing them...teaching them..." (vv. 19-20)
- **A scope statement** – "all nations" (v. 19)
- **Assurance of Christ's presence** – "I am with you always" (v. 20)

First, Jesus asserts His authority to His disciples ("All authority in heaven and on earth has been given to me"), and then charges the eleven to lead God's people in accomplishing a particular task, the task of making disciples of all nations. Jesus' "brand" of evangelism is "a kind of evangelism that does not stop"[270] with conversion but continues in "teaching them to observe all that I have commanded you" (28:20). He outlines the scope of that task – "all nations" – and charges His disciples to bring in new disciples as an official part of the body of Christ by baptizing them into the church, in a public and formal ceremony. This evangelistic commission is wide-ranging and succinct. **According to Jesus, this charge is the chief strategic task in the life of God's people as we shall see.**

This commission of Jesus is also of historic significance since the Great Commission finds its conclusion at the second coming of Christ. "Together with [Mt.] 10:23

---

268 John Nolland, *The Gospel of Matthew: A Commentary on the Greek Text* (NIGTC) (Grand Rapids, MI; Carlisle: W.B. Eerdmans; Paternoster Press, 2005), p. 1261.

269 "The words of Jesus to His disciples in Matthew 28:18-20, the so-called Great Commission, could be seen as a Christological mutation of the original Abrahamic commission – 'Go...and be a blessing...and all nations on earth will be blessed through you.'" Wright, *The Mission of God*, p. 213.

270 Blomberg, *Matthew* (NAC), p. 431.

and 24:14, the concluding commission of 28:16-20 also places the Christian mission firmly within an **eschatological**[271] **framework: mission is the church's primary task between Christ's first coming and his return"** (emphasis mine).[272] This task is specific to carrying the message of the gospel to all nations. It is not a charge to make social justice the primary aim of the church, which many have done. It is not a charge to reform society.[273] While believers **should** care about justice, corruption, poverty, hunger, violence, immorality, and other social concerns in the societies in which they live, **the ultimate task of the church is to introduce lost souls to the redemption available only in Christ.** When individuals are transformed by the Holy Spirit at work through the gospel, society will be changed. It is "a mission that reaches out to Jews and Gentiles alike with a message of repentance and faith in Jesus the Messiah."[274] Jesus' commission is a charge to call individuals to repent of their sins and place their trust in Christ and in what He accomplished on the cross. "Human goodness will avail nothing for lost souls; ye must be born again"[275] (cf. Jn. 3:3, 5; 2 Cor. 5:17-21).

> *This 'good news' of salvation in Jesus, however, must be made known. Thus, mission is the ingredient that both precedes Christian existence and constitutes a major motivation for Christian living: the saving mission of Jesus forms the foundation for Christian mission, and the gospel is the message of this mission, a mission that is not optional but mandatory.*[276]

---

271 Eschatology is a broad topic, but in general is concerned with the last things and the end of the world; a doctrine that addresses Christ's second coming in judgment of those who have rebelled against Him and in salvation of His elect.

272 Andreas J. Köstenberger and T. Desmond Alexander, *Salvation to the Ends of the Earth: A Biblical Theology of Mission*, series ed. D. A. Carson, Second Edition, vol. 53, New Studies in Biblical Theology (London; Downers Grove, IL: Apollos; IVP Academic, 2020), p. 67.

273 J. Gresham Machen, *Christianity & Liberalism* (Grand Rapids, MI: Wm. B. Eerdmans Publishing Co., 1923), pp. 47-48, 156.

274 Köstenberger and Alexander, *Salvation to the Ends of the Earth*, p. 67.

275 Machen, *Christianity & Liberalism*, p. 156.

276 Köstenberger and Alexander, *Salvation to the Ends of the Earth*, p. 1.

At this point in Jesus' ministry on the earth, the disciples have been trained, officially commissioned, and will soon be empowered by God's Spirit to fulfill this task to make disciples.

Luke 24:44-49. In another post-resurrection appearance, Jesus speaks to a group of disciples, the eleven plus "those who were with them" (Lk. 24:33). Luke is not clear precisely when this appearance takes place, but he has placed it at the end of his Gospel. **It is of profound significance to Jesus' disciples and the church.**

> *Then he said to them, "These are my words that I spoke to you while I was still with you, that everything written about me in the Law of Moses and the Prophets and the Psalms must be fulfilled." Then he opened their minds to understand the Scriptures, and said to them, "Thus it is written, that the Christ should suffer and on the third day rise from the dead, and that repentance for the forgiveness of sins should be proclaimed in his name to all nations, beginning from Jerusalem. You are witnesses of these things. And behold, I am sending the promise of my Father upon you. But stay in the city until you are clothed with power from on high."*
>
> *Lk. 24:44-49*

Jesus emphasized that **"everything written"** about Him "in the Law of Moses and the Prophets and the Psalms must be fulfilled. Then he opened their minds to understand the Scriptures..." (24:45). As the passage continues, Jesus states specifically what was prophesied in the Old Testament writings that must be fulfilled. The list includes events already fulfilled in the life of Christ and events that will be fulfilled in the future through His followers. Jesus specifically names:

- The cross (v. 46) – Ps. 22; Isa. 52:13-53:12 – **fulfilled by Jesus**
- The resurrection (v. 46) – Ps. 16:10 – **fulfilled by Jesus**
- Proclamation of the gospel – "repentance for the forgiveness of sins should be proclaimed" (v. 47) – Ps. 22:30-31; Isa. 12:4-5; 49:6; 66:19; Mal. 1:11, 14 – **begun by Jesus and to be fulfilled by His followers**

- To all nations (v. 47) – Gen. 12:1-3; 22:18; Isa. 11:10-16; 42:6; 49:6; 66:18-24; Mal. 1:11, 14 – **begun by Jesus and to be completed by His followers**
- You are my witnesses (v. 48) – Isa. 43:8-13; 44:6-8 – **to be fulfilled by His followers**
- You will receive the Holy Spirit (v. 49) – Joel 2:28-31; Ez. 36:22-27 – **initiated by Jesus and to be experienced by His followers**

It is significant that everything Jesus did and experienced on the earth was the fulfillment of Old Testament prophesies. **And what He is commissioning the disciples to do going forward will also be in fulfillment of Old Testament prophesies.** The witness of God's people in the last days was ordained by God long before Jesus' incarnation. The prophet Isaiah saw this and prophesied the massive evangelism task to be carried out in the New Testament times (Isa. 11:1, 10-16; 12:1-6; 66:18-24; see the sections of chapter 4 in this book covering Isa. 12 and 66). This evangelistic mandate is the proclamation of the gospel, the message of "repentance for the forgiveness of sins." The chief strategic task of God's people in this epoch of the "last days" (Acts 2:17) is **a mandate predicted in the Old Testament and illuminated, restated, authorized, and empowered by Jesus.** There is no higher authority than Jesus. Therefore, Jesus' evangelistic mandate has an historic purpose during the last days before His return (Mt. 24:14; Mk 13:9-10).

> *And this gospel of the kingdom will be proclaimed throughout the whole world as a testimony to all nations, and then the end will come.*
>
>

Mt. 24:14

In Luke 24:47, "repentance for the forgiveness of sins should be proclaimed," is another way of saying "the gospel must be proclaimed." "The OT basis for the thought [of Lk. 24:47] is probably to be found in Is. 49:6 (quoted in Acts 13:47)."[277] Paul specifically cited Isa. 49:6 in Acts 13:47 as the basis for his commission from the Lord and as his

---

277 Marshall, *The Gospel of Luke* (NIGTC), p. 906.

authority to take the gospel to the Gentiles. The story of Jonah in the Old Testament demonstrates that the idea of gospel outreach to the Gentiles is close to God's heart. This recurring theme is seen throughout the Old Testament. Jesus' Great Commission is not really new. It is a new expression of a commission that has been planned by the triune God and ordained from eternity past (Gen. 12:1-3; Isa. 49:6; 1 Cor. 2:7).

Jesus' statement in Luke 24:48, "You are witnesses of these things," is nearly identical to the writings of Isaiah (Isa. 43:10, 12; 44:8). We saw in chapter 4 of this book that in Isaiah 43:8-13, the words of Isaiah were like a sarcastic rebuke of God's people for failing to be a witness to His glory. Jesus seems to be restating Isaiah and making application of Isaiah's writings to the church for this last period of world history before His second coming.[278] In Jesus' hands Isaiah's words, which were a rebuke to God's people at that time, become an obligation that has a shadow of warning and an implied note of reproof if it is not heeded. His word is a double-edged sword that cuts both ways. Notice the similarity between Isaiah 43:10, 12; 44:8 and Luke 24:48.

You are witnesses of these things (Lk. 24:48)

- "'You are my witnesses,' declares the Lord" (Isa. 43:10)
- "'you are my witnesses,' declares the Lord" (Isa. 43:12)
- "the people whom I formed for myself that they might declare my praise" (Isa. 43:21)
- "And you are my witnesses!" (Isa. 44:8)

According to the books of Isaiah and Luke, the Great Commission has been ordained by God from eternity past, prophesied by the prophets of the Old Testament, and expressed by Jesus in the language of Isaiah. We surveyed examples of similar prophecies in the first part of this book such as Gen. 3:14-15; 12:1-4; Ps. 22:31; 96:2-3; Isa. 11; 12; 49:6; 66:19; and Mal. 1:11, 14.

---

278 "He [T. S. Moore] adds that Luke 24:48 'verbally recalls Isaiah 43:10, 12; and 44:8, and in so doing picks up the Isaianic background in which Israel, God's servant, is summoned to testify of God's saving acts on behalf of His people.'" Citing T. S. Moore 1997a: 53–55. Köstenberger and Alexander, *Salvation to the Ends of the Earth,* p. 120, footnote 66.

Acts 1:7-8. Immediately prior to Jesus' ascending into heaven, He has a final conversation with His disciples. This statement is shorter than Luke 24:44-49 but it is the same evangelistic charge. However, the distinction in Acts 1:7-8 is that these are the last words of Jesus to the disciples before He ascends into heaven. It is like a short version of His last will and testament. The writer, Luke, has made clear exactly when this charge from Jesus occurs (Acts 1:9) because it matters. His ascension immediately following His commission provides a dramatic exclamation point to His words.

> *He said to them, "It is not for you to know times or seasons that the Father has fixed by his own authority. But you will receive power when the Holy Spirit has come upon you, and you will be my witnesses in Jerusalem and in all Judea and Samaria, and to the end of the earth."*
>
> *Acts 1:7-8*

There are two obvious lessons here from Jesus' last words on earth. First, Jesus through the disciples would not be establishing an earthly political kingdom at this time with military and political power. The disciples, who had certainly been hoping for that, are being told that an earthly political reign is not part of Jesus' plan at this point in history. Second, they would receive power to be His witnesses "to the end of the earth." "Jesus is speaking of the final success of his eschatological purpose. There is a sense of promise, participation, and guaranteed fulfillment." This was not only an encouragement to the disciples, but clarifying as to their purpose as it is for the church today.

Acts 1:7-8 is Jesus' last conversation with the disciples before His ascension into heaven. This reiteration of His commission just before His feet leave the earth is equivalent to an architect adding the capstone as the successful completion of a structure. It is the crowning achievement to the monumental work of his earthly ministry – his life, proclamation of the good news, the cross, and the resurrection. In a real sense, all of His teachings come to their ultimate expression in these last words. The church's mission, in these "last days" (Acts 2:17), is a saving mission larger than anything the world has ever seen. It will even eclipse the exodus of Israel out of Egypt (Isa. 11:1, 10-16; 66:19-20).

His disciples had no idea how they would accomplish this "impossible" task, so Jesus ordered "them not to depart from Jerusalem, but to wait for the promise of the Father" because they "will be baptized with the Holy Spirit not many days from now" (Acts 1:4-5). When that happens, their equipping for this central task of the church in the "last days" will be complete. Jesus then departs into heaven. **Again, this dramatic departure immediately following the third expression of His Great Commission is an exclamation point for how important this charge is to the church.**[279]

What Can We Learn About God's Purpose for His People from the Great Commission?

First, clarity of purpose. Understanding the similarities and the distinctive features of these three evangelistic commissions, from Jesus to His disciples, gives believers a triple affirmation of their importance. In all three commissions: (1) authority is expressed or asserted; (2) a directive is given; (3) the scope is provided; and (4) God's presence and empowerment is assured.

The distinctive characteristics of each of Jesus' evangelistic commissions are as follows. In **Matthew**, the commission is formal, comprehensive, and strategically oriented. In **Luke**, the commission is presented as foreordained by God, rooted in the prophets of the Old Testament, and expressed by Jesus in the language of the prophets. In **Acts**, the dramatic departure of Jesus into heaven, immediately following His reiteration of the commission, dramatizes and emphasizes its supreme importance.

> *The disciples are given the mission of the Servant of Isaiah 49:6 and will receive the Spirit to enable them to proclaim the good news of Jesus' saving death and resurrection (cf. Acts 1:8; 2:11).*[280]

---

279 The great commission is also seen in John 20:21-23 with reflections of it in John chapter 15 and especially verses 16 and 26-27. The Gospel of Mark has a great commission passage in 16:14-18, but 16:9-20 is generally considered not a legitimate part of the gospel. This will be discussed in more detail in the chapter on the Gospel of Mark under the heading "The Ending of the Gospel of Mark.".

280 Köstenberger and Alexander, *Salvation to the Ends of the Earth*, p. 120.

Second, intentionality. The three texts we have focused on imply a coordinated effort to accomplish a specific task that Jesus defines. Mt. 28:18-20 says we are to "go make disciples", baptize,", and "teach" (my paraphrase). Lk 24:44-49 and Acts 1:8 tell us we are to proclaim the gospel to all nations. None of this will happen without a focused effort. If you are a leader in your church, what is your formal plan to fulfill this Great Commission given by Christ to His people? I know that is understandably a difficult question for today's church because many churches have no evangelistic plan. As a long-time leader in a business environment, I know how important written plans are to organizational effectiveness. It has been my experience that if you aim at nothing, you will hit it every time. Biblical churches **must** develop an evangelistic plan and update it each year. In addition to developing a plan, effective churches should during the year, and at a minimum annually, evaluate how faithful the church has been in sharing their faith with a lost world.

If you are a pastor, elder, deacon, or other leader within your church, there is another perspective to consider. It is not enough that you are personally active in evangelism. If you are modeling evangelism, I applaud you. That is outstanding! If you are not, you should. But as a spiritual leader in the church, you are also charged with equipping and training God's people to do the work of ministry (Eph. 4:11-12). And fulfilling the Great Commission is at the top of God's list of strategic purposes for His people. Is it at the top of yours?

I am convinced that every church can benefit from having a written plan for how it will fulfill the Great Commission. Every leader of the church should have buy-in for the plan. **Every church member should know the plan and be trained in how to carry it out.**

Some may object that the apostles never had a written plan for how they would fulfill the Great Commission and yet they did an outstanding job. I would agree whole heartedly that they did an outstanding job and most gave their lives because of their loyalty to Jesus and because of their loyalty to His Great Commission. We can credit their success at least in part to the clear and concise commission Jesus articulated for them. But I would also point out that most churches today have at least one written plan, and that would be the church budget. In addition, most churches have a church calendar for the year where the major events are noted. Most churches also have a written plan for worship every Sunday known as the order of worship or something similar.

A logical question follows. Is the Great Commission incorporated into or noted in the church budget, church calendar, and the order of worship? Hopefully the answer is yes. Just as most churches have a written children's ministry plan, having a separate written plan for how the church body will be obedient to the Great Commission is also important. It is a way to get participation by everyone in the congregation and to set some benchmarks for the goals and objectives of the local body of believers.

Third, prayer. Even if a church has the best plans humanly possible to create an evangelistic ministry, nothing can be achieved for God's kingdom in human power alone. Believers need God's power and presence if they are to be faithful in obeying the Great Commission. My strong encouragement is to incorporate regular prayer for the fulfillment of the Great Commission into the life of the church. Incorporate prayer for this great task into the worship service. Include it in the Wednesday night prayer service. Churches can start small prayer groups praying only for local and world evangelization. **Regardless of the plan or method, the church must spend time in prayer focused on God's purpose.** Make sure it is on the church prayer list that circulates among the members. Prayer is a primary means God uses to accomplish His purpose.

As noted earlier in this chapter, Jesus' Commission was to a group of nobodies to carry on with His mission. This charge continues to the nobodies who followed them and to the nobodies of the 21st century. The Holy Spirit works well with nobodies, as He has proven over the last twenty centuries. As a matter of fact, He seems to delight in nobodies.

> In the very place, He says, **where ye are afraid**, that is, in Jerusalem, there preach ye first, and afterwards unto the uttermost part of the earth.[281]
>
> *John Chrysostom on Acts 1:8 (A.D. 347-407)*

---

281 Philip Schaff. Ed., *Saint Chrysostom: Homilies on the Acts of the Apostles and the Epistle to the Romans*, trans. J. Walker et al., vol. 11, A Select Library of the Nicene and Post-Nicene Fathers of the Christian Church (New York: Christian Literature Company, 1889), p. 13.

PART THREE

THE NEW TESTAMENT – TELLING THE GOSPEL

CHAPTER 11

THE BELIEVER'S CALL TO EVANGELISM

But thanks be to God, who in Christ
always leads us in triumphal procession,
and through us spreads the fragrance of the
knowledge of him everywhere...

...entrusting to us the message of reconcil-
iation. Therefore, we are ambassadors for
Christ, God making his appeal through us.
                              2 Corinthians 2:14 and 5:19-20

It is surprising that God's call to evangelize receives such clear expression in Paul's letter to the Corinthians because they were a church rocked by conflicts and problems. Many were turning to a false gospel, a "rival gospel" that "had corrupted their thoughts."[282] But Paul expected them to follow his example as he followed Christ, and that included evangelism. As we will see, Paul confirms in 2 Corinthians that God calls all ordinary believers, to share the gospel with the lost. In this chapter we will see that God's call to evangelize is not limited to the apostles, the clergy, or people with special gifts. The laity are to evangelize. Paul in this case expected even a bad laity to evangelize.

---

282 Murray J. Harris, *The Second Epistle to the Corinthians* (NIGTC) (Grand Rapids, MI; Milton Keynes, UK: W.B. Eerdmans Pub. Co.; Paternoster Press, 2005), p. 71.

The values and behaviors of the culture of Corinth had infiltrated the Corinthian church. The church was characterized by many challenges that threatened their walk with Christ and their fulfillment of God's purpose for them. Many in the Corinthian church were succumbing to the pressures of the culture around them.

Paul founded this church on his second missionary journey probably around AD 50 [283] and wrote 2 Corinthians most likely in AD 56.[284] The city of Corinth was a prosperous city with a wide mix of people. The church was equally diverse, comprising multiple nationalities and languages, affluence and poverty, and both Jew and Gentile. The church had a history of problems such as factions, disunity, immorality, and lawsuits. They wrestled with questions about marriage, worship, food sacrificed to idols, spiritual gifts, and the resurrection. There were arrogant leaders that not only failed to stop developing factions in the church, but seemed to encourage them and admitted into the church cultural influences that were in opposition to the gospel.[285] These leaders challenged Paul's authority and "claimed to be wise and philosophically informed; undoubtedly they were influenced by the Greek philosophy of their day (compare 1:20–25; 2:1–5, 12–14; 3:18–22; 12:3). They were not Gnostics but opponents of Paul's efforts to teach and apply Christ's gospel."[286] In other words, there was the infiltration of cultural values into the church through its leaders. There were also false apostles, most likely outsiders, who claimed apostolic authority of their own and contradicted the gospel of Christ, leading some astray.[287]

The church at Corinth was a supreme test even for the Apostle Paul. It was in many ways a combative church that "did not excel in stability."[288] Paul had to consistently take a strong stand with the various issues in the Corinthian church. Even though Paul was harshly criticized by this church, he never gave up on them. He considered it a battle worth fighting.

---

283 Simon J. Kistemaker, *Exposition of the First Epistle to the Corinthians* (Grand Rapids, MI: Baker Books, 1993), p. 9.

284 Kistemaker, *Exposition of the Second Epistle to the Corinthians*, p. 18 and Harris, *The Second Epistle to the Corinthians* (NIGTC), pp. 50-51. Some date the writing of this letter in AD 55 (R. Kent Hughes and Daniel Wallace).

285 This characterization of the church at Corinth in the five preceding sentences is taken from Kistemaker, *Exposition of the First Epistle to the Corinthians*, pp. 10-11.

286 Kistemaker, *Exposition of the First Epistle to the Corinthians* p. 11.

287 R. Kent Hughes, *2 Corinthians: Power in Weakness* (Wheaton, IL: Crossway Books, 2006), p. 181.

288 Kistemaker, *Exposition of the First Epistle to the Corinthians*, p. 10.

Believers today are the great beneficiaries of the Apostle Paul having come under severe attack by his enemies in the church at Corinth. His defense of his apostleship provides us with a large amount of detail about authentic gospel ministry. We will examine not only the principles that Paul embraced but his modeling of them in his own life.

Second Corinthians 2:14-7:4 is a section of Scripture that could be carved out and used as a standalone 1,845-word[289] **manifesto** on gospel ministry.[290] Some of its highlights include: the lifestyle model for every believer (2:14-16); the greater glory of the New Testament in contrast with the glory of the Old Testament (3:1-18); the transformational nature of what it means to walk with Christ (3:18); explicit principles for sharing the gospel – God's role, the believer's role, and the importance of gospel integrity (4:1-7); proper motivations and necessary transformations in Christ (5:9-17); the entrusting of the gospel to believers for sharing with others (5:18-20); the believer's call to holiness (6:14-7:1); and the cost of following Christ (6:1-10). In my view it is the most important section on evangelism in the Bible.[291]

In this chapter we will focus primarily on three aspects of Paul's discourse: **A Life Model, A Life Motivation**, and **A Life Commission**. They go together and are integral to each other. Paul shows this troubled church what he is committed to, how it is lived out, and the qualifications, motivations, and transformations that drive it. He expects the Corinthians to follow his example.

A Life Model (2 Cor. 2:14-16)

Paul begins his manifesto by using a visually striking image to portray the model for his life. Paul is an example for all believers, and the image he uses is the lifestyle model for every believer. It is not an "apostles only" or a clergy-centric model as we shall see.

---

289 The word count of 2 Corinthians 2:14-7:4 in the ESV is 1,845.

290 Many scholars refer to this section as "the great digression" or a "major digression" since it is where Paul lays out his ministry and its "grandeur and superiority, its suffering and glory, and its essence and exercise." Harris, *The Second Epistle to the Corinthians* (NIGTC), pp. 240-241.

291 Pastor John Chapman, an Australian evangelist, referred to 2 Cor. 4:1-6 as the most important passage on evangelism in the New Testament. I agree with him completely and have expanded on his comment to include the entire section of 2 Cor. 2:14-7:4 as the most important extended discourse on evangelism in the Bible. It is an exposition by Paul devoted to authentic gospel ministry.

Paul begins this text with a profound illustration – the triumphal procession. It is a metaphor that includes conquered slaves. It dramatizes the fact that every believer is a slave, albeit a willing and voluntary one. **The triumphal procession is important to Paul, and he uses it here because of its powerful imagery and its foundational role for all who will follow Christ.**

To put this image into the proper perspective, and before we examine it in detail, we should consider how Paul often referred to himself. Thirteen times in Paul's letters, he referred to himself as a "servant" or "prisoner" of the Lord – such as "servant of Christ" (e.g., Rom. 1:1) or "a prisoner of Christ Jesus" (e.g., Eph. 3:1). In addition, more than two dozen times Paul used the metaphor of dying such as dying to self (2 Cor. 5:15), dying to the law (Rom. 7:4-6), and dying to sin (Rom. 6:2; also, Peter in 1 Pet. 2:24). We are made alive in Christ and set free from the law (its consequences) and set free from sin (its bondage). Paul's use of this rare metaphor – the triumphal procession (2 Cor. 2:14) – is consistent with his self-portrayal in his letters.

The Greek word translated as "triumphal procession" is used only one other time in the New Testament in Colossians 2:15.[292] There may be a reflection of this idea in Ephesians 4:7-14, where Ps. 68:18 is cited (note the phrase "captives"). It is the most dramatic image of all the figures of speech Paul used to describe himself and believers.

> *But thanks be to God, who in Christ always leads us in **triumphal***
> ***procession**, and through us spreads the fragrance of the knowledge of*
> *him everywhere.*
>
> (2 Cor. 2:14)

This triumphal procession is a portrayal of dying to self and living for Christ that should stir our emotions. This image opens a window to how all of what follows relates to ordinary believers. Paul's imagery sweeps all of us along and *into* his narrative.

A triumphal procession evokes the image of a conquering king or general returning from a significant military victory and parading the spoils of his triumph for all to

---

292 Arndt et al., *A Greek-English Lexicon of the New Testament* (BDAG), p. 459. The root word θριαμβεύω (*thriambeuo*) is used only twice in the New Testament. The other use of it is in Col. 2:15 where it is translated as "triumphing over."

admire, all while basking in the adulation of throngs of people. R. Kent Hughes says Paul had this in mind:

> *A triumph of the first order featured the conquering general riding in a triumphal chariot drawn by four horses...He was clothed in a purple toga and a tunic stitched with palm fronds...In Paul's day, triumphal processions were conducted with grand theatrical pomp, always with a train of conquered subjects in a vast vanguard...Add to this the pagan priests burning incense and musicians and cultic rhythms, and we have the picture.*[293]

The first thing to think about is, how did Paul view himself in relation to this "triumphal procession"? Did he see himself as riding alongside the victorious general in the lead chariot? Was he one of those burning incense along the way? Or was he one of the musicians beating a tambourine arousing the crowd? **It was none of those. Paul viewed himself as a conquered slave or prisoner, but in this instance (unlike the slaves and prisoners of a conquering Roman general) Paul was willingly and joyfully following Christ as Christ presided at the head of the parade.**[294] Paul "will dramatically restate the idea in 4:8-12."[295]

Kent Hughes provides additional insight to this image:

> *Startling as this idea may be, the application goes beyond that to frankly shocking—because conquered enemies (or a representative group of them) were put to death at the end of the processional as a sacrifice to the Roman gods. Thus Paul viewed himself as God's captive being led to death. This is confirmed by the only other occurrence of the Greek word translated "triumphal procession" in the New Testament, in Colossians 2:15 where God, having conquered*

---

293 Hughes, *2 Corinthians: Power in Weakness,* p. 55.
294 Simon J. Kistemaker, *Exposition of the Second Epistle to the Corinthians* (Grand Rapids: Baker Book House, 1997), p. 89.
295 Hughes, *2 Corinthians: Power in Weakness,* p. 56.

the rulers of this age, has led them in triumphal procession and a
public display of their destruction.[296]

"The Roman general at the head of the triumphal parade was the one being glorified. The train of captives bore witness to the power, genius, and glory of the Roman general and therefore of Rome. It is an image of the believer living for the glory of Christ the triumphal King."[297] The world views the life of a believer who is living for the glory of Christ as a life of defeat. But in actuality it is the only path to real and lasting triumph – eternal life.

The second thing to notice in this passage is that Christ, in leading this triumphal procession, is using Paul to "spread the fragrance of **the knowledge of him** everywhere." This "fragrance" is both the life example of Christ's followers, often characterized by suffering and hardships, and the spoken gospel message. Knowledge of Jesus comes through the spoken word, the gospel. **Christ's followers are a life fragrance and a message fragrance.** To those who embrace the message of salvation, it is a sweet-smelling message of eternal life and to those who reject it, it is a foul-smelling message of death (2:14-16). Following Jesus is a life of dying to self and living for Christ, which means living in moral purity **and** being a witness to Christ.

The third thing to notice is that Christ is the triumphal King and is leading His followers in victory. In His triumph He has given His "captives" amazing benefits. "He disarmed the rulers and authorities and put them to open shame, by triumphing over them" (Col. 2:15) through the cross. He destroyed death (1 Cor. 15:54-57), forgave our sins "by cancelling the record of debt that stood against us with its legal demands" (Col. 2:13-14), appeased God's wrath (Rom. 3:25), redeemed His followers from being owned by sin (Rom. 3:24), declared His followers justified before a holy God (Rom. 3:24), and reconciled them to God (Rom. 5:10). His triumph rescued believers from slavery to their sin and from its consequences just as God rescued Israel out of slavery in Egypt. There is a cost of following Christ (which we will discuss in more detail later in this chapter), but the benefits far outweigh any difficulties a believer may experience.

---

296 Hughes, *2 Corinthians: Power in Weakness,* pp. 55–56.

297 Pastor Matthew Bradley, Interview by author, Nashville, TN, March 1, 2022. See also Wayne Grudem, General Editor, *ESV Study Bible,* (Wheaton IL: Crossway, 2008), note for 2 Cor. 2:14 and Wikipedia: https://en.wikipedia.org/wiki/Roman_triumph, September 10, 2022.

Paul's life model, as illustrated in the triumphal procession, is a foundation for following Christ. It establishes the platform for Christ's leading of His followers. It is a procession to ultimate victory in the same victorious path Jesus walked on his way to the cross. Believers are called to the path of the cross with the assurance of resurrection as the final destination. It is a model for believers and churches to imitate. Paul is not a perfect model, as Christ Jesus is the only sinless example. But Paul is the quintessential example among followers of Christ.

A Life Motivation (2 Cor. 5:9-18)

How can Paul be a servant of the gospel? How can he be a good example for believers to imitate? He had been a murderer of Christians! How could he not be permanently disqualified because of this previous sin? He had been an arch enemy of Christ. What had changed him and qualified him? What motivated him to be engaged like this?

This section contains the answers to those questions. It is not surprising that he addresses these issues since, as we have already seen, his critics and enemies were challenging his suitability for the role of apostle.[298] His answer points to God's work in his life, along with motivations, attitudes, and lifestyle changes that emerge out of that work.

Paul bases his suitability as a minister (or servant) of the gospel on four central facts. First, one day the Lord would judge him for all his actions at the judgment seat of Christ (2 Cor. 5:10). Second, Jesus had died for all believers including him (2 Cor. 5:14-15) and paid the price for his sins. Third, Paul had become a new creation in Christ (2 Cor. 5:17). And fourth, he had been reconciled to the God of creation (2 Cor. 5:18). The first of these facts was an action God would take in the future, and the other three were actions God had already taken on his life. All four of these truths shaped and transformed him in significant ways.

Emerging out of these actions taken by God are two foundational components of his motivations: **"the fear of the Lord"** (5:11) and **the dominating love of Christ** (5:14). The first, **"knowing the fear of the Lord,"** Paul relates to his impending ap-

---

298 Paul further defends his apostleship later in this second letter to the Corinthians in chapters 10-13.

pearance before the judgment seat of Christ. It was not a dread of Jesus but a reverential fear of Him. Just as Noah "in reverent fear constructed an ark for the saving of his household" (Heb. 11:7) and Moses, when he met God on the mountain said, "I tremble with fear" (Heb. 12:21), so Paul came to know the reverent and awesome fear of the Lord. It caused him to redirect his life in a way that was pleasing to Jesus and caused him to evangelize the lost. The judgment Paul anticipated was not a judgment to determine if he would be admitted into heaven, but it would be an event where a record of his life would be brought before a holy God, and he would be judged for how he lived his life and how he handled the responsibility that came with being a follower of Christ (1 Cor. 3:10-15).

R. C. Sproul has a good working definition of fearing the Lord:

> *For the Christian the holy war [with God] is over; the peace has been established. Access to the Father is ours.* **But we still must tremble before our God. He is still holy. Our trembling is the tremor of awe and veneration, not the trembling of the coward or the pagan frightened by the rustling of a leaf.** *Luther explained it this way: We are to fear God not with a servile fear like that of a prisoner before his tormentor but as children who do not wish to displease their beloved Father. We come to Him in confidence; we come to Him in boldness; we have access. We have a holy peace.*[299] *(Emphasis mine.)*

Many today seem to be uncomfortable with "fear" as a motivator of one's life. But not so for Paul. He grabs on to it and asserts it as a valid motivator of his life. One logical result of "knowing the fear of the Lord" for Paul was **to persuade others of the great salvation available to them in Christ** (2 Cor. 5:11). He makes a direct connection between the two.

The second foundational component comes a few sentences later – **"For the love of Christ controls us…"** (2 Cor. 5:14). He was overwhelmed by the love of Christ.

---

299 R. C. Sproul, *The Holiness of God* (Carol Stream, IL: Tyndale House Publishers, 1998, 2nd Edition), pp. 153-154.

The word translated "controls" in the ESV is συνέχω (*sunéchō*) and deserves additional elaboration. It is explained in the *Theological Dictionary of the New Testament* as follows:

> *"To be claimed, totally controlled" is also the meaning of the verb in two passages in Paul's letters: 2 Cor. 5:14 and Phil. 1:23.* **It is the love of Christ which "completely dominates" Paul (2 C. 5:14) so that on the basis of Christ's death the only natural decision for him, as for all other believers, is no longer to live for self but to live for Christ.** *This is how Paul defends his conduct before the Corinthians here; Christ's love claims him in such a way that in relation to others he can no longer exist for himself—in contrast to his opponents, who boast to the Corinthians that they are religious and spiritual, that they are something in themselves.*[300] *(emphasis mine)*

The "fear of the Lord" and "the controlling love of Christ" were a powerful combination of forces shaping Paul's life. The two motivations balance each other and coexist in perfect harmony. One without the other would be a gross distortion and create a caricature of Christianity that moves to one of two extremes. Fear without love could result in severity of actions, extreme legalism, no mercy toward others, and a perverting of the gospel message. Love without fear could result in sentimentalism, licentious actions, and a perverting of the gospel message. The fear of the Lord and the controlling love of Christ are the two dominant motivations Paul names. They produced in his life dramatic transformation.

Here is a list of truths, motivations, transformations, and actions in the order in which they appear.

1. "we make it our aim to please him" (5:9)
2. "For we must all appear before the judgment seat of Christ" (5:10)

---

300 Helmut Köster, "Συνέχω, Συνοχή," ed. Gerhard Kittel, Geoffrey W. Bromiley, and Gerhard Friedrich editors, *Theological Dictionary of the New Testament* (Grand Rapids, MI: Eerdmans, 1964), pp. 883–884.

3. **"knowing the fear of the Lord"** (5:11)
4. "we persuade others" (5:11)
5. **"For the love of Christ controls us"** (5:14)
6. "one (Jesus) has died for all" (5:14)
7. We live for Christ (no longer for self) (5:15)
8. We have a new kingdom perspective – no more superficial appraisal or valuation of others (5:16)
9. We are a new creation in Christ (5:17)
10. We are reconciled to God – no longer an enemy of Christ (5:18)

It is important to keep in mind that this discussion is in the context of Paul defending his qualifications as an apostle. It is a blend of God's saving actions on his life and transformations springing from that salvation.

A Life Commission (2 Cor. 5:18-20)

Moving to 2 Cor. 5:18-20, Paul brings us to an important application of the triumphal procession. It is a distinctive point of strategic significance. He states it as a logical outworking of the preceding facts. It has the force of a commission to all who follow Christ. He gives Christ's followers a title and an identity – **"Ambassadors for Christ."**

> *All this is from God, who through Christ reconciled us to himself and gave us the ministry of reconciliation; that is, in Christ God was reconciling the world to himself, not counting their trespasses against them, and entrusting to us the message of reconciliation.* ***Therefore, we are ambassadors for Christ, God making his appeal through us.***
> 2 Cor. 5:18-20

A slave of the Roman empire did what the Roman empire wanted them to do. A slave of Christ does what Christ wants them to do. These three verses outline a fourfold description of the role Christ has given to His "captives."

First – God "gave us **the ministry of reconciliation**" (5:18). The "ministry of reconciliation" Paul is referring to is the reconciliation of sinful man with a holy God. The word translated "ministry" in the ESV is "διακονία" [*diakonia*], which means service[301] and "here refers not to an office but to the function of serving, the role of presenting for acceptance God's offer of reconciliation."[302]

Second – God "entrusted to us **the message of reconciliation**" (5:19). The "message of reconciliation" is the gospel. Paul gave a short summary of it in 2 Cor. 5:21 – "For our sake he made him to be sin who knew no sin, so that in him we might become the righteousness of God."

Third – "Therefore, we are **ambassadors for Christ**" (5:20). "In the OT, an ambassador was a messenger, envoy, or negotiator sent on a special, temporary mission as an official representative of the king, government, or authority who sent him."[303] The ambassador carried the message of the king he represented. Christ's followers carry His message.

Fourth – "**God [is] making his appeal through us**" (5:20). This statement continually amazes me. The fact that God would entrust to His people such an important responsibility is a bit overwhelming. It's a big responsibility to say the least.

As we reflect on the triumphal procession model, based on what follows it, we can define what it means to "spread the fragrance of the knowledge of him everywhere" (2:14). He has given believers an outline of the work. Paul also provides additional information about what it means in 4:1-7, which we will examine in the next chapter of this book.

What Can We Learn About Evangelism from Paul's Declaration?

First, the triumphal procession is described by Kent Hughes as the "spiritual reality that we ought to embrace but that is not so easy to do."[304]

> *That reality is this: A vibrant, useful spiritual life is a death march*
> *in which the marcher repeatedly dies. It is the path pioneered and*

---

301 διακονία means "1) service rendered in an intermediary capacity, mediation, assignment, 2) performance of a service, 3) Functioning in the interest of a larger public" Arndt et al., *A Greek-English Lexicon of the New Testament* (BDAG), p. 230.

302 Harris, *The Second Epistle to the Corinthians* (NIGTC), p. 439.

303 Elwell, "Trades and Occupations," *Baker Encyclopedia of the Bible*, p. 2083.

304 Hughes, *2 Corinthians: Power in Weakness*, p. 53.

mastered by Christ. And it is the course that Paul strode as he said,
"I die every day!" (1 Corinthians 15:31). It is the course celebrated
in the triumphal procession, which is at the heart of the passage
before us [2 Cor. 2:14-17].[305]

This is the fundamental calling in Christ of all believers. It separates a genuine believer from a nominal believer. It is what it means to live a holy life, and its roots in the New Testament precede Paul. They begin with Jesus. His call to anyone who would follow Him is in Mark 8:34-38. We examined that passage in chapter 8 of this book. This spiritual reality, however, is opposed on multiple fronts today.

Christ's call is a difficult one to follow. It is a counterintuitive call and is certainly countercultural. To live the lifestyle of following Christ, one will encounter massive headwinds from the culture and even from within the church. And make no mistake about it – His call and the call of culture are in a cosmic battle with life and death consequences hanging in the balance.

The life and message of the follower of Christ are arrayed in battle against two opposing forces. The first of these forces is our own human nature. We all want to be in control of what is happening in our lives, and we resist turning our life over to God daily. We take pride in being in charge, but in reality we give ourselves a false sense of control. It is sin not to yield our life to Him. This struggle to trust God and live in obedience to Him is a battle. It is an internal struggle in which the battle is waged on a daily basis. Every believer has difficulty denying self-determination and denying self-gratification.

The second opposing force to the normal Christian life is the culture we live in. It opposes believers on two levels: one, it seduces Christians by appealing to their human nature and two, it confronts them with opposition. On the first, the culture promotes its own views of the ideals and values we should live by. It works overtime to make the old idols of the world look new and fresh and compelling. Our self-centered tendencies are inflamed by being "constantly bombarded in our culture by appeals to our native narcissism."[306] Practically every movie, TV program, and nearly every commercial assails

---

305 Hughes, *2 Corinthians: Power in Weakness*, p. 53.
306 Michael Horton, *Christless Christianity: The Alternative Gospel of the American Church* (Grand Rapids, MI: Baker Books, 2008), Kindle iOS edition, p. 91.

us with appeals to sensuality, greed, and materialism along with encouraging our desires for power, wealth, and fame.

The culture we live in opposes Christians on a second level. It is speaking out against Christianity with increasing intensity. The culture deifies the self,[307] removes the transcendent God from society,[308] opposes "Christianity [as] a corrupt ideology,"[309] sees "the traditional patriarchal family [as] a unit of oppression,"[310] and believes "the dismantling and abolition of the nuclear family are essential."[311] **In its idolization of "the genius of human happiness"[312] it sees Christianity as opposing true happiness. Consequently, Christianity must be destroyed.**

In the context of these battlegrounds, what does it mean when 96% of our churches are ineffective evangelistically?[313] I believe it means the vast landscape of evangelical Christianity has made friends with the culture and abandoned Christ's calling to evangelize the lost. We are seeing the result of the infiltration of the philosophies and values of the culture into the pulpits of evangelical churches and into the lifestyles of believers. In that process of cultural accommodation, we have redefined what it means to be a follower of Christ and, consequently, what it means to be saved.

It is easy to slip into a type of Christ followership that is at peace with the culture. When this happens, the biblical lifestyle and purpose for the believer are redefined so that God and the Bible become merely an enhancer or supercharger of self-inspired goals. This is what it means to move quietly from genuine biblical discipleship into nominal Christianity – where a person is Christian in name only and his or her hope of salvation is a delusion.

Second, believers are called to be ambassadors for Christ. The immediate context, as well as the larger context of the New Testament, supports the conclusion that Paul intended the label "ambassadors for Christ" to apply to every believer and not in a

---

307 Carl R. Trueman, *The Rise and Triumph of the Modern Self: Cultural Amnesia, Expressive Individualism, and the Road to Sexual Revolution* (Wheaton, IL: Crossway, 2020), pp. 164-165.

308 Trueman, *Rise and Triumph,* pp. 76-77, 96-97.

309 Trueman, *Rise and Triumph,* p. 196.

310 Trueman, *Rise and Triumph,* p. 234.

311 Trueman, *Rise and Triumph,* p. 235.

312 Trueman, *Rise and Triumph,* p. 155.

313 Rainer, *Effective Evangelistic Churches,* p. 50.

restricted way to him and his small group of assistants, the clergy, or people with special gifts.[314]

In this section of Scripture, Paul listed his motivations and inspirations for gospel ministry. It is significant what he names. He lists: (1) being led in triumphal procession by Christ, (2) living to please Jesus, (3) standing before the judgment seat of Christ, (4) "knowing the fear of the Lord," (5) controlled by the love of Christ, (6) Jesus' death on the cross, (7) dying to self and living for Christ, (8) possessing a new kingdom perspective, (9) being a new creation in Christ, and (10) reconciled to God in Christ. After listing these qualifications, he then brings those facts to their logical conclusion: "Therefore, we are ambassadors for Christ, God making his appeal through us" (2 Cor. 5:20). His conclusion is a statement of fact that also conveys obligation of all believers.

An important question is: Are all of the attributes listed by Paul characteristic of every believer? The answer is, of course, a resounding "Yes!" Does the triumphal procession metaphor apply to every believer? Again, the answer is "Yes." In that case, it follows that ordinary believers "are ambassadors for Christ." Believers possess every attribute and qualification that Paul listed, and believers are under the same call of Christ.

Paul could have compiled a list of his supernatural credentials as qualifying him for gospel ministry, such as: (1) the Damascus road experience (Acts 9:1-9), (2) his having received direct revelation from God (Gal. 1:11-12; 2:2; Eph. 3:3), (3) the many miracles he performed (Acts 13:8-12; 14:3, 9-10; 19:11-12; 28:7-10), (4) his raising of Eutychus from the dead (Acts 20:7-12), (5) his being bitten by a venomous snake with no adverse reaction (Acts 28:3-5), and (6) casting out demons (Acts 19:12-17). That set of qualifications placed him in a small elite group of believers, namely the apostles. But he listed none of those and instead grounded ambassadorship in the miracle of simply being a follower of Christ.

---

314 There are different opinions as to who Paul is referring to when he says, "Therefore, *we* are ambassadors for Christ..." (5:20). Does the *"we"* refer to Paul and his associates or to the Corinthians and other believers as well? Köstenberger and Alexander take the position that it applies to other believers as well: **"While in the first instance Paul is referring to his own mission and that of the apostles, he is including the Corinthian (and, by implication, other) believers as well when he speaks of their being 'ambassadors for Christ.'"** Andreas J. Köstenberger with T. Desmond Alexander, *Salvation to the Ends of the Earth: A Biblical Theology of Mission*, ed. D. A. Carson, Second Edition, vol. 53, New Studies in Biblical Theology (London; Downers Grove, IL: Apollos; IVP Academic, 2020), p. 169.

Two specific sections of Scripture, 2 Cor. 2:14-16 and 5:9-20 (also 4:1-7 as we shall see in the next chapter), give us important insight as to how Mt. 28:18-20 and Acts 1:8 are to play out in the life of the believer and in the life of the church. In those two passages there is no restriction placed on who is to spread the gospel. John Stott has this to say about Acts 1:8:

> *Christ expects His witnesses to take the initiative. 'You shall receive power when the Holy Spirit has come upon you, and you shall be my witnesses...' (Acts 1:8). This is the risen Lord's standing order to all his followers.* **We can no more restrict the command to witness than we can restrict the promise of the Spirit.**[315] *(Emphasis mine.)*

I think it is more amazing, and not what we expect, that the Holy Spirit is given to every believer (i.e., not restricted to a special class of believers) than that the obligation to witness is given to every believer. Both are clearly unlimited. Many believe that evangelism is an obligation only for those who are specially gifted in some way. But that is to add a restriction that is never made in Scripture.

Third, most believers and churches do not meet the standards for evangelism given by Paul. The data collected by Thom Rainer, as noted earlier, showed that less than 4% of the 40,000 Southern Baptist churches were effective evangelistically.[316] (Other denominations do not appear to be any better.) This is a massive and widespread failure by any measure. This failure is not because the gospel has lost its power. John Dickerson has an apt summary:

> *What we do know is this: The United States church is moving with speed and momentum in a direction that includes lethargic discipleship, sputtering evangelism, abandoned unity, pending bankruptcy, and failed ambassadorship to the lost. We are in need of a historic course correction, lest we run aground.*[317]

---

315 Stott, *Our Guilty Silence*, p. 62.
316 Rainer, *Effective Evangelistic Churches*, p. 50.
317 John S. Dickerson, *The Great Evangelical Recession* (Grand Rapids, MI: Baker Books, 2013), Kindle loc. 3162-3164.

We also know the gospel is a dynamic force.[318] As he writes in 1 Thess. 1:5, Paul believes the gospel has a power infused by God, "because our gospel came to you not only in word, but also in power and in the Holy Spirit and with full conviction." Paul had seen before the effect the gospel of Jesus Christ could have on people. The gospel he preached came to people: **in word – in power – in the Holy Spirit – with full conviction.** We know that Paul never removed the offensive parts of the gospel (Gal. 5:11) such as sin, wrath, and the cost of following Christ, and that he preached the whole gospel centered on the cross. **If we remove the offensive parts of the gospel, it is no longer a dynamic force.**

God's people are a worshipping and witnessing people. It is time to rediscover the witnessing component, which is God's chief outward purpose for His people, that we "may proclaim the excellencies of him who called [us] out of darkness into his marvelous light" (1 Pet. 2:9). Believers have been entrusted with this dynamic gospel, and we must spread it so it can do its work.

Fourth, as noted in previous chapters, we should pray Scripture. We should meditate on Scripture, confess our sins, and repent with God's help.

Example One: Lord Jesus, I too often live for my own selfish purposes. You "died for all, that those who live might no longer live for themselves but for [you] who for [my] sake died and was raised" (2 Cor. 5:15). Lord, please give me the desire to live for you. Help me to recognize and to abandon my self-centered ways of thinking and living. Help me, Lord Jesus, to follow you joyfully in your "triumphal procession" as your captive. Amen.

Example Two: Lord Jesus, the influence of the culture around me is overwhelming. It pulls me into its orbit and shapes what I value. Please forgive me for allowing these influences into my life. Please give me discernment to recognize the influence of the culture. Enable me to turn away from these influences and to be reshaped and transformed by your word. Give me the desire every day to no longer live for myself but for you (5:15). Amen.

---

318 "Several scholars have noted this evangelistic reference to the dynamic 'word of the Lord' in 1 Thessalonians 1:8. James Patrick Ware, for example, comments on the text: 'The word is pictured as an active force, radiating out from the Thessalonians by its own power.' Along the same lines Plummer quotes J. Lambrecht as writing, 'God's initiative is irresistible; the Lord's word is a dynamic, outreaching and contagious power,'" Plummer, *Paul's Understanding of the Church's Mission,* pp. 56, 62.

Example Three: Help me, Lord Jesus, to "spread the fragrance of the knowledge of [you] everywhere" (2 Cor. 2:14). Help me to live a life that is not only pleasing to you but that speaks the words of your gospel to those around me. Give me the courage, the grace, and the passion to be a witness to your glory, to your loving kindness, and to your great salvation. Help me to "spread the fragrance of the knowledge of [you] everywhere." Amen.

All Churches and Believers are Ambassadors for Christ

Ambassadors for Christ – who does that apply to? Does it apply to all churches and to all ordinary believers? Here are four additional reasons from Scripture that support my (and many others') conclusion that it applies to every believer.

1. **"Therefore, we [all] are ambassadors for Christ"** (2 Cor. 5:20). I added the "all" because it is required by the immediate context (5:17-20a). It is not in the original Greek. Paul alternately references himself and the Corinthians in this section of Scripture. Consider a few examples. At the beginning of this section at 2 Cor. 2:14 Paul uses "us" to refer to the Corinthians and thus all Christians and maintains that meaning until we come to 3:1. At that point he is referring to himself until we come to 3:18 where the meaning is back to "we all." The meaning goes back and forth like that throughout the section.

    When we come to 5:17 the pronoun shift is to all believers with, "Therefore, if **anyone** is in Christ, he is a new creation." This meaning of "all believers" is maintained until we come to the second sentence of 5:20 which begins "We implore you." Notice the flow and the unbroken connectivity in 5:17-20a.

    - 5:17 – "Therefore, if **anyone** is in Christ he is a new creation." – all believers
    - 5:18 – "All this is from God, who through Christ reconciled **us** to himself..." – all believers
    - 5:18 – "...and gave **us** the ministry of reconciliation;" – all believers
    - 5:19 – **"that is**, in Christ God was reconciling the world..." – the application is drawn in the context of all believers

- 5:19 – "...and entrusting to **us** the message of reconciliation." – all believers
- 5:20a – **"Therefore, we** are ambassadors for Christ, God making his appeal through **us."** – a big application word, "therefore," applied to the pool of **all believers**
- 5:20b – **"We** implore you..." – the shift back to Paul
- 5:21 – "so that in him **we** might become the righteousness of God" – all believers

There is a battle over these pronouns among interpreters. There are differing opinions as to who the pronouns refer to and who the biblical truths apply to. Despite the differing opinions, I consider that "the ambiguity throughout is intentional because it distinguishes Paul as an apostle and at the same time draws all believers into his model. As believers read through this section they recognize that all of what Paul says applies to them. **Paul is an exemplar**, someone to imitate, a great example to follow as he followed Christ."[319]

"'Ambassador' language is consistent with our being made in the image of God and our responsibility to represent God. The entire arc of redemptive history points to our being ambassadors for Christ – we are His representatives made in the image of Christ. This goes back to the garden and man's responsibility to tend and grow the garden."[320]

The passage that immediately follows reinforces this application to all believers. "Working together with him, then, we appeal to you not to receive the grace of God in vain" (2 Cor. 6:1). "How might the Corinthians let God's grace come to nothing? Answers are necessarily speculative, but they would probably include the following. In general, God's grace would be ineffective if the Corinthians squandered God-given opportunities for bringing spiritual benefit to themselves and to unbelievers (cf. Col. 4:5b, 'making the most of

---

319 Bradley, Interview, March 1, 2022; with much appreciation for his assistance in sorting out this rich section of Scripture with Paul's constant interchanging of pronouns.
320 Bradley, Interview, March 1, 2022.

opportunity'), and if they failed to exercise the ministry of reconciliation (5:18) and to fulfill their role as Christ's ambassadors (5:19)."[321] God has given us His grace not so we can put it in the bank and collect interest. Properly understood, His grace motivates believers and enables them to bear fruit in His kingdom. Paul said that grace caused him to work harder than anyone else: "But by the grace of God I am what I am, and his grace toward me was not in vain. On the contrary, I worked harder than any of them, though it was not I, but the grace of God that is with me" (1 Cor. 15:10).

2. **Imitation of Paul.** Paul's life is a **representational model for churches and believers.** Eight times in four different letters Paul charges the recipients, either directly or by implication, to imitate him and his ministry (1 Cor. 4:16; 11:1; Phil. 3:15, 17; 4:9; 2 Thess. 3:7, 9; 2 Tim. 1:13). Three additional times he acknowledges and is obviously pleased with the body of Christ imitating his ministry (1 Thess. 1:6-8; 2:14; 2 Tim. 3:10-15). Here is a look at one of those passages.

> And you became **imitators of us and of the Lord,** for you received the word in much affliction, with the joy of the Holy Spirit, so that you became an example to all the believers in Macedonia and in Achaia. For not only has **the word of the Lord sounded forth from you** in Macedonia and Achaia, but your faith in God has gone forth everywhere, so that we need not say anything.
>
> 1 Thess. 1:6-8

It is important to note that in Paul's mind, imitation of him was grounded in his imitation of Christ. We know that from this passage and from his statement to the Corinthians, "Be imitators of me, as I am of Christ" (1 Cor. 11:1). Here it is again in this passage, **"you became imitators of us and of the Lord"** (1:6).

---

321 Harris, *The Second Epistle to the Corinthians* (NIGTC), p. 459.

In 1 Thess. 1:6-8, Paul was delighted at their evangelism efforts and the several other ways they were imitating him. Here is how they were imitating Paul.

1) They **"received the word in much affliction"** – their turning away from idols to follow Christ brought suffering into their lives. In spite of suffering, they continued in faithfulness to Christ.

2) In their suffering they experienced **"the joy of the Holy Spirit."** This is the joy and peace that defies circumstances and human explanation. (Phil. 4:7).

3) **"The word of the Lord sounded forth"** from the Thessalonian believers throughout a large region (Macedonia and Achaia). This is nothing less than an evangelistic proclamation of the gospel.[322]

4) **Reports of their conversion and faith in God went everywhere.** They were a witnessing, living testimony of a vibrant faith in Christ.

5) They **"became an example to all the believers in Macedonia and in Achaia."**

The phrase, **"the word of the Lord sounded forth"** is a powerful statement of their evangelism efforts. "The term translated *rang out* ['sounded forth' in the ESV] *(exechetai)* appears only here in the NT, but in other literature of the era it could be used to describe a clap of thunder (Sir. 40.13), the loud cry of a multitude...**The proclamation from Thessalonica was set at high volume and went out with great force over a large area...[this] speaks of a tremendous effort by the Thessalonian believers to carry the word of the Lord to all**

---

322 Gene L. Green, *The Letters to the Thessalonians* (PNTC) (Grand Rapids, MI; Cambridge, UK: Wm. B. Eerdmans Publishing Co., 2002), pp. 101-108. "The result of this great evangelistic effort on the part of the Thessalonians was that *Therefore we do not need to say anything about it* [1 Thess. 1:8]. The words *about it* are not part of the Greek sentence and need not be supplied in translation to clarify the sense. Following the previous interpretation of this verse, the idea is not that Paul did not have to say anything about the reputation of the Thessalonians (cf. 2 Thess. 1.3-4) but rather that they did not find it necessary to preach in certain places because of the previous evangelistic efforts of this church" (pp. 104-105).

parts"[323] (emphasis mine). Their effort was intentional and carried out "with the joy of the Holy Spirit" (1 Thess. 1:6).

3. **The ordinary witnesses.** In Acts 8:1-4, there was a great persecution of the church, led by none other than the future apostle, Paul himself. The persecution that arose on that occasion caused believers to flee Jerusalem, "and they were all scattered throughout the regions of Judea and Samaria, except the apostles" (Acts 8:1). Notice that the apostles stayed in Jerusalem. This is significant because of what follows in verse 4: "Now those who were scattered went about preaching the word." The phrase translated as "preaching the word" is from the Greek word εὐαγγελίζω (*euaggelizo*) which means "to evangelize, proclaim the good news, preach the gospel."[324] These non-elite, non-clergy believers were driven by the love of Christ and were doing what that love compelled them to do – tell the good news.

Historian Kenneth Scott Latourette makes this observation about the spread of the gospel:

> *The chief agents in the expansion of Christianity appear not to have been those who made it a profession or a major part of their occupation, but men and women who earned their livelihood in some purely secular manner and spoke of their faith to those whom they met in this natural fashion.*[325]

In noting the evidence for the witness of the church in the first century, Plummer writes, "A variety of evidence in the New Testament and early Christian history indicates not only that early Christians suffered, but that the gospel

---

323 Green, *The Letters to the Thessalonians* (PNTC), pp. 101-102.

324 Spiros Zodhiates, General Editor, *The Complete Word Study Dictionary: New Testament (electronic edition)*, word no. 2097.

325 Tim Beougher, (https://www.9marks.org/article/journalmust-every-christian-evangelize/, August 27, 2013, accessed August 21, 2021) quoting from Kenneth Scott Latourette, *A History of the Expansion of Christianity* (Harper & Brothers, 1937), 1:116.

was advancing through the ministry of ordinary believers. The book of Acts alone is a treasury of the entire church's active and constant witness."[326] In a supplemental footnote to that statement he writes, "Luke consistently reports a vibrant witness by all persons in the church (e.g., Acts 4:23-31; 6:7; 8:1-4; 11:19-21; 12:24; 13:49; 15:35; 16:5; 19:10, 18-20)."[327]

4. **Evangelists – "to equip the saints for...the work of ministry."** In Paul's letter to the believers in Ephesus, he spells out that Christ "gave the apostles, the prophets, the evangelists, the shepherds and teachers, **to equip the saints for the work of ministry,**[328] for building up the body of Christ" (Eph. 4:11-12). The purpose of these gifted individuals is to equip those whom he refers to as "saints," ordinary believers, "for the work of ministry [service]." It is easy to overlook the purpose of these gifted men that Paul spells out.

We could paraphrase the passage like this without distorting its meaning: "Christ gave evangelists to equip the saints for the work of evangelism." The same principle works if we apply it to the other gifts named in that passage. "Christ gave prophets to help the saints discern right ways of living and to avoid the subtle infiltration of cultural values into the church." Or "Christ gave teachers to equip believers to understand clearly the word of God and equip them to teach their families and others the truths of God's word." The significant point I am calling attention to here is that these gifted individuals are not the only ones called to do "the work of ministry." They are to prepare others, the body of believers, for sharing that workload.

This brings out more clearly that the immediate purpose of Christ's gifts is the ministry to be rendered by the entire flock; their ultimate

---

326 Plummer, *Paul's Understanding of the Church's Mission*, p. 127.
327 Plummer, *Paul's Understanding of the Church's Mission*, p. 127, footnote 57.
328 *"to prepare God's people for **productive service** Eph 4:12."* Arndt et al., *A Greek-English Lexicon of the New Testament* (BDAG), p. 230. (emphasis mine).

purpose is the building up of the body of Christ, namely, the church.
The important lesson taught here is that not only apostles, prophets,
evangelists, and those who are called 'pastors and teachers,' but the
entire church should be engaged in spiritual labor. 'The universal
priesthood of believers' is stressed here. [329]

One question that emerges out of this text is, **"Are churches and pastors
today equipping the saints for the work of ministry?"** My observation is:
not very well. This represents a huge opportunity for leaders who care about
the biblical model for ministry which includes "equipping the saints." Many
leaders seem to believe that preaching from the pulpit or in a classroom is
enough to equip believers in their various areas of biblical ministry, including evangelism. As important as both of those tasks are, they are inadequate
by themselves. Equipping the saints for the work of ministry must include
modeling, instructing, training, mentoring, and accountability. The church
is missing out on robust service in all areas of ministry when spiritual gifts
are not developed and deployed.

Clergy vs Laity

There is much confusion about the roles of clergy and laity in the church. In *The
History of the Christian Church,* Philip Schaff includes a section titled "Clergy and
Laity" that is worth noting.

The idea and institution of a special priesthood, distinct from the
body of the people, with the accompanying notion of sacrifice and
altar, passed imperceptibly from Jewish and heathen reminiscences
and analogies into the Christian church. The majority of Jewish

---

329 William Hendriksen, *Exposition of Ephesians* (Grand Rapids: Baker Book House, 1967, first printing
1995), p. 198. Peter T. O'Brien agrees and writes, "The notion of equipping or preparing, in the sense of
making someone adequate or sufficient for something, best suits the context. However, it does require an object: people are prepared for some purpose. That purpose is 'for the work of ministry', an activity of the saints
for which the leaders are to prepare and equip them." Peter T. O'Brien, *The Letter to the Ephesians* (PNTC)
(Grand Rapids, MI: Wm. B. Eerdmans Publishing Co., 1999), pp. 303.

converts adhered tenaciously to the Mosaic institutions and rites, and a considerable part never fully attained to the height of spiritual freedom proclaimed by Paul, or soon fell away from it. He opposed legalistic and ceremonial tendencies in Galatia and Corinth; and although sacerdotalism does not appear among the errors of his Judaizing opponents, the Levitical priesthood, with its three ranks of high-priest, priest, and Levite, naturally furnished an analogy for the threefold ministry of bishop, priest, and deacon, and came to be regarded as typical of it. Still less could the Gentile Christians, as a body, at once emancipate themselves from their traditional notions of priesthood, altar, and sacrifice, on which their former religion was based. Whether we regard the change as an apostasy from a higher position attained, or as a reaction of old ideas never fully abandoned, the change is undeniable, and can be traced to the second century. **The church could not long occupy the ideal height of the apostolic age, and as the Pentecostal illumination passed away with the death of the apostles, the old reminiscences began to reassert themselves.**

In the apostolic church preaching and teaching were not confined to a particular class, but every convert could proclaim the gospel to unbelievers, and every Christian who had the gift could pray and teach and exhort in the congregation. **The New Testament knows no spiritual aristocracy or nobility, but calls all believers "saints" though many fell far short of their vocation. Nor does it recognize a special priesthood in distinction from the people, as mediating between God and the laity. It knows only one high-priest, Jesus Christ, and clearly teaches the universal priesthood, as well as universal kingship, of believers.** *[Schaff is not saying there is no place for offices and officers in the church* *today; please see footnote below.*[330]*] It does this in a far deeper and larger sense than the Old [Ex. 19:6]; in a sense, too, which even to this day is not yet fully realized. The entire body of Christians are called "clergy" (κλῆροι) [kleroi], a peculiar people, the heritage of God.*[331] *(emphasis mine)*

In other words, as believers moved away from the illumination and power of the Holy Spirit with the passing of the apostles, their dependence on God's power in their lives waned. The spiritual freedom proclaimed by Paul and the other apostles could not long be maintained. Believers could not "bear" the responsibility that came with that freedom. It takes courage to walk in the way of freedom in Christ. It is much easier to outsource ministry responsibility to someone else. It is much easier to even outsource our faith to someone else.

So, "the old reminiscences" were brought forward not unlike the people of Israel dragging the paganism of Egypt with them after God rescued them from Egyptian slavery. Then "high-priest, priest, and Levite" of the Old Testament were brought forward into the New Testament. The old structures which had been a good thing when established by God became a bad thing when they were brought forward into the New Testament after they had been rendered obsolete by God. "And no one puts new wine into old wineskins. If he does, the wine will burst the skins – and the wine is destroyed, and so are the skins. But new wine is for fresh wineskins" (Mk. 2:22). Dragging the OT priesthood forward was like bringing old wineskins to hold the new wine of the NT. The wine and the skins are destroyed when that happens. Those offices no longer had a place or function in God's purpose after Pentecost.

---

330 I think Schaff overstates this principle though he does clarify it in the paragraph that follows: "On the other hand it is equally clear that there was in the apostolic church a ministerial office, instituted by Christ, for the very purpose of raising the mass of believers from infancy and pupilage to independent and immediate intercourse with God, to that prophetic, priestly, and kingly position, which in principle and destination belongs to them all [footnote: comp. Eph. 4:11-13]." Philip Schaff and David Schley Schaff, *History of the Christian Church, vol. 2* (New York: Charles Scribner's Sons, 1910), pp. 123–124.
331 Schaff, *History of the Christian Church, vol. 2*, pp. 123–124.

Pastors, elders, and deacons were given a place and purpose in the New Testament, but there was no priest standing between man and God. Every believer was a priest with direct access to God through the Lord Jesus Christ (1 Pet. 1:9; Rev. 1:5-6, 9). Pastors, elders, and deacons have an important role in the spiritual growth of followers of Christ, in mentoring believers to maturity in Christ-like living, and in the exercise of their spiritual gifts for the growth of God's kingdom.

CHAPTER 12

WHAT IS BIBLICAL EVANGELISM?

¹ Therefore, having this ministry by the mercy of God, we do not lose heart. ² But we have renounced disgraceful, underhanded ways. We refuse to practice cunning or to tamper with God's word, but by the open statement of the truth we would commend ourselves to everyone's conscience in the sight of God. ³ And even if our gospel is veiled, it is veiled to those who are perishing. ⁴ In their case the god of this world has blinded the minds of the unbelievers, to keep them from seeing the light of the gospel of the glory of Christ, who is the image of God. ⁵ For what we proclaim is not ourselves, but Jesus Christ as Lord, with ourselves as your servants for Jesus' sake. ⁶ For God, who said, "Let light shine out of darkness," has shone in our hearts to give the light of the knowledge of the glory of God in the face of Jesus Christ.

2 Corinthians 4:1-6

Pastor John Chapman, an Australian evangelist, often referred to 2 Corinthians 4:1-6 as the most important passage on evangelism in the New Testament. It is situated in the middle of Paul's great manifesto on gospel ministry and provides believers with boundaries that govern, shape, and transform their engagement in the great undertaking of evangelism.

Evangelism is a broad term that covers a broad range of activities. For example, if a believer does not know their work colleague or their neighbor, they must introduce themselves and get to know them. This can take time but is part of what is often called pre-evangelism. Pre-evangelism is an important step toward the goal of having the opportunity to share the whole gospel with those who do not know Jesus. Second Corinthians 4:1-6 is a passage of Scripture that equips believers for the God-ordained work of evangelism.

Paul spells out three biblical truths that are at the center of biblical evangelism: **God's Sovereignty**, **Gospel Integrity**, and **Our Service**.[332] In these three fundamental truths, Paul contrasts God's role with the believer's role and unveils the heartbeat of evangelism.

Before we examine these three truths, we should note the context of evangelism. It is a mercy ministry (2 Cor. 4:1). It was bestowed on Paul based on God's great mercy extended to him, and it is through Paul and other believers (including believers in the 21st century) that God's great mercy is extended to others. Paul understood that taking possession of the gospel, becoming a believer in Christ, conveyed an "obligation" to its possessor (every believer) (Rom. 1:14). In this passage, Paul sets forth three pillars that biblical evangelism stands on.

Three Pillars of Evangelism

First Pillar – God's Sovereignty. Paul spells out God's role in evangelism. Since the challenge in evangelism lies in the fact that Satan has blinded the minds of non-believers (2 Cor. 4:4), something extraordinary must happen to heal the lost person's blindness. Paul reveals that a miracle by God is the only way that spiritual blindness can be healed in a non-believer. As Jesus said to Nicodemus "you must be born again" (Jn. 3:3, 7) and as Paul wrote to the Corinthians, "if anyone is in Christ he is a new creation" (2 Cor. 5:17). No human has the capability to make themselves into a "new creation" or to cause someone else to "be born again." Paul states it another way in his letter to the Colossians: "And you, who were dead in your trespasses and the uncircumcision of your flesh, God made alive together with him" (Col. 2:13). It is an act of God requiring the power of God.

---

332 From Christianity Explored Ministries training materials used in training conferences held around the world.

For God, who said, "Let light shine out of darkness," has shone in our
hearts to give the light of the knowledge of the glory of God in the face
of Jesus Christ.

2 Cor. 4:6

Paul is alluding to Genesis 1:3: "And God said, 'Let there be light,' and there was light." It is not an exact quote, but he is clearly alluding to the creation of the world. By doing so, he is saying that the power that brought the world into existence is the same power required to make a "new creation" (2 Cor. 5:17) of a lost soul.

What role did the world God created have in creating itself? What ability does a child have to cause their own birth? The answer is that neither the world nor the child has any ability to create themselves and to bring themselves into being. The action needed for a person to become a "new creation" in Christ is beyond human ability. Every single time a non-believer is converted to Christ, nothing short of a miracle has taken place.

Second Pillar – Gospel Integrity. In the miracle-working power of God, the gospel is what God uses to remove the blindness or the "veil" (2 Cor. 3:14-16; 4:3-4) that shrouds the eyes and hearts of the lost (1 Pet. 1:23-25; Rom. 1:16), so Paul instructs the believer that God's servants must handle the gospel with care and respect. Believers do not own the gospel but have been made custodians of it and must not allow it to become contaminated. Believers must not misuse it or abuse it. Paul describes God's requirement of *Gospel Integrity* with four negatives and one positive all from 2 Cor. 4:2.

First, the negatives. The believer **must not** employ methods that are:

- Disgraceful – αἰσχύνη (*aischunē*), "disgraceful ways";[333] "what one conceals from a feeling of shame";[334]
- Underhanded – κρυπτός (*kruptos*), "the things that are hidden out of a sense of shame";[335]

---

333 Harris, *The Second Epistle to the Corinthians* (NIGTC), p. 324.
334 Arndt et al., *A Greek-English Lexicon of the New Testament* (BDAG), p. 30.
335 Arndt et al., *A Greek-English Lexicon of the New Testament* (BDAG), p. 571.

- Cunning – πανουργία (panourgia) "craftiness, trickery, lit. 'readiness to do anything'";[336] or that
- Tamper (with God's word) – δολόω (doloō), "to make false through deception,"[337] **as a noun, "'bait' for fish."**[338]

Next, he ends with one strong positive. The believer **must** tell the whole gospel:

- "By the open statement of the truth" – φανέρωσις (phanerōsis) "the open proclamation of the truth"[339]

Murray Harris provides a paraphrase of 2 Corinthians 4:2b: "Rather, we state the truth candidly and boldly, as we seek to commend ourselves and our teaching to the conscience of every last person."[340] The believer's role is to express the "mighty works of God" (Acts 2:11) in redemption through Christ. It entails telling who Jesus is, what he accomplished on the cross, who the non-believer is, how they should respond, and what the consequences are of that response. Those facts must include all the elements of the gospel, as I have repeatedly detailed in this book from the first chapter.

Third Pillar – Our Service. This spells out the believer's role in evangelism.

> *For what we proclaim is not ourselves, but Jesus Christ as Lord, with ourselves as your servants for Jesus' sake.*
>
> *2 Cor. 4:5*

The **servant's** (believer's) task is to proclaim the gospel. "The phrase 'Jesus Christ as Lord' is shorthand for the gospel."[341] The word "proclaim" is from the Greek root word κηρύσσω (kērussō), which means "to make public declarations, proclaim aloud...

---

336 Arndt et al., *A Greek-English Lexicon of the New Testament* (BDAG), p. 754.
337 Arndt et al., *A Greek-English Lexicon of the New Testament* (BDAG), p. 256.
338 Harris, *The Second Epistle to the Corinthians* (NIGTC), p. 325.
339 Arndt et al., *A Greek-English Lexicon of the New Testament* (BDAG), p. 1049.
340 Murray J. Harris, *The Second Epistle to the Corinthians (Expanded Paraphrase of 2 Corinthians)* (Grand Rapids, MI; Milton Keynes, UK: W.B. Eerdmans Pub. Co.; Paternoster Press, 2005), 2 Co 4:2.
341 R. Kent Hughes, *2 Corinthians: Power in Weakness*, p. 85.

generally speak of, mention publicly."[342] The word includes a full range of activities from preaching sermons to conversationally sharing the gospel message with a friend at a coffee shop. The believer's role is to speak of Jesus and to make His name and His great work of salvation known to others.

Paul uses the word "servant" to describe himself and by implication other followers of Christ. It is a willing servitude. He joyfully and enthusiastically submits his life to Jesus. He is living his life for the glory of another, Jesus, and not for his own glory. He understood that to serve Christ was to place "all one's possessions, aspirations, time, and labor" in the service of Christ.[343] So in this context, followers of Christ, are under orders as "slaves" of Christ, to proclaim the gospel message of "Jesus Christ as Lord."

There are several ways of thinking about this third pillar of *Our Service*. We can think of it as *Our Creativity* – we serve others by finding creative ways to engage the lost with the gospel. Paul expresses his willingness to "become all things to all people, that by any means I might save some" (Cor. 9:19-27). We can think of it as *Our Energy* – we invest our time and energy at finding ways to engage the lost. It takes individual initiative and time to engage people to tell of the name and saving acts of Jesus.

Integrating All Three Pillars in Evangelism

These three evangelistic pillars Paul gives us reveal God's role, the believer's role, and the gospel's role in evangelism. To aid in understanding how these interact and complement each other, there is an exercise we can do. We can pose and answer a hypothetical question for each one of these pillars.

The first question is, "If a believer **fails** to understand **God's Sovereignty** in evangelism, but does understand Gospel Integrity and Our Service, how will that affect the believer's efforts in evangelism?"

The result: If a believer fails to understand *God's Sovereignty* and fails to recognize that only God can open blind eyes, then they will not pray. If the believer sees many people turning to Christ because of their efforts, they will tend to become arrogant and think, "What great skills I have." Conversely, if no one is turning to Christ, the

---

342 Arndt et al., *A Greek-English Lexicon of the New Testament* (BDAG), p. 543.
343 David E. Garland, *2 Corinthians* (NAC) (Nashville: Broadman & Holman, 1999), p. 215.

believer may become discouraged and give up sharing the gospel with the lost entirely. Or, they may move toward the manipulation of people and put too much pressure on them to "pray the sinner's prayer." The believer will feel that it is up to them to get someone saved. But believers must remember that only God can cause someone to be "born again" (Jn. 3:3; 2 Cor. 5:17).

All of those responses are, of course, inappropriate. The believer must be faithful to their God-assigned role and share the gospel in love and compassion and let God be God. Only God can raise someone from the dead to "walk in newness of life" in Christ (Rom. 6:4). Believers can rest in the fact that this is God's responsibility and not theirs. Praying a prayer does not save anyone, only a heart of genuine repentance that turns one's life (and lifestyle) over to Christ as Lord and Savior.

The second question is, "If a believer **fails** to understand **Gospel Integrity,** but does understand God's Sovereignty and Our Service, how will that affect their efforts in evangelism?"

The result: If a believer fails to understand *Gospel Integrity,* they will water down the gospel. They will not guard the gospel and will allow cultural values to influence their understanding and speaking of the gospel to the lost. In doing so, believers will remove the hard parts such as sin, repentance, judgement, wrath, and the cost of following Christ. In other words, believers will tamper with the gospel to make it more acceptable to lost people. That will turn Christianity into a means to achieve personal ambitions and not what it really is, a dramatic rescue from the wrath of God.

The believer must remember that when someone turns to Christ, they must come to God on His terms and not on their own terms. They must come in genuine repentance of their sins trusting in Christ's finished work on the cross, recognizing that following Him may be difficult (Mk. 8:34-38; Lk. 14:25-33; Jn 15:18-16:4), but that the benefits far outweigh any cost. The only way a person can come on Jesus' terms is if they know the terms. A person must know the reality about themselves, that they are a sinner deserving the wrath of God and that they are without hope apart from Christ. They must know the facts about Jesus, His saving action on the cross, where He suffered the wrath of God in place of sinners who turn to Him, and His triumphant resurrection from the dead. A person must know the whole gospel message, and that means the believer must be committed to presenting the full and unvarnished facts of the gospel – all of it.

The third question is, "If a believer **fails** to understand **Our Service,** but does understand God's Sovereignty and Gospel Integrity, how will that affect their efforts in evangelism?"

The result: If a believer fails to understand *Our Service,* they will not tell the gospel to the lost. The disobedient believer will not invest their time to meet non-believers and get to know them. Instead, they will fill up their time with work, career, sports, favorite hobbies, and leisure. When that believer is around non-believers, they will not make the effort to engage them with the gospel. The result in this hypothetical situation is very simple: they will not engage.

Life at the Epicenter of All Three Pillars

There is significant spiritual power when a believer integrates these three evangelistic pillars into their lives. The goal for the follower of Christ is to live at the epicenter of all three fundamentals of biblical evangelism. It is the epicenter of evangelism. **It is the combustion chamber of evangelism.** When a believer lives at this center, they will experience maximum freedom from failure and from the guilt of too few results. It is a freedom that prevents believers from pressuring people inappropriately and releases them to allow God to accomplish His work in His timing. It is a freedom to love people and to take interest in their lives. Evangelism is rarely easy, but standing on these three pillars gives the believer a solid foundation.

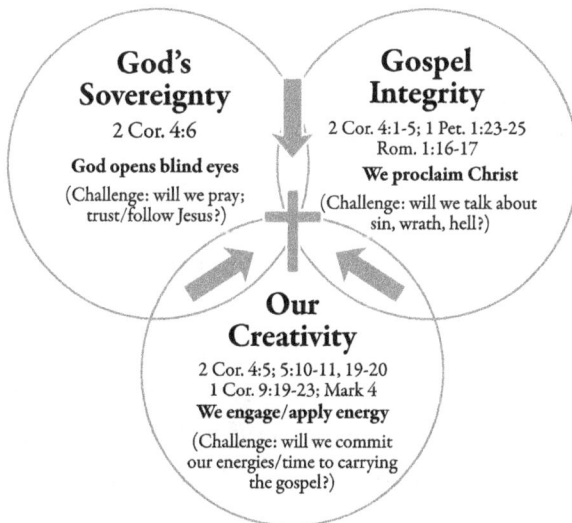

God's Sovereignty
2 Cor. 4:6
God opens blind eyes
(Challenge: will we pray; trust/follow Jesus?)

Gospel Integrity
2 Cor. 4:1-5; 1 Pet. 1:23-25
Rom. 1:16-17
We proclaim Christ
(Challenge: will we talk about sin, wrath, hell?)

Our Creativity
2 Cor. 4:5; 5:10-11, 19-20
1 Cor. 9:19-23; Mark 4
We engage/apply energy
(Challenge: will we commit our energies/time to carrying the gospel?)

What Can We Learn About the Gospel and Evangelism from this Section?

First, in recognition of God's sovereignty, believers should be actively engaged in prayer for the lost. I encourage using a prayer list. Believers can use a scrap of paper, a single sheet of paper, or a small notebook. I have used all of those at different times. At one point I had about six or eight scraps of paper held together by a paper clip. It was not very elegant, but it worked. I've graduated to a small notebook now. But regardless of what you use, include the names of loved ones, friends, work friends, and neighbors. Using a list adds a level of discipline that is useful and helps us to be more consistent in our prayers.

Many years ago, during a six-year span when I worked in a different city than I live in now, I kept a prayer list for lost people. About eight or nine years after moving away from that city, I came across the list. I had written across the top of the page "The Impossible," meaning that apart from God acting in those lives nothing would happen. I used that label because I wanted to be reminded that God is a God who does the impossible. As I scanned the list of 20 or more names, one name stood out. It was the name Will, a man who came to faith in Christ about the time I was relocating to where I now live. I circled that name on the page and paused to reflect on the many times I had prayed for the people on that list and how at times it seemed very discouraging, even like a waste of time. But as I looked at the list many years later and reflected on it, it was a moment of absolute joy and praise to the Lord that He had brought salvation into that one individual's life. Maybe some others on that list will eventually come to faith. We should take the long view in our prayers. It is in God's hands.

Second, gospel integrity is crucial. This important pillar separates real Christianity from a false version of it. All believers share in the responsibility to "guard the deposit entrusted to" us (1 Tim. 6:20). There are persistent forces acting in never-ending opposition to the gospel. We must tenaciously protect God's word, of which the gospel message is a crucial part, and we must faithfully communicate all of it.

The culture we live in is always pressuring God's people to make the gospel message more acceptable to them. Exposure of sin is often met with "that's none of your business" or "you are intolerant." Calling people to repentance from sin is deemed "not your prerogative" or is met with "who are you to tell me how to live?" Lovingly warning people about judgment and God's wrath is totally unacceptable, meeting with "you are being mean-spirited" or "that is the angry God of the Old Testament and not the loving God of the New."

Non-believers tend to think they are "no worse" than other people they know, and they believe they "will get through the judgment just fine, if there even is a judgment." But there is a judgment, and it should be feared. Those who reject God will face a terrible future that will never end. The apostle Paul writes, "For you yourselves are fully aware that the day of the Lord will come like a thief in the night. While people are saying, 'There is peace and security,' then sudden destruction will come upon them as labor pains come upon a pregnant woman, and they will not escape" (1 Thess. 5:2-3). Fortunately, there is hope, and that hope is found only in Christ for those who repent of their sins and trust in Him.

The prophet Jeremiah would add a strong amen to Paul's exhortation to not tamper with God's word. He faced off against false prophets for the 40 years of his ministry and was a great example of speaking the whole gospel by the "open statement of the truth." His appraisal of the situation in his time was:

> *An appalling and horrible thing*
> *has happened in the land:*
> *the prophets prophesy falsely,*
> *and the priests rule at their direction;*
> *my people love to have it so,*
> *but what will you do when the end comes?*
> *Jer. 5:30-31*

Please note that Jeremiah is speaking of a triad of evil: **(1) false prophets, (2) false priests, and (3) the people loved it that way.** Every person loved the situation in which they could go about their sinful lifestyles and self-aggrandizing purpose with God as their "Protector." They loved being free to pursue their every desire and did not want God spoiling their fun. They wanted God's protection and security without any obligation to live for His purpose. They would not allow any interference from God in their lives. But this threefold embrace of falsehood put the nation on a dangerous path that led to the perfect storm – the Babylonian catastrophe.

Jeremiah attempted to avert this national tragedy. He exposed the sins of the nation (2:1-37), called for repentance (3:1-4:4), and warned of God's judgment and wrath (4:5-6:30).[344] He pleaded for them to trust in God, who would preserve their lives if they would only repent and turn to Him in obedience. Otherwise, judgment was coming. But Jeremiah's opponents, the false prophets, proclaimed "a false sense of security which was preventing the nation from responding to Yahweh's call to repentance."[345]

These false prophets were not devoid of truth altogether but took selected truths out of their historical and biblical context.[346] The context was that Israel had abandoned obedience to God's covenant obligations and had degenerated into morally reprehensible lifestyles (Jer. 23:14), corruption of political and religious life (Jer. 7), and idolatry (Jer. 10). The "nothing-but-salvation-prophets"[347] misapplied truth about God and ignored the reality of the nation's sins. They embraced the truth of God's protection, mercy, and grace and ignored the truth of God's holiness and righteousness. They removed God's demand for righteous living, repentance from sin, and His warnings of judgment from their message. They focused exclusively on God's covenant promises of security and ignored the covenant obligations set out by God. They preached "All is well!" whereas Jeremiah preached "but nothing is well" (Jer. 6:14).[348] The false prophets and the people of Israel had "a false notion of what it meant to be a chosen people."[349] They preached that "[God] will do nothing; no disaster will come upon us, nor shall we see sword or famine" (Jer. 5:12), but Jeremiah said, "The prophets will become wind; the word is not in them" (Jer. 5:13). In other words, the false prophets "will be shown to be windbags who have no substance to their words."[350]

This is a sample of what Jeremiah proclaimed to his disobedient nation. This is where godly leaders dwell:

---

344 These three points are taken from the outline in J. A. Thompson, *The Book of Jeremiah* (NICOT) (Grand Rapids, MI: Wm. B. Eerdmans Publishing Co., 1980), p. 125.

345 Thomas W. Overholt, *The Threat of Falsehood: A Study in the Theology of the Book of Jeremiah* (London: SCM Press Ltd., 1970), p. 1.

346 Overholt, *The Threat of Falsehood*, pp. 40-48.

347 Overholt, *The Threat of Falsehood*, p. 41.

348 Both quotes in this sentence are translated by Thompson, *The Book of Jeremiah* (NICOT), p. 256.

349 Overholt, *The Threat of Falsehood*, p. 3.

350 Thompson, *The Book of Jeremiah* (NICOT), p. 244, footnote 11.

Behold, the storm of the LORD!
  Wrath has gone forth,
a whirling tempest;
    it will burst upon the head of the wicked.
                                    Jer. 23:19

But if they [the grace-only prophets] had stood in my council,
    then they would have proclaimed my words to my people,
and they would have turned them from their evil way,
    and from the evil of their deeds.
                                    Jer. 23:22

There is a similar phenomenon occurring today. J. I. Packer addresses this issue in his well-known book *Knowing God.*

> ***A certain type of ministry of the gospel is cruel.*** *It does not mean to be, but it is. It means to magnify grace, but what it does is rather the opposite.* ***It scales down the problem of sin and loses touch with the purpose of God.*** *The effect is twofold: first, to depict the work of grace as less than it really is; second, to leave people with a gospel that is not big enough to cover the whole area of their need.*[351] *(Emphasis mine.)*

Based on my observation, preaching today in America places a heavy emphasis on grace to the exclusion of sin, repentance, God's wrath, the difficulties of following Christ, and the need to persevere in faith to the end. But is this emphasis on grace really an accurate interpretation of biblical teaching on grace? Packer writes: "There are four crucial truths in this realm which the doctrine of grace presupposes, and if they are not acknowledged and felt in one's heart, clear faith in God's grace becomes

---

351 Packer, *Knowing God,* p. 243

impossible."[352] He names those "crucial truths" as: (1) "the moral ill-desert of man," (2) "the retributive justice of God," (3) "the spiritual impotence of man," and (4) "the sovereign freedom of God."[353]

Biblical grace is grace that not only saves the sinner from the consequences of their sins and redeems their life for the glory of God. It also propels the believer to do the hard work of growing in sanctification, mortification of sin, persevering and trusting God through the hard times, and living for God's purpose of worshiping and witnessing to His great glory. "But by the grace of God I am what I am, and his grace toward me was not in vain. On the contrary, I worked harder than any of them, though it was not I, but the grace of God that is with me" (1 Cor. 15:10). God's grace had a discernible impact on Paul's life and drove him to the hard work of life transformation and ministry; in other words, it drove him to holiness and living for God's purpose.

The false prophets of Jeremiah's day were essentially cruel. The nation of Israel followed the message of "All is well!" to their utter destruction. Had the nation repented of their sins and followed God, they would have been able to remain in their homeland to carry on with their lives.

When was the last time the pastor of your church exposed your sins, warned of God's wrath, or explored the difficulty of following Christ during a Sunday morning sermon? I am not suggesting that he called you out by name, but specifically named the sins that all believers wrestle with in the generation in which we live. Admittedly that does not happen very often in today's pulpits in America. But believers should take note that after the Babylonian disaster, Jeremiah put in writing some of his thoughts and emotions of what it was like to experience God's heavy hand of judgment. In his reflections, recorded in the Book of Lamentations, one of the issues that still haunted his mind was the reality that it didn't have to end that way. It was an absolute failure of the false prophets, the false priests, and the idolatrous worship of ordinary people who loved falsehood that caused the ultimate failure of God's people.

---

352 Packer, *Knowing God,* p. 129.
353 Packer, *Knowing God,* pp. 129-131.

Your prophets have seen for you
false and deceptive visions;
they have not exposed your iniquity
to restore your fortunes,
but have seen for you oracles
that are false and misleading.

Lam. 2:14

This "threat of falsehood"[354] to the biblical gospel is real in the 21st century, and its damage is being realized as I write these words. Falsehood is like poison wherever it is ingested, whether in a family, business, society, government, judicial system, or church. It has a corrosive and destructive force that runs its course over time unless arrested. False prophets are with us today, just like those of Jeremiah's time, but they don't wear a sign around their neck. Within evangelicalism they can be difficult to identify, but they invariably distort the biblical view of human nature (by saying we are all basically good), refuse to expose and confront sin, fail to call for repentance from sins, refuse to give the biblical emphasis to judgment and God's wrath, and focus almost solely on God's love, mercy, and grace. Paul warns believers that they must embrace **all of God's attributes** when he writes: "Note then the kindness and the severity of God" (Rom. 11:22). Christians cannot pick and choose what they like and don't like about God, His character, and His message. If believers ignore who He fully is, they place themselves on a treacherous path.

Kent Hughes notes several ways in which pastors fail the "open statement of the truth" test given by Paul. Today, rather than denying the supernatural, "it is far more common for the evangelical preacher to edit God's Word: (1) by removing the text from its context, and using it to say whatever the preacher likes, (2) by moralizing the text, so that it is reduced to an ethical maxim that fits any religion, (3) by using the text to promote hobbyhorses, and (4) by dogmatic insistence that the text says things it does not truly say."[355] Hughes goes on to add: "But most often God's Word gets watered down by

---

354 Overholt, *The Threat of Falsehood,* from the title.
355 Hughes, *2 Corinthians: Power in Weakness,* p. 84.

the preacher's laziness. He simply will not do the hard work to engage and preach a text in its context."[356] I would expand Hughes' criticism to confront ordinary believers who love falsehood and are "lazy" and "will not do the hard work to engage" and understand the biblical gospel. It may be laziness driven by modern day idolatry, love of the things of this world more than the things of God. Whatever the cause, there is no excuse for any follower of Christ to fail to do the work of understanding the biblical gospel. It is the responsibility of all believers to know the gospel and to guard it with loving care.

Third, what are we to do? The answer is simple, but not easy. **Believers proclaim Christ, and God opens blind eyes.** We have a job to do, and we do it trusting in Christ. Results are His. We all pray for and long to see results, but we must guard against moving into God's area of responsibility. It is a delicate balance, but it is never a good thing when we step into God's role. We simply do not have the spiritual power. Whenever we see a conversion occur, we are witnessing a miracle of God. He receives the glory "so that as grace extends to more and more people it may increase thanksgiving, to the glory of God" (2 Cor. 4:15).

> *I charge you in the presence of God and of Christ Jesus, who is to judge the living and the dead, and by his appearing and his kingdom: preach the word; be ready in season and out of season; reprove, rebuke, and exhort, with complete patience and teaching. For the time is coming when people will not endure sound teaching, **but having itching ears they will accumulate for themselves teachers to suit their own passions, and will turn away from listening to the truth and wander off into myths.** As for you, always be sober-minded, endure suffering, do the work of an evangelist, fulfill your ministry.*
>
> 2 Tm. 4:1-5

---

356 Hughes, *2 Corinthians: Power in Weakness*, p. 84.

CHAPTER 13

THE GOSPEL OF MARK: INTRODUCTION, PROLOGUE, PART ONE

The beginning of the gospel of Jesus Christ,
the Son of God.

Mark 1:1

As a reminder, the purpose of this book is twofold: (1) to reveal the biblical gospel of Jesus Christ as seen throughout the entire Bible and (2) to make it crystal clear that the sharing of this amazing gospel with the lost is the responsibility of all Christians. My greatest desire for all believers in Jesus Christ is to understand the biblical gospel and to know that they are called to live and to share it with the lost. This responsibility is not only for the "professional Christians" but is the call to all professing believers. We will see all of this and more in the Gospel of Mark.

I have selected the Gospel of Mark for extensive study for two reasons: (1) to arm you as a follower of Christ to have an in-depth knowledge of one of the Gospels and (2) because the evangelism material I am recommending is based on the Gospel of Mark. That material can be found in chapter 15.

INTRODUCTION

The Gospel of Mark is a prophetic voice standing on the shoulders of all the prophets of the Old Testament. Jesus emerges out of that voice in fulfillment of all their predictions and promises. Though Jesus is greater than all the prophets, His incarnation is not the end of that voice but the continuation and amplification of it. His gospel proclamation is in the tradition of all the prophets from Enoch to Malachi. His message cuts through the spiritual darkness of the world. He shines a bright light into the spiritual blindness of lost souls. But not everyone can stand the brilliance of that light.

The force of this prophetic voice comes in two basic expressions: (1) "declaring the truth about God" and (2) "predicting what God will do."[357] For example, a prophetic voice confronts sin (declaring the truth about God) and warns of judgment (predicting what God will do). A true prophetic message builds a highway in the desert of human hearts to salvation in Christ (Isa. 40:3). **The prophetic voice of The Gospel of Mark identifies who Jesus is, defines His mission, and calls people to repentance – Identity, Mission, and Call.**[358] These three themes are crucial in our evangelism efforts and will be discussed in detail as we go through Mark's Gospel.

The Gospel of Mark is a "single flowing narrative"[359] that follows the pattern of the apostolic evangelistic preaching of the first century. It incorporates drama, suspense, and the artistic use of paradox and irony. It captures the reader's attention from its opening statement, "The beginning of the gospel of Jesus Christ, the Son of God," and never lets it go. There are surprises along the way as people grapple with the person and message of Jesus. Along the journey of Mark's Gospel, today's reader will be drawn into the story and come face to face with the real Jesus. There are unexpected twists and turns as we travel Mark's path, and it even ends on an improbable note that forces deep personal reflection (16:8). Based on what we know of John Mark, the author, this should be no surprise since he was mentored by Peter and steeped in the tradition of the apostolic evangelistic thrust of the first century. John Mark's aim is the salvation and transformation of the reader's life.

---

357 Elwell, "Prophet, Prophetess," *Baker Encyclopedia of the Bible*, p. 1782.

358 From Christianity Explored Ministries. "Identity" will be used to refer to the precise identification of who Jesus is and how the Gospel of Mark defines Him. "Mission" will be used to address the specific mission of Jesus and principally why He came to earth. "Call" will be used to refer to Jesus' claim on every life; it is what Jesus requires of everyone on the planet with no exceptions.

359 France, *The Gospel of Mark* (NIGTC), p. 13.

The outline of the Gospel of Mark I will use is based on the outline by R. T. France in his commentary on the Gospel of Mark, but with different labels.[360] The Gospel of Mark fits broadly into a prologue plus three parts.

Prologue – Standing on the Shoulders of the Prophets (1:1-1:13)
Part One – The Identity of Jesus (1:14-8:21) – Ministry in Galilee
Part Two – The Mission and Call of Jesus (8:22-10:52) – Journey to Jerusalem
Part Three – Salvation Through Judgment (11:1-16:8) – Jerusalem and the Cross

We will focus primarily on four themes. **Who is Jesus? (Identity); Why did He come? (Mission); and How should we respond? (Call).**[361] **The fourth theme is spiritual blindness.** All four are interwoven throughout as Mark reveals spiritual blindness in the lives of others in contrast to the vivid reality of Jesus. Mark weaves these four together in a way that enables non-believers to see themselves under the bright light of Christ's righteousness and against the darkness of their own sins.

As Jesus' ministry progresses, we learn that most people (including religious leaders, political leaders, ordinary people, *and the disciples*) struggle to understand who He is. Even the disciples closest to Jesus have great difficulty in accurately understanding Him, His purpose, and consequently, His purpose for their lives. Through the course of Jesus' earthly ministry, we will discover that "corresponding to the increasingly supernatural character of the portrait of Jesus is the increasing inability of his disciples to cope with it."[362]

Many church people today have trouble coping with the biblical Jesus. The more they learn of His character, His purpose, and His call on their lives, the less they are able to deal responsibly with who He really is. The cultural Jesus leaves out passion for the lost and instead focuses Jesus' power on fulfilling selfish desires. Many come to terms with Jesus by simply downgrading the full reality of Him ("dumbing Him down").

---

360 France, *The Gospel of Mark* (NIGTC), pp. 11, 13-15.
361 The labelling of these three themes as Identity, Mission, and Call with the three accompanying questions are from the resources and training materials of Christianity Explored Ministries, *Christianity Explored Handbook* (4th Edition, 2016) and *Video Series* (2011) (Epsom, UK: The Good Book Company Ltd, 2016).
362 France, *The Gospel of Mark* (NIGTC), p. 270.

They create instead a low risk, truncated version of Jesus incorporating the traits they prefer and leaving out anything that is not safe or is too authoritative over their lives.

In the United States a popular version of Jesus empowers a person to achieve their greatest ambitions. He is a Jesus who will guide one to marry the right spouse, make the right job decisions, achieve financial goals, and lead to a life without stumbles. In other words, Jesus will empower one to live a flawless life free from pain, suffering, and struggles – a life with no bumps in the road. It is also a Jesus who is not offensive to the surrounding culture and is there to help them realize all of their dreams in life. Some will even think they are being complimentary of Jesus when they refer to Him as a great man, a prophet, a wise man, or an ethical teacher, but not God.

A human-centered Jesus is a narcissistic substitution of a counterfeit Jesus for the real thing. The disciples in their spiritual blindness did this and tried to pour Jesus into their own mold and to leverage Him for their own personal ambitions (Mk. 8:32; 9:33-34; 10:35-37). Jesus would have no part of it and rebuked them sternly (Mk. 8:33; 9:35-37; 10:38-45).

All of this about the typical misperceptions of Jesus is to prepare you, the reader, to look for the biblical Jesus as we explore the Gospel of Mark. Jesus' purpose for His followers is that they serve Him and follow Him along the same path that He walked.

Who is John Mark?

"John whose other name was Mark" (Acts 12:12) is the author of this Gospel. Here are some useful facts to help us understand that John Mark is the author of the Gospel with his name attached to it.

- Daniel B. Wallace: "'So strong was the early Christian testimony that Mark was the author of this gospel that we need do little more than mention this attestation' (Guthrie, 81). It is cited by Papias, Irenaeus, the Muratorian Canon (most likely), Clement of Alexandria, Tertullian, Origen, and Jerome. Further, this testimony is universal in connecting this gospel with Peter."[363]

---

363 Daniel B. Wallace, *Mark: Introduction, Argument, and Outline* (Biblical Studies Press, http://www.bible.org, 1998), p. 1, accessed February 3, 2023, https://bible.org/seriespage/2-mark-introduction-argument-and-outline.

- William Hendriksen: "Papias...born between A.D. 50 and 60, and thought to have died shortly after the middle of the second century," wrote: "When Mark became Peter's interpreter, he wrote down accurately, although not in order, whatever he remembered of what was said or done by the Lord." [364]

But who is this John Mark, and what qualifies him as a writer of one of the canonical books of the Bible? As we examine the limited but informative biblical record of Mark, a remarkable set of qualifications comes into view. Mark had an abundance of exposure to the apostolic preaching that emerged from Pentecost. His name is mentioned six times in the Book of Acts and four times in three epistles (three by Paul and one by Peter). There is speculation that Mark was the man who "ran away naked" (Mk. 14:51-52) when Jesus was arrested at a place called Gethsemane, but that is only speculation. It may be a good guess, but there is no evidence to substantiate it.[365]

John Mark is first mentioned in Acts 12:12 when Peter is miraculously rescued from certain death, shortly after Herod killed the apostle James in AD 44[366] (Acts 12:1-5, 20-23). When Peter was released by an angel, "he went to the house of Mary, the mother of John whose other name was Mark, where many were gathered together and were praying" (Acts 12:12). Mark's mother Mary was a follower of Jesus and probably a widow with enough means to afford a home large enough for Christians to meet in.[367] We do not know what age Mark is at this point but most likely a young man. *If* (a big "if") Mark was the young man in AD 33 who fled the scene of

---

364 William Hendriksen, *Exposition of the Gospel According to Mark* (NTC) (Grand Rapids: Baker Book House, 1975), p. 12. See also Papias, "Fragments of Papias," in *The Apostolic Fathers with Justin Martyr and Irenaeus*, ed. Alexander Roberts, James Donaldson, and A. Cleveland Coxe, vol. 1, The Ante-Nicene Fathers (Buffalo, NY: Christian Literature Company, 1885), pp. 154–155.

365 "This reference occurs only in Mark...The most common suggestion, now more than a century old, is that the young man is actually Mark, making vv. 51–52 an 'anonymous signature' of the author of the Gospel. This is an attractive hypothesis, and not impossible; but if it is Mark, it is a very obscure byline." Edwards, *The Gospel According to Mark* (PNTC), pp. 440-441.

366 "Josephus supplies the information that Herod died after five days in pain, 'in the fifty-fourth year of his life and the seventh of his reign.' That is, Herod died in A.D. 44. A persecutor of the church, he came to a shameful death relatively soon after he had killed James and incarcerated Peter." Simon J. Kistemaker, *Exposition of the Acts of the Apostles* (NTC) (Grand Rapids: Baker Book House, 1990), p. 447.

367 Kistemaker, *Exposition of the Acts of the Apostles* (NTC), pp. 439-440.

Gethsemane when Jesus was arrested (Mk. 14:51-52), and *if,* hypothetically speaking, we assume he was 13 years old at that time, in AD 44 he would be 24 years old. It is safe to assume that Mark would have known Peter prior to this event in AD 44, given the assumption that Christians were likely meeting regularly in his home in Jerusalem. Peter knew exactly where to go when released by the angel.

By the time Mark published his gospel, he would have personally known many of the apostles and would have had more than 20 years of firsthand experience with several of them. Some of those years would have been spent on evangelistic missionary tours. Here is a synopsis of the mention of Mark's name in Scripture with approximate dates.[368] Together they give us a sketch of John Mark over a span of about 20 years.

- AD 33 – The crucifixion of Christ[369]
- AD 44 – Peter is rescued from Herod's clutches and comes to Mark's house (Acts 12:12)
- AD 46 – Mark travels from Jerusalem to Antioch with Paul and Barnabas (Acts 12:25)
- AD 46 – Mark embarks with Paul and Barnabas on Paul's first missionary journey (Acts 13:4-5)
- AD 46 – Mark abandons the missionary journey in Perga and returns to Jerusalem (Acts 13:13)
- AD 48 – Paul is not happy about Mark leaving them in Perga two years earlier and refuses to take Mark on another missionary expedition at this time; Barnabas disagrees with Paul and takes Mark and splits with Paul on a second missionary journey (Acts 15:37-39)

---

368 The main purpose of listing these dates is not to pinpoint specific dates but to give a sense of the span of time. To simplify this timeline, the dates of events in the Book of Acts that I have chosen are early in the range, when a range is given, and for the epistles I have chosen a date named as most probable or one in the middle of the range based on Carson and Moo, *An Introduction to the New Testament,* pp. 369, 522, 578, 592, 646-7.

369 Hoehner, *Chronological Aspects of the Life of Christ,* p. 114. Carson and Moo differ slightly and write that the two most likely dates for the crucifixion are April 3 AD 33 or April 6 or 7 AD 30. "But the A.D. 30 date is slightly preferable." Carson and Moo, *An Introduction to the New Testament,* pp. 126-127.

- AD 61 – Mark is mentioned in epistles to the Colossians (4:10) and to Philemon (24). Notice that Paul views Mark as an important part of his ministry team by this time. This indicates Mark was reconciled with Paul sometime earlier. The split had occurred about fifteen years prior to the writing of these two letters. So, sometime before AD 61 Mark is fully embraced by Paul and is a vital part of his ministry team.
- AD 62 – **Mark is with Peter when he writes 1 Peter; refers to him as "Mark, my son"** (1 Pet. 5:13).
- AD 64 – **Paul instructs Timothy to "get Mark and bring him with you, for he is very useful to me for ministry"** (2 Tim 4:11). This illuminates Mark's ongoing participation on this ministry team.

Mark was shaped during that 20-year span of spreading the gospel with Paul, Barnabas, and Peter. He would have been intimately familiar with their preaching. He would have known their theology and their method of presenting the gospel of Jesus Christ. He would have prayed and sung hymns with them. He would have known success and failure. He likely would have undergone hunger, danger, and persecution with them. He would have experienced the joys of seeing many turn "to God from idols to serve the living and true God" (1 Thess. 1:9).

Peter must have had a special bond with Mark, and possibly from a young age, as Christians may have met in his home in Jerusalem on many occasions. Mark was a ministry partner in this historic evangelistic missionary endeavor of the first century. What a privilege to have learned theology under Paul and to have been shaped by the preaching ministry of Peter, with his vivid eyewitness accounts of Jesus' ministry. Twenty years of being mentored by these great leaders doing evangelistic ministry is astonishing to think about. It is hard to imagine better preparation for writing the Gospel of Mark.

Mark's Purpose in Writing This Gospel

This brings us to an important question. **Why did Mark write his Gospel?** What did Mark expect his account of Jesus to accomplish? There are a wide range of opinions, expressed by scholars, as to the occasion for writing it and Mark's intended purpose. Those opinions include "catechetical, liturgical, apologetic, conflict with the Twelve, Christological, ecclesiastical, pastoral, and editorial."[370] "the threat of persecution" prior to AD 64,[371] "the Neronian persecution following the great fire of Rome (AD 64)",[372] and others. There may be some truth in several of those stated purposes, and Mark may have intended to accomplish multiple objectives. Any accurate account of the biblical gospel usually does that. In terms of persecution and the cost of following Christ, the content of Mark matches what we find throughout the Book of Acts, all of which occurs prior to the Neronian persecution of AD 64.

There was an emerging need to have a written account of Jesus' actions and words as the apostles were nearing the end of their lives. Yet there is another bit of information that sheds light on Mark's purpose. I have alluded to it above and we can see it in the preaching of Peter – specifically, Peter evangelizing the Gentile Cornelius and his family. Carson and Moo compare the parallels between Peter evangelizing Cornelius and the Gospel of Mark. I have added four points of my own to their table and each are marked with an asterisk.

---

370 Citing Guthrie, Wallace, *Mark: Introduction, Argument, and Outline*, p. 1.

371 James A. Brooks, *Mark* (NAC) (Nashville: Broadman & Holman Publishers, 1991), pp. 29–30.

372 William L. Lane, *The Gospel of Mark (NICNT)*, (Grand Rapids, MI: Wm. B. Eerdmans Pub. Co., 1974), p. 18. Also, Edwards, *The Gospel According to Mark* (PNTC), p. 10.

How the Structure of the Gospel of Mark Mirrors Peter's Preaching to Cornelius and Family[373]

	Peter's Sermon in Acts 10:34-43	Gospel of Mark
	"good news" (v. 36)	"The beginning of the gospel" (1:1)
*	"the prophets bear witness" (v. 43)	"As it is written in Isaiah the prophet" (1:2-3)
*	Jesus Christ (he is Lord of all) (v. 36)	"So the Son of Man is Lord even of the Sabbath." (2:27; also 14:62)
*	baptism by John (v. 37)	"baptized by John in the Jordan" (1:9)
	"God anointed Jesus of Nazareth with the Holy Spirit" (v. 38)	"the Spirit descending on him like a dove" (1:10)
	"beginning from Galilee" (v. 37)	The Galilean ministry (1:14-8:26)
	"He went around doing good and healing all who were under the power of the devil" (v. 38)	Jesus' ministry focuses on healings and exorcisms
*	"in every nation anyone who fears him" (v. 35)	Healings and miracles in Gentile territory (5:1-20; 7:24-8:10)
	"we are witnesses of all that he did in the country of the Jews and in Jerusalem (v. 39)	Training for witness and ministry in Jerusalem (6:7-13; chaps. 11-14)
	"They put him to death" (v. 39)	The death of Christ (chap. 15)
	"God raised him from the dead on the third day" (v. 40)	"He has risen" (16:6)
	* = Added by me to the table by Carson and Moo	

---

373 Carson and Moo, *An Introduction to the New Testament*, p. 193. Lane, writing prior to Carson and Moo, takes the same position: "The repeated statements that the background for Mark's Gospel was provided by Peter's preaching are supported by the striking fact that the outline of the Gospel is already suggested in the sermon summarized in Acts 10:36–41." Lane, *The Gospel of Mark* (NICNT), pp. 10-11.

The parallels between the two must be more than coincidental. This may have been Peter's standard format for much of his preaching, which he would have adjusted to meet the needs of each audience he addressed. Peter's telling the gospel message to Cornelius and his family of lost Gentiles in Acts 10:34-43 is similar in content and flow to the Gospel of Mark. It is not identical in every way, but it is strongly reflective of it.

Based on this and other evidence, it seems appropriate to say that Mark was mentored not only by Paul and Barnabas but especially by Peter. This evidence supports my conclusion that though there are multiple purposes the Gospel of Mark serves, there is an overriding twofold purpose of Mark in writing his gospel that stands above all others. **Mark wrote this gospel so that sinners may come to a saving faith in the Lord Jesus Christ**[374] **and so that believers may be equipped to fulfill the Great Commission.**[375] The evident influence of Peter explains why the Gospel of Mark is more like the delivery of a single evangelistic sermon than the other three Gospels.

Place and Date of Writing

Many interpreters believe Mark wrote his gospel account in Rome to the predominantly Gentile Christians in Rome. "The tradition of the early church then affirms consistently that this gospel was written by Mark in Rome as a record of Peter's teaching, most probably while Peter was still alive and therefore not later than the early sixties of the first century."[376] An issue important to the date of this Gospel is the Neronian persecution that arose after "the disastrous fire that swept Rome in the summer of A.D. 64."[377] Though some commentators believe the Gospel of Mark was written in response to that turn of events, it seems the evidence fits better for an earlier date. The suffering, persecution, and difficulties of following Jesus addressed in the Gospel of Mark seem to fit better the suffering and persecution that occurs throughout the Book of Acts. There

---

374 I agree with William Hendriksen who said, "Mark's aim is that men everywhere may accept this Jesus Christ, "Son of man" and "Son of God," this conquering King... as their Savior and Lord." Hendriksen, *Exposition of the Gospel According to Mark* (NTC), p. 18.

375 Carson and Moo add, "The focus in the gospel on Jesus' actions, the similarity between the gospel's structure and the early Christian evangelistic preaching, and Mark's announced intention to write a book about 'the gospel' all suggest that Mark wanted to arm his Christian readers with a knowledge of the 'good news of salvation'". Carson and Moo, *An Introduction to the New Testament,* p. 186.

376 France, *The Gospel of Mark (NIGTC),* p. 38.

377 Lane, *The Gospel of Mark (NICNT),* p. 13.

is enough persecution in that historical timeframe (AD 33 to approximately AD 60) to warrant Mark's treatment of the difficulties in following Christ.

Many scholars date the Gospel of Mark in the decade of the A D 60s. My preference is for a date in the mid-50s to the early 60s. Here are two opinions that strike me as accurate: (1) Dan Wallace concludes, "Mark should be dated before the production of Luke's gospel which we date no later than 62 CE. Sometime in the mid-50s is most probable."[378] And (2) D.A. Carson and Douglas Moo conclude: "A decision between a date in the 50's and one in the 60's is impossible to make. We must be content with dating Mark sometime in the late 50's or the 60's."[379] The mid AD 50s to the early AD 60s seems a good range for dating the writing of this gospel.

The Style of John Mark

"Literacy in the ancient Mediterranean world was probably 'no more than 10 percent, although the figure may have risen to 15 or 20 percent in certain cities.'"[380] This leads many scholars to conclude that, "Mark was designed for oral transmission – and for transmission as a continuous whole."[381] "It takes about two hours to recount Mark's Gospel, not an unusual length of time for an ancient storyteller or for an ancient audience to embrace...As such, the written text of the Gospel of Mark functioned as a script for storytelling, much as a script functions for a play or sheet music for a musical performance."[382] Mark's style is perfectly suited for an oral tradition society. The British actor Alec McCowen has proven that with his well known dramatic recitation from memory of the Gospel of Mark in performances in the UK and in the US. He first performed it in 1978 after spending nearly a year and a half memorizing it. "Mr. McCowen noted that 'Mark had constructed his Gospel with the skill of a great dramatist.'"[383] A

---

378 Wallace, *Mark: Introduction, Argument, and Outline,* p. 6.

379 Carson and Moo, *An Introduction to the New Testament,* p. 182.

380 France, *The Gospel of Mark* (NIGTC), p. 9.

381 France, *The Gospel of Mark* (NIGTC), p. 9. Quoting C. Bryan, *A Preface to Mark* (Oxford: Oxford University Pres, 1993), p. 152.

382 David Rhoads, Joanna Dewey, Donald Michie, *Mark as Story: An Introduction to the Narrative of a Gospel* (Minneapolis, MN: Fortress Press, Third Edition, 2012), pp. xi-xii.

383 Greg Kandra, https://aleteia.org/blogs/aleteia-blog/rip-alec-mccowen-who-performed-st-marks-gospel-in-a-one-man-tour-de-force/, February 8, 2017, accessed February 3, 2023.

recording can be found of his performance on the internet.[384] The actor David Suchet, well known for his portrayal of Agatha Christie's Hercule Poirot, more recently performed a dramatic reading of the Gospel of Mark in St. Paul's cathedral in London in 2017.[385] A recording of his live performance can be found on the internet (https://www.stpauls.co.uk/resources/gospel-according-to-mark-read-by-david-suchet).

Mark is a man endowed with storytelling skill extraordinaire. He uses "brilliantly vivid"[386] descriptions (5:1-20) and "paradoxes [that] are maintained and never fully resolved"[387] (e.g., the parables of chapter 4). "The Second Gospel is characterized by irony"[388] (e.g., the request of James and John, 10:35-40, stands ironically in contrast with the request of blind Bartimaeus, 10:46-52). **Mark "is a past master at the narrative art of 'sandwiching' one story or scene within another."**[389] He interweaves "contemporary events in such a way that one helps to interpret the other."[390] Some of Mark's sandwiches are simple three-part sandwiches, two parallel scenes with a middle section (1:21-28; 3:22-30; 11:12-21), whereas others are more complex and include multiple phases (14:1-12).[391]

Mark employs an "expansive storytelling"[392] style that is well known for its attention to detail. The typical Gospel of Mark miracle account is twice as long as the same

---

384 https://www.theguardian.com/stage/2017/feb/14/alec-mccowen-obituary-letter, accessed April 22, 2023. Also, it can be purchased on Amazon at https://www.amazon.com/St-Marks-Gospel-Alec-McCowen/dp/B00IK52TTC, accessed April 22, 2023. I found it in the past on YouTube.

385 Joseph Hartropp, https://www.christiantoday.com/article/poirot.star.david.suchet.will.read.the.entire.gospel.of.mark.in.st.pauls.cathedral/103654.htm, January 6, 2017, accessed February 3, 2023.

386 R. Kent Hughes, *Mark: Jesus, Servant and Savior*, Vol. 1 (Westchester, IL: Crossway Books, 1989), p. 15.

387 France, *The Gospel of Mark* (NIGTC), p.20.

388 Edwards, *The Gospel According to Mark* (PNTC), p. 12.

389 France, *The Gospel of Mark* (NIGTC), p.19.

390 France, *The Gospel of Mark* (NIGTC), p.18

391 In 14:1-12, "Three scenes are set parallel to each other, with the devotion of the unnamed woman at Bethany enclosed between two phases of the plotting of the priests, the latter itself enclosed within two mentions of the arrival of the Passover festival. All this suggests that 'sandwich' is too simple a term for what Mark is doing [in this case]; nor are all his interweavings 'concentric'. Not only does he enclose one story within another, but he likes to set up parallel scenes and move the spotlight successively between them. This is a proven narrative and dramatic technique, to maintain interest and to allow the reader/hearer to gain a wider perspective on the constituent elements of the story, placing one alongside another so that they become mutually illuminating." France, *The Gospel of Mark* (NIGTC), p.19.

392 France, *The Gospel of Mark* (NIGTC), p. 9.

account in Matthew.[393] One scholar provides a list "of some 200 'elements peculiar to Mark' in the first six chapters of the gospel, most of which consist of additional details in the telling of the stories which Mark shares with one or more of the other evangelists."[394]

We can conclude that:

Mark was a skilled literary artist and theologian. – Edwards [395]

The newer approaches to Mark as literature have revealed the artistry and power of Mark's narrative. – Carson and Moo [396]

It is evident that [Mark] was a charismatically endowed teacher and evangelist. – Lane [397]

A skilled storyteller immersed in the apostolic evangelistic preaching and with a special relationship with Peter, Mark gives us a two-hour evangelistic sermon from the historic period that began at Pentecost. It is a period dominated by the Holy Spirit illuminating the work of Christ and the gospel in power in the face of significant opposition.

In view of the evidence, it is entirely appropriate to bestow the title "Prophet of Evangelism" on John Mark.[398]

---

393 France, *The Gospel of Mark* (NIGTC), p. 17.

394 France, *The Gospel of Mark* (NIGTC), p. 17. Quoting Vincent Taylor, *The Gospel According to St. Mark* (London: Macmillan, 1952), p. 135-139

395 Edwards, *The Gospel According to Mark* (PNTC), p. 3.

396 D. A. Carson and Douglas J. Moo, *An Introduction to the New Testament* (Grand Rapids, MI: Zondervan, 2005), p. 192.

397 Lane, *The Gospel of Mark* (NICNT), p. 23.

398 This is an honorary title I have bestowed on John Mark.

PROLOGUE

(1:1-1:13)

Mark is an evangelist with an urgent message and a compelling purpose to save lost souls. He uses the word "immediately" 42 times as he maintains urgency and keeps his fast-paced narrative charging along. His urgency is matched by his confidence as displayed in the opening declaration (1:1) which is bold, courageous, and assertive. From the beginning he sets himself up for a massive failure if he cannot deliver the evidence. But he can and does deliver.

Mark uses the Old Testament as his launch pad. He brings the prophets Isaiah, Malachi, and John the Baptist onto the scene and demonstrates that their message is his message. Many people do not understand that the gospel Jesus taught is the same gospel message seen throughout the Old Testament. I have heard people say that the God of the Old Testament is an angry God and that the God of the New Testament is a God of love. Both of those statements are grossly incorrect when placed in opposition. The God of the Old Testament and the God of the New Testament are the same God. The attributes of God did not change when Jesus was born in "either December, 5 B.C. or January, 4 B.C." [399] God is, and always has been, a God of mercy, grace, and love just as much as He is a God of righteousness, justice, and wrath. God is all of His attributes, all of the time, and always in perfect harmony. [400]

Drawing from the Old Testament prophets in Mark 1:2-3, Mark provides "a composite quotation from Ex. 23:20, Mal. 3:1, and Isa. 40:3." [401] The first quotation is from

---

399 "Although the exact date of Christ's birth cannot be known either December, 5 B.C. or January, 4 B.C. is most reasonable." Hoehner, *Chronological Aspects of the Life of Christ*, p. 27.

400 See Grudem's discussion of the "unity of God". Wayne Grudem, *Systematic Theology*, (Leicester, GB, and Grand Rapids, MI: Inter-Varsity Press and Zondervan, 2000), pp. 177-181.

401 Lane, *The Gospel of Mark (NICNT)*, p. 45.

Malachi 3:1 (which pulls from Ex. 23:20), "Behold, I will send my messenger ahead of you, who will prepare your way" (1:2). The second is from Isaiah 40:3, "the voice of one crying in the wilderness: 'Prepare the way for the Lord, make his paths straight'" (1:2). Both refer to John the Baptist, the last of the Old Testament prophets. Though Mark does not cite it, Malachi adds another prediction of John the Baptist in Mal. 4:5-6 (Mt. 17:10-13).

When a passage from the Old Testament is quoted in the New Testament, it is essential to examine the context it is drawn from. In this case, both citations, in their original contexts in Isaiah and Malachi, are preceded by warnings of judgment. In Isaiah, a warning of judgment and of the national catastrophe of the Babylonian captivity is issued to Hezekiah (Isa. 39:5-7) and immediately precedes the statement of salvation and hope which begins at Isa. 40:1. The Malachi passage is preceded by multiple exposures of specific sins with warnings of judgment (1:6-10; 2:1-17) and is followed by more warnings of judgment (3:2-5; 4:5-6). It is a judgment/salvation sandwich in Malachi. If we are to understand Mark's use of these passages, we must understand their Old Testament contexts. We cannot fully appreciate his meaning without doing so. Mark is alerting his readers to the fact that this book is about salvation and will contain warnings of judgment. Those who reject the salvation of Jesus and who reject His purpose of being a light to the nations will face the judgment of God's wrath.

An additional note of context is important here. The "wilderness" in Mark is not merely a geographic notation, but often a reference to the exodus events that were so ingrained in the Jewish mindset and in the Jewish sense of belonging to God. The three passages cited by Mark, Ex. 23:20, Isa. 40:3, and Mal. 3:1, are linked to the exodus. In this Gospel, both John the Baptist and Jesus are introduced to us in the "wilderness." Mark first brings Jesus onto the scene in the wilderness setting. Each Gospel introduces Jesus to its readers in a different fashion. Jesus first appears in Matthew via a genealogy going back to Abraham (Mt. 1:1-17). Luke introduces Jesus through Gabriel's appearance to the virgin Mary (Lk. 1:26-38). And John introduces Jesus from creation (Jn. 1:1-18).

John the Baptist is a man of the wilderness, his dress is of the wilderness, his diet is of the wilderness, he lives in the wilderness, and his public ministry is in the wilderness. Jesus too emerges in the wilderness at His baptism by John and is then immediately thrust more deeply into the wilderness, where Satan tries to derail Him from His purpose. This wilderness connection is intentional and significant. Jesus represents the new exodus. He is "the Prophet" like Moses who is to come (Jn. 6:14-15; Deut. 18:15, 18). He is the greater Moses, the perfect Son of God who leads His people (Heb. 3:1-6). As we go through the Gospel of Mark, Jesus invites us to follow Him in the way of the wilderness, to walk with Him in the way of the cross (Mk. 8:34-38). These are parallel images conveying what it means to walk with Christ. The way of Christ is a difficult way and a way that has many dangers, but it is the only way that has real joy, real meaning, real purpose, and real hope – the hope of eternal life. It is the way of salvation, and Jesus invites us to follow Him along this way.

"The wilderness in Mark 1:3 carries with it the full weight of a great religious tradition embracing high hopes and promises as well as the deep shadows of judgment and despair, and this is imposed upon the succeeding verses, molding them as counterparts of Israel's experience in the desert."[402] The Apostle Paul, saw the wilderness wanderings of the exodus as analogous to the Christian life (1 Cor. 10:1-13). "All Israelites were in possession of divine aid, yet most of them incurred the displeasure of God (1 Cor. 10:5). The wilderness was the scene of singular grace, but it becomes a huge and terrifying grave; it is strewn with dead." [403] Most of the Israelites, having received God's grace, rebelled against Him and received His judgment, "thus the place of God's saving help was turned into a place of disaster for many."[404]

It is easy to miss these "deep shadows of judgment" with their implications. Isaiah and Malachi understood them and were both fearless proclaimers of the gospel exposing sin, warning of judgment, and urging all to repent and place their trust in the only one who can save from the coming judgment. John Mark, an evangelist of the order of Isaiah and Malachi, begins his message of good news with these Old Testament prophets as his foundation.

---

402 Ulrich Mauser, *Christ in the Wilderness: The Wilderness Theme in the Second Gospel and Its Basis in the Biblical Tradition* (London: SCM Press Ltd, 1963), p. 82. Also, Rikki E. Watts, *Isaiah's New Exodus in Mark* (Grand Rapids, MI: Baker Academic, 1997, 2000), p. 58.
403 Mauser, *Christ in the Wilderness*, p. 65.
404 Mauser, *Christ in the Wilderness*, p. 65.

PART ONE
THE IDENTITY OF JESUS

(1:14-8:21)

Mark unfolds the first of the three themes of Identity, Mission, and Call in this section. The focus is primarily on Identity – "Who is Jesus?" Was He a great teacher, an anti-establishment revolutionary, a great healer, or a misguided idealist who lost His life because He went too far? Mark boldly stakes his claim in his opening sentence – Jesus is the Messiah, the Son of God (1:1). He then proceeds to pile up an overwhelming amount of evidence to support his claim. It is important we understand the identity of Jesus, otherwise we will relate to Him in the wrong way. Mark is clear who Jesus is and that He came for redemption.

Mark transitions from the prologue to this section with a summary of the beginning of Jesus' ministry and His message: "Now after John was arrested, Jesus came into Galilee, proclaiming the gospel of God, and saying, **'The time is fulfilled, and the kingdom of God is at hand; repent and believe in the gospel'**" (Mk. 1:14-15; emphasis mine). Though this is a high-level summary of the gospel message Jesus would preach, it revealed His purpose to evangelize the lost.

The Gospel of Mark, the shortest of the four Gospels, is very dense with miracle accounts by comparison with the other three. It has a total of 21. (Part One is especially dominated by them with 17.) The Gospels of Matthew and Luke contain 22 and 20 respectively, while John has the fewest at eight.[405] The Gospel of Mark has fewer lengthy discourses of Jesus than the others. Mark is not only giving us clear identification of who Jesus is, through His supernatural works, but is teaching theology through His actions.

---

405 The miracle account numbers used here are based on my count that includes only accounts of miracles performed by Jesus. I did not include all supernatural events that happened in His life such as God's voice at His baptism, the transfiguration, darkness in the middle of the day at the cross, or the resurrection.

John Stott writes about the miracles of Jesus: "They were 'signs' as well as 'wonders'. They were never performed selfishly or senselessly. Their purpose was not to show off or to compel submission. They were not so much demonstrations of physical power as illustrations of moral authority. They are in fact the acted parables of Jesus. They exhibit his claims visually. His works dramatize his words."[406]

Mark gives us five or six categories of evidence (depending on how one classifies them) of Jesus' power and authority. The historical facts demonstrate that His power and authority extend over: (1) His words and teaching, (2) every disease and sickness, (3) the forgiveness of sins, (4) the power of nature, (5) cosmic powers of the universe, and (6) even over death itself. In short, there is nothing Jesus does not have total authority and power over. His dominion is unlimited.

I have selected four groups of miracle accounts that Mark has arranged together. They are labeled A through D, and we will follow Mark's order of them.

A. – A Blizzard of Grace (1:21-2:17)

The Amazing Love of Jesus to Redeem!

Mark arranges individual stories and miracle accounts together for a purpose and feeds them to us in rapid succession. The miracle accounts themselves tell a theological story of redemption. They not only validate that Jesus is God, but they reveal His purpose to redeem lost souls.

It is appropriate that **the first miracle** account in Mark is a miracle "sandwich" (1:21-28) that dramatizes the importance and power of Jesus' words. The Gospel of John begins with "In the beginning was the Word, and the Word was with God and the Word was God" (Jn. 1:1). This miracle in Mark conveys the same message and dramatizes the same truth. It is Mark's version of John 1:1. It sets the stage for everything that follows.

The paragraph opens with Jesus teaching at the synagogue in Capernaum and those present "were astonished at his teaching" as He taught "as one who had authority" (1:22). In the middle of the story, a demon raised its ugly head and confronted Jesus.

---

406 John Stott, *Basic Christianity* (Downers Grove, IL: InterVarsity Press, 2nd ed., 1971, 2006), p. 41.

Jesus rebuked the demon and threw him out of the man and out of the synagogue (1:25-26). Mark closed the story with these words: "A new teaching with authority" (1:27) and adds, "his fame spread everywhere" (1:28).

The demonstration of power in casting out the demon is "sandwiched" between "he taught them as one who had **authority**" at the beginning of the story and "a new teaching with **authority**" at the end of the story. It forms a "sandwich" with a visible demonstration of power in the middle. Each part of the sandwich illuminates the other. This story within a story shows us that Jesus' words have a special authority and power never before seen. It establishes the fact that Jesus' words have real consequences, and the listener or reader should pay close attention to everything He has to say. His teaching and His words are supernatural.

The second miracle in this series shows Jesus' healing Peter's mother-in-law (1:29-31). Following that, **the third miracle** account reveals that "the whole city was gathered together at the door. And he healed many who were sick with various diseases, and cast out many demons" (1:32-34). Jesus basically healed everyone in the city who had a disease. It established His authority over every human ailment.

Mark continues to build Jesus' resume. **In the fourth miracle** Jesus expanded His public declaration of dominion by cleansing a leper (1:40-45). Leprosy was a life devastating illness with religious implications. A person with leprosy was not only banished from family and from society but was spiritually unclean and unable to participate in corporate worship. It was the ultimate form of isolation. Although no Jewish person would dare touch a man with leprosy, Jesus did touch this man. Instead of becoming unclean Himself, He freed the man from the disease and made him spiritually clean by merely speaking a word to him. "Moved with pity, he stretched out his hand and touched him and said to him, 'I will; be clean'" (1:41). Jesus has the authority and the power to make someone "clean" spiritually and physically simply by speaking a word. This miracle dramatizes that Jesus can cleanse a lost soul from sin. In the next miracle account, he explicitly declared that He had the authority to forgive sins.

In the fifth miracle Jesus returned to His home in Capernaum and was presented with a man who was paralyzed. Four friends of the paralytic could not get their friend into the house because of the crowd of people, so they took him up onto the roof. There they dug a hole above Jesus and lowered the man down through it. "And when Jesus saw their faith, he said to the paralytic, 'Son, your sins are forgiven'" (2:5). This made the scribes very angry because they knew only God could forgive sins (Ps. 32:1-2; 51-1-2; Isa. 43:25; Jer. 31:34). Jesus was thus equating Himself with God. But Jesus did more than talk a good talk. He dramatized that His words were true with supernatural action. "'But that you may know that the Son of Man has authority on earth to forgive sins' – he said to the paralytic – 'I say to you, rise, pick up your bed, and go home.' And he rose and immediately picked up his bed and went out before them all, so that they were all amazed and glorified God, saying, 'We never saw anything like this!'" (2:10-12). Jesus said things that only God could say, and they were backed up by actions that only God could accomplish. The scribes' hearts were so hard they could not see Jesus for who He truly is, and they remained lost in their sins, alienated from God, and under His wrath.

Mark now brings this arrangement of miracles to a fitting conclusion. Jesus' encounter with Levi was a **miracle of redemption** (2:13-17). It illuminated the central purpose of His coming – the redemption of people dead in their sins. And Levi was dead in his sins. This encounter is not typically counted as a miracle, but it was nothing less.[407]

Jesus passed by Levi's tax collecting operation. Levi was a Jewish man working for the oppressor Roman government. If he was like most tax collectors, he would have been corrupt, enriching himself at the expense of subjects of the Roman Empire, extracting from ordinary people more taxes than authorized for his own personal gain. He would have been hated by the Jews for being a traitor and banished from polite society. **But as Jesus passed by, He called Levi to follow Him "and he rose and followed him"** (2:14).

There is a parallel between the healing of the paralytic and the "healing" of Levi that we must not miss. The ESV translation uses the same expression, "and he rose", for the response of both the paralytic and Levi to Jesus' command (2:12 & 14). The parallelism in principle and textually is very strong. Both men rose from their respective positions forgiven, their dead souls brought to life, and reconciled to God. Jesus brought His cleansing, forgiving, transforming authority to tax collectors and sinners.

---

407 Craig Dyer, Training Director for Christianity Explored Ministries, highlighted this miracle of Levi's conversion and its place in Mark's sequence in a talk at the annual Christianity Explored Conference in Colorado in 2015. He does not claim originality for this observation.

That is the purpose of His coming – the redemption of lost souls. It is the great accomplishment of the cross.

In these events we have seen a virtual blizzard of grace pouring forth from Jesus. In the first miracle we saw the people in the synagogue wowed by the authority of His word. In the second He healed Peter's mother-in-law and followed that by healing all diseases in Capernaum. Then He cleansed a leper and healed a paralytic after forgiving his sins. The final miracle was the calling of Levi, the traitor and terrible sinner, into God's kingdom. None of these people deserved God's grace. They were all sinners deserving God's wrath but received His grace. It is an amazing display of grace. Levi is our poster child as the most unlikely recipient of God's grace so far in the story. Jesus did not come to earth to simply perform miracles.

B. – Three Storms (4:35-5:43)

The Absolute Power of Jesus to Redeem

Mark now strings together a triad of storms consecutively in the narrative that demonstrate Jesus' ability to accomplish three things: (a.) to reverse the curse placed on the earth at the fall of Adam and Eve, (b.) to defeat the cosmic enemies of God in the universe, and (c.) to redeem a person from actual death. Nothing is too powerful for Him. We have in this order: (1) the raging storm on the Sea of Galilee (4:35-41), (2) the cosmic storm of demons raging inside a man (5:1-20), and (3) the storm of death that swept away the 12-year-old daughter of Jairus (5:21-43). There are four parallels that run through all three of these events: (a) they represent new categories of miracles in Mark's narrative – dominion over nature, over cosmic (non-human) hostile powers, and over death, (b) in each Jesus faces an overpowering force that no human power can overcome, (c) death is common to all three — the threat of death or actual death,[408] and (d) the conquering

---

408 "The three miracles...have been brought together as a unit, presumably by the evangelist, to illustrate the vanquishing of powers hostile to God. The cosmic dimensions of Jesus' encounter with Satan are emphasized in the first of these stories, where the sea is understood as a manifestation of the realm of death, with overtones of the demonic in its behavior. This in turn prepares for the account of Jesus' healing of the demoniac from Gerasa. Between the two narratives there are parallels too obvious to be incidental." Lane, *The Gospel of Mark* (NICNT), p. 174.

power of Jesus is spectacularly on display in each, with both friendly and hostile witnesses for corroboration. No one could deny these miracles had occurred. All three demonstrated in dramatic terms that Jesus could do what only God can do. In other words, Jesus is God and only He can save. But could the participants see who Jesus is? Or did their spiritual blindness obscure His reality and prevent them from turning to him for salvation?

The first storm is the familiar story of **a storm on the Sea of Galilee** (4:35-41). At the end of a long day of teaching, Jesus and the disciples got into a boat to cross the sea. During the crossing a "great windstorm" came upon them and threatened their lives. Jesus, exhausted from a day of teaching and interacting with people, "was in the stern, asleep on the cushion" (4:38). The disciples woke Jesus and reproached Him saying, "Teacher, do you not care that we are **perishing**?" (4:38). Jesus "awoke and rebuked the wind and said to the sea, 'Peace! Be still!'" (4:39). The wind "ceased" and "there was a great calm" (4:39) on the sea. Jesus then said to the disciples, "Why are you so afraid? Have you still no faith?" (4:40). After the danger from the storm was over, they were more afraid of Jesus than they were of the storm.

> *And they were filled with great fear and said to one another, "Who*
> *then is this, that even the wind and the sea obey him?"*
>
> *Mark 4:41*

That is the central question, isn't it? The disciples put into words the question on all of our minds. Who is this man? What we learn from this event is that Jesus has two natures. He has the nature of a man and the nature of God in one person. He is fully human and fully divine. But most people could only see His human nature, including those closest to Him. They were blind to the reality of who Jesus actually is. In this situation, Jesus subdued the raging storm by uttering mere words of command. It is an abrupt command that required immediate obedience. It had a double force. The untamable storm immediately obeyed His words.

The second of the three storms (5:1-20) occurred when Jesus and the disciples crossed over to the eastern shore of the Sea of Galilee and came "to the country of the Gerasenes" (5:1). Here Jesus encountered **a raging army of demons** living inside a man. Jesus had ventured into Gentile territory. Most of His ministry was spent in predominantly Jewish areas, but some notable ministry occurred in areas inhabited mostly by Gentiles. Jesus came for all the nations.

"And when Jesus had stepped out of the boat, immediately there met him out of the tombs a man with an unclean spirit" (5:2). This was the second opposing force attempting to prevent Jesus from doing ministry in Gentile territory. Just as the storm on the sea opposed Jesus' going to this area, so now a man possessed with many demons "immediately" confronted Him as He came ashore. The man was a living disaster with superhuman demonic strength. "Night and day among the tombs and on the mountains he was always crying out and cutting himself with stones" (5:5). He was walking death and destruction. No one wanted to be near this man who was more like a wild animal than a human.

When this wild man, under the control of an army of cosmic villains, arrived in front of Jesus, he "fell on his knees ... [and] shouted at the top of his voice, ... 'Swear to God that you won't torture me!'"[409] In this confrontation Jesus demanded his name. The demon obeyed, "My name is Legion, for we are many" (5:9). At the time of Jesus, a "legion" was a unit of about 6,000 men in the Roman army with 120 calvary added to it.[410] "Because it represented a large body of men, the word 'legion' came to be used symbolically for an indefinitely large number."[411] Legion had been in charge of this territory, but King Jesus arrived.

Legion was terrified of the wrath of the Lamb (Rev. 6:6). Legion knew exactly who Jesus was and knew that Jesus would one day cast him and his many friends into hell. But he did not know the time of his impending destruction. This army of demons was no match for Jesus. Legion had to depart, but Legion begged Jesus "not to send them out of the country" (5:10). As a herd of pigs was feeding nearby, "They begged him, saying, 'Send us to the pigs; let us enter them'" (5:10). And Jesus granted permission. So, about 2,000 pigs race down the hill and drown in the sea (5:13). This was a huge economic loss of over $1,000,000 in terms of today's U.S. dollars.[412] Due to the law of

---

409 Translation by Edwards, *The Gospel According to Mark* (PNTC), p. 156.

410 Elwell, "Legion," *Baker Encyclopedia of the Bible*, p. 1322.

411 Elwell, "Legion," *Baker Encyclopedia of the Bible*, p. 1322.

412 This estimate of economic value is based on the assumption of an average weight per pig in the herd of 150 pounds and a market price of $3.50 per pound. In the U.S. in 2022 the average market weight of a pig is 265 pounds. For the herd in this story, I assumed a mix of young pigs as well as mature pigs. Price and average weight are based on an internet search on September 27, 2022.

supply and demand, with this significant loss of protein, I suspect the price of chickens shot up on the eastern side of the lake after this incident.

The herdsmen of the pigs ran into the city and reported the loss. People from the city came out to see what had happened. They looked at Jesus, looked at the man now in his right mind, and considered the pigs that just went down the steep bank into the sea. Their response: "And they began to beg Jesus to depart from their region" (Mk. 5:17). These Gentiles made an on-the-spot value-based assessment of the situation. They saw the man now saved from the wrath of the demons and in his right mind. They saw the total loss of a herd of 2,000 pigs. For them, the value of a herd of pigs was greater than the value of a human soul. It was not worth the cost of having Jesus around. He was just too expensive. They valued economic wealth over a human life. Before departing, Jesus sent the man home and said to him, "Go home to your friends and tell them how much the Lord has done for you, and how he has had mercy on you" (Mk. 5:19). God's purpose to redeem lost souls was once again brought to the fore. Jesus sent him to the Gentiles to tell of the Lord's mercy.

The third storm in this flow of accounts is actual death (5:21-43). Whereas the storm on the lake and the army of demons represented the threat of death, **the raising of Jairus' daughter is actual death.** This account is sandwiched around the healing of a woman who had been suffering from a hemorrhage for 12 years. She was getting worse and had been ill for as long as Jairus' daughter had been alive. Death had been stalking in the previous two events, and Jesus prevented its victory. Now death had actually happened. Did Jesus have power over death once it had taken place?

This story began as Jairus, the ruler of a synagogue, came to Jesus and "implore[d] urgently" that He come and heal his daughter who is at death's doorstep (5:23). Jesus agreed and went with him. Along the way, as a large crowd was all around Jesus, a woman who was ill got close enough to Jesus to touch His garment. Jesus perceived that power went out from Him and turned to look for the one who drew the healing power from Him. When the hemorrhaging woman realized she had been discovered, she fell down before Jesus in "fear and trembling" (5:33). Jesus responded to her tenderly and told her to "go in peace, and be healed of your disease" (5:34).

While Jesus was still speaking with the now-healed woman, someone from Jairus' house arrived with the tragic news that his daughter had died and advised him not to bother Jesus any further. But Jesus overheard the conversation and intervened, telling Jairus, "Do not fear, only believe" (5:36). Jairus had enough faith to approach Jesus in the first place, but now that his daughter was dead a test of his faith was upon him. This was clearly more difficult for Jairus, but he continued with Jesus.

When Jesus arrived at Jairus' home, there was loud weeping and wailing (5:39). Jesus asked them, "Why are you making a commotion and weeping? The child is not dead but sleeping" (5:39). Their response was to ridicule Jesus with laughing mockery. Jesus booted them all out and only allowed the mother and father in the room along with Himself, Peter, James, and John.

Jesus walked over to the young girl lying dead on her bed. "Taking her by the hand he said to her...Little girl, I say to you, arise" (5:41). Immediately this twelve-year-old girl got up and started walking around. Everyone at the scene was overwhelmed with amazement. **Jesus brought this young girl back to life as easily as you or I would awaken someone from sleep.** In dramatic fashion, Jesus had answered the question, "Does Jesus have power over death?" The answer was strikingly, "Yes!"

Jesus could save from impending death, He could save from a living hell, and he could save from the condition of actual death. Once again, we saw that there was nothing Jesus did not have power over. He was and is the one and only capable redeemer.

C. – An Exodus Sandwich (6:30-8:10)

The Historic (Proven) Ability of Jesus to Redeem

Beginning at Mark 6:30 there is a series of six miracles which form an "Exodus Sandwich." It begins with the feeding of 5,000 and ends with the feeding of 4,000. The feeding miracles, and the water miracle, are reminiscent of the exodus of Israel out of Egyptian bondage, which included water miracles (parting the Red Sea, Ex. 14; water from the rock in the desert, Ex. 17:1-7; also see Job 9:8-11) and massive feeding miracles (manna in the wilderness for 40 years, Ex. 16).

Before looking at a few details, here is a diagram of the six miracles with an account of a confrontation with the religious elite in the middle. The religious elite, comprising the Pharisees and Scribes (Mk. 7:1), are a mirror image of the disobedient people of

God in the wilderness wanderings. "For who were those who heard and yet rebelled? Was it not all those who left Egypt led by Moses? And with whom was he provoked for forty years? Was it not with those who sinned, whose bodies fell in the wilderness? And to whom did he swear that they would not enter his rest, but to those who were disobedient? So we see that they were unable to enter because of unbelief" (Heb. 3:16-19). Spiritual blindness is deadly.

- **Feeding of 5,000** (6:30-44)
  - Jesus walks on water (6:45-52)
  - The healing of many (6:53-56)
    - *Confrontation with Pharisees and Scribes (7:1-13)*
    - *Teaching about sin (7:14-23)*
  - Gentile woman's daughter freed (7:24-30)
  - Deaf mute healed (7:31-37)
- **Feeding of 4,000** (8:1-10)

The two feeding miracles, in context with the other miracles embedded with them, bring us to a pinnacle of sorts in the Gospel of Mark. It is a pinnacle revealing that Jesus is the great redeemer, the great "I AM" of the exodus (Ex. 3:13-14). He is the one Moses predicted: "The LORD your God will raise up for you a prophet like me from among you, from your brothers—it is to him you shall listen..." (Dt. 18:15; Jn. 6:14). And though Jesus is the prophet like Moses, He is far superior to Moses in every way. "For Jesus has been counted worthy of more glory than Moses – as much more glory as the builder of a house has more honor than the house itself" (Heb. 3:3; see also 3:4-6).

The first three of the six miracles – feeding 5,000, Jesus' walking on water and healing many – occurred in Jewish territory. The second three – freeing the Gentile woman's daughter from demon possession, healing the deaf mute, and feeding 4,000 – occurred in predominantly Gentile territory in Tyre and Sidon and on the east side of the Sea of Galilee. This "exodus" (salvation) is for both Jews and Gentiles.

In the feeding of the 5,000 there are ten points of contact with the first exodus events, when God used Moses as His shepherd to liberate the children of Israel out of Egyptian bondage.

1. It occurred in a "desolate place" (Mk. 6:31, 32, 35; Ex. 3; 4:27; 5:1, 3; 7:16; 8:27; 13:18; 16:32).

2. Jesus' intention was to give the disciples physical and spiritual "rest" (Mk. 6:30-32; also 6:7-13); "rest" was a recurring theme in the first exodus[413] (Ps. 95:11; Isa. 63:11-14; Heb. 3:7-4:13).

3. It was a miraculous feeding of a massive crowd (Mk. 6:34, 44; Ex. 16:4, 8, 12).

4. "The arrangement of the crowd into field-groups of hundreds and fifties recalls the order of the Mosaic camp in the wilderness (e.g., Ex. 18:21)"[414] (Mk. 6:39-40).

5. "The provision of food by Jesus symbolized what it symbolized with Moses – God's saving grace in rescuing His people from bondage."[415]

6. The water miracle late on the night of feeding the 5,000 parallels the water miracles of the exodus event (Mk. 6:45-52; Ex. 14).

7. The religious elite mirror the rebellious people of God led by Moses out of Egyptian bondage to slavery (a metaphor for sin).

The Gospel of John adds four connecting elements to the exodus that are not found in the Synoptic Gospels.

8. It occurred at the time of "the Passover, the feast of the Jews" (Jn. 6:4; Ex. 12).

9. The people recognized it as a "sign" and identified Jesus as the prophet Moses pointed to (Jn. 6:14; Deut. 18:15-19).

10. The people were going to force Jesus to become their king and lead them in an "exodus" out from under Roman oppression (Jn. 6:15).[416]

---

413 Lane, *The Gospel of Mark* (NICNT), p. 225.

414 Lane, *The Gospel of Mark* (NICNT), p. 229.

415 Hughes, *Mark: Jesus, Servant and Savior*, Vol. 1, pp. 146–147.

416 "An unusual number of signs thus suggest that the wilderness commotion was aflame with messianic fervor, and that the crowd hoped to sweep Jesus up as a guerrilla leader. These clues are confirmed in John's account of the feeding of the five thousand, where we are told that the people 'intended to come and make him king by force' (John 6:15). It is nevertheless clear from the account that Jesus will not march to a populist and militarist drumbeat. He will not be a militant-messianic shepherd of the sheep." Edwards, *The Gospel According to Mark* (PNTC), pp. 194–195.

Mark has placed on full display, through the fast-moving sequence of miracles, the full humanity and the full divinity of Jesus. There should be no mistaking who Jesus is. Yet, most are not able to see Him clearly. Mark ends this section of his narrative with an ironic twist that reveals spiritual blindness among even those closest to Him.

D. – A Pandemic of Blindness (8:11-21)

Spiritual Blindness – The Barrier to Redemption

Two stories bring this section to a close and emphasize the theme of spiritual blindness. It is ironic that Mark closes this section of his narrative, and its many miracles, with the theme of spiritual blindness. But spiritual blindness is a major block to salvation and stands as an obstacle in the path of evangelism.

In the first story, immediately following the feeding of 4,000, Mark recounts the Pharisees' "seeking from him [Jesus] a sign from heaven to test him" (8:11-13). If we pause and think about their request, within this context of a multitude of miracles performed over a period of about two years, it is nothing short of incredible. It would be laughable if it weren't so tragic. For Jesus it was no laughing matter.

> *And he sighed deeply[417] in his spirit and said, "Why does this generation seek a sign? Truly, I say to you, no sign will be given to this generation." And he left them, got into the boat again, and went to the other side.*
>
> *Mk. 8:12-13*

---

417 "The word for 'groaned' ["sighed deeply" in the ESV] (Gk. *anastenazein*) is a rare word, occurring only here in the NT, and fewer than thirty times in all of Greek literature. A survey of its uses reveals that it is not an expression of anger or indignation so much as of dismay or despair... The antagonism of the Pharisees parallels the antagonism of the Israelites to Moses in the wilderness – and Jesus' groaning in dismay seems to reflect God's disgust with the bent and recalcitrant Israelites (Exod 33:5!). The reference to 'this generation' signals the Pharisees' alienation from Jesus and recalls the disbelieving generation of Noah's day (Gen 7:1) and the stubbornness of the Exodus generation in the wilderness (Ps 95:10–11)." Edwards, *The Gospel According to Mark* (PNTC), p. 236.

Jesus had demonstrated through His many miracles His mastery over every area of life, and yet the Pharisees still came seeking a sign to prove who He is. They had been following Jesus' words and actions over many months, but with hearts of hardened opposition to Him. They saw Him as a threat to their sin and their personal idols which they refused to abandon.

Their hard hearts had blinded them to the truth of who Jesus is, and the more they resisted Jesus the deeper they descended into darkness. They loved their positions in society, their culture, their religious traditions, and other comforts and routines of life more than they loved God. This did not go over well with Jesus. He had appealed to them on many occasions to repent of their sins and place their trust in Him. But at this juncture, **Jesus groaned deeply and turned His back on them.** He refused their request and turned away. "Jesus' abrupt departure from the Pharisees gave visible expression to his indignation."[418] "What a terrible thing it is to have Christ turn his back on you and sail away."[419]

In the second story, Mark reveals with striking clarity the spiritual blindness of the disciples. Back again in the boat, the disciples discovered "they had forgotten to bring bread, and they had only one loaf with them" (8:14). Jesus "cautioned them, saying, 'Watch out; beware of the leaven of the Pharisees and the leaven of Herod'" (8:15). The disciples did not understand Jesus' meaning and "began discussing with one another the fact that they had no bread" (8:16). Jesus was beyond not happy with them and proceeded to castigate them about their blindness. Jesus excoriated them with these words:

> *Why are you discussing the fact that you have no bread? Do you not yet perceive or understand? Are your hearts hardened? Having eyes do you not see, and having ears do you not hear? And do you not remember? When I broke the five loaves for the five thousand, how many baskets full of broken pieces did you take up?" They said to him, "Twelve." "And the seven for the four thousand, how many baskets full of broken pieces did you take*

---

418 Lane, *The Gospel of Mark* (NICNT), p. 279.
419 Hughes, *Mark: Jesus, Servant and Savior, Vol. 1*, p. 189.

up?" And they said to him, "Seven." And he said to them, "Do you not yet understand?"

Mk. 8:17-21

Jesus' rebuke of the twelve was severe. They had been with Him for about two years and had seen numerous miracles, including two massive feeding miracles. They had experienced His miraculous saving of their own lives on the lake. He expected them to understand the meaning of His caution "Watch out." Yet they did not understand, and they appeared as rather obtuse and lacking in practical intelligence. They took Him literally when He was speaking metaphorically. It is not a happy ending for this section, but it prepares us for what follows – the only cure for spiritual blindness is Jesus' opening someone's eyes.

As Mark transitions the reader to the next section, Jesus did not turn His back on His disciples, as He did to the Pharisees. The Pharisees and the disciples were both afflicted with spiritual blindness, yet each appears to have had a different kind of spiritual blindness. The Pharisees had hardened, defiant blindness undergirded by a love of their sins and a hatred of Jesus. The disciples' blindness was a result of wrong expectations and worldly idols perhaps, but at the same time was undergirded by a love for Jesus. Both types of blindness lead to failings with different negative consequences.

If Mark's narrative pace has been swift up to this point, he slows it down now as he moves to his next subject. He knows that we, like the disciples, will not be able to keep up if he doesn't.

CHAPTER 14

THE GOSPEL OF MARK: PART TWO AND PART THREE

PART TWO

THE MISSION AND CALL OF JESUS

(8:22-10:52)

A change in geography signals a shift in the focus of Jesus' ministry. He and His disciples moved from Dalmanutha (which is probably near Magdala[420]) to Bethsaida, located on the northeastern shore of the Sea of Galilee, and then on to Caesarea Philippi (8:10, 22, 27) about 25 miles to the north. Caesarea Philippi had a population that was chiefly non-Jewish[421] and was away from the crowds that had been following Him throughout Galilee. It was away from Jerusalem, the stronghold of His enemies. Here Jesus began His ultimate journey, the journey to the cross.

By my estimate, this occurred six to twelve months prior to the cross.[422] From this point on, Jesus mostly avoided the large crowds He accommodated during the first two years of His ministry and focused His attention on preparing the disciples for His departure.

---

420 Edwards, *The Gospel According to Mark* (PNTC), p. 234.

421 Edwards, *The Gospel According to Mark* (PNTC), p. 246.

422 The estimates are based on the dating of Passover in April AD 32 (Jn. 6:4; Mk. 6:30-44), the Feast of Tabernacles in September AD 32 (Jn. 7:2, 10), and the Feast of Dedication in December AD 32 (Jn. 10:22-39) by Harold Hoehner, *Chronological Aspects of the Life of Christ,* p. 143, and are compared with a harmony of the Gospels by Robert L. Thomas, *Charts of the Gospels and the Life of Christ,* pp. 26-30.

Significantly, this middle section of the narrative, the journey to the cross, is framed or sandwiched by two healings of blind men. The center of this sandwich is filled with three teachings of the cross. The two healings of blind men stand like two giant floodlights illuminating the mission and the call of Jesus.

Mark slows the narrative pace as we come to this section. The disciples were struggling to understand what Jesus was teaching and doing. We will have the same struggle. The challenge of the cross is twofold. First, do we understand what occurred in that event? And second, is our life in conformity with the demands of it? The cross is not only a matter for the intellect, but a serious test of the heart. The cross for Jesus' followers means faithfulness to Him and faithfulness to telling His message of salvation.

Healing a Blind Man in Two Steps (8:22-26)

The first healing of blindness was an acted parable by Jesus (8:22-26). It was a historical event, but it also was a dramatization of spiritual truth that communicates a deeper meaning. It was the only miracle accomplished by Jesus in two stages and is only recorded in the Gospel of Mark. It immediately followed a series of rebukes of the disciples that included, *"Are your hearts hardened? Having eyes do you not see, and having ears do you not hear?...Do you not yet understand?"* (8:17-21). Mark wants us to know that the previous episode, highlighting the blindness of the disciples, is connected to this one. In fact, this event explains the previous situation of spiritual blindness and reveals the only solution for that blindness.

The healing of blind Bartimaeus at the end of this section (10:46-52) is connected to this event and dramatizes even further this idea. In a real sense, this may be the biggest theological sandwich that Mark provides in his Gospel. There is a lot in the middle, and we will not understand any of it unless Jesus heals our own blindness. To be more specific, if you want to understand the mission of Jesus and God's purpose for your life, you will need to experience God's healing of your spiritual blindness on a daily basis.

This event began when Jesus and the disciples arrived in Bethsaida (8:22). People brought a blind man to Him for healing. Jesus took the man by the hand and led him outside of the village. **In the first step,** Jesus "spit on his eyes and laid his hands on him" (8:23) and asked him what he could see. The man said, "I see people, but they look like trees, walking. **In the second step,** Jesus laid his hands on his eyes again" (8:24-25) and he could immediately see everything clearly.

It was a two-step healing process. After the first step the man's vision was partial. After the second step he could see everything clearly. Jesus was not having a "bad power day" and unable to heal the man in one step. It was intentional and dramatized that the disciples (and all of us) were in need of Jesus' healing their blind eyes and softening their hard hearts. The lost will not be able to see their lost condition nor understand the terrible danger they are in, and believers will not be able to understand Jesus' purpose of being a light to the nations. It is an ongoing process. In the next sequence we will see that the disciples could partially see and were partially blind.

Grand Central Station (8:27-38)

We now come to the theological center of Mark's Gospel. It was a pivotal moment because for the first time the disciples recognized that Jesus is the Messiah (8:27-38).[423] This was immediately followed by what it means to be Messiah (death on the cross, 8:31), which was then followed by what it means to be a follower of Messiah (deny self and take up one's own cross, 8:34-38). This section reveals Jesus' purpose and the believer's purpose. His mission and our mission.

Rico Tice has called this section the "Grand Central Station" of Mark. The entire Gospel of Mark flows into and out from it. There is a special force here "because so many of the paradoxes come together in a great knot."[424] It is like a Gordian knot that is so complex as to be nearly unsolvable. In fact, there is only one solution. And that solution is Jesus Christ healing a person's spiritual blindness. If that does not happen, a person may study the facts of this puzzle all they want but will never be able to comprehend its meaning for their life.

In three successive paragraphs Mark brings together the Gordian knot of the Identity (27-30), Mission (31-33), and Call (34-38) of Jesus.

Identity – Who is Jesus? (27-30). After the healing of the blind man in two steps they left Bethsaida and headed due north to the villages of Caesarea Philippi. Along the way

---

423 Lane, *The Gospel of Mark* (NICNT), pp. 288-289.
424 France, *The Gospel of Mark* (NIGTC), p. 20 citing Frank Kermode, *The Genesis of Secrecy: On the Interpretation of Narrative, 1979, p. 141.*

Jesus asked the disciples, "Who do people say that I am?" (8:27). They responded, "John the Baptist; and others say, Elijah; and others, one of the prophets" (8:28). Then Jesus asked the penetrating question, "But who do you say that I am?" (8:29). Peter responded with his famous statement, **"You are the Christ"** (8:29). Peter got this question precisely correct which leads us to conclude that **Peter could "see" and was not blind.**

Mission – Why did Jesus come? (31-33). Jesus, for the first time, explicitly taught the disciples that He must die on the cross and would be subsequently raised from the dead (8:31-33). This was the first of Jesus' three predictions of the cross in Mark (8:31-33; 9:30-32; 10:32-34). We will examine three features of these predictions: (1) elements common to all three, (2) differences among the three which are significant, and (3) the disciples' response in each case.

Divine Necessity.[425] **The first prediction of the cross and resurrection** occurred approximately six to twelve months prior to His death:[426]

> *And he began to teach them that the Son of Man must suffer many things and be rejected by the elders and the chief priests and the scribes and be killed, and after three days rise again.*
>
> *Mk. 8:31*

The three teachings have four elements in common: "1) the Son of Man 2) will be killed and 3) after three days 4) he will rise."[427] In this first teaching of the cross, **the distinctive element unique to it is that the cross is a divine necessity.** "The verb translated 'must' (*dei*) [8:31] suggests divine necessity, probably as it is indicated in the Scriptures. The most obvious Scripture is Isa 52:13–53:12..."[428]

Earlier, when Jesus asked the disciples, "But who do you say I am?" Peter's response was on target. This time, however, Peter did not respond well. In fact, he got it cata-

---

425 Peter G. Bolt, *The Cross from a Distance: Atonement in Mark's Gospel* (Downers Grove, IL: InterVarsity Press, 2004), p. 49.

426 Parallel accounts for this event are in Matthew 16:21-28 and Luke 9:22-27.

427 Bolt, *The Cross from a Distance*, p. 48.

428 Brooks, *Mark* (NAC), p. 136. Peter Bolt agrees and writes, "R. H. Smith (1973: 332) states that Mark's *dei* [must] is equivalent to 'according to the Scriptures', and is echoed in Mark's Old Testament allusions and quotations." Bolt, *The Cross from a Distance*, p. 49, footnote 4.

strophically wrong. He went from profoundly correct to embarrassingly wrong. We are told that "Peter took him aside and began to rebuke him" (8:32). But Jesus rebukes Peter severely saying, "Get behind me, Satan! For you are not setting your mind on the things of God, but on the things of man" (8:33). Peter was trying to stop Jesus from going to the cross. Peter could not accept a suffering Messiah. So, what happened? Peter was brilliant in answering the first question, but here he could not have been more diametrically opposed to the purpose of God.

In this instance we must conclude that **Peter was blind.** So how could Peter see clearly one moment and be blind the next? The healing of the blind man in two stages holds the answer to that question. Just like the blind man in the process of being healed, Peter could partially see and was partially blind. He would need ongoing healing of his spiritual blindness. It was not to be a single step but a progression of multiple steps. It would be a series of small steps throughout Peter's life. And that will be the case for all followers of Jesus.

What had blinded Peter? We are not told specifically, but we can make an educated guess. Peter and the other disciples were steeped in the values of their culture and of their world. He seems to have presupposed a conquering and triumphant Messiah, not a suffering Messiah. Peter perhaps wanted to win in the political arena and among the world national powers. Peter may have desired a life without struggles, pain, or stumbles. But Jesus rebuked him for having his mind set on the "things of man." Peter had an expectation of a Messiah that was the opposite of the real Messiah. And he recoiled at the thought of a suffering Messiah. Peter did not realize it, but he was rejecting the central purpose of Jesus' incarnation, His offering of Himself for the sins of the world.

Before moving to the succeeding paragraph, it is important to examine the other two predictions of the cross and the resurrection. They are highly instructive as we seek to understand the cross. We can learn from the spiritual blindness of the disciples.

Divine Judgment without Mercy.[429] **The second teaching of the cross** occurs in Mark 9:30-32.[430] Jesus and the disciples had returned from the area of Caesarea Philippi

---

429 Bolt, *The Cross from a Distance,* p. 53.
430 Parallel accounts for this event are in Matthew 17:22-23 and Luke 9:43-45.

and were passing through Galilee on their journey to Jerusalem and the cross. Jesus taught the disciples a second time:

> *The Son of Man is going to be delivered into the hands of men, and they will kill him. And when he is killed, after three days he will rise.*
>
> Mk. 9:31

The same four elements common to all three teachings of the cross are present in this second teaching. **The element unique to this one is "delivered into the hands of men."** "When God is the one handing people over, the expression has overtones of divine judgment (e.g. Ezek. 39:23), sometimes explicitly paralleled with a reference to the wrath of God (Judg. 2:14; Ps. 78 [LXX]:61, cf. v. 59...Rom. 1:18ff.). When threatened with judgment after numbering the people of Israel in an illegal census, David said that he would rather fall into the hands of the Lord, whose mercies are great...than into human hands, for, by implication, human beings are not known for their compassion (1 Chr. 21:13)."[431]

The response of the disciples to this second prediction of the cross was to argue among themselves as to who was the greatest (9:33-37). This was another inappropriate response revealing spiritual blindness. In fact, it went beyond inappropriate and was actually a ridiculous response. But can we determine the source of their persistent spiritual blindness? It was another unveiling of their core values which were aligned with their culture. It seems they had a longing for personal significance and craved being great in the eyes of others. It was about life with me at the center. It was a self-focus that desired greatness and personal significance according to the world's terms and was a form of idolatry of the heart. They had no desire to walk in the way of the cross with Jesus.

Jesus corrected them and gave them an object lesson about real greatness. "And he said to them, 'If anyone would be first, he must be last of all and servant of all.' And he took a child and put him in the midst of them, and taking him in his arms, he said to them, 'Whoever receives one such child in my name receives me, and whoever receives me, receives not me but him who sent me'" (9:35-37).

---

431 Bolt, *The Cross from a Distance*, p. 53.

Divine Wrath.[432] **The third teaching of the cross** is in Mark 10:32-34.[433] This took place within three months of His death. Jesus was leading the disciples on the road to Jerusalem. The disciples were apparently lagging behind Jesus and not eager to go to Jerusalem since the text says they were "amazed" and "afraid" as they followed Him. The disciples knew that Jesus' enemies wanted to put Him to death, and they also feared for their own lives. They were walking toward danger. And He began to teach the twelve again and said,

> *"See, we are going up to Jerusalem, and the Son of Man will be delivered over to the chief priests and the scribes, and they will condemn him to death and deliver him over to the Gentiles. And they will mock him and spit on him, and flog him and kill him. And after three days he will rise."*
>
> *Mk. 10:33-34*

The element unique to the third teaching is that Jesus will be handed over to the nations. "The horror of this action should be apparent to all who are familiar with Old Testament history. To hand someone over to the nations (Gentiles) is equivalent to handing someone over to God's wrath."[434] The phrase is a "theologically loaded term."[435]

The response of the disciples in this instance was no better than the first two. It was driven by the same set of values instilled in them by their culture. In Mark 10:35-45 we see James and John asking Jesus for positions of power in His coming kingdom. James and John were not only blinded to the mission of the Son of Man, which Jesus had disclosed to His disciples for a third time, but they were also incorporating their personal ambitions into Jesus' teaching. They were searching for a way to leverage Jesus for their own desires for power and all the benefits that come with it. Their request was incredibly inappropriate in the context of Jesus' facing the horrendous ordeal of the cross. **Jesus was not going to the cross to die a painful death to supercharge their personal ambitions.** In today's

---

432 Bolt, *The Cross from a Distance,* p. 56.
433 Parallel accounts for this event are in Matthew 20:17-19 and Luke 18:31-33.
434 Bolt, *The Cross from a Distance,* p. 56.
435 Bolt, *The Cross from a Distance,* p. 56. Bolt lists the following Old Testament references in support of the phrase being linked to "God's wrath": Lev. 26:32-33, 38; Hos. 8:10 in the Septuagint (also Hos. 10:10 ESV*); Ps. 106:41 (in the context of 106:40-43*); Ezra 9:7. *Added by me.

world many slip into that way of thinking. For that matter, many sitting in the pews on Sunday morning seem to have embraced the Jesus of this fabrication.

Jesus unsparingly rebuked James and John (10:37-40). The other disciples were "indignant" at them, probably because the two of them made their request before the rest of them could (10:41). But Jesus called all of them to Himself and gave them further instructions about the values of the kingdom of God in contrast to the values of the world. They should view themselves, not as ruling potentates nor as great men in the world, but as servants or slaves of Christ. The disciples' eyes were partially blind at this point, and they could only partially see.

In all three of the disciples' responses, we witness a clash of values. The disciples' values were in direct opposition to Jesus' values. **He had called the disciples, and anyone who will follow Him, to live out His values.** He issued an explicit call to repent of one's self-centered purpose. Many people today think they can be saved by praying a sinner's prayer and continue living their lives in pursuit of their world-shaped ambitions. But that is a lie. The world's value system is set in opposition to the values of the kingdom of God. When our value system is aligned with the world's system, our lives will be out of alignment with what God is doing. Discerning whether our values are in accord with God's values is a great challenge for every follower of Christ and can rightly be discerned only if Jesus is healing our spiritual blindness on an ongoing basis. It can only be discerned if we are actively repenting of being aligned with the world and if we are actively infusing our lives with biblical values daily. The primary way God does this is through His Word.

Call – How should we respond? (8:34-38). Back to 8:34, in the third paragraph of this sequence Jesus, "calling the crowd to him with his disciples" (8:34), opened this part of His teaching to a larger group. This is significant in two respects. First, this larger group would have a mix of believers and non-believers in this predominantly non-Jewish area. Based on that fact, we know this is an evangelistic call. Second, it means "the harsh demands of the following verses apply not only to the Twelve but to anyone who may wish to join the movement...this is not a special formula for the elite, but an essential element in discipleship."[436] Here's what Jesus said:

---

436 France, *The Gospel of Mark* (NIGTC), p. 339.

*And calling the crowd to him with his disciples, he said to them,
"If anyone would come after me, let him deny himself and take up
his cross and follow me."*

Mk. 8:34

We can think of this as ***the Great Call of Jesus.***[437] It is His claim on every life. It is an evangelistic call to salvation. Jesus followed His invitation by explaining what it means.

First, being saved means yielding to the two conditions Jesus established: "For whoever would save his life will lose it, but whoever loses his life for my sake and the gospel's will save it" (8:35). Jesus' invitation to salvation is a call to embrace: (1) living a life of faithfulness to Jesus **and** (2) faithfulness to His gospel. Jesus underscored the importance of these requirements by restating them two sentences later, "For whoever is ashamed of me and of my words...of him will the Son of Man be ashamed when he comes in the glory of his Father with the holy angels" (8:38). These two conditions are spelled out twice here in summary form, but they capture two broad areas of what salvation is all about. It is a call to worship and obey Jesus Christ as Lord and a call to be a light to the nations through our witness and telling the gospel. This is Jesus' twin purpose for His people – living life under His Lordship (including worship which is implied here) and bearing the fruit of the gospel. There are consequences if we corrupt or forsake this twofold purpose. We will see those repercussions in Mark 11-13. There God's judgment was pronounced on His people because they had corrupted obedience to God and had blocked the purpose of being a light to the nations. The two conditions spelled out by Jesus twice – His Lordship and faithfulness to His gospel – are wrapped around alarming consequences for those who reject His call, as we shall see below.

Second and to further emphasize the gravity of these two conditions, Jesus wrapped them around two difficult questions (Mk. 8:36, 37). They are heart-stopping questions and should stop every one of us in our tracks.

---

437 This is not an isolated statement by Jesus calling would be followers to follow Him in the way of the cross. Matthew and Luke both record this teaching on this same occasion. And there are two additional occasions given in the Gospels where this truth is taught. One is in Matthew as he records Jesus' teaching the necessity of carrying one's cross in 10:38-39. Luke adds another identical teaching in 14:25-33. This means a total of five times this teaching of carrying one's cross is recorded across the four Gospels.

    –   *What does it profit a man to gain the whole world and forfeit his soul?*
        and

    –   *What can a man give in return for his soul?*

The conditions of following Jesus, coming under the Lordship of Christ and becoming part of His purpose to be a light to the nations, are sandwiched around the salvation of one's soul. That is what is at stake. They are interlocking pieces. It is a sobering invitation He issued to this crowd, which is the invitation that comes to us. (See chapter 7 of this book for more on Mark 8:34-38.)

A follower of Jesus is synonymous with our words "believer" and "Christian." Jesus was not describing some radical fringe sect of believers that are hyper-obedient. His statement in Mark 8:34, along with the verses that follow, provides a dramatic portrayal of what it actually means to be a Christian. These truths spoken by Jesus in 8:34-38 apply to every would-be follower of Him. The surprising tragedy is that these words of Jesus are rarely taught from the pulpits of evangelical churches. Many "believers" have no idea what Jesus is talking about here if they even notice it. Many "believers" apparently think this passage does not apply to them. One evidence of a genuine follower of Christ is that they share their faith. What does it say about a person if they have no concern for the lost and if they never share the gospel with others?

> *"The heart of the gospel is 'Jesus is Lord', not 'Jesus saves'.*
> *Jesus saves those over whom He is Lord."*[438]
>
> **Rico Tice**

"The heart of the gospel" is found at this theological center of the Gospel of Mark. It is placed in the context of Jesus' identity, as the sovereign Lord of the universe, His mission, which is to die on the cross and rise from the dead, and the purpose for His people, which is to tell the gospel to the lost. These truths are inseparable. Jesus framed His invitation to be saved within this context. He is the one who establishes the terms on which a person comes to Him.

---

438 Rico Tice, Christianity Explored Annual Conference (St. Louis, MO, USA), November 12, 2022.

"Confessing Christ means we must follow him to crucifixion."[439] "'Following' in this context...refers to that common commitment to Jesus which distinguishes all Christians from those who fail to recognize him as God's appointed Savior."[440]

> *Following Christ in self-denial and even in suffering is a necessary means of salvation, not of being worthy or of becoming worthy by so doing. One cannot follow Jesus except "on the way" of self-denial and the cross. – James Edwards* [441]

Salvation is by grace alone through faith alone. Make no mistake about that. However, James 2:14-26 makes it clear that not all kinds of faith are created equal. James defines genuine saving faith as a faith that is not dead but is alive and visible in a person's life. It is a faith that bears fruit. A person can have a "faith" in Jesus that is "intellectual only." But biblical faith is not "faith in faith." Saving faith, which is a miracle of the new birth (Jn. 3:3; 2 Cor. 5:17; Gal. 6:15), is grounded and rooted in the reality of Jesus and His purpose. It manifests itself in the life of the believer following Jesus in the way of the cross.

There are two kinds of people who do not share the gospel with others in my estimation. And God's grace is sufficient for both. The first kind is made up of genuine believers who are in a state of immaturity and without much evident fruit of the Spirit. There are many possible reasons for this situation, and I will not try to explore them here. But God's grace meets every one of us where we are and enables us in a one small step at a time succession to grow in Him. The first step in that process is repentance. "And we all, with unveiled face, beholding the glory of the Lord, are being transformed into the same image from one degree of glory to another. For this comes from the Lord who is the Spirit" (2 Cor. 3:18). God delights in the ongoing repentance and transformation of our lives into Christ's likeness.

A second kind of person is a nominal Christian, someone who has all of the trappings of being a genuine Christian but is not. They may attend church often, even

---

439 Hughes, *Mark: Jesus, Servant and Savior*, Vol. 1, p. 202.
440 Lane, *The Gospel of Mark* (NICNT), p. 307.
441 Edwards, *The Gospel According to Mark* (PNTC), p.256.

regularly, speak the Christian language and participate in the fellowship. But there is one thing missing. They have never truly repented of their sins and placed their trust in Christ as Lord. A nominal Christian is someone who is not saved from God's wrath and does not have the hope of heaven after this life. But there is grace for this person as well. Paul wrote to the Corinthian church about this kind of person, "Examine yourselves, to see whether you are in the faith. Test yourselves. Or do you not realize this about yourselves, that Jesus Christ is in you? – unless indeed you fail to meet the test! I hope you will find out that we have not failed the test" (2 Cor. 13:5-6). The solution is repentance and trust in Jesus as Lord. For "everyone who calls on the name of the Lord will be saved" (Rom. 10:13).

All across the New Testament there is consistency and clarity about this commitment level. It is the same commitment for every believer, but the fruit may vary. The lack of fruit may indicate an area of need for growth, but it may indicate an unsaved status. The epistles illuminate further this calling for the believer. Here are some images used by the biblical writers:

1. being led in "triumphal procession" (2 Cor. 2:14; see chapter 10 of this book),
2. "buried with him" (Rom. 6:4),
3. "death like his," "die," or "dying" (Rom. 6:5; 1 Cor. 15:31; 2 Cor. 4:10; 5:15), and
4. being servants of Christ (Rom. 1:1; 1 Cor. 9:19; Jas. 1:1; 2 Pet. 1:1).

The biblical meaning of being a follower of Christ has been obliterated from many churches by being dumbed down and ignored. It must be recaptured and mainstreamed into our theology and into our hearts. Churches are often ignoring the hard parts of what it means to be a follower of Christ to make the message easier on their listeners. That is something Jesus never did.

Healing of Blind Bartimaeus (10:46-52)

This section closes the same way it opened, with the healing of a blind man – blind Bartimaeus. This too was an acted parable by Jesus revealing not only that Jesus is the only one who can open blind eyes, but that people with eyes to see Jesus align their lives with His purpose in redemption. Bartimaeus was one of the few in this section who could see spiritually. He is shown to have had superior spiritual sight to the rich man of 10:17-22. In some respects, he could even see more clearly than the disciples as evidenced by their responses to Jesus' three teachings of the cross. When Jesus asked Bartimaeus what he wanted Him to do for him, his request was a far better request than the request of James and John in 10:36-37. It was a request each of us should make each time we pick up the word of God to read. Bartimaeus responded, "Rabbi, let me recover my sight" (10:51). Jesus immediately healed him, and Bartimaeus followed Jesus on the way (10:52).

Remember that earlier James and John had come to Jesus with a request of their own. Jesus asked them the same question He asked Bartimaeus: "What do you want me to do for you?" (10:36). In dramatic contrast to Bartimaeus, they brazenly asked for power and authority. They tried to leverage their relationship with Jesus for their personal ambitions. They did not understand what Jesus' mission was (despite Jesus' explaining it to them three different times), and they did not comprehend Jesus' purpose for their lives of being a light to the nations. His claim on their lives was to follow Him in the way of the cross and to proclaim the great news of redemption to the nations. It seems they were steeped in the values of the culture around them. They should have asked Jesus to heal their spiritual blindness. Just as Bartimaeus was physically blind, they were spiritually blind. Jesus responded to James and John with a rebuke and to Bartimaeus with healing and restored vision.

PART THREE
SALVATION THROUGH JUDGMENT

(11:1-16:8)

And the gospel must first be proclaimed to all nations.

Mark 13:10

As we come to Mark chapters 11-16, we need to brace ourselves. In chapters 11, 12, and parts of 13, Jesus pronounces a horrific judgment on His people. They have sold themselves to religious corruption, including corruption of the gospel, and have forsaken God's purpose as a light for the nations. Consequently, they are blinded by their sin and reject their Messiah.

John Mark presents truths that Jesus revealed in the amazing confrontation with a fig tree, wrapped around His casting out the money changers at the temple. Following that, Mark reveals Jesus' condemnation of the religious elite through the parable of the wicked tenants and then Jesus' explicit prediction of the destruction of the temple. This should be shocking to 21st century Christians who are steeped in the values of their culture. Jesus revealed the absolute and unyielding danger of God's judgment and wrath to those who think they are right with God but are not.

> *The fact is that the subject of divine wrath has become taboo in modern society, and Christians by and large have accepted the taboo and conditioned themselves never to raise the matter...*
> *One cannot imagine that talk of divine judgment was ever very popular, yet the biblical writers engage in it constantly. One of the most striking things about the Bible is the vigor with which*

both Testaments emphasize the reality and terror of God's wrath.[442]

J. I. Packer

There are two triumphs in this section, the triumphal entry and the triumph of the cross. There is one massive failure – the failure of God's people to be a light, a witness to the nations through theological corruption and rejection of Jesus. The temple represents Jesus Christ. It was the repository of the gospel and was to be a light to all nations drawing the Gentiles into God's family. But the Jews have corrupted the temple and the gospel, and Jesus is angry about it.

The dominant themes in this section are salvation and judgment. Interwoven through it is God's purpose for His people to take the gospel to the nations. The fruit that God demands of His people is the fruit of bearing witness.

The Triumphal Entry (11:1-10)

Jesus' triumphal entry into Jerusalem on Sunday was a dramatic and public display and, along with His forceful denunciation of the temple the following day, placed Him on a collision course with the authorities. Jesus whacked the proverbial hornets' nest with His entry into Jerusalem and into the temple. The Jewish leaders were forced to respond.[443]

Messiah was on His way to the cross. His purpose was clear to Him and His path was unobstructed. The Son of God was on a different track than the Jewish messianic expectation of the day.

Judgment on Israel (11:11-13:2)

Mark introduces his readers to some solemn facts that most of us would rather avoid. The reality was that God's judgment was coming on God's people for their failure to fulfill His purpose.

---

442 Packer, *Knowing God*, p, 151.
443 France, *The Gospel of Mark* (NIGTC), pp. 427-428.

In this lengthy section of Scripture, we will find two dramatizations of judgment – the cursing of the fig tree (11:12-14; 20-21) and Jesus' denouncing the temple (11:15-19). We will find a parable of judgment about the wicked tenants (12:1-12) plus a plain language declaration of judgment (13:1-2).

A Dramatization of Judgment

The cursing of the fig tree and the condemnation of the temple on the Monday before the cross were intertwined dramatizations of judgment. They go together. These twin acted parables began late on the previous day. After His triumphal entry on Sunday, Jesus went into the temple and "looked around at everything" (11:11). It seems anticlimactic, but Jesus was not a tourist going to see the beautiful buildings. He was the "Lord of the Temple" who had come to "determine whether the purpose intended by God is being fulfilled."[444] After this He went to Bethany to spend the night. The next day He would have much to say.

Cursing the fig tree. Monday, on His way back to the temple, Jesus saw a fig tree in leaf and went to gather some fruit because He was hungry. When He found it had no fruit, Jesus cursed the fig tree (11:12-14). At first glance, this seems an unreasonable expectation on the part of Jesus because "it was not the season for figs" (11:13). Some see this as a spiteful act by Jesus and use it to reject Him.[445] Even some Christian scholars are "perplexed by this story."[446]

The proper lens to understand this event is the Old Testament prophets. "The earliest commentary on the Gospel of Mark by Victor of Antioch in the fifth century already understood the event as an *enacted parable*, in which the cursing of the fig tree symbolized the judgment to befall Jerusalem."[447] Jesus in this situation was acting "in the tradition of the Old Testament prophets."[448] Consider Isaiah who walked around naked to "symbolize the stripping of Egypt" (Isa. 20:1-6) and Jeremiah who wore a

---

444 Lane, *The Gospel of Mark* (NICNT), p.398.

445 "The late Bertrand Russell, who wrote an essay titled 'Why I Am Not a Christian,' cited this narrative as one of his reasons for repudiating Christianity. He said this incident displays Jesus as a man who expressed vindictive fury to an innocent plant, manifesting behavior that was not that of a righteous man, let alone the Son of God." R. C. Sproul, *Mark* (Orlando, FL: Reformation Trust, 2011), p. 284. Bertrand Russell is an example of how God's word, and particularly parables, will harden some and draw others into God's Kingdom.

446 Sproul, *Mark*, p. 284.

447 Edwards, *The Gospel According to Mark* (PNTC), p. 339.

448 Brooks, *Mark* (NAC), p. 180.

rotten waist band to symbolize the humiliation of Judah (Jer. 13:1-11). Jeremiah also broke an earthenware jar to dramatize the breaking of Judah (Jer. 19:1-3, 10-11) and wore an oxen's yoke around his neck to symbolize enslavement to the king of Babylon (Jer. 27:1-15; 28:10-17).[449] Some of those *enacted parables* were a bit bizarre. Much more so than the cursing of the fig tree.

But Jesus actually honored this fig tree.[450] He made it the most famous fig tree that has ever lived.[451] Its silent witness has carried an important message down through the centuries and will continue to convey that message until the return of Christ. Jesus valued the people of Israel more than He valued the fig tree. The fig tree served Jesus' purpose to warn Israel of the terrible judgment that was bearing down on them.

I think there is another application here. It was not the season for figs when Jesus came upon the fig tree and held it accountable for its lack of fruit. This creates a shock factor. I think it implies that judgment comes when least expected. Paul writes to Timothy, "Preach the word; be ready in season and out of season; reprove, rebuke, and exhort, with complete patience and teaching" (2 Tim. 4:2). In Mark 13 we are told, "Therefore stay awake—for you do not know when the master of the house will come, in the evening, or at midnight, or when the rooster crows, or in the morning — lest he come suddenly and find you asleep" (Mk. 13:35-36). The fig tree did not know when its Creator would come.

Condemnation of the temple leadership. After arriving in Jerusalem, Jesus entered the temple and "began to drive out those who sold and those who bought in the temple, and he overturned the tables of the money-changers and the seats of those who sold pigeons" (11:15). Jesus combined writings from Isaiah 56:7 and Jeremiah 7:11 and said, "Is it not written, 'My house shall be called a house of prayer for all the nations'? (Isa. 56:7) But you have made it a den of robbers" (Jer. 7:11; Mk. 11:17). Jesus condemned the temple leadership for their perversion of faithful obedience to God. The temple was not serving as a "light for the nations" as intended by God (Isa. 42:6; 49:6; Acts

---

449 Brooks, *Mark* (NAC), pp. 180-181.

450 Hughes, *Mark: Jesus, Servant and Savior*, Vol. 2, p. 86.

451 Kent Hughes calls it "the most useful tree that ever grew!" Hughes, *Mark: Jesus, Servant and Savior*, Vol. 2, p. 86.

13:47). Merchants in the temple, in the court of the Gentiles, were blocking the nations from access to God. Jesus was angry.

When Jesus or a writer of the New Testament cites an Old Testament passage, it can be like the tip of an iceberg with much more beneath the surface. So, let's look at both the Isaiah and Jeremiah passages more closely.

The citation from Isaiah 56:7 is truly the tip of a massive redemption iceberg. The preceding four chapters in Isaiah lead us from Messiah dying on a cross to "make many to be accounted righteous" (53:11) to people from all nations being aggressively sought out by God and gathered into His house (56:7-8) and closes with condemnation of the shepherds of Israel for their corruption of God's purpose. God's people are to play a vital role in His purpose.

- **Chapter 52:13-53:12** – predicts and portrays Messiah dying on the cross to "make many to be accounted righteous" (53:11).
- **Chapter 54** – reveals God's family enlarging through God's supernatural means.[452]
- **Chapter 55** – all nations are summoned to God's great feast.[453]
- **Chapter 56:1–8** – depicts the gathering of all nations who are aggressively sought out by God (56:8). [454]
- **Chapter 56:9** – God pronounces judgment on Israel for their failure to fulfill His purpose.
- **Chapter 56:10-12** – the failure of the spiritual shepherds of Israel is condemned, and specific sins of these ungodly leaders are named and exposed.

The shepherds of Israel were thwarting God's intent to reach the nations. They had long since stopped looking out for the spiritual welfare of God's people. They had stopped caring about lost Gentiles. They had become blind watchmen, silent guard dogs "lacking the basic qualifications for their office,"[455] indolent, slothful, insatiably

---

452 Motyer, *The Prophecy of Isaiah*, p. 444.
453 Motyer, *The Prophecy of Isaiah*, pp. 444, 463.
454 Motyer, *The Prophecy of Isaiah*, p. 463.
455 Motyer, *The Prophecy of Isaiah*, p. 468.

greedy, narcissistically ambitious, intoxicated by alcohol (and likely other pleasures of life), and seduced into complacency, thinking that there will be no judgment and no accountability (Isa. 56:10-12).[456]

The citation from Jeremiah 7:11 is from what some scholars refer to as Jeremiah's "temple sermon" (Jer. 7:1-15).[457] It can more accurately be labeled as Jeremiah's "destruction of the temple sermon." Here is the immediate context of Jer. 7:11 (please read the whole passage of 7:1-15).

> *⁴ Do not trust in these deceptive words: 'This is the temple of the LORD, the temple of the LORD, the temple of the LORD.'*
>
> *⁸ "Behold, you trust in deceptive words to no avail. ⁹ Will you steal, murder, commit adultery, swear falsely, make offerings to Baal, and go after other gods that you have not known, ¹⁰ and then come and stand before me in this house, which is called by my name, and say, 'We are delivered!'—only to go on doing all these abominations? ¹¹ **Has this house, which is called by my name, become a den of robbers in your eyes? Behold, I myself have seen it, declares the LORD.** ¹² Go now to my place that was in Shiloh, where I made my name dwell at first, and see what I did to it because of the evil of my people Israel. ¹³ And now, because you have done all these things, declares the LORD, and when I spoke to you persistently you did not listen, and when I called you, you did not answer, ¹⁴ therefore I will do to the house that is called by my name, and in which you trust, and to the place that I gave to you and to your fathers, as I did to Shiloh. ¹⁵ And I will cast you out of my sight, as I cast out all your kinsmen, all the offspring of Ephraim.*
>
> *Jer. 7:4, 8-15*

---

456 Motyer, *The Prophecy of Isaiah*, pp.467-469.

457 J. A. Thompson, *The Book of Jeremiah* (NICOT) (Grand Rapids, MI: William B. Eerdmans Publishing Company, 1980), pp. 271-283.

Jeremiah began his ministry in 627 BC about 70 years after Isaiah passed from the scene.[458] The situation Jeremiah faced was identical to what Isaiah encountered. Jeremiah warned that God would destroy the temple and Jerusalem if they did not repent. The leaders' response was that God would surely not destroy His temple, that He was a God of grace and would certainly not do a thing like that, and they refused to repent. Jeremiah warned (my loose paraphrase): "If you think God will not destroy this temple, go check out Shiloh and see if you can find the sanctuary that was once located there" (7:12, 14).[459]

Jeremiah said they had turned God's temple into a "den of robbers." This refers to a hideout or safe place where robbers would retreat to for their own safety after committing their crimes. Jeremiah was saying to the leaders of Israel that if they think they can "steal, murder, commit adultery, swear falsely, make offerings to Baal, and go after other gods" (Jer. 7:9) and then come to "church" (the temple) and go through the rituals of religion and think they are delivered, then they had better think again. The marketplace in the court of the Gentiles, at the time of Christ, was full of money changers and the selling of sacrificial animals with throngs of people surging through it. Whether or not there was excessive profiteering, and there could well have been, it was blocking access to the nations. Financial exploitation was only the tip of the iceberg. Jesus' pronouncements went much deeper. They went to the heart of the system that had become corrupt to the core by the Jewish leadership and it would be replaced from its roots. The marketplace "robbers" were emblematic of the deeper corruption.

Six hundred years after Jeremiah's warning to Israel and the destruction of the temple by the Babylonians, Jesus came to His temple and this temple system was similarly debased, rotten to the core, and refused to fulfill God's purpose of glorifying God and

---

458 Thompson, *The Book of Jeremiah* (NICOT), pp. 10-11.

459 "As further warning that the temple was not exempt from God's wrath, he [Jeremiah] reminded them to consider the fate of Shiloh (Ps 78:56–64). Located about eighteen miles north of Jerusalem, it was the first permanent location of the tabernacle in Canaan (Josh 18:1) and the place where the land was divided among the tribes (Josh 18:8–10; 19:51). The shrine was still located there when Eli was high priest (1 Sam 1:3) and Samuel was called to be God's prophet (1 Sam 3:1, 21). Nevertheless, the city apparently was destroyed by the Philistines around 1050 b.c. after the battle described in 1 Sam 4. If God would destroy the city where the tabernacle and ark were located because of Israel's sins, how could Jerusalem expect to escape a similar fate?" Huey, *Jeremiah* (NAC), p. 107.

reaching the nations. The corruption of the system had distorted true worship and was blocking fulfillment of God's chief strategic task for His people: being an open door for the gospel to the Gentiles (or lost people). The Gentiles were crowded out and Jesus was angry about it. He delivered the same message that Isaiah and Jeremiah delivered. The response Jeremiah received to his message was not repentance but: "You shall die!" (Jer. 26:7-9). The response Jesus received was identical: "the chief priests and the scribes... were seeking a way to destroy him" (Mk. 11:18).

God had destroyed the temple twice in history, and under Jesus' words, it was under judgment for a third and final time. The nation still had time to repent of their corruption, but time was running short. In less than 40 years the temple would be leveled to the ground.

The temple was, in a very real sense, God's gospel to the nations. It was the place where the gospel was expressed to the world. The indicator of the Jews' lostness was that they had distorted the gospel and were failing to fulfill God's purpose to be a light (witness) to the nations. The church today has largely lost its way, and the chief indicator of our lostness is that the church, by and large, has sterilized the gospel and forsaken evangelism. When the church strips the gospel message of its backbone of sin, judgment, wrath, the cost of following Jesus, and repentance, it follows that the need to evangelize will disappear. When sin, judgment and wrath are removed, there is no need to go to the trouble of evangelizing the lost.

The church today has moved into a cave of self-satisfaction and complacency. It has done what God's people in both Jeremiah's and Jesus' day had done. The church has been turned into a good luck charm to enhance its own comfort and has failed to do the hard work of proclaiming the gospel to the lost.

Should we in the 21st century think that God has ceased caring for lost people and is happy when we ignore His mandate to evangelize the world around us? We should not! In fact, as we in the United States observe the deteriorating conditions in the culture, government, sports, education, etc., could this be God's judgment rolling out slowly but visibly on His people who still go by His name but have, for the most part, corrupted His gospel message and abandoned His purpose to evangelize the lost? We can never separate following Jesus from telling the gospel to others. Holiness includes being faithful to His command to share the gospel with the lost.

But even though many churches may have drifted away from God's purpose, the church is absolutely and unequivocally God's answer to the problem. "His [God's] solution...is the church. That is, every individual follower of Christ relearning what it is to share the Good News with their neighbors, coworkers, family members, and friends. This is the only fuel combustible enough to re-ignite the stalled engine of evangelism in the United States."[460] We do not need to look for a new model, we have that already in the church.

Though it seems that the gospel voice of many churches has been swept away by an onslaught of cultural influences, apathy, and complacency, there are a small number of churches who remain faithful to the Lordship of Christ and to His gospel. These churches may even be small congregations and seemingly without political or cultural power, but they are treasured by God (Mal. 3:16-18). God never gives up on His chosen structure for His people, the church. We must not abandon the church but work to make it better. We as believers must support and be part of those churches who remain faithful.

> *We must not be ashamed of being a remnant, weak and small. We must cease to think in terms of numbers, we must think in terms of the purpose of God and the purity of the witness and testimony. God will preserve this seed. He will carry it on in spite of everything.*[461]
>
> Martyn Lloyd-Jones

The next day, Tuesday morning, on the way to the temple, "they saw the fig tree withered away to its roots" (11:20). Mark wrapped the cursing of the fig tree around Jesus' pronouncement of judgment on the temple. The imagery is unmistakable. As certainly as the fig tree withered under Jesus' words of judgment, so will the barren temple be destroyed to its roots under God's judgment. The fruitless fig tree is an apt parable

---

460 John S. Dickerson, *The Great Evangelical Recession: 6 Factors that will Crash the American Church...and How to Prepare* (Grand Rapids, MI: Baker Books, 2013, 2016), p. 202.

461 Martyn Lloyd-Jones cited by Bill Muehlenberg in *On Being a Remnant* (https://billmuehlenberg.com/2021/03/08/on-being-a-remnant/, March 8, 2021), accessed February 24, 2024.

of what is happening to the church in America today. There are very few churches (less than 4% according to a study done in the 1990s[462]) that are faithful to God's mandate of carrying the gospel to the world around them.[463] Those of us in the American church should be alarmed. Yes, we should be alarmed at the condition of God's people. We should be alarmed at the condition of our own church if it is not proclaiming the biblical gospel and carrying it to those around us. We should be alarmed to such an extent that we repent of this failure. Self-centered ambition and God cannot both reign in the church at the same time.

That same day, Jesus warned the leadership again. He told a parable about the failure of wicked tenants to produce fruit for a vineyard's owner. It is a parable of judgment against them (12:1-12). In the parable, a man planted a vineyard, leased it out to others, and expected a share in the fruit of the vineyard in its season. After the harvest he sent many servants to collect his share, yet they abused many and killed some. Finally, he sent his beloved son whom they also killed. In the story the "man" represents God the Father, the "vineyard" represents Israel, the "tenants" represent the ruling elite, and the "beloved son" represents Jesus. And like the tenants in the story, the chief priests, scribes, and elders refused to produce fruit for God, and they kept all the "produce" for their own selfish purposes. They used the temple system to build their own little fiefdom to promote their own comfort, power, authority, and glory.

The imagery in the parable is so clear that even the ruling elite recognized themselves in it. They were the bad guys, and they knew it "for they perceived that he told the parable against them" (12:12). Unrepentant, they continued their efforts to destroy Jesus. They were determined to find a way to get rid of this troublemaker. He was a threat to their power and authority. God saw them as a threat to His kingdom and to

---

462 Rainer, *Effective Evangelistic Churches,* p. 50.

463 The survey by Thom Rainer was based primarily on results such as conversions. It is entirely possible that there are churches making the effort to carry the gospel to the lost but are not seeing much in the way of results. They are being faithful, but the place where they minister may be very hardened toward the gospel. So even if we assume there are an equal number of churches being faithful to the gospel but without results, the number of faithful churches is less than 10%. That means 90% of evangelical churches are unfaithful in carrying the gospel to the lost. This is massive apathy or disobedience to God's purpose and may be why the church appears to be under judgment.

the salvation of the nations. This was a collision course that ultimately did not end well for the enemies of God.

Conclusion: A Plain Language Declaration of Judgment

As they came out of the temple, Jesus was not finished speaking about judgment. He had much more to say. He gave an explicit explanation in plain language of what He had been warning about in the two acted parables and in the spoken parable.

> *And as he came out of the temple, one of his disciples said to him, "Look, Teacher, what wonderful stones and what wonderful buildings!" And Jesus said to him, "Do you see these great buildings? There will not be left here one stone upon another that will not be thrown down."*
>
> Mk. 13:1-2

God was not pleased, and the temple was under judgment. It was a judgment on God's people for rejection of Messiah and for rejection of His intended purpose to reach the lost. One cannot accept Messiah and not His purpose. They rejected Messiah **AND** counterfeited God's purpose. Israel was at the eleventh hour. The clock was about to strike midnight. There was very little time to repent. In AD 70 judgment did fall, and not one stone of the temple was left on top of another.

Do you place your trust in the beautiful building of your church? Do you take comfort in the safe space that it provides? Have you turned it into a "den of robbers" so that you can avoid obedience to God's intended purpose of reaching the lost? Sadly, and even tragically, many today have done just that.

The temple was a physical structure and a beautiful one. There is nothing wrong with a beautiful building. But the temple revealed God's relationship with man. It was about access to God and serving His purpose. Worse than loving a building is using our relationship with God to our own glory and making God our servant and not us His. It may be that many today are trying to leverage their relationship with Christ to serve their own ends. That is a tragedy. But God's grace is available to us if we recognize we are living this way. And access to His grace is through repentance.

How to Live in the Last Days

(Olivet Discourse, 13:3-37)[464]

It is still Tuesday of the week that Jesus will die on Friday. On the Mount of Olives after leaving the temple, He prepared the disciples for following Him after He ascends into Heaven. It was a powerful message of purpose and preparation that is often obscured by Jesus' predictions of the future. We must not allow that to happen. They are both important.

The Olivet discourse is "by far the most difficult passage in the book of Mark."[465] "Widely divergent interpretations of the discourse have been proposed, and it remains the most disputed area in the study of Mark's gospel."[466] The difficulty pertains primarily to Jesus' predictions of the future. God's purpose for His people, the command to be watchmen, the warnings about hazards to be faced, and the commands to action are all quite clear. We must not let one overshadow the other.

The predictions of the future give us one certainty that is clear – Jesus is coming again in salvation through judgment. He will save His people from the presence and from the effects of sin. The details may be difficult to interpret, but His coming again in great power is clear.

My view of the discourse is that two events of history are interwoven in the narrative. They are like "widely separated mountain peaks of historic events [that] merge and are seen as one...two momentous events are here intertwined, namely, (a.) the judgment upon Jerusalem (its fall in the year A.D. 70), and (b.) the final judgment at the close of the world's history."[467]

Here is my interpretation of the future predictions of this passage. I hold this opinion with modest confidence.

13:4-23 – this is a dual reference with a near term imperfect fulfillment in the destruction of Jerusalem and the temple in AD 70 and ultimately a perfect fulfillment at the second coming of Jesus Christ.

---

464 Parallel passages are in Matthew 24:3-44 and Luke 21:7-36.

465 Hughes, *Mark: Jesus, Servant and Savior*, vol. 2, p. 135.

466 France, *The Gospel of Mark* (NIGTC), p.498.

467 Commenting on the Olivet Discourse in the Gospel of Matthew, Hendriksen, *Exposition of the Gospel According to Matthew* (NTC), p. 844–846.

13:24-27 – the second coming of Jesus Christ in "cosmos shaking" power and in final judgment.

13:28-31 – the destruction of Jerusalem and the temple are signs that we are in the last period of history and are signs of assurance of the second coming of Christ.

13:32-37 – an admonition to be prepared and to be dedicated to God's purpose because the timing of Jesus' return is uncertain, unpredictable, and imminent. The fact of His return is certain.[468]

R. Kent Hughes sums it up quite well when he writes, "The fact is, we have yet to find a scholar who can perfectly unravel the knotty problems of the Olivet Discourse. Study of it requires a proper humility and a willingness to admit that we do not know everything."[469]

If details of the future are somewhat obscure, the details of God's purpose and what He requires of His people are quite clear. **First, God's overriding purpose**, which spans from Genesis through Revelation, is stated clearly by Jesus: **"…you will stand before governors and kings for my sake, to bear witness before them. And the gospel must first be proclaimed to all nations"** (13:9-10). This is the Great Commission commanded in the context of the tribulations of the world and in the face of the fierce opposition of God's enemies.

Second, there are 20 imperatives, calls to action, in Jesus' teaching. The imperatives can be summarized in one phrase: **All of God's people are called to be action-oriented witnesses and watchmen** (13:9-10, 32-37). This applies not only to pastors, elders, Sunday school teachers and the like, but to every believer – "And what I say to you I say to all" (13:37). Jesus charges all His people to "be on guard," "keep awake," "stay awake," "stay awake," and "stay awake." The redundancy in these six verses (13:32-37) – five imperatives – is significant. Jesus could not have been more emphatic. (Please see the Table of 20 Imperatives at the end of this chapter.)

---

468 An acknowledgment and thank you to Pastor Matt Bradley for helping me to have a better grasp of Mark 13.
469 Hughes, *Mark: Jesus, Servant and Savior*, vol. 2, p. 135.

"'Watch!' is the final and most important word of the Olivet discourse. The point of Mark 13 is not so much to inform as to admonish; not to provide knowledge of arcane matters but to instill obedience in believers."[470]

Third, there is a cost of following Jesus and being faithful in spreading the gospel, but the benefits far outweigh any difficulties we may encounter, even the loss of life. Jesus names 17 hazards that His followers will encounter. These dangers fit into two categories: (1) all manner of falsehoods to avoid – believers must be on guard against false teaching, false leaders, false witnesses, false christs, and false prophets and (2) all manner of tribulations to contend with – believers must be prepared for national upheavals, natural disasters, opposition, hatred from those unknown, hatred from close family, physical harm, and possible death. His purpose in naming these risk factors is for believers to be prepared and remain faithful to the end. (Please see the Table of 17 Hazards at the end of this chapter.)

God never abandons the chief strategic purpose for His people. He expects His followers to be faithful to it as well.

Judgment Falls on Jesus (14:1-15:47)
(The Most Important Event in the History of the World)

There was a storm of judgment coming. And in this case it was taking aim at Jesus. Jesus will fall under the judgment of God and become the recipient of God's wrath for man's sins. It is in fact His main purpose in coming to earth.[471] The false religious leaders of Israel, driven by their hatred of God and of His Anointed, had dedicated themselves to the destruction of Jesus. God, paradoxically, used their hatred to accomplish His purpose.

---

470 Edwards, *The Gospel According to Mark* (PNTC), p. 409.

471 A less summarized way of saying this is: "The work of Jesus Christ, the God-man, is redemption and is understood in terms of his active and passive obedience, his humiliation and exaltation, and his offices of prophet, priest, and king. This redemption is accomplished by meeting the demands of the Covenant of Works (perfect obedience) and removing the curse of that Covenant (death, alienation from God, the wrath of God, all under the heading of the curse of the Covenant of Works)." Matthew Bradley, *The Doctrine of Christ* (Sunday School Class Handout, February 5, 2023). The covenant of works is the covenant God made with Adam where life was promised to Adam conditioned on his perfect obedience (Gen. 2:16-17; Hos. 6:7).

We will examine Jesus' celebrating the Passover with His disciples, blindness at the cross, and His resurrection. What appeared to be the ultimate defeat, Jesus' death on the cross, was His greatest triumph.

The Passover – The Lord's Supper – The Cross

As the disciples of Jesus were preparing a lamb without blemish for the Passover meal (Mk. 14:12-16), the religious authorities were preparing "the Lamb of God" for the cross (Mk. 14:1-2; Jn. 1:29). The religious leaders, including the high priest, elders, and scribes, were acting out of their self-delusional purpose, supposing it was God's purpose. Jesus, the true High Priest, was acting out of a perfect understanding of God's purpose.

Though highly ironic, it was no coincidence the Jews and Jesus were on parallel tracks. Jesus is the real Passover Lamb without blemish. Mark wants us to see the connection.

> *It was now two days before the Passover and the Feast of Unleavened Bread. And the chief priests and the scribes were seeking how to arrest him by stealth and kill him, for they said, "Not during the feast, lest there be an uproar from the people."*
> *Mk. 14:1-2*

The Passover Feast was initiated during the exodus event and was established as an annual commemoration of this great act of salvation. The exodus was the most important salvation event in the history of Israel. The Old Testament prophets repeatedly referred to it in their writings. At the time of that event, God revealed what He was doing: "I am the LORD...and **I will redeem you with an outstretched arm and with great acts of judgment**" (Ex. 6:6). It was a portrayal of what Christ would accomplish on the cross. In order for salvation to occur, evil had to be judged and defeated. God gave them an image or acted parable of this salvation event – the Passover meal.

God told Moses and Aaron that he was going to pass through Egypt in judgment (Ex. 12:1, 12-13). Both Israel and Egypt were under judgment.[472] Only those protected by

---

472 This insight conveyed to me by Dale Ralph Davis.

the blood of the lamb (a symbol for the shed blood of Christ) would survive. "The story makes two things clear: first, that on Passover night there was a death in every house in Egypt without exception. In Egyptian houses, where there was no sheltering blood, there was the grim, sad death of the firstborn (Ex. 12:29–30), but in the houses of Israel lay the dead body of the lamb providing the Passover meal (12:8–11) for those who took shelter beneath its blood."[473] The sword of judgment fell on the firstborn of every Egyptian household, whereas the sword of judgment fell on the lamb in every household of Israel.

Judgment and salvation go hand in hand. The same is true in God's actions on the cross. God's wrath is poured out on Jesus in judgment for the sins of God's people as He saves His people through the propitiation of God's wrath.[474] The cross was the fulfillment of what the Passover meal portrayed. Jesus suffered God's wrath that you and I deserved so that we might be reconciled to this holy God. **It was a great act of judgment and a great act of salvation.**[475]

The Great Salvation and Blindness at the Cross

The cross is the most important event in the history of the world. This event is like a hinge about which every life will turn. How a person responds to the cross and its call on their life (Mk. 8:34-38) will determine the trajectory of their life. Most who witnessed the cross in person failed to understand what was happening. Many today who are "eyewitnesses" to the cross, as they hear the cross proclaimed in churches across America, fail to understand its significance for their lives. Blindness to the cross is an obstacle to salvation.

---

473 Alec Motyer, *Look to the Rock: Old Testament Background To Our Understanding Of Christ* (Leicester, England: Inter-Varsity Press, 1996), p. 50.

474 "To 'propitiate' somebody means to appease or pacify his anger" (p. 169). "It is God himself who in holy wrath needs to be propitiated, God himself who in holy love undertook to do the propitiating, and God himself who in the person of his Son died for the propitiation of our sins" (p. 175). John Stott cites David F. Wells: "In Pauline thought, man is alienated from God by sin and God is alienated from man by wrath. It is in the substitutionary death of Christ that sin is overcome and wrath averted, so that God can look on man without displeasure and man can look on God without fear. Sin is expiated and wrath is propitiated" (David F. Wells, *Search for Salvation*, p. 29). Stott, *The Cross of Christ*, pp. 169, 175. See also the only four uses of this word in the N.T.: Rom. 3:25; Heb. 2:17; 1 Jn. 2:2; 4:10.

475 Salvation and judgment are often depicted together (Gen. 6:7-8, 18; 7:11-24; Ex. 6:6-7; 12:1-32). In the case of the salvation of lost souls, salvation can only be achieved if justice is accomplished. Man cannot be saved from sin without God's righteous anger at sin being satisfied. God is a righteous God, and the righteous response to sin is wrath. Jesus took on Himself God's wrath for the sins of many. He does not propitiate God's wrath for everyone. Only for those who repent and trust in Him.

Though we have seen spiritual blindness throughout Mark's narrative, it reaches a pinnacle of sorts in this narrative. The significance of the event is astounding, yet in the shadow of the cross spiritual blindness was pervasive.

Mark's description of Jesus' death shows the reactions of people who witnessed it. There were individuals and groups of individuals through whose eyes we can view this event. There may be a bit of all of us in each of these reactions.[476]

The great irony was the blindness of **the religious leaders.** They were the spiritual shepherds of God's people. They considered themselves to be righteous and moral people who knew God's purpose. But they actually did not know God's purpose. Thinking they were doing a righteous act in destroying Jesus, they were raging against God the Father and His Anointed (Ps. 2:1-3). They were blinded by lust for power.

Pontius Pilate was blinded by his desire to please the crowd and he gave in to evil. He was a crowd-pleaser. **The soldiers** were blinded by the excuse of just doing their job and missed the greatest act of salvation in the history of the world happening a few feet away from them. The legacy of the cross for them was dividing Jesus' clothes. **Others** were there for the spectacle of it all.

But there was another person at the scene that we must not miss. **The Roman centurion** was someone important whose reaction Mark records. We don't know much about this centurion, but this man had likely fought many campaigns and had seen many men die. Yet he had never seen a man die like this. He was a hard-bitten soldier who was a high-ranking military officer. This is how Mark describes it.

> *And when the centurion, who stood facing him, saw that in this way he breathed his last, he said, "Truly this man was the Son of God!"*
>
> *Mk. 15:39*

Notice that the centurion "stood facing him." He looked into Jesus' eyes. He saw how he behaved. He heard His strong authoritative voice. He heard Jesus declare, "It is

---

476 Discussion of the blindness of individuals in this section is drawn from the CE Leader's Handbook and shortened to fit this context. *Christianity Explored Leader's Handbook* (4th edition), pp. 62, 146-147.

finished" (Jn. 19:30). He heard Jesus "calling out with a loud voice, 'Father, into your hands I commit my spirit!'" (Lk. 23:46, citing Ps. 31:5). These were not whispers from the last ounce of waning strength. Mark makes sure we know this by stating that Jesus spoke "with a loud voice" and "a loud cry" (15:34, 37; also Lk. 23:46).

Jesus' death was a supernatural death – a miracle. "Normally the crucified, through progressive loss of strength, fell unconscious and died feebly."[477] Jesus didn't die in out-of-control desperation gasping for air. The Roman centurion recognized this miracle of Jesus' death. The centurion saw that Jesus chose the exact moment of His death. **The centurion must have felt and heard the power of God's Word which prompted him to exclaim, "Truly this man was the Son of God!"**

Unlike the others, this centurion recognized who Jesus is: "the Son of God." We know he got Jesus' identity right, but we don't know what he did after that. Recognizing who Jesus is isn't all we need to do – we then need to put our trust in him to rescue us from the problem of sin and to help us live as his followers.

The Resurrection. On Sunday morning around sunrise, 36 to 40 hours after Jesus' death on Friday afternoon, some women went to the tomb to anoint Jesus' body. They were fully expecting to find a corpse. There was no doubt in their minds that He was dead as they would not have spent so much money on spices if they had not been convinced of His death. But they were in for two major shocks.

The first shock was that the huge, heavy stone covering the entrance to the tomb had been rolled away. Then came the second shock as they went inside the tomb. Jesus was nowhere to be seen. Instead, they saw a young man dressed in a white robe. He told them the reason Jesus was not there.

> *And he said to them, "Do not be alarmed. You seek Jesus of Nazareth, who was crucified. He has risen; he is not here. See the place where they laid him. But go, tell his disciples and Peter that he is going before you to Galilee. There you will see him, just as he told you."*
>
> *Mk. 16:6-7*

---

477 Hughes, *Mark: Jesus, Servant and Savior*, vol. 2, p. 208.

But Mark is under no illusions about the outrageousness of this claim. He doesn't gloss over the struggle to believe what has just happened. In fact, he says this:

> *And they went out and fled from the tomb, for trembling*
> *and astonishment had seized them, and they said nothing to*
> *anyone, for they were afraid.*
>
> Mk. 16:8

Even though Jesus had told them repeatedly in advance that it was all part of the plan, it was still too much for them to fully understand or accept. Someone has captured in hyperbolic fashion what Jesus had been telling the disciples for the last six to twelve months: "Brothers, we are going up to Jerusalem in a bit and we'll have a bad day on Friday. I will need to borrow a tomb for a few days, but I'll meet you for lunch in Galilee on Monday."[478] They heard His teaching, but they could not "see" it. The disciples were likely blinded by their own presuppositions.

The resurrection is a struggle, not only for non-believers, but for many believers today as well. It is easy to view it through a culturally colored lens and not understand its impact on our lives. It is not a hope we sit on and cover up. The reality of the resurrection means believers can risk their lives proclaiming the good news.[479] It is fantastic news that must be proclaimed.

The Ending of the Gospel of Mark

Mark's account ends on the surprising note already mentioned. "And they went out and fled from the tomb, for trembling and astonishment had seized them, and they said nothing to anyone, for they were afraid" (16:8). This has caused much debate among scholars. Two questions emerge. Did Mark write the longer ending of 16:9-20? And if not, did he intend to end at 16:8?

---

478 I heard this statement from Craig Dyer who is not sure if it is original with him. Another individual thinks he may have heard it from Alistair Begg. The origin is unclear.

479 The Apostle Paul's lengthy treatment of the resurrection in 1 Corinthians 15 demonstrates that believers can risk everything in ministry for Christ.

To the first question, there "is the virtually unanimous verdict of modern textual scholarship, that the authentic text of Mark available to us ends at 16:8."[480]

To the second question, opinions are somewhat divided. "The prevailing view in contemporary scholarship is that Mark intended to end his Gospel with v. 8. The problem then becomes to explain why he did so."[481]

There were primarily 10 theologians I consulted, through their commentaries or sermons, for this chapter on the Gospel of Mark. They were unanimous on the first question, that what follows Mark 16:8 was not written by him. They were, however, evenly divided on the second question. Four concluded that Mark did not intend to end his Gospel at v. 8, four concluded he did intend to end at v. 8, and two did not say. But an important fact is evident. Whatever Mark intended, the Spirit intended it to end here because that is all he gave us.

I lean toward the opinion that Mark intended to end his Gospel at v. 8. The enigmatic ending is totally consistent with his use of irony, surprise, and paradox throughout the entire narrative. "Mark refrains from making many editorial comments about the significance of the history he narrates. He lets his story speak for itself, forcing his readers to discover the ultimate significance of much of the story of Jesus. A somewhat enigmatic ending to the gospel suits this strategy perfectly."[482]

So, what is the significance that we need to discover in this ending? The significance has already been alluded to. The resurrection of Jesus is a shocking fact of history. It was so shocking to the women who first encountered it that they were too overwhelmed to comprehend it. They left the scene in "trembling," "astonishment," and fear. They were commanded to "go, tell," and to our astonishment Mark writes "they said nothing to anyone, for they were afraid." It is understandable for them to be there in the middle of all of this history playing out and not understand what was going on. And we know

---

480 France, *The Gospel of Mark* (NIGTC), p. 685. James Edwards agrees and provides this: "The two oldest and most important manuscripts of the Bible, codex Vaticanus (B) and codex Sinaiticus (ℵ), omit 16:9–20, as do several early translations or versions, including the Old Latin, the Sinaitic Syriac manuscript, about one hundred Armenian manuscripts, and the two oldest Georgian manuscripts. Neither Clement of Alexandria nor Origen shows any awareness of the existence of the longer ending, and Eusebius and Jerome attest that vv. 9–20 were absent from the majority of Greek copies of Mark known to them." Edwards, *The Gospel According to Mark* (PNTC), p. 497.
481 Brooks, *Mark* (NAC), p. 274.
482 Carson and Moo, *An Introduction to the New Testament*, p. 189. They consider the possibility that Mark intended to end his gospel at v. 8 to be "the most likely" scenario.

from the other Gospels and the Book of Acts that they came to their senses spiritually speaking eventually and put it all together. They and the other disciples went on to impact the nations with the gospel.

But Mark is an ancient writer dramatically posing, through his narrative art, a piercing question: "What will you do?" Will you remain in a catatonic state throughout your Christian life and say nothing to anyone? Or will you break out of your spiritual sleep and fulfill the task God has ordained for His people – telling the gospel?

It is a powerful ending that will not allow us to sleep!

What Can We Learn About the Gospel and Evangelism from the Gospel of Mark?

There may be an infinite number of applications that can be drawn from the Gospel of Mark, and I have made many in this chapter so far. To narrow this down to some extent, I will choose what I think are the four most urgent actions for the church in the United States as demanded by the Gospel of Mark. Even though you may not live in the United States, these may also apply to your church in your country as well.

First, the Gospel of Mark is a prophetic voice that demands amplification and imitation. It is a model to emulate with its integration of grace and wrath. The voice of many pulpits in America today has grown quiet and timid. This voice contains almost no exposures of sin, warnings of God's wrath, calls for repentance, or admonitions to count the cost of following Christ in a hostile world. The Gospel of Mark, however, is a two-hour sermon that contains every element of the gospel fully integrated and with the proper emphasis. The style is courageous, direct, informative, artistic, interesting, loving, and urgent. It is a "gospel proclaiming and sharing" model to aspire to.

A church that is teaching a truncated, disintegrated gospel is engaged in false teaching and on a path away from God. If exposure of sin, calls for repentance, cautions about the cost of following Jesus, and warnings of judgment and the wrath of God to come are removed, then it is no longer the biblical gospel. It may take time for that to become obvious, but that is where it inevitably leads. The eight elements of the gospel that I have articulated throughout this book are a good measuring stick. (See the Elements of the Gospel in Mark at the end of this chapter.) We should pose this question: Are all of these elements being thoroughly taught and explained from the pulpit and in the classrooms of our church regularly? If not, that is a serious red flag that something is not right. Nominal Christianity flourishes in that environment.

Second, Jesus' purpose of being a light to the nations must be every believer's purpose and every church's purpose. This means bearing witness and proclaiming the gospel to all nations (13:9-10). The center of Mark's gospel, where Jesus stakes His claim on all who will follow Him, makes this clear (8:34-38). Jesus demands denial of self and the embrace of His purpose of disseminating the gospel to the lost. A church that has forsaken this purpose should consider itself under God's wrath (11:12-21).

Third, believers must be prepared for the cost of following Christ. Jesus makes this clear in His teaching to the disciples on the Mount of Olives (chapter 13). It is an extensive teaching of what it means to follow Jesus in the midst of this cosmic conflict we are all in. Courage is a necessary character trait for the follower of Christ.

Fourth, all believers are charged to be watchmen. A faithful watchman warns of dangers both outside and inside the church. It is a difficult job with a challenging job description (13:5-37). It can be quite lonely pulling guard duty. We must guard the power of the gospel.

Watchmen guard the truth and pray for themselves and for God's people to be faithful followers of Christ. Complacency is the great enemy of watchmen.

> At that time I will search Jerusalem with lamps,
>   and I will punish the men
> who are **complacent,**
>   those who say in their hearts,
> The Lord will not do good,
>   nor will he do ill.
>
> *Zep. 1:12*

Watchmen grow weary. It is easier to go with the flow of the culture and to think that God does not really care how people live or how the gospel is treated. It is easy to think that God is not really angry about sin. It is easy to think that we don't need any unhappy talk about sin and wrath. It is easy to think that there will be no judgment. But God does care.

Jesus charged all of us with guard duty: "And what I say to you I say to all: Stay awake" (Mk. 13:37). Ezekiel received, and was faithful to, a similar charge from God.

> *Son of man, I have made you a watchman for the house of Israel. Whenever you hear a word from my mouth, you shall give them warning from me.*
>
> *Ezk. 3:17*

Table of 17 Hazards

1	v. 5	False teaching in general and false leaders	10	v. 13	Hatred from the world
2	v. 6	False messiahs, leaders	11	v. 14	Abomination of desolation, religious sacrilege
3	v. 7	Wars and rumors of wars	12	v. 19	Significant tribulation
4	v. 8	Worldwide national upheavals	13	v. 21	False witnesses
5	v. 8	Natural disasters	14	v. 22	False Christs
6	v. 9	Opposition and persecution by religious leaders	15	v. 22	False prophets
7	v. 9	Opposition and persecution by political leaders	16	v. 32, 36	The final judgment of Christ at His second coming (a hazard for those who do not know Jesus and for the irresponsible)
8	v. 11	Being put on trial	17	vv. 32-36	Complacency
9	v. 12	Family opposition and physical harm			

Table of 20 Imperatives

No.	Ref.	Imperatives	No.	Ref.	Imperatives
1	13:5	See that no one leads you stray			
2	13:7	Do not be alarmed			
3	13:9	Be on your guard			
		13:9 Purpose of God in the last epoch of history: ## "to bear witness"			
		13:10 Purpose of God in the last epoch of history: # "And the Gospel must first be proclaimed to all nations."			
4	13:11	Do not be anxious what to say	13	13:23	But be on guard
5	13:11	Say whatever is given you in that hour	14	13:28	From the fig tree learn its lesson
6	13:14	Let the reader understand	15	13:28	You know that summer is near
7	13:14	Let those who are in Judea flee.	16	13:29	Know that he is near
8	13:15	Let the one on the housetop not go down	17	13:33	Be on guard
9	13:15	Nor enter his house to take anything out	18	13:33	Keep awake
10	13:16	Let the one who is in the field not turn back		13:34	Stay awake (a mini parable)
11	13:18	Pray that it may not happen in winter	19	13:35	Stay awake
12	13:21	Behold, do not believe it [false messiah sightings]	20	13:37	Stay awake

Elements of the Gospel in Mark

	Description	Gospel of Mark
1.	God – creator, father, judge	1:1, 11; 9:2-8; 13:24-27; 14:62; 16:1-8; 21 miracle accounts.
2.	Holiness – God is holy and requires absolute holiness, perfection, and obedience of mankind	1:9-11; 8:34-38; 9:2-8; 10:17-31; 12:29-31; 16:1-8
3.	Sin	4:1-20; 7:14-23; 8:14-21, 33; 9:33-37, 42-50; 11:12-21; 12:1-11, 38-40.
4.	Judgment and wrath	9:42-50; 11:12-21; 12:1-12; 13:1-2; 24-27.
5.	The cross and resurrection	8:31-32; 9:31,10:32-34; 10:45; 14:1-2, 22-25; 15:1-47; 16:1-8.
6.	Grace	1:40-45; 2:1-12, 13-17; 10:13-31; 10:46-52; 21 miracle accounts.
7.	Counting the cost of following Jesus	6:14-29; 8:34-38; 10:28-31; 13:5-37.
8.	Repentance and faith	1:4-5, 14-15; 8:34-38.

CHAPTER 15

CHRISTIANITY EXPLORED: HOW TO RUN THE COURSE

When I was in search of something to help me in the area of evangelism, one of the provisions God made was to place me in contact with Christianity Explored Ministries (CEM). The material and the training provided by CEM were exactly what I needed. It is not the only way to do evangelism effectively, but it is one of the finest programs and trainings I have encountered. If you have an effective way of doing evangelism, by all means keep using it. And if you do, you may also find this can be a good complement to it.

In this chapter, I will focus on a course called Christianity Explored (CE) because it is what I know, and I have many years of experience with it. This chapter is an introduction to CE and how to use it. CE is designed to introduce nonbelievers to Christ in a relational setting. However, the course is multifaceted. Not only is it highly effective in sharing the gospel with individuals, but also in equipping churches to become actively involved in sharing the gospel with the lost. CE and its training can accomplish two important functions: (1) it walks non-believers through the gospel in a highly effective way and (2) it can serve as an anchor to a church's evangelism efforts.

Before we go into the specifics of using Christianity Explored, it may be important to step back and to think about how a church functions. Specifically, it is important to think about how an organization, any organization, accomplishes work. The short answer is that organizations accomplish work through systems.

As a practical definition, we can think of a system as a group of interrelated components and people forming a functional organism that can accomplish a task. Even though most pastors and church leaders may not think in terms of systems, churches do use systems in similar ways that businesses use them. Churches typically have multiple systems in place to accomplish their work. A worship service is a good example of the end product of a system. Most worship services have multiple elements such as a call to worship, prayer, liturgy/Scripture reading, music, a sermon, affirmation of faith, the Lord's Supper, and a benediction. Various individuals are in charge of selecting the specific hymns, Scriptures, liturgy, etc., to be used each Sunday. Various individuals are involved in leading the service. All these people and components are part of a system to accomplish worship.

Something similar is needed for a church to be intentional and faithful in evangelism. A system for evangelism is essential. All of the church's members should be included. Christianity Explored can be the anchor to a church's system for intentional evangelism. It is not the system all by itself, but it can be a foundational part of it.

Christianity Explored materials and training can (1) equip believers to understand and explain the gospel, (2) train leaders, and (3) be used in actual evangelism. Churches can use it as a platform to build an ongoing evangelistic ministry that can be effective year after year. It can be used as an evangelism tool in large groups, small groups, and one-to-one settings. Individuals can use it to engage the lost in their neighborhoods. CE is highly versatile and multifaceted in what it can accomplish. It is one of the most effective tools a church can employ in the area of evangelism.

As an anchor for a system of evangelism, Christianity Explored can support other programs of the church, outreach ministries, and evangelistic efforts. For example, many churches have women's Bible studies every week and often nonbelieving friends come along. It is difficult in that setting for nonbelievers to ask their questions and to examine the gospel. But if they show interest in Christianity, they can be invited to a CE course where they can ask whatever question they want without fear of being seen as uninformed about Bible teachings.

When the membership of a church is trained in using Christianity Explored and has been through its training in a biblical foundation for evangelism, the church can then build a "superstructure" on top of it using tools such as gospel tracts like the Gospel of Mark or *Two Ways to Live*,[483] special meet and greet events, church picnics

---

483 https://www.twowaystolive.com/; hard copies of the tract can be purchased through https://matthias-media.com/products/two-ways-to-live.

with invited guests, street evangelism, and many other ministries of the church. CE is where a person can be directed to hear the whole gospel in a setting that welcomes their questions, gives them biblical answers, and allows them space to contemplate the implications of the gospel.

Since most people need to hear the gospel multiple times before making a commitment to follow Christ, CE is the forum for allowing the gospel to do its work. As another example, if a nonbeliever is presented the gospel by someone using an Evangelism Explosion[484] presentation, and that person expresses interest in knowing more, CE is a great follow up for that individual. And since we should never place high pressure on someone to pray the sinner's prayer, CE provides the perfect forum for a nonbeliever to have time and space to digest the gospel. On the other hand, if a person genuinely prays a sinner's prayer, and becomes a new creation in Christ on the spot, CE is still the perfect place for them to get the gospel ingrained in their hearts and to get started in their spiritual growth in Christ.

Here is a brief diagram of CE as the anchor to a system for evangelism.

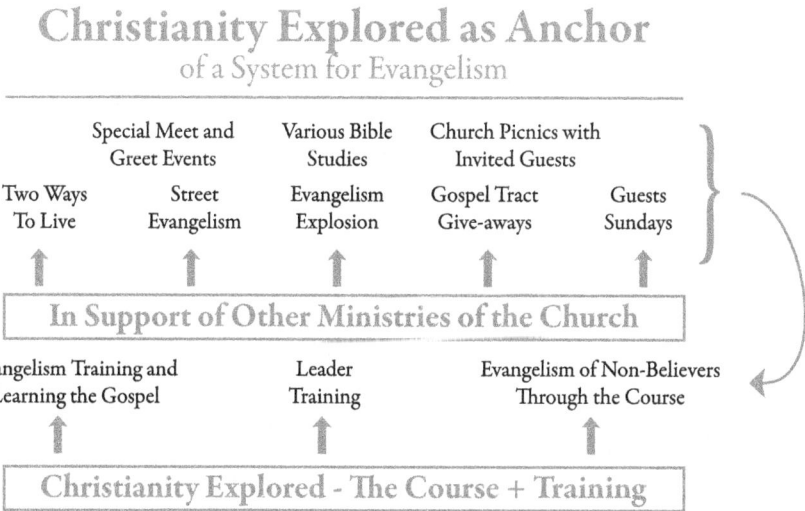

Christianity Explored as Anchor
of a System for Evangelism

Special Meet and Greet Events	Various Bible Studies	Church Picnics with Invited Guests	
Two Ways To Live	Street Evangelism	Evangelism Explosion	Gospel Tract Give-aways	Guests Sundays

↑ ↑ ↑ ↑ ↑

In Support of Other Ministries of the Church

Evangelism Training and Learning the Gospel	Leader Training	Evangelism of Non-Believers Through the Course

↑ ↑ ↑

Christianity Explored - The Course + Training

---

484 https://evangelismexplosion.org/.

All of what follows is from the "How to Run the Course" section of the "Christianity Explored Leader's Handbook" (3rd and 4th Editions). It has been edited to fit this context.[485]

Introduction

When *Christianity Explored* first started running more than twenty-five years ago at All Souls, Langham Place in London, we were uncertain how it would be received. We were pretty sure that opening up the message of Jesus by walking through the Gospel of Mark would be a great thing to do. But we have been amazed by how God has honored and blessed this simple approach to outreach.

We are so thankful that, since those early days, hundreds of thousands of people throughout the world have encountered the real Jesus as he walks off the pages of Scripture. The course has stimulated thought and discussion – and people have been challenged to consider the claim of Christ on their lives. *Christianity Explored* has been translated into over 100 languages and continues to grow.

What makes this course – and the Christian gospel – distinctive is its insistence on God's remarkable grace: the clear teaching that although we have rebelled against God, we are deeply loved by him. Loved with an outrageous, costly, and incomprehensible love that was poured out for us on a little hill just outside Jerusalem.

Christianity Explored is a seven-session course with a creative mixture of Bible studies, talks, videos, group discussions, and home Bible-reading. Participants will discover the identity, mission, and call of Jesus – who Jesus is, what he came to do, and how he calls us to   respond.

And you are an important part in bringing this good news to your friends, family, or neighborhood. Trust in the Holy Spirit's power to open blind eyes, because this ancient story with its many life-changing truths will find its way into the hearts and souls of those who hear it. And by the miracle of God's grace, you will be part of others coming to know the love and salvation that only Christ can give.

---

485 *Christianity Explored Leader's Handbook* (4th Edition), pp. 8-27. The introduction is from *Christianity Explored Leaders Guide* (3rd Edition) (New Malden, UK: The Good Book Company, Ltd, 2011), p. 3. Used with permission.

There are two Christianity Explored websites to help you:

1) **www.christianityexplored.org**. This website is for non-Christians, whether or not they are on a course. It features a visual gospel outline based on the Gospel of Mark, video answers to common questions, and testimonies from a wide variety of people, as well as information about the Christianity Explored course.

1) **www.ceministries.org**. This is for leaders looking for information, downloads, and resources.

Rico Tice, Barry Cooper, Craig Dyer
and the Christianity Explored Team,
February 2011

Getting Started

Telling people about Jesus Christ is a stunning privilege and a huge responsibility. It's a stunning privilege because Almighty God is pleased to call us his "fellow workers" (1 Corinthians 3:9) as he seeks and saves the lost. And it's a huge responsibility because it can be tempting to present a watered-down gospel that has no power to save and is "no gospel at all" (Galatians 1:7). Our evangelism must always be careful, prayerful, and faithful.

Christianity Explored has been developed to let the Gospel tell the gospel: it takes your group members on a seven-session journey through Mark's Gospel to discover who Jesus is, what he achieved, and how he calls us to respond.

Structure of the Course

How and when you meet will depend on your situation. Many courses run on a midweek evening for seven weeks, with a day away on the Saturday between sessions 6 and 7. But your circumstances may be different.

The course material can be adapted to suit your situation, including meeting one to one with a friend or neighbor. However, you will find it helpful to meet as regularly as possible – and please don't skip any sessions or change the order. (Please use the day away material between sessions 6 and 7, even if you don't go "away" to use it.)

If this is the first time you have run Christianity Explored, you will find helpful tips at www.ceministries.org. This includes guidance on:

- setting up your venue
- choosing and training leaders
- inviting people to come

The chart below shows how the course is structured, and how the themes fit together.

	Session	Explore (Bible Study)	Listen (Talk/Video)	Discuss	Follow Up (At Home)
Identity	**Session 1: Good News** Christianity is about Christ.	Welcome	Good News	Discuss talk/video	Mark 1:1-3:6
Identity	**Session 2: Identity** Jesus is the Christ (God's only chosen King) and God's Son.	Mark 4:35-41	Identity	Discuss talk/video	Mark 3:7-5:43
Mission	**Session 3: Sin** Jesus came to cure our heart problem – our sin.	Mark 2:1-12	Sin	Discuss talk/video	Mark 6:1-8:29
Mission	**Session 4: The Cross** Jesus died to rescue us from sin, by taking the punishment we deserve.	Mark 8:22-33	The cross	Discuss talk/video	Mark 8:30-10:52
Mission	**Session 5: Resurrection** The resurrection proves that God accepted the ransom Jesus paid, that death has been beaten, and that Jesus will come back to judge everyone.	Mark 14:27-31	Resurrection	Discuss talk/video	Mark 11:1-13:37

Call	**Session 6: Grace** Jesus died to reconcile us to God, rescuing us from our sin by taking the punishment we deserve. This is grace – God's undeserving gift to us.	Mark 10:13-16	Grace	Discuss talk/video	Mark 14:1-16:8
Call	Day Away 1. The Sower. We must listen to Jesus, and act on what we hear. 2. James and John. Following Jesus is about service, not status. We need to ask Jesus for mercy, not a reward. 3. King Herod. Rejecting Jesus' call to repent and believe will eventually earn us the rejection of Jesus.	Mark 4:1-9 and 13-20	The Sower James and John King Herod	Discuss talk/video	
Call	**Session 7: Come and Die** A follower of Jesus "must deny himself and take up his cross". But what is given up is nothing compared to what is gained.	Mark 1:14-15	Come and Die	Discuss talk/video	

The first five weeks focus on who Jesus is and what he achieved – his identity and mission. Then during the final two sessions and the day away the emphasis is on how we should respond to Jesus – his call. In particular, course members will explore Jesus' words in Mark 8:34: "If anyone would come after me, he must deny himself and take up his cross and follow me".

Structure of a Session

Below is the suggested structure for an evening session. Of course, depending on your circumstances, you might want to change the exact times, or offer coffee and cake instead of a meal. Equally, you might want to run the course during the day if that is a more suitable time for those you're trying to reach.

6:30 p.m.	Leaders' prayer meeting
7:00 p.m.	Guests arrive for the meal
7:45 p.m.	Explore (Bible study)
8:05 p.m.	Listen (Talk/video)
8:30 p.m.	Discuss
9:00 p.m.	End of the evening – "One-to-One"

Note: All times are approximate. You can make certain sessions shorter or longer depending on your circumstances.

You can run Christianity Explored with Bible talks presented by the course leader or by using the course DVD or downloadable videos, presented by Rico Tice, who is Senior Minister (Evangelism) at All Souls Church, Langham Place in London.

If you decide to run the course with the talks, you can download the talk outlines from the Christianity Explored website. You can either download the talks as pdfs, or as Word documents so that you can adapt them for your own situation. They are available from www.ceministries.org.

If you decide to run the course with the DVD/videos, please note that because each episode features on-screen Bible text, it is inadvisable to use them with large groups unless you have access to a projection screen and projector.

Everyone involved in the course – leaders, guests and the course leader – will need a copy of Mark's Gospel or a Bible. It is important that everyone use the same version and edition so that page numbers will be the same. (The version used throughout the course material is the New International Version.*)

- Guests should each be given a Mark's Gospel or Bible at the beginning of the course, preferably one they can keep when the course ends.
- They should also be given a copy of the Handbook.
- Pens should be made available to allow guests to make notes or jot down questions.

Note: Christianity Explored uses the 1984 edition of the New International Version (NIV). The 2011 revised edition includes a number of changes to the English text in Mark's Gospel. Where these changes involve significant words or phrases that are used within the course, there are notes in this Leader's Handbook to help you adapt the material if you are using the 2011 NIV.

Before the Course

Before the course starts, there are a number of things you should do:

Get to know Mark's Gospel, the Handbook, and the Videos

Read through Mark at least three times. Familiarize yourself with the Handbook that your group will be using, and the guidance on the answers to questions in the study guide section of this Leader's Handbook.

As you prepare, you might find it helpful to make notes in your copy of the group members' Handbook. Some people prefer to use an annotated Handbook to lead their group instead of referring back to this Leader's Handbook. Either way, you will feel much more confident to lead your group once you've prepared for the Bible studies and discussions.

As your group members read through Mark, you will need to be prepared to answer questions that arise from the Bible text. There is a section in the Leader's Handbook that will help you prepare for these questions in advance. If, during the session, you don't know the answer to someone's question, just acknowledge the fact, and ask if you can find the answer in time for the next session.

If you are using the Christianity Explored DVD, or downloadable videos, watch each episode through several times. This will help you to become more familiar with the material, and also enable you to refer back to it during discussion: "Do you remember what was said in the video?"

Prepare Your Personal Story

"Always be prepared to give an answer to everyone who asks you to give the reason for the hope that you have. But do this with gentleness and respect..." (1 Peter 3:15).

A personal story or testimony is an account of God's work in your life. Everybody who has been born again and who is becoming like Christ has a unique, interesting and powerful story, regardless of whether or not it appears spectacular.

At some point during the course, you may feel it appropriate to share your story with the group. Often someone will ask you directly how you became a Christian and you will need to have an answer ready.

You may find the guidelines below helpful as you prepare your story:

- Keep it honest, personal and interesting.
  *Tip: Your first sentence should make people sit up and listen.
  Anything too general, for example: "Well, I was brought up in
  a Christian home..." may make people switch off immediately.*
- Keep it short.
  *Tip: Any more than three minutes may stretch people's patience. They can
  always ask you questions if they want to know more.*
- Keep pointing to Christ, not yourself.
  *Tip: Your story is a great opportunity to communicate the gospel. Always
  include what it is that you believe, as well as how you came to believe it.
  As a general guide, try to explain why you think Jesus is God, how
  his death affects you personally, and what changes God has made
  in your life.*
- Prepare your personal story. (Write the main points on a sheet of paper.)
  You might find it useful to share your story with other leaders and get
  their feedback.

Prepare for Difficult Questions

Session 1 finishes by asking the group members to answer this question: "If you could ask God one question, and you knew it would be answered, what would it be?" This will draw out a number of questions that will need careful handling. The appendices (in the Christianity Explored leaders guide; not printed in this book) will help you deal with some of the most common questions that people may ask about Christianity in general, and about Mark's Gospel in particular.

Pray

- That those invited will attend the course.
- That God would enable you to prepare well.
- For the logistics of organizing the course.
- For good relationships with your co-leaders and group members.
- That God would equip you to lead faithfully.
- That the Holy Spirit would open the blind eyes of those who attend.

God's Role in Evangelism and Ours

This topic was covered in Chapter 11 of this book, "What is Biblical Evangelism?" but this is a good refresher and summary with a short exercise.

We need to distinguish between God's role in evangelism and our role. It's going to be incredibly frustrating if we try to fulfill God's role – because only the Creator of the universe is able to do that.

Read 2 Corinthians 4:1-6

Answer the following questions from the verses you've just read:

What is God's role in evangelism?

Why can't people see the truth of the gospel?

What is our role in evangelism?

How should we do our role in evangelism?

God's Role in Evangelism

What is God's role in evangelism? God makes "his light shine in our hearts to give us the light of the knowledge of the glory of God in the face of Christ" (2 Corinthians 4:6).

In other words, God enables us to recognize that Jesus is God. God makes it possible – by his Holy Spirit – for a person to see who Jesus is. When Paul is on the Damascus road, he asks, "Who are you, Lord?" and is told, "I am Jesus" (Acts 9:5). That is the moment of his conversion – when he recognizes for the first time who Jesus actually is.

The beginning of 2 Corinthians 4:6 reminds us that God said, "Let light shine out of darkness". That is a reference to the miracle of creation in Genesis 1:3. This same God who brought light into the world at creation now shines light into the hearts of human beings, enabling them to see that Jesus is God. In other words, for people to recognize that Jesus is God, God must perform a miracle.

People do not become Christians just because we share the gospel with them. God must shine his light in people's hearts so that they recognize and respond to the truth of the gospel.

And we know from 2 Corinthians 4:4 that people can't see the truth of the gospel because "the god of this age has blinded the minds of unbelievers".

Here, Paul reminds us that we are in the middle of a supernatural battlefield. The reason so many reject the gospel is that the devil is at work, preventing people from recognizing who Jesus is.

The devil blinds people by making them chase after the things of this world, which are passing away and which cannot save them. Their concerns are confined to the here and now: their popularity, their family, their relationships, their material possessions. They are blind to anything beyond that.

As a result, they can only see Jesus in the here and now, perhaps as a great moral teacher; his eternal significance is completely obscured. And, according to verse 4, Satan is determined to prevent people from seeing "the light of the gospel of the glory of Christ, who is the image of God". Satan does not want people to recognize who Jesus is.

Our Role in Evangelism

What then is our role in evangelism? "We ... preach ... Jesus Christ as Lord."

The word "preach" can evoke negative images, but it derives from a word simply meaning "herald": someone who relates important announcements from the king to his kingdom. Our role is to tell people the gospel and leave the Spirit of God to convict them of its truth.

These verses also reveal the attitude we should adopt as we preach. We are to be like "servants for Jesus' sake" (2 Corinthians 4:5). The word translated "servants" literally means "slaves" in Greek. Paul was determined to present Christ to others without any hint of self-promotion.

We must remember that the only difference between ourselves and an unbeliever is that God, in his mercy, has opened our blind eyes and illuminated our hearts by his Holy Spirit. We should be forever grateful, and so seek to promote Christ, not ourselves.

We must keep preaching Christ as Lord and, remembering that only a miracle from God can open blind eyes, we must keep praying that God will shine his light in the hearts of unbelievers.

2 Corinthians 4:1-6 also helps us to carry out our role in the right way: "We do not use deception, nor do we distort the word of God ... By setting forth the truth plainly we commend ourselves to every man's conscience in the sight of God ... For we do not preach ourselves, but Jesus Christ as Lord."

When we tell people about Christ, we should demonstrate the following qualities:

Integrity – "We do not use deception." We are straight with people; we are genuine and sincere, and we never use any kind of emotional manipulation.

Fidelity – We do not "distort the word of God". We have to tell people the tough bits. If, for example, we don't tell people about sin, about hell, and about the necessity of repentance, then we are distorting God's word. Preaching these hard truths means trusting in the work of the Holy Spirit to draw people to Christ, however "difficult" the message.

Humility – "We do not preach ourselves, but Jesus Christ as Lord." We must draw people to Jesus, not to ourselves. We must remember that some people are very impressionable, and that we want them to make a decision to follow Christ because they are convinced by the truth and are being led by the Holy Spirit, rather than being manipulated by their admiration of the course leader.

As we use Christianity Explored to preach the gospel, we must remember that it is up to God whether somebody becomes a Christian or not. Only he can open blind eyes, so we must trust him for the results.

Get to Grips With Mark's Gospel

As a Christianity Explored leader, it's important to familiarize yourself with Mark's Gospel before the course starts. Here's one exercise to help you do that.

Most Bibles divide Mark up with subheadings. As you finish reading each of these short sections, ask yourself: What is this section telling me about...

- Jesus' Identity? (who he is)
- Jesus' Mission? (what he set out to achieve)
- Jesus' Call? (how he's calling me to respond)

You'll find that every section of Mark's Gospel has something to say about one or more of those three themes. A great way to prepare for the course is to write "I", "M" or "C" next to each section you read.

Christianity Explored takes each theme in turn:

- Sessions 1-2 Identity
- Sessions 3-5 Mission
- Sessions 6-7 Call

The great drama of Mark – and Christianity Explored – is people's blindness to Jesus' identity, mission and call. Even those closest to Jesus repeatedly failed to see it.

The great joy of Mark – and Christianity Explored – is that as they spend time with Jesus, many are cured of that blindness. They come to see that Jesus is infinitely more valuable to them than anything else in the universe, and they are prepared to follow him whatever the cost.

Getting Our Expectations Right

Jesus was the most brilliant teacher who ever lived. Nevertheless, a glance through Mark chapter 3 reminds us that:

- those in authority wanted him dead (v 6).
- the public were often more interested in his miracles than in his teaching (v 9-10).
- one of his own followers would eventually betray him (v 19).
- his own family thought he was out of his mind (v 21).
- many religious people thought he was evil (v 22).

Yet, in spite of all this pressure, rather than change his approach or water down his message, Jesus continued to teach: "With many similar parables Jesus spoke the word to them, as much as they could understand" (Mark 4:33).

We, too, will face pressure. So why should we persist in teaching God's word to people who don't seem to be listening, or who openly oppose us?

Jesus gives us the answer in Mark chapter 4: God's word produces dramatic results (v 8, 20, 32). But Jesus begins by warning us to expect disappointment and delay.

Expect Disappointment
Read Mark 4:1-8, 14-20

The seed (which is "the word," as Jesus explains in v 14) can fall in unfruitful places:

- along the path (v 15)
- on rocky places (v 16)
- among thorns (v 18)

There will be those who delight us by turning up for the first session, but who never come again. There will be those who joyfully make a commitment in Session 7 but, because of family pressure, they soon decide it's just not worth the trouble. Then there are those who diligently attend each week of the course but decide right at the end that their material possessions mean more to them than anything they've heard.

It can be desperately disappointing to see group members apparently respond to the gospel message, but then show no sign of lasting change. But Jesus warns us to expect it.

Expect Delay
Read Mark 4:26-29

Jesus uses the metaphor of the seed with good reason: it takes time for seed to grow.

The farmer has to be patient: "Night and day, whether he sleeps or gets up, the seed sprouts and grows, though he does not know how" (Mark 4:27). He just has to trust that the seed will grow, even though it may seem that nothing much is happening.

We live in an instant culture – instant food, instant information, instant credit – and we may find ourselves expecting guests to acquire an instant relationship with God. But delay is as much a part of our work as it is the farmer's. We must be prepared to stay in touch with group members for weeks, months, or even years after the course ends.

There will be those who seem to agree with everything they learn through the course. You decide to meet up with them on a regular basis and, a year later, they still agree with everything they've learned. But they're not Christians.

There may be times when we lose patience and are tempted to give up. But we must continue to plant the word in people's lives, trusting in its power, and remembering that God's timescale is very different from our own.

Expect Dramatic Results
Read Mark 4:30-32

Despite the inevitable disappointments and delays, there is a good reason to continue sowing God's word in people's lives, just as Jesus did: "When planted, it grows and becomes the largest of all garden plants, with such big branches that the birds of the air can perch in its shade" (Mark 4:32). Even a tiny seed – like the mustard seed – can produce dramatic results.

There will be those who bring up the same difficult issues week after week. Then suddenly one of those people will arrive one week and tell you that he or she has become a Christian. A few months after that, that person is taking every opportunity to grow in their own understanding in order to be able to teach the gospel more clearly to others. And a year later that same person is a Christianity Explored leader.

As Jesus tells us in Mark 4:20, there will be those who hear the word, accept it, and go on to "produce a crop – thirty, sixty or even a hundred times what was sown".

It is a great encouragement to remember that the power to change lives dramatically is not in our eloquence – it is in God's word. So, whatever disappointments we suffer, and whatever delays we endure, keep teaching the word faithfully.

CHAPTER 16

ENGAGING OTHERS

I find evangelism hard. The problem with being an evangelist is that people assume that you find evangelism effortless; but I don't find it easy, and never have. For me, telling people about Jesus has often been nerve wracking. But it has been joyful.

Rico Tice, Evangelist[486]

I was doing an internet search using key words such as "work of evangelism" and this popped up: "Free Downloadable Guide – Evangelism Made Easy." For most people, evangelism is not easy. I don't find these kinds of headlines useful. In fact, I find them discouraging. But even though evangelism can be challenging, it is something every ordinary follower of Christ can do.

There are good books on evangelism available to believers. I have benefited from several of them. In this chapter, I will not attempt to rewrite what has already been produced but will provide a few ideas to help those who are getting started in this important task. Everyone needs a bit of encouragement and guidance, so I will provide some pointers that I think will be helpful. Please know from the start that there is a learning curve in evangelism. Training and preparation are essential. At the end of this chapter, I will provide a list of recommended books to help you continue this journey.

In this chapter we will cover (1) personal preparation, (2) people in our lives, (3) practical motivations, (4) practical thinking about evangelism, (5) practical things we can do, and (6) practical readings.

---

486 Rico Tice, *Honest Evangelism* (Epsom, Surrey, UK: The Good Book Company, 2015, 2016), p. 11. Please read this really fine book. It will be a tremendous encouragement to those who find evangelism difficult.

Evangelism is best viewed as a team sport. God called together a team, His people the church, to engage in this important endeavor. Teams encourage, sharpen, and support each other in numerous ways. And teams can accomplish more than any one individual acting alone. We can see that across practically all sports. Evangelism needs the foundation of the church and the encouragement and prayer support that comes from the team members. None of us can walk in the way of the cross as a solo mountain climber.

Personal Preparation

I have had several great hobbies in my adult lifetime – softball, jogging, flying, fishing, and photography to name a few. In fact, I believe everyone should have a hobby. We all need to engage our minds in something other than the regular work routine that we carry. We should be careful not to let a hobby become an idol of the heart. But kept in the proper perspective, hobbies can refresh us for the work we are engaged in. My point here is that each hobby I have engaged in required a learning process to be able to enjoy it. That was part of the fun. I spent a lot of time reading about photography, for example, and learning about f-stops, aperture openings, shutter speeds, film speeds, exposure meters, medium tones, depth of field, and about placing a tree in just the right spot in the frame. I acquired about 14 books on photography during that hobby and devoured each of them. It was all great fun.

We should expect no less when we engage in evangelism. There is a learning process that includes reading, talking with others, training, and practice. Here are some things you can begin to do to prepare for evangelism.

Learn the biblical gospel. By now you probably know what I mean by that. If we don't know the biblical gospel, we have no message. We must understand it, protect its integrity, and be prepared to discuss all of it. We should prepare ourselves mentally, spiritually, and emotionally to speak the whole gospel message and understand that certain parts of the gospel may not improve our personal popularity.

Pray, as Paul prayed, for open doors for the sharing of the gospel. "At the same time, pray also for us, that God may open to us a door for the word, to declare the mystery of Christ, on account of which I am in prison – that I may make it clear, which is how I ought to speak" (Col. 4:3). Also refer to: Acts 14:27; 1 Cor. 16:9; 2 Cor. 2:12; Rev. 3:8. Pray also for the combination of love and courage to speak the hard parts such as God's righteousness, judgment, and wrath. Pray for the lost.

Prepare your testimony of coming to faith in Christ. Write it out on paper, or at least write it in outline form. It should be about three to five minutes in length. Incorporate elements of the gospel into it, and present it in a way that exalts Christ and how He has saved your soul. The sharing of one's testimony is not the same thing as sharing the gospel, but it can be a bridge to sharing the full gospel message. The more you incorporate the individual elements of the gospel into your testimony, the more effective it will be.

When I share my testimony, I discuss the struggle I had in turning from a life centered on myself to trusting in Christ and living for His purpose. Even though I knew the gospel message, I rejected Jesus as Lord. And in that rejection, I knew I was under the wrath of God. **The wrath of God was very troubling to me, as it should have been.** I could never get away from that inconvenient reality. It was distressing to me and there was only one solution. Christ was the only one who could rescue me from the coming wrath.

Cultivate friendships among non-believers. Many people over the years have told me that they do not have any non-Christian friends. But this is not how it should be. We have too often walled ourselves off from the non-Christian world, and that is not a good thing. Jesus never did that. He hung out with some notable sinners. He made friends with people who had terrible reputations in the eyes of the world. It was so flagrant at times that it destroyed Jesus' reputation among the arrogantly self-important. May we be so blessed.

Establish an evangelism partner. A few years ago, an evangelistically minded friend and I began *unofficially* acting as evangelism partners. When I was to meet with someone I wanted to share the gospel with, I would ask my friend, Matt to pray for me that I would have the courage to raise the subject of the gospel. He would make the same request of me, and I would pray for him as he engaged a friend for Christ. It became a habit with us, and we continue this practice nearly 10 years later. It has been a source of encouragement, prayer support, and accountability. I highly recommend this practice. Pray for God to give you an evangelism partner.[487]

Commit to learning about evangelism and to becoming faithful in this great work that God is doing in the world. There is a learning curve, and most of us need help and encouragement along the way.

There is one other aspect of evangelism that I should mention. It's called "crossing the pain line."[488] We can talk to people about the weather, sports, work life, and many other topics, but when we bring up the subject of the gospel, we are crossing the pain line. Many people think they are okay with God and that when they die, surely they will go to heaven. In practically every movie or TV program, when someone dies, it is said of them, "They are in a better place now." But that may not be true. And lost people sometimes become offended or even angry if we share what the gospel has to say about life after death.

When we talk about sin, the need for repentance, and the coming judgment, we are "crossing the pain line." People in general do not want to hear about sin and may respond negatively. When we tell others that Jesus is the only way to heaven, they may become offended and think we are being intolerant. This does not mean we refrain from speaking the gospel, but that we should prepare ourselves for a possible negative response. A good preparation for crossing the pain line is to plan an escape route if things go in the wrong direction.[489] If the response is anger or a vitriolic outburst, politely retreat and talk about

---

487 One day in Sunday school Matt Bonner and I were discussing our evangelism partnership, and another gentleman overheard us. He suggested that what we were doing would be a good model to teach others to replicate. So, a thank you to Doug Hixson for his observation and suggestion.

488 Rico Tice, *Honest Evangelism*, pp. 14-15. Rico Tice discusses the "pain line" throughout this outstanding, must-read book. My strong recommendation for first readings and preparation for evangelism is to read *Honest Evangelism* and then read *Tell the Truth* by Will Metzger. You will be off to a great start with these two books.

489 Credit to Rico Tice.

the weather or something else. Not everyone, though, will respond negatively. Many people I talk to respond merely with apathy. I hate apathy. That may be a worse response. But some, maybe a small minority, will respond to the call of the gospel message and give their life to Christ and avoid the wrath of God that awaits them otherwise.

People in Our Lives

The goal in evangelism is to have a meaningful conversation about the gospel with those who are lost. The gospel is the message that God uses to remove the veil, the blindness that is covering the eyes of those who are perishing (2 Cor. 4:3-6; also Acts: 11:13-14; Rom. 1:17; 1 Pet. 1:23-25).

The concentric diagram below can be helpful in visualizing the work of evangelism. We can think of the non-believing world around us in terms of family, friends, neighbors, work associates, random contacts, and others. All these relationships provide opportunities for engaging someone with the gospel. The best opportunities I have had to discuss the gospel are with people who know me and trust me and with whom I have a relationship.

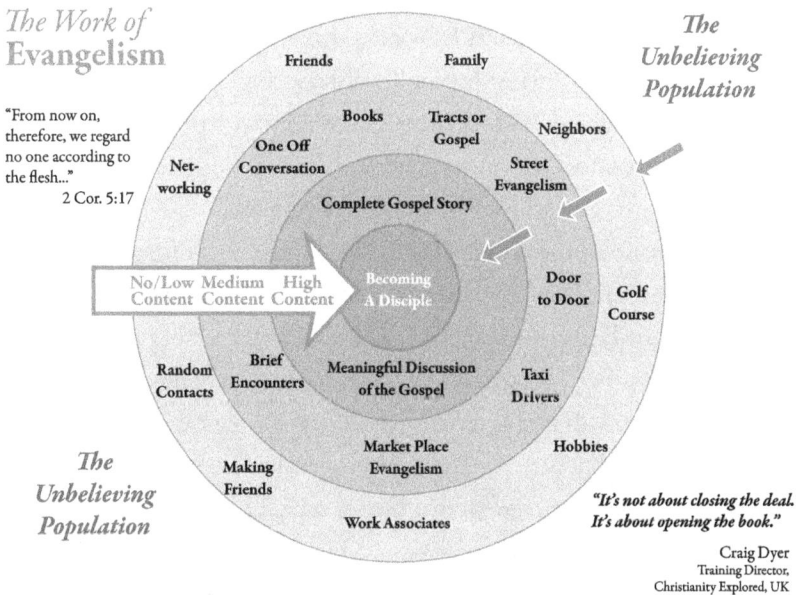

The Work of **Evangelism**

"From now on, therefore, we regard no one according to the flesh..." 2 Cor. 5:17

The **Unbelieving** *Population*

The **Unbelieving** *Population*

Friends — Family — Neighbors

Books — Tracts or Gospel — Street Evangelism

One Off Conversation — Networking

Complete Gospel Story

No/Low Content — Medium Content — High Content

Becoming A Disciple — Door to Door — Golf Course

Random Contacts — Brief Encounters — Meaningful Discussion of the Gospel — Taxi Drivers

Market Place Evangelism — Hobbies

Making Friends — Work Associates

"It's not about closing the deal. It's about opening the book."
Craig Dyer
Training Director,
Christianity Explored, UK

Parents. If you are a father or mother, your children are obviously a top priority for teaching the gospel. There are many good helps for teaching children the Bible's story. I have listed a few below. Spend time with your children telling them your story of repentance and trust in Christ. Teach them the doctrines of the gospel.

Grandparents. You can play a vital role in shaping grandchildren. A few years ago, I read through *The Action Bible* with two of my grandchildren. Now I am reading a biography of John Newton with them. After each chapter we discuss what Newton was going through or his courage in speaking the gospel, along with other aspects of God's acting in his life. They will remember their grandfather telling them about his faith and how Christ saved his life when he was a young adult. They will remember discussions with him about the gospel. This is something they will remember all their lives. My prayer is that it will encourage them to walk in the way of the cross.

Siblings, family members, and friends. Many in this category may live in different cities than we do, but they can be engaged via telephone, Skype, Zoom, or other media. We can invite them to read through a book of the Bible with us. It is nonthreatening to a non-believing friend and does not require much preparation. It can lead to meaningful discussions of the gospel. Currently, I am reading through a book of the Bible with one of my sons who lives 250 miles away. We began doing this more than a year ago. Two days ago, I sent a friend a link to a Christianity Explored video, and he has promised to watch it. He too lives in a different city, and I am hoping he will be willing to discuss the gospel by phone.

Coworkers and others. We have many connections with people through the course of our lives. Some are brief encounters, and some become long-term working relationships. Can we see the lost people in this group of contacts?

You may have heard the saying: "Right living begins with right thinking." This is especially true in evangelism. It is essential that we have a biblical theology of evangelism. If we do, we will view the people in our lives through a biblical lens. Paul gives us that lens when he writes: "From now on, therefore, we regard no one according to the flesh" (2 Cor. 5:16). This means we are not to view people based on the standards of the culture around us but based on the measuring stick of the gospel message. Paul goes on to write in that same paragraph that God is using His people to make His appeal to the lost (2 Cor. 5:20). But what do we see when we see other people? Do we see the possessions they own or the way they dress or the car they drive? Do we only see the trappings of success, or do we see lost people? Jesus can see lost people everywhere. He is not blind. Can we see lost people everywhere? Are we blind?

Our goal is to engage our relationships for God's glory and for the good of others. If we care about lost people, as we certainly should (just ask Jonah about that!), we will try to entice them to examine the gospel with us. This often takes time and may involve many invitations and promptings over several years for a person to be willing to hear the gospel. We should think of people as being in a process of coming to faith. We should think in terms of moving friends from no gospel content to a discussion of the whole gospel story. People need to hear the full gospel. This may take time and a significant amount of persistence and pre-evangelism work. But the stakes are huge. Where a person spends eternity really matters. It is truly a life and death drama that is playing out before our very eyes. But can we see it? And do we have enough courage and love to act accordingly? If you do not, please consult Jonah (chapter 3 of this book) and ask him what he would have done differently if he could have a do-over of that moment in his life.

Practical Motivations

I addressed motivations in Chapter 10. But to keep them in focus it may be worth a brief review. These are the top four motivations driving my life.

1. **Love.** If we love other people, we will warn them of the impending disaster of God's wrath. The perfect love of Christ compels us to share this story of redemption with the lost (2 Cor. 5:14). Love for other people is the most powerful motivator for me. If I care about my friend, I will cross the pain line to share this message with them.

2. **Accountability.** We will stand before the judgment seat of Christ and give an account of whether we were faithful in sharing the gospel with the lost (2 Cor. 5:9-11).

3. **God has commanded it.** We have seen this mandate from Genesis through the Old Testament and into the New Testament. Reaching the lost is an ingrained part of God's character.

4. **People who die without Christ spend eternity in hell.** This is the great tragedy of the fall in Genesis 3. The only relief from the curse of death is trusting in Christ. Believers must fully digest this reality and let it shape their view of everyone around them.

Practical Thinking About Evangelism

Most people do not know the biblical gospel. Some, depending on their upbringing and the culture they grew up in, may know certain aspects of the gospel or possibly a distorted version of it. We should not take for granted that people among our family and friends have an accurate understanding of the gospel.

Lost people are in a process of coming to faith. We can envision that process as a continuum or a timeline with one end being far away from God and the other end being near God. For someone to move from the far end to the near end may take a considerable amount of time. One book on evangelism that I read many years ago stated that a person needs to hear the gospel 7.6 times on average before coming to faith.[490] This means we must take the long view about evangelism. The proper understanding of evangelism is that it is not a "one and done" event. It is not "present the gospel, make a decision, and move on." People need time to process what the gospel means, the cost of following Christ, and how they should respond. And this takes time.

For some believers, a serious impediment to engaging others with the gospel is fear of being asked a question they cannot answer. It is good to be prepared with as many answers as possible, but it is okay if a believer does not have the answer to a particular question. In fact, it provides an opportunity to have a follow-up conversation when an answer has been found. Even though having good answers is useful, it is the content of the gospel that God uses to bring dead souls to life. We should link answers to questions with gospel content as much as possible. We should always point people to Scripture as the only source of spiritual truth.

Practical Things We Can Do

Once the believer has an opportunity to engage someone with the gospel message, there are multiple ways to go about it. Here are a few ideas to consider. I have used all these methods at different times.

1. **Small group or large group** using the Christianity Explored course. This material leads people through the Gospel of Mark in seven sessions. Each

---

490 William Fay with Linda Evans Shepherd, *Share Jesus Without Fear* (Nashville, TN: B&H Publishing Group, 1999), pp. 11, 19.

session has a short video (11 to 18 minutes in length), and there is a handbook with questions for discussion. It gives people time to digest the content of the gospel in a safe environment.

2. **One to one** using the Christianity Explored course, simply reading through one of the four Gospel accounts in the Bible together, reviewing a gospel tract, or sharing a sequence of Bible passages. This can be over a cup of coffee or over the phone once a week. It provides an opportunity for the non-believer to ask questions and to have dialogue over passages in the Bible.

3. **Technologies** today afford the opportunity to do both the above methods over Skype, Zoom, other video conferencing apps, and even over the telephone. I have used the Christianity Explored materials over Skype and over the telephone, with small groups and one to one.

4. **Books and resources to give away.** I find it useful to have a gospel tract or a Gospel of Mark to give away to people. In fact, the Gospel of Mark is my favorite gospel "tract" to give away. It is short, concise, and rich with all the elements of the gospel written by an expert evangelist under the inspiration of the Holy Spirit.

Practical Reading

Honest Evangelism by Rico Tice (Epsom, Surrey, UK: The Good Book Company, 2015, 2016). This book has been such an encouragement to me and to many others. It covers the basics of evangelism and helps the average believer realize that they too can be active in evangelism and that evangelism is not for "professionals" only.

Tell the Truth: The Whole Gospel to the Whole Person by Will Metzger (Downers Grove, IL: InterVarsity Press, 2002, 3rd Ed). This is like a handbook for evangelism. It was most helpful to me when I discovered it in about 2007.

Evangelism and the Sovereignty of God by J. I. Packer (Downers Grove, IL: InterVarsity Press, original edition 1961, Americanized 2008). This is an absolute classic on the theology of evangelism.

Questioning Evangelism: Engaging People's Hearts the Way Jesus Did by Randy Newman (Grand Rapids, MI: Kregel Publications, 2004). This book equips believers to be better listeners and to be armed with engaging questions.

Becoming a Contagious Christian Participants Guide: Communicating Your Faith in a Style That Fits You by Mark Mittleburg, Lee Strobel, and Bill Hybels (Grand Rapids, MI: Zondervan, 1995, 2007). Everyone has a different style in relating to people. This book is excellent, especially for its teaching on six styles of evangelism.

The Cross of Christ by John R. W. Stott (Leicester, UK: Inter-Varsity Press, 1986, 2004). A classic on the accomplishments of the cross.

Resources for Children and Youth

The Action Bible (Colorado Springs, CO: David C. Cook, 2010). It covers both the Old and New Testaments and is for ages 9 and up.

The Jesus Storybook Bible by Sally Lloyd-Jones (Grand Rapids, MI: Zonderkidz, 2007). Excellent for younger children.

ESV Student Study Bible (Wheaton, IL: Crossway, 2011).

Books/Materials to Give Away

The Gospel of Mark (Christianity Explored Edition, ESV), (Epsom, Surrey, UK: The Good Book Company, 2016). This small paperback in the ESV has 13 pages of helps to assist someone unfamiliar with the Bible. https://www.thegoodbook.com/ce-marks-gospel-esv-pack-of-20.

The Case for Christ by Lee Strobel (Grand Rapids, MI: Zondervan, 1998).

Mere Christianity by C. S. Lewis (New York: HarperCollins, 2001, first published 1952).

Why I Am a Christian by John Stott (Downers Grove, IL: InterVarsity Press, 2003).

The Way of the Righteous in the Muck of Life by Dale Ralph Davis (Fearn, Scotland: Christian Focus Publications Ltd., 2016).

Basic Christianity by John Stott (Downers Grove, IL: InterVarsity Press, first edition 1958, Americanized 2006).

EPILOGUE

In the second century, the church was a marginal sect within a dominant, pluralist society... This is where we are today.[491]

Carl Trueman

Jesus wrote an epilogue for His people, about three days before the cross, that prescribed their future. He prepared them for how to live after His departure into heaven and until His return to earth in His second coming. It is recorded in Mark 13. Let's consider it in the context of the 21st century.

Society in the United States today is racing headlong into causes, pursuits, and beliefs that, in many respects, defy comprehension. Our society promotes and often demands affirmation of various immoralities, including co-habitation outside of marriage, homosexuality, adultery, and transgenderism. The government attempts to usurp the authority of parents and take children out from under their parents' protection. We have corruption at many levels of government. Laws are even being enacted to make it illegal to resist many of these tragic undertakings. And Christianity is viewed as an evil, oppressive system that must be destroyed. To say these endeavors are destructive is an understatement.

So where do believers in Jesus Christ turn? How do God's people focus their energies, manage their expectations, and not merely cope with this environment, but faithfully follow Christ in these tumultuous times? I don't know how to turn around society in the short run. Individual Christians should stand against these forces of

---

491 Trueman, *Rise and Triumph,* p. 406-407. In the second century the church was relatively new. Today the church has been around a long time. It has baggage and people know many of the church's failures that we have to contend with. The true church of God today also has many counterfeits to contend with. These counterfeits resemble real Christianity in many ways but are in fact not the real thing.

evil as best we can. Individual believers living as salt and light can and should take on that task. But the church faces a significant question: Will it be faithful to the biblical gospel, and will it be a faithful witness in these difficult times? It is not the church's central task to reform society. The church is to make disciples of all nations and that begins with evangelism.

Being faithful as a believer means rejecting the morals society is embracing when they conflict with biblical standards and mandates. God told Jeremiah that he must not adopt the false ways of the society of his day. God said to him, "They shall turn to you, but you shall not turn to them" (Jer. 15:19). There are many good things in many societies and cultures around the world. "But the culture is only neutral in the abstract and we kid ourselves if we think culture is not against biblical Christianity."[492] Therefore, believers must be careful and not drink deeply from the wells of the arts, philosophy, hedonistic lifestyles,[493] and moral values promoted by the surrounding culture. Much of the content in public media, such as TV, movies, print, various websites, and blogs is full on promotion of destructive ideas and lifestyles. When we immerse ourselves in society's standards, morals, and worldview, like the proverbial frog, we become boiled in the water of the culture. This leads to spiritual death at worst and spiritual blindness at best.

Though there are quite a few passages of Scripture that address the challenges believers face today, in Mark 13, Jesus prepares His disciples for life after His ascension. In His teaching on the Mount of Olives on the Tuesday before His death on the cross, He writes the script for their lives until He returns. Their era was tumultuous, as is the era in which we live. His disciples were people of no political power, like most believers today, and a distinct minority. In His teaching on that occasion, Jesus assures them of His return one day in great power and in great acts of judgment. He articulates the central task for them, and for all His followers, during the time before He comes again. Jesus warns them they will face great opposition to His message. He gives them 20 commands and 17 warnings of hazards to avoid. The disciples' central covenantal task,

---

492 Insight provided by Pastor Matt Bradley, February 2024.

493 Definition of Hedonism: 1) the doctrine that pleasure or happiness is the highest good; 2) devotion to pleasure and self-gratification as a way of life. *Random House Kernerman Webster's College Dictionary*. S.v. "hedonism." Retrieved July 28, 2023, from https://www.thefreedictionary.com/hedonism.

He tells them, is to bear witness to Him and to proclaim the gospel: "But be on your guard. For they will deliver you over to councils, and you will be beaten in synagogues, and you will stand before governors and kings for my sake, to bear witness before them. And the gospel must first be proclaimed to all nations" (Mk. 13:10). This task, the proclaiming of the gospel, possesses eschatological[494] urgency and is a divine mandate during this epoch of history.[495] It is the urgent task of the church during the last days. (See chapter 14, part 3 of this book for more discussion.)

The charge in Mark 13 is to: guard the gospel, protect its integrity, avoid being seduced by false teachings, persevere with courage, endure hardships and persecution – these are to be expected as the norm. The church in the United States has enjoyed an abnormal existence with peace, prosperity, and lack of persecution over the past 200 years or even from its founding. Yet the church has squandered its opportunity and failed in its responsibility to tell the world of the saving grace of Jesus Christ. The church became prosperous and complacent and distorted the gospel to conform to its self-centered desires for prosperity and a hassle-free lifestyle.

The culmination of decades of false teaching has turned the gospel inward and degraded it to a self-help formula for successful living. The biblical gospel, however, has an implied mandate for evangelism embedded in it that cannot be tampered with nor separated without distorting the character of God. We become false teachers when we alter God's attributes by distorting His message, and by changing its posture (i.e., its priorities, emphases, applications, and bearing). The gospel and evangelism are two sides of the same coin, as are worship and witness. Sadly, many churches and believers have gutted the gospel and forsaken evangelism. This is a sin that needs to be repented of.

The church must embrace an accurate expression of the gospel that maintains the biblical posture of the gospel. Gresham Machen, writing in the 1920s, accurately articulates these principles:

---

494 Eschatology is a broad topic, but in general is concerned with the last things and the end of the world; a doctrine that addresses Christ's second coming in judgment of those who have rebelled against Him and in salvation of His elect.

495 "This epoch of history" and "the last days" are phrases used synonymously in this paragraph. The last days began at Jesus incarnation and Pentecost and will continue until Christ comes for the second time to wrap up history as we know it.

> *The character of Christianity as founded upon a message is summed up in the words of the eighth verse of the first chapter of Acts — "Ye shall be my witnesses both in Jerusalem, and in all Judea and Samaria, and unto the uttermost part of the earth"… From the beginning Christianity was a campaign of witnessing. And the witnessing did not concern merely what Jesus was doing within the [inner] recesses of the individual life. To take the words of Acts in that way is to do violence to the context and to all the evidence…Christianity is based, then, upon an account of something that happened, and the Christian worker is primarily a witness.*[496]

False teaching in the United States, and for that matter all over the world, too often flies under the banner of orthodoxy, inerrancy, and expositional preaching. These are good and true principles, but if a church holds to these and neglects the hard parts of the message in favor of truths such as love, grace, and mercy, then that is a serious problem. If expositional preaching consistently ignores the warnings in Scripture of God's coming judgment or disregards the consequences of sin and the need for repentance, then the effect is false teaching. When the gospel is perverted by deemphasizing or removing any of the elements that are not easy to deal with such as conviction of sins, calling for repentance, preparation of believers for the difficulties of following Christ, and warnings of God's judgment and wrath, then the abandonment of God's purpose for His people logically follows. Believers must remember that God established His plan of redemption, which was revealed in the gospel "before the ages began" (2 Tim. 1:9; Tit. 1:2-3). It was God's expressed purpose from the fall in Genesis 3 that the Great Commission would be an irrevocable part of His plan (Gen. 3:15; 12:1-3; Isa. 49:6; 56:7; 66:19; Mal. 1:11, 14; decreed before the creation of the world, 1 Cor. 2:7; 1 Pet. 1:20).

All believers have been assigned the role of "watchman" (Mk. 13:37). Watchmen have two basic responsibilities: (1) to guard the assets of the owner, and (2) to accom-

---

496 Machen, *Christianity & Liberalism*, pp. 52-53.

plish the work assigned by the owner while he is away. The asset in this context is the gospel. The task assigned by the owner Jesus, while He is away, is proclaiming the gospel to the lost and training believers as His followers.

We have seen the primacy of proclaiming the gospel to all nations throughout this book. A brief review of some highlights shows that in the New Testament it is central in two important models of the Christian life: following Christ in the way of the cross (Mk. 8:34-38) and following Jesus in triumphal procession (2 Cor. 2:14-16). These vivid images of following Christ have witness as a central component. In the extended metaphor of the vine, witness is prominent (Jn. 15:16). We have it in commission form three times in Mt. 28:18-20, Lk. 24:44-49, and Acts 1:7-8. In Acts 1:7-8, Jesus is dramatically passing the mantle of witness to His disciples with His command to witness immediately before His feet leave the ground for heaven. It reminds us of Elijah's ascension and the passing of his mantle to Elisha (2 Kgs. 2:9-14). And Paul writes that we have been declared "ambassadors for Christ," God having "entrusted to us the message of reconciliation" (2 Cor. 5:19-20).

If Jesus commands witness as the chief strategic task of His people, we should expect accountability. As with any command Jesus gives to His followers, there are consequences for failing to embrace it. Jesus issues a warning to the church in Ephesus for the failure to be a faithful witness. Revelation 2:1-7 is a letter from Jesus Christ to the church in Ephesus. God's people there had many things for which to be commended. They worked hard and patiently endured difficulties on behalf of Christ. They hated evil and separated themselves from those who practiced such things. And they rejected false teachers and false doctrine. Most Christians and pastors today would call this a successful church, a healthy church. Yet, Jesus was highly displeased. There was something missing that was serious. "But I have this against you, that you have abandoned the love you had at first" (Rev. 2:4). Most interpreters consider having left "the love you had at first" to mean either they were no longer loving one another as they did at first or that they had lost their love for Christ in general.

However, there is another view, a minority view, that I believe is the correct interpretation of this passage. It is the view that the church in Ephesus had abandoned their love for Jesus that resulted in a zealous witness for Christ.

*That the primary meaning of lampstand is that of witness is
confirmed from Rev. 11:3–7, 10, where the "lampstands" refer
to those who are God's "prophetic witnesses." Similarly, Mark
4:21 and Luke 8:16 say that a "lamp" is to be put on a "lampstand" to shine in order to emphasize the witnessing role of those
who truly possess God's revelation (cf. also Mt. 5:14–16!) in
close connection to the basic formula "if anyone has ears to hear
let him hear" (Mark 4:23; Luke 8:8). These two texts also imply that those among God's people who do not shine their light
will have their lamps removed (Mark 4:25; Luke 8:18).[497]*

Revelation 2:4 is an indictment by Jesus. And it comes with a threat of judgment.
Jesus commands them to "repent and do the works you did at first. If not, I will come to
you and remove your lampstand from its place..." (Rev. 2:5). Their witness had grown
cold and dim. If they failed to repent, their witness would be extinguished, God would
remove His presence, and they would no longer be a church of God. God always requires of His people, in every century and in every environment, faithful following of
Christ in the way of the cross. The way of the cross is a way of witness (Mk. 8:34-38).
Jesus said, "If you love me, you will keep my commandments" (Jn. 14:15).

The church at Ephesus "will cease to exist as a church when the very function that
defines the essence of their existence is no longer performed."[498] Sadly, there are many
churches today that bear the spiritual heritage and have the spiritual DNA of the church
in Ephesus. This is a DNA that has no future. Jesus firmly and lovingly warned them of
this reality. They were in danger of losing the presence of Jesus Christ.

As an example of the accountability demanded by Jesus, we can look to His actions
against the Jews who had so corrupted the use of the temple that they were blocking
access to God for the Gentiles. Jesus' turning over the tables of the temple, sandwiched
by the withering of the fig tree (Mk. 11:12-21) and the parable of the tenants (Mk. 12:1-
12), demonstrates that witness matters and there will be accountability and judgment

---

497 G. K. Beale, *The Book of Revelation* (NIGTC), p. 231; see pages 230-233 in his commentary for more
discussion.
498 Beale, *The Book of Revelation* (NIGTC), p. 232.

(see chapter 14 part 3 of this book for a more detailed discussion). Paul understood this accountability and cited as one of his foundational motivations the judgment seat of Christ, "For we must all appear before the judgment seat of Christ...Therefore, knowing the fear of the Lord, we persuade others" (2 Cor. 5:10-11). We should not be surprised by the threat of the removal of the lampstand from the church at Ephesus for their failure to witness. Without accountability the Great Commission is merely the Great Suggestion.

After Jesus' call for repentance and warning of judgment in verse 5, He urges them with this admonition, "He who has an ear, let him hear what the Spirit says to the churches. To the one who conquers I will grant to eat of the tree of life, which is in the paradise of God" (Rev. 2:7). Jesus assumes a "mixed audience"[499] in the church at Ephesus, and that means some will respond positively and some will reject His exhortation. "Those who do accept the message are promised the inheritance of salvation blessings. νικάω [nikáō] ('conquer') is repeated in the concluding promise in all the letters as the condition for inheriting salvation."[500] Failure to repent and conquer will result in separation from Christ's presence.

The clarion call of Scripture to be a light to the nations is and always has been the central charge to the church. May we as believers in Jesus Christ and may His church return to the great message of redemption and disseminate it widely. This is my prayer for you, the reader of this book. Lord, grant us courage to conquer.

---

499 Beale, *The Book of Revelation* (NIGTC), p. 234.
500 Beale, *The Book of Revelation* (NIGTC), p. 234.

APPENDIX

THE TERM GOSPEL AS USED IN THE NEW TESTAMENT

There are many opinions as to what constitutes the biblical gospel of Jesus Christ. "Ask any hundred self-professed evangelical Christians what the good news of Jesus is, and you're likely to get about sixty different answers. Listen to evangelical preaching, read evangelical books, log on to evangelical websites, and you'll find one description after another of the gospel, many of them mutually exclusive."[501] Many pastors I have heard from the pulpit over the years have preached a gospel with an emphasis only on the positive elements of the gospel to the neglect of the holiness of God, sin, judgment, wrath, the cost of following Jesus, and even to the neglect of repentance.

The term gospel, as used in the New Testament, is, in a sense, the name of a doctrine encompassing the complex evangelistic message that incorporates the eight key elements that I have articulated throughout this book. For convenience, here are those eight elements that summarize the gospel: (1) God, (2) holiness, (3) sin and rebellion, (4) judgment and wrath, (5) the cross and the resurrection of Christ, (6) grace, (7) the cost of following Jesus, and (8) His call on every life to repent and believe.

This appendix will provide the data that supports my view that the true gospel must include all eight elements, otherwise it is something other than the biblical gospel. I will frame the issue around two questions: Does the term gospel, as used in the New Testament, convey anything other than good news? And, Do the truths about sin, judgment, wrath, the cost of following Christ, and repentance belong under the label of gospel?

To answer those questions, we will explore the use of the word gospel outside of the Bible and how it is used in the Bible. I will begin with the Septuagint's use of the

---

501 Greg Gilbert, *What Is the Gospel?* (Wheaton, IL: Crossway, 2010), p.18.

word gospel and then move to a Greek-English lexicon. From there we will consider examples of sin, judgment, and wrath as an expressed part of the gospel, and then we will observe other contextual evidence. I will close with six theologians who have an opinion on these questions.

The Septuagint (commonly abbreviated as LXX), a translation of the Hebrew Bible into Koine Greek (the Greek of the New Testament), was completed from the third to the second century BC. The LXX is a translation of inspired Scripture just like the NIV or the ESV are translations of inspired Scripture. The Septuagint was the copy of the Old Testament that most of the New Testament authors were using. It provides insight into how the word gospel was used and thought of in close proximity to the New Testament.[502] The word gospel occurs in the LXX 28 times. Sixteen times it is used as an announcement of victory in battle. In each case there is the element of salvation for the victor and destruction of the enemy.[503] Ten times it is used as news of God's salvation in general.[504] Once it is used as a birth announcement and once as an announcement to Adonijah of Solomon being anointed king.[505] Some of those occurrences are predictive in nature of God's coming victory. G. K. Beale comments: "In the LXX of Isaiah the 'announcement of good news' in context included not only salvation but also judgment of the impious (see Isa. 40:9; 52:7; 61:1; and in particular 60:6–14)."[506]

Outside of the New Testament among the Greeks, gospel (euaggelion) "is a technical term for 'news of victory'...[and] is closely linked with the thought of victory in battle."[507] "The εὐάγγελος [good messenger] comes from the field of battle by ship...or...as a swift runner, and proclaims to the anxiously awaiting city the victory of the army, and the death or capture of the enemy."[508] The word gospel applies to the news, the announcement, and

---

502 For a thorough discussion of the history of the word gospel see Friedrich, "Εὐαγγελίζομαι, Εὐαγγέλιον, Προευαγγελίζομαι, Εὐαγγελιστής," *Theological Dictionary of the New Testament*, pp. 707-736.
503 1 Sam. 31:9; 2 Sam. 1:20; 4:1 (2x's); 18:19-31 (9x's); 2 Kgs. 7:9; 1 Chron. 10:9; and Ps. 68:11.
504 Ps. 96:2; Ps. of Sol. 11:1 (apocrypha); Isa. 40:9 (2x's); 52:7 (2x's); 60:6; 61:1; Joel 2:32; Nah. 1:15.
505 Jer. 20:15 (Jeremiah curses the "good news" of his birth); 1 Kgs. 1:42 (Adonijah is terrified at the "good news" of the appointing of Solomon to the throne by King David and by the prophet Nathan; he had earlier exalted himself to the throne).
506 Beale, The Book of Revelation (NIGTC), p. 748.
507 Friedrich, "Εὐαγγέλιον," *Theological Dictionary of the New Testament*, p. 722.
508 Friedrich, "Εὐαγγελίζομαι, Εὐαγγέλιον, Προευαγγελίζομαι, Εὐαγγελιστής," *Theological Dictionary of the New Testament*, p. 710.

not to the viewpoint of the hearer. News of victory over one's enemies invariably meant there were winners and losers such as when the Philistines defeated Israel and killed Saul and Jonathan. They sent messengers to announce good news (euaggelizo) throughout their land (1 Sam. 31:9). The word often contained this hard edge of bad news for one side and the welcome news of victory for the other. The Greeks also used the word as an announcement of news in general such as "the birth of a son," "an approaching wedding," "the death of someone", and "other communications."[509]

Now, turning to a Greek-English lexicon we see that the noun form of the word gospel, εὐαγγέλιον (euaggelion) in the Greek, means: "1) God's good news to humans, good news as proclamation, 2) details relating to the life and ministry of Jesus, good news of Jesus, 3) a book dealing with the life and teaching of Jesus, a gospel account that deals with the life and teaching of Jesus".[510] The verb form of the word gospel, εὐαγγελίζω (euaggelizo) in the Greek, means: "1) generally bring good news, announce good news, 2) **mostly specifically proclaim the divine message of salvation, proclaim the gospel**" (emphasis mine).[511] Passages as a message of salvation include – Ps. 68:11 (LXX 67:12); Acts 8:25, 40; 14:21; 16:10; Gal. 1:9; Lk. 9:6; 20:1; Acts 14:7; Rom. 15:20; 1 Cor. 1:17; 9:16, 18.[512]

There are 134 occurrences in the New Testament of the noun and verb form of the word gospel. Many of these occurrences are broad uses such as: "the gospel of Christ" eight times, "the gospel of God" seven times, and "the gospel of the kingdom" four times. Based on those nineteen occurrences, the gospel is about: (1) what Christ has done and will do in redemption, (2) God's character, all of his attributes, including His mercy, righteousness, and aversion to all that is evil, and (3) the certain victory of His coming Kingdom which includes the salvation of His people and the destruction of all that is evil. God's coming kingdom will be a worldwide flood sweeping His people to salvation and sweeping to destruction all who have rejected him and lived for their own glory. It is about the victory of God, and all of it is good news for God's people.

---

509 Friedrich, "Εὐαγγέλιον," *Theological Dictionary of the New Testament*, p. 722.
510 William Arndt et al., *A Greek-English Lexicon of the New Testament and Other Early Christian Literature* (BDAG) (Chicago: University of Chicago Press, Third Edition, 2000), pp. 402-403.
511 Arndt et al., *A Greek-English Lexicon of the New Testament* (BDAG), p. 402.
512 Arndt et al., *A Greek-English Lexicon of the New Testament* (BDAG), p. 402.

Another example of a broad use of the word gospel is how the author of the Gospel of Mark uses the term to label the contents of the entire Gospel (1:1). All eight elements of the gospel are included in the Gospel of Mark with judgment of the Jews (chapters 11-12) and God's wrath falling on Jesus (chapters 14-15) dominating chapters 11-15. Plus, he uses the word gospel as a summary of Jesus' message of salvation (1:14-15).

The New Testament uses the word gospel explicitly to include the negative elements such as sin, judgment, warnings of wrath, and calls for repentance. In Rom. 2:16, Paul states: "on that day when, according to my gospel, God judges the secrets of men by Christ Jesus." He explicitly and unequivocally names the coming judgment of Christ as part of his gospel. The broad context of that statement (1:16-3:20) overwhelmingly supports judgment as an element of the gospel as I will discuss below.

Revelation 14:6-20 is an example of a message labeled as the gospel, explicitly including the hard edge of judgment and wrath, and it is directed to lost people. In this text we have an account of three angels "with an eternal gospel to proclaim to those who dwell on earth, to every nation and tribe and language and people" (14:6). The angels' message is directed to the entire lost world. And God names it "an eternal gospel." The details that follow specifically link gospel with calls to fear and worship God (v. 7), warnings of coming judgment (vv. 7, 8), warnings of God's wrath and eternal punishment (vv. 9-11), a call for God's people to endure (v. 12) which implies there is a cost of being faithful to Christ, comfort promised to God's people (v. 13), and predictions of judgment, destruction, and wrath for those who have rejected God (vv. 14-20). "The meaning of the word [gospel] here must be determined ultimately by the immediate context. **The angel announces not a different gospel, but one that carries dire consequences if it is rejected, as Paul underscores in Rom. 1:16ff.; 2 Cor. 2:14–16; and Acts 17:18–32**" (emphasis mine).[513]

Luke, in similar fashion to the apostles Paul and John, provided specific details of the content of the gospel. He does so in the context of the preaching of John the Baptist. He writes of John in Luke 3:18: "So with many other exhortations he preached good news to the people." We can examine what those "exhortations" were that John preached.

---

513 Beale, The Book of Revelation (NIGTC), p. 748.

In 3:7-17 John called out sinners (7), named sins (10-14), warned of judgment (17), warned of wrath (7-10), and called for repentance (7-8). These "exhortations" were placed by Luke under the label of *gospel*. This demonstrates that these hard truths are included under the term gospel.

Paul used the gospel of coming judgment as good news to encourage the church in Thessalonica who were suffering affliction for their faithfulness to the gospel. He writes that their suffering was "evidence of the righteous judgment of God" (2 Thess. 1:5). Paul explained that Jesus is coming in great power and will repay with vengeance those who were afflicting them. He wrote that their enemies will "suffer the punishment of eternal destruction" (1:9) and will be removed from the presence of the Lord (1:5-10). This is news of God's ultimate victory as well as a warning to those who oppose Jesus Christ. The hard edged components of Paul's gospel served as a motivation for individuals to turn away from their sin and place their trust in Christ. Paul was speaking "the gospel of God" (1 Thess. 2:2, 8, 9) into these suffering Christians lives as it is "news of God's victory" which encouraged them to remain faithful. Peter also spoke "the gospel of God" into the lives of Christians undergoing trials: "For it is time for judgment to begin at the household of God; and if it begins with us, what will be the outcome for those who do not obey the [**the news of God's victory**]?" (1 Pet. 4:17) (emphasis and [paraphrase] mine, in place of "the gospel of God").

In 1 Corinthians 1:17-2:5 Paul sees the cross as the heart of the gospel. In this passage Paul uses "the gospel" (1:17), "the cross of Christ" (1:17), "the word of the cross" (1:18), "Christ crucified" (1:23), and "Jesus Christ and him crucified" (1 Cor. 2:2) as interchangeable words and phrases. He uses these phrases synonymously.

I stated in the introduction of this book that Jesus' death on the cross cannot be explained without addressing the eight elements of the gospel. The gospel is diminished and stripped of its power when we remove the hard elements such as sin, judgment, wrath, the cost of following Jesus, and repentance. A gospel stripped of these elements is a gospel rendered "with words of eloquent wisdom" with the result that "the cross of Christ [is] emptied of its power" (1 Cor. 1:17). Jesus rebuked the scribes and Pharisees saying to them, "Woe to you, scribes and Pharisees, hypocrites! For you travel across sea and land to make a single proselyte, and when he becomes a proselyte, you make him twice as much a child of hell as yourselves" (Mt. 23:15). The religious leaders of Jesus' day had perverted God's truth, including the way of salvation, and were producing children of hell. A sterilized gospel cannot produce Godly offspring. In fact, it produces quite the opposite.

There is yet another aspect of the gospel that we can see in this passage (1 Cor. 1:17-2:5) and that is its power to divide. Paul explains that those "who are perishing" (1:18) view the cross as folly (1:18, 23) and as a stumbling block (1:23). Those "who are being saved" view it as "the power of God and the wisdom of God" (1:18, 24). Paul lays out this discussion under the label of the gospel (1:17ff). Jesus is the gospel, and we must understand that he is the dividing line of history (Mt. 10:34-39; Lk. 2:32-35; 12:49-53; Jn. 7:40-44; 9:16; 10:19-21). The good news about Jesus is a lightning bolt in every society. It will offend many and save some.

Emphasizing the same point regarding the offense of the cross in Galatians 5:11, Paul states as a fact that the cross is offensive or scandalous. Paul is essentially saying the same thing about the gospel in 1 Cor. 1:17, 18, 23; 2:2. It is offensive to Jews for at least two reasons. First, because they were looking for a politically and militarily powerful Messiah and second, because they believed they were saved by keeping the law. The cross offended these religious leaders at both levels as the cross was a sign of weakness in their view and it demonstrated that they were inadequate to save themselves. The true gospel called for the religious leaders to humble themselves before a scandalized savior. It called for them to stop trusting in their ability to keep the law for salvation. Consequently, they viewed the cross as "folly."

Paul opens his letter to the Romans with the statement: "Paul...set apart for the gospel" (1:1). He then gives a summary of the gospel as part of his greeting (1:2-6) After more introductory remarks he brings us to a transitional statement that he uses to launch his great treatise on the gospel: "So I am eager to preach the gospel to you who are in Rome" (1:15). This is followed by the opening line of his gospel presentation. Notice how these statements flow and are connected.

> **Introduction:** (1:1-2, 15) "Paul...set apart for the gospel of God, which he promised beforehand through the prophets in the holy Scriptures...So I am eager to preach the gospel..."

A **Launch of gospel dissertation:** (1:16) "**For** I am not ashamed of the gospel, for it is the power of God for salvation to everyone who believes..."

B (1:17) "**For** in it the righteousness of God is revealed..."

C (1:18) "**For** the wrath of God is revealed from heaven against all ungodliness and unrighteousness of men, who by their unrighteousness suppress the truth."

For Paul, these three strong connectors, the word "For", means all of what precedes and what follows is connected under the label of gospel. Paul's gospel dissertation runs through at least the end of chapter 8 of Romans and maybe beyond. In case we lose track that he is writing about the gospel, in Romans 2:16 Paul is quite explicit and writes, "on that day when, **according to my gospel, God judges the secrets of men by Christ Jesus.**" This is significant. The gospel is the full story of God's victory over sin, evil, and death and it is a story that includes every aspect of the truth of God's character, the terrible reality of man's sinful condition, and God's absolute and ultimate triumph over evil. The meaning of these words by Paul is good news for those who trust in Him, but terrifying news to those who refuse to heed them and go their own way.

Statements by selected theologians:

Consider these statements by some fine theologians and pastors on this topic.

John Murray. "While it is true that knowledge of the fact of judgment is derived from other sources than the gospel, yet the proclamation of God's righteous judgment of all men and of all the secrets and deeds of men is an outstanding feature of the gospel." [514]

John Stott. "God's judgment is part of the gospel...We cheapen the gospel if we represent it as deliverance only from unhappiness, fear, guilt, and other felt needs, instead of as a rescue from the coming wrath." [515]

---

514 John Murray, *The Epistle to the Romans* (Grand Rapids, MI: Wm. B. Eerdmans Publishing Co., 1971), p. 77.
515 John Stott, *Romans: God's Good News for the World (with study guide)* (Downers Grove, IL: InterVarsityPress, 1994), p. 88.

J. I. Packer. "In a word, the evangelistic message is the gospel of Christ, and him crucified; the message of man's sin and God's grace, of human guilt and divine forgiveness, of new birth and new life through the gift of the Holy Spirit."[516]

"The gospel is a message about sin. It tells us how we have fallen short of God's standard; how we have become guilty, filthy and helpless in sin, and now stand under the wrath of God. It tells us that the reason why we sin continually is that we are sinners by nature, and that nothing we do, or try to do, for ourselves can put us right or bring us back into God's favor. It shows us ourselves as God sees us, and teaches us to think of ourselves as God thinks of us. Thus it leads us to self-despair. And this also is a necessary step. Not till we have learned our need to get right with God, and our inability to do so by any effort of our own, can we come to know the Christ who saves from sin."[517] (Bold is in the original; it is numbered point 2.)

"He [Jesus] did not desire to make disciples under false pretenses. He had no interest in gathering vast crowds of professed adherents who would melt away as soon as they found out what following him actually demanded of them. In our own presentation of Christ's gospel, therefore, we need to lay a similar stress on the cost of following Christ, and make sinners face it soberly before we urge them to respond to the message of free forgiveness. In common honesty we must not conceal the fact that free forgiveness, in one sense, will cost everything; or else our evangelizing becomes a sort of confidence trick. And where there is no clear knowledge, and hence no realistic recognition of the real claims that Christ makes, there can be no repentance, and therefore no salvation. Such is the evangelistic message that we are sent to make known."[518]

"One of the miserable ironies of our time is that whereas liberal and radical theologians believe themselves to be restating the gospel for today, they have for the most part rejected the categories of wrath, guilt, condemnation and enmity of God, and

---

516 Packer, *Evangelism and the Sovereignty of God*, p. 66.
517 Packer, *Evangelism and the Sovereignty of God*, pp. 67-68 (emphasis in original).
518 Packer, *Evangelism and the Sovereignty of God*, p. 81.

so have made it impossible for themselves ever to present the gospel at all, for they cannot now state the basic problem which the gospel of peace solves." [519]

James Montgomery Boice. "Today's preaching is deficient at many points. But there is no point at which it is more evidently inadequate and even explicitly contrary to the teachings of the New Testament than in its neglect of 'the wrath of God.' God's wrath is a dominant Bible teaching and the point in Romans at which Paul begins his formal exposition of the gospel."[520] From an exposition of Rom. 1:18.

Thomas Schreiner. "The wrath of God is part of the righteousness of God that is revealed in the gospel, so that the wrath of God (like the righteousness of God) is also disclosed in the gospel...The saving and judging righteousness of God find their resolution, as [Rom.] 3:21-26 illustrates, in the gospel. The revelation of God's saving righteousness exposes the full wickedness of human sin and the depth of God's wrath against it."[521] Commenting on Rom. 1:18.

C. H. Spurgeon. "'According to my gospel,' saith Paul; and he meant, that the judgment is an essential part of the gospel creed."

"The doctrine of judgment to come is the power by which men are to be aroused. There is another life; the Lord will come a second time; judgment will arrive; the wrath of God will be revealed. Where this is not preached, I am bold to say the gospel is not preached."

"The gospel is as truly a two-edged sword against sin, as ever the law can be. There is grace for the man who quits his sin, but there is tribulation and wrath upon every man that doeth evil. 'If ye turn not, he will whet his sword; he hath bent his bow,

---

519 Packer, *Knowing God,* p. 196.
520 James Montgomery Boice, *Romans: Justification by Faith*, vol. 1 (Grand Rapids, MI: Baker Book House, 1991), p. 129.
521 Thomas R. Schriener, *Romans (BECNT)* (Grand Rapids, MI: BakerBooks, 1998), pp. 77-78.

and made it ready.' The gospel is all tenderness to the repenting, but all terror to the obstinate offender." These three quotes are from a sermon by Spurgeon on the text of Rom. 2:16 preached on July 12, 1885. [522]

Conclusion

A literal interpretation of the word gospel (that it can only mean good things) is impossible given the way it is used both outside and inside the New Testament. It is a word with broad shoulders and carries a weight of evangelistic power that either softens hard hearts or hardens those hearts. Every culture opposes this message and will do everything it can to change it, disparage it, and to silence it. It takes personal spiritual strength and preparation to carry this message which has such significant consequences. Those who tell others this great gospel will get messy...and dirty...and may be scorned. Only men and women filled with the Holy Spirit and who are actively engaged in personal spiritual preparation will be able to faithfully communicate this message of the King.

---

522 C. H. Spurgeon, *Coming Judgment of the Secrets of Men,* in *The Metropolitan Tabernacle Pulpit Sermons,* vol. 31 (preached July 12, 1885) (London: Passmore & Alabaster, 1885), pp. 382–384.

BIBLIOGRAPHY

Baldwin, Joyce G., *Haggai, Zechariah and Malachi: An Introduction and Commentary* (Vol. 28) (Downers Grove, IL: InterVarsity Press, 1972).

Bassett-Brody, Lisette, *Etched in Stone* (Washington, D.C.: WND Books, 2017).

Beale, G. K. and Carson, D. A., Editors, *Commentary on the New Testament Use of the Old Testament* (Grand Rapids, MI; Nottingham, UK: Baker Academic; Apollos, 2007).

Beale, G. K., *Isaiah VI 9–13: A Retributive Taunt against Idolatry* (Vetus Testamentum, Vol. 41. July, 1991), pp. 258-278.

Beale, G. K., *The Book of Revelation: A Commentary on the Greek Text* (NIGTC) (Grand Rapids, MI, USA; Carlisle, Cumbria, UK: W.B. Eerdmans; Paternoster Press, 1999).

Blomberg, Craig L., *Matthew,* Vol. 22 (NAC) (Nashville: Broadman & Holman Publishers, 1992).

Boice, James Montgomery, *Genesis: An Expositional Commentary* (Vol. 1 & 2) (Grand Rapids, MI, Baker Books, 1982, 1998).

Boice, James Montgomery, *The Minor Prophets: An Expositional Commentary* (Vol. 1 & 2) (Grand Rapids, MI: Baker Books, 1986, 2002).

Boice, James Montgomery, *Psalms 1–41: An Expositional Commentary* (Grand Rapids, MI: Baker Books, 1994, 2005).

Boice, James Montgomery, Psalms 42–106: An Expositional Commentary (Grand Rapids, MI: Baker Books, 1996, 2005).

Boice, James Montgomery, *Romans: Justification by Faith*, vol. 1 (Grand Rapids, MI: Baker Book House, 1991)

Bolt, Peter G., *The Cross from a Distance: Atonement in Mark's Gospel* (Downers Grove, IL: InterVarsity Press, 2004).

Borchert, Gerald L., *John 1–11* (NAC) (Nashville: Broadman & Holman Publishers, 1996).

Borchert, Gerald L., *John 12–21* (NAC) (Nashville: Broadman & Holman Publishers, 2002).

Brooks, James A., *Mark* (NAC) (Nashville: Broadman & Holman Publishers, 1991).

Buechner, Frederick, *Telling the Truth: The Gospel as Tragedy, Comedy, and Fairy Tale* (New York: HarperCollins Publishers, 1977)

Carson, D. A., *The Gospel According to John* (PNTC) (Leicester, England; Grand Rapids, MI: Inter-Varsity Press; W.B. Eerdmans, 1991).

Carson, D. A. and Moo, Douglas J., *An Introduction to the New Testament* (Grand Rapids, MI: Zondervan, 1992, 2005).

Currid, John D., *A Study Commentary on Exodus: Exodus 1–18* (Vol. 1) (Darlington, England; Carlisle, PA: Evangelical Press, 2000).

Dallimore, Arnold A., *Spurgeon: A Biography* (Edinburgh, UK: Banner of Truth, 1984, reprinted 2018).

Davis, Dale Ralph, *Faith of Our Father: Expositions of Genesis 12-25* (Fearn, Scotland: Christian Focus Publications, 2015).

Davis, Dale Ralph, *Stump Kingdom: Isaiah 6–12* (Fearn, Scotland, UK: Christian Focus, 2017).

Dickerson, John S., *The Great Evangelical Recession* (Grand Rapids, MI: Baker Books, Kindle Ed., 2013).

Duriez, Colin, *AD 33: The Year that Changed the World* (Downers Grove, IL: Inter-Varsity Press, 2006).

Edwards, James R., *The Gospel According to Mark* (PNTC) (Grand Rapids, MI; Leicester, England: Eerdmans; Apollos, 2002).

Edwards, Jonathan, *Sinners in the Hands of an Angry God* (Enfield, MA, July 8, 1741).

France, R. T., *Matthew: An Introduction and Commentary* (TNTC) (Downers Grove, IL: Inter-Varsity Press, 1985, 2008).

France, R. T., *The Gospel of Mark: A Commentary on the Greek Text* (NIGTC) (Grand Rapids, MI; Carlisle: W.B. Eerdmans; Paternoster Press, 2002).

Gilbert, Greg, *What Is the Gospel?* (Wheaton, IL: Crossway, 2010).

Green, Gene L., *The Letters to the Thessalonians* (PNTC) (Grand Rapids, MI; Cambridge, UK: Wm. B. Eerdmans Publishing Co., 2002).

Green, Michael, *Evangelism in the Early Church* (Grand Rapids, MI: William B Eerdmans, 1970, 1977).

Harris, Murray J., *The Second Epistle to the Corinthians* (NIGTC) (Grand Rapids, MI; Milton Keynes, UK: W.B. Eerdmans Pub. Co.; Paternoster Press, 2005).

Hendriksen, William, *Exposition of Ephesians* (Grand Rapids: Baker Book House, 1967, 1995).

Hendriksen, William, *Exposition of Paul's Epistle to the Romans*, Vol. 12–13 (NTC) (Grand Rapids: Baker Book House, 1980, 1981).

Hendriksen, William, *Exposition of the Gospel According to John*, vol. 1 & 2 (NTC) (Grand Rapids, MI: Baker Book House, 1953).

Hendriksen, William, *Exposition of the Gospel According to Luke* (NTC) (Grand Rapids: Baker Book House, 1978).

Hendriksen, *Exposition of the Gospel According to Mark* (NTC) (Grand Rapids, MI: Baker Books, 1975).

Hendriksen, William, *Exposition of the Gospel According to Matthew* (NTC) (Grand Rapids: Baker Book House, 1973).

Hoehner, Harold, *Chronological Aspects of the Life of Christ* (Grand Rapids, MI: Zondervan Publishing House, 1977).

Horton, Michael, *Christless Christianity: The Alternative Gospel of the American Church* (Grand Rapids, MI: Baker Books, Kindle Ed, 2008).

Horton, Michael, *The Gospel-Driven Life* (Grand Rapids, MI: BakerBooks, 2009).

Huey, F. B., *Jeremiah, Lamentations* (NAC) (Nashville: Broadman & Holman Publishers, 1993).

Hughes, R. Kent, *2 Corinthians: Power in Weakness* (Wheaton, IL: Crossway Books, 2006).

Hughes, R. Kent, *Mark: Jesus, Servant and Savior* (Westchester, IL: Crossway Books, 1989).

Keener, Craig S., *The Gospel of John: A Commentary, vol. 1 & 2* (Grand Rapids, MI: Baker Academic, 2003, electronic ed., 2012).

Kistemaker, Simon J., *Exposition of the Acts of the Apostles* (NTC) (Grand Rapids: Baker Book House, 1990).

Kistemaker, Simon J., *Exposition of the First Epistle to the Corinthians* (NTC) (Grand Rapids, MI: Baker Books, 1993).

Kistemaker, Simon J., *Exposition of the Second Epistle to the Corinthians* (NTC) (Grand Rapids, MI: Baker Books, 1997).

Kistemaker, Simon J., *New Testament Commentary: Exposition of Peter and Jude* (NTC) (Grand Rapids: Baker Books, 1987).

Köstenberger, Andreas J. and Alexander, T. Desmond, *Salvation to the Ends of the Earth: A Biblical Theology of Mission*, ed. D. A. Carson, 2nd Ed., vol. 53, New Studies in Biblical Theology (London; Downers Grove, IL: Apollos; IVP Academic, 2020).

Lane, William L., *The Gospel of Mark* (NICNT) (Grand Rapids, MI: Wm. B. Eerdmans Pub. Co., 1974).

MacArthur, John, *The MacArthur Study Bible (NASB)* (Nashville, TN: Thomas Nelson, Inc., 2006).

Machen, J. Gresham, *Christianity & Liberalism* (Grand Rapids, MI: Wm. B. Eerdmans Publishing Co., 1923).

Mackay, John L. *A Study Commentary on Isaiah* (Vols. 1 & 2) (Darlington, England; Carlisle, PA: EP Books, 2009).

Marsden, George M., *Jonathan Edwards: A Life* (Harrisonburg, VA: R. R. Donnelley and Sons, Kindle Ed., 2003).

Marshall, I. Howard, *The Gospel of Luke* (NIGTC) (Exeter: Paternoster Press, 1978).

Matthews, Kenneth A., *Genesis 1-11:26,* Vol. 1A (NAC) (Nashville, TN: Broadman & Holman Publishers, 1996).

Mauser, Ulrich, *Christ in the Wilderness: The Wilderness Theme in the Second Gospel and Its Basis in the Biblical Tradition* (London: SCM Press Ltd, 1963).

Metzger, Will, *Tell the Truth: The Whole Gospel to the Whole Person by Whole People* (Downers Grove, IL: InterVarsity Press, third edition 2002).

Motyer, Alec, *6 Ways the Old Testament Speaks Today: An Interactive Guide* (Wheaton, IL: Crossway, Kindle Edition, 2016).

Motyer, Alec, *Look to the Rock: Old Testament Background To Our Understanding Of Christ* (Leicester, England: Inter-Varsity Press, 1996),

Motyer, Alec, *The Message of Exodus: The Days of Our Pilgrimage* (Nottingham, England: Inter-Varsity Press, 2005).

Motyer, J. Alec, *The Prophecy of Isaiah: An Introduction & Commentary* (Downers Grove, IL: InterVarsity Press, 1993).

Murray, John, *The Epistle to the Romans* (Grand Rapids, MI: Wm. B. Eerdmans Publishing Co., 1971).

Nolland, John, *The Gospel of Matthew: A Commentary on the Greek Text* (NIGTC) (Grand Rapids, MI; Carlisle: W.B. Eerdmans; Paternoster Press, 2005).

O'Brien, Peter T., *The Letter to the Ephesians* (PNTC) (Grand Rapids, MI: Wm. B. Eerdmans Publishing Co., 1999).

Oswalt, John N., *The Book of Isaiah, Chapters 1-39* (Grand Rapids, MI: Wm. B. Eerdmans Publishing Co., 1986).

Overholt, Thomas W., *The Threat of Falsehood: A Study in the Theology of the Book of Jeremiah* (London: SCM Press Ltd., 1970).

Packer, J. I., *Knowing God* (Downers Grove, IL: InterVarsity Press, 1993).

Packer, J. I., *Evangelism and the Sovereignty of God* (Downers Grove, IL: InterVarsity Press, 1961, Americanized and Forward, 2008).

Plummer, Robert L., *Paul's Understanding of the Church's Mission: Did the Apostle Paul Expect the Early Christian Communities to Evangelize?* (Bletchley, UK: Paternoster, 2006).

Polhill, John B., *Acts* (NAC) (Nashville: Broadman & Holman Publishers, 1992).

Rainer, Thom S., *Effective Evangelistic Churches* (Nashville, TN: Broadman & Holman Publishers, 1996).

Rhoads, David, Dewey, Joanna, and Michie, Donald, *Mark as Story* (Minneapolis, MN: Fortress Press, 3rd edition, 2012).

Ross, Allen P., *Creation and Blessing: A Guide to the Study and Exposition of Genesis* (Grand Rapids, MI: Baker Books, 1998).

Schaff Philip, Ed., *Saint Chrysostom: Homilies on the Acts of the Apostles and the Epistle to the Romans*, trans. J. Walker et al., vol. 11, A Select Library of the Nicene and Post-Nicene Fathers of the Christian Church (New York: Christian Literature Company, 1889).

Schaff, Philip and Schaff, David Schley, *History of the Christian Church*, vol. 2 (New York: Charles Scribner's Sons, 1910).

Schreiner, Thomas R., *1, 2 Peter, Jude* (NAC) (Nashville: Broadman & Holman Publishers, 2003).

Schreiner, Thomas R., *Romans* (Grand Rapids, MI: BakerBooks, 1998).

Shaeffer, Francis, *The Complete Works of Francis A. Shaeffer: A Christian Worldview* (Wheaton, IL: Crossway Books, 1976, 1982, *2nd Edition*).

Smith, Billy K. and Page, Frank S., *Amos, Obadiah, Jonah* (NAC) (Nashville: Broadman & Holman Publishers, 1995).

Smith, Gary V., *Isaiah 1–39* (NAC) (Nashville: B & H Publishing Group, 2007).

Smith, James E., *The Minor Prophets* (Joplin, MO: College Press, 1994).

Spence, H. D. M. (Ed.), *Jonah,* The Pulpit Commentary (London; New York: Funk & Wagnalls Company, 1909).

Sproul, R. C., Gen. Ed., *The Reformation Study Bible (ESV)* (Sanford, FL: Reformation Trust Publishing, 2015).

Sproul, R. C., *Mark* (St. Andrew's Expositional Commentary) (Orlando, FL: Reformation Trust, 2011).

Sproul, R. C., *What is Reformed Theology?: Understanding the Basics* (Grand Rapids, MI: Baker Books, 2006, Third Printing).

Spurgeon, C. H., *The New Park Street Pulpit Sermons* and *The Metropolitan Tabernacle Pulpit Sermons* (London: Passmore & Alabaster).

Stein, Robert H., *Luke* (NAC) (Nashville: Broadman & Holman Publishers, 1992).

Stott, John, *Our Guilty Silence: The Church, The Gospel, and The World* (Leicester, England: Inter-Varsity Press, first published 1967, 1997).

Stott, John, *The Cross of Christ (with study guide)* (Leicester, England: Inter-Varsity Press, 1986, 2004).

Stott, John, *The Marks of a Renewed Church* (https://www.preachingtoday.com/sermons/sermons/2013/april/marks-of-renewed-church.html, 2013), accessed June 16, 2020.

Stott, John, *The Message of Acts* (Downers Grove, IL: InterVarsity Press, 1990).

Stott, John, *Romans: God's Good News for the World (with study guide)* (Downers Grove, IL: InterVarsityPress, 1994).

Stuart, Douglas K., *Exodus,* Vol. 2 (NAC) (Nashville: Broadman & Holman Publishers, 2006).

Taylor, Richard A. and Clendenen, E. Ray, *Haggai, Malachi,* vol. 21A (NAC) (Nashville, TN: Broadman & Holman Publishers, 2004).

Thomas, Derek, *God Delivers: Isaiah Simply Explained* (Auburn, MA: Evangelical Press, 2002 *electronic ed.*).

Thomas, Robert L., *Charts of the Gospels and the Life of Christ* (Grand Rapids, MI: Zondervan, 2000).

Thompson, J. A., *The Book of Jeremiah* (NICOT) (Grand Rapids, MI: William B. Eerdmans Publishing Company, 1980).

Tice, Rico, *Honest Evangelism* (Epsom, Surrey, UK: The Good Book Company, 2015, 2016).

Trueman, Carl R., *The Rise and Triumph of the Modern Self: Cultural Amnesia, Expressive Individualism, and the Road to Sexual Revolution* (Wheaton, IL: Crossway, 2020).

Watts, Rikki E., *Isaiah's New Exodus in Mark* (Grand Rapids, MI: Baker Academic, 1997, 2000).

Wright, Christopher J. H., *The Mission of God: Unlocking the Bible's Grand Narrative* (Downers Grove, IL: InterVarsity Press, 2006).

Young, Edward J., *The Book of Isaiah* (vol. 1) (Grand Rapids, MI: Wm. B. Eerdmans Publishing Co., 1965).

REFERENCE WORKS

Arndt, William et al., *A Greek-English Lexicon of the New Testament and Other Early Christian Literature* (BDAG) (Chicago: University of Chicago Press, Third Edition, 2000).

Elwell, W. A. (General Editor), *Baker Encyclopedia of the Bible* (Grand Rapids, MI: Baker Book House, 1988).

Gerhard Kittel, Geoffrey W. Bromiley, and Gerhard Friedrich, editors, *Theological Dictionary of the New Testament* (Grand Rapids, MI: Eerdmans, 1964).

Louw, Johannes P. and Nida, Eugene Albert, *Greek-English Lexicon of the New Testament: Based on Semantic Domains* (New York: United Bible Societies, 1996).

Mandryk, Jason, *Operation World* (Colorado Springs, CO: Biblica Publishing, 7th Edition, 2010).

Zodhiates, Spiros (General Editor), *The Complete Word Study Dictionary: New Testament* (Chattanooga, TN: AMG Publishers, 1993).

www.ingramcontent.com/pod-product-compliance
Lightning Source LLC
LaVergne TN
LVHW051623250125
802024LV00004B/73